Workflow Modeling

Tools for Process Improvement and Application Development

Second Edition

For Karen and our family
—AS

For Lilian
—PM

For a listing of recent related Artech House titles,
turn to the back of this book.

Workflow Modeling

Tools for Process Improvement and Application Development

Second Edition

Alec Sharp
Patrick McDermott

ARTECH
HOUSE

BOSTON | LONDON
artechhouse.com

Library of Congress Cataloging-in-Publication Data
A catalog record for this book is available from the U.S. Library of Congress.

British Library Cataloguing in Publication Data
A catalogue record for this book is available from the British Library.

ISBN-13: 978-1-59693-192-3

Cover design by Yekaterina Ratner

© 2009 ARTECH HOUSE, INC.
685 Canton Street
Norwood, MA 02062

10 9 8 7 6 5 4 3

Contents

CHAPTER 7

PART III

CHAPTER 8

PART IV
Phase 3: Design the To-Be Process   299

CHAPTER 12
Conduct Final As-Is Process Assessment   301

CHAPTER 13
Determine To-Be Process Characteristics and Workflow   323

Preface

How the First Edition Came to Be

I've been asked many times why I decided to write a book, often in a tone that makes the question seem more like "What on earth possessed you to do *that*?" The truth is, I've asked myself the same question, in the same tone, more than once. Let's start the second edition of *Workflow Modeling* by answering it.

I met Patrick McDermott in October 1997, at a DAMA[1] conference in Sacramento, California. We became coauthors of the first edition of this book, but when we met, neither of us had any idea that would happen. Both of us were speaking on topics that were relatively obscure at the time, but would get more attention in the coming years. Mine was business modeling in the world of packaged applications, and Patrick, whose book *Solving the Year 2000 Crisis*[2] had just been published, naturally spoke about Y2K. I loved Patrick's presentation and his easy way of involving everyone, and he apparently thought well of my presentation, so we ended up talking about our interests and our work. Later, while we were out to dinner in Old Sac with a large group from the conference, I told Patrick how much I admired him for having a book published. I told him I wished I could say I'd written a book too. The conversation went roughly like this:

Patrick: "Why would you like to write a book?"

Alec: "I think my mother would be really pleased if I had a book published."

"What would you write about?"

"Hmmm... I think I'd write a book about workflow modeling."

"Workflow modeling? Why workflow modeling?" (Patrick looked interested, not dubious.)

"Well, with all the Internet hysteria these days, everyone seems to have forgotten how important business processes are. But companies are going to get into trouble, and business processes and workflow modeling and all that stuff will come back."

"Sounds interesting..."

---

1. Data Administration and Management Association.
2. An editorial comment: The media by and large sniggered that the world didn't end on January 1, 2000, but the Year 2000 problem (Y2K, as it came to be known) certainly wasn't a sham. I was in many companies whose Y2K remediation programs uncovered problems that would have stopped the business in its tracks. My favorite was the dairy that found its cows were not Y2K compliant because of the embedded ID tags that tracked their movements in and out of the barn—that would have left them legally unable to ship milk.

I don't actually remember if Patrick said it sounded interesting or not. What I do remember is returning our attention to the matter at hand—dinner and some good West Coast microbrew.

The next day, back at the conference, Patrick greeted me with a reminder of the previous night's conversation:

"Say, about that book you want to write…"

"Book? What book?"

"You know, the one on workflow modeling."

"Oh, yeah… that book."

"Well, I e-mailed my editor Jonathan Plant about it last night, and he says Artech wants it."

"Really?"

"Yes. And if you want to write it, I'll help."

I thought about it for roughly half a second and said "Sure—that sounds great." A book seemed like a good idea, but I knew that without making a commitment to another person, I'd never be able to finish writing one.

What I *didn't* know was how hard it would be, but it would be a while before I was going to find that out. The publishing process being what it is, there were many things to be done before we would actually start writing the book, and our consulting schedules being what they were, these things were going to take a long time. Over the next 11 months we developed overviews and outlines, created a table of contents, wrote a sample chapter, completed a marketing proposal, responded to the comments of anonymous reviewers, and so on. Almost a year after we'd met, on September 24, 1998, I received a brief e-mail from Patrick: "Good news: looks like the book's been accepted. Bad news: now we've got to write it."

Soon I found out just how much work writing is. Over the next two years, between autumn 1998 and summer 2000, I worked on the book—in hotel rooms, airplanes, restaurants, the library, and anywhere else I happened to be when a bit of time opened up. Patrick kept busy at his end, and because work took me to Northern California regularly, we were often able to arrange working sessions in San Francisco or Sacramento. Throughout those two years, I was constantly grateful for Patrick's ideas, writing, and great stories, and especially grateful to have a sounding board and someone to keep the project moving forward. This second edition has been a solo project, but without Patrick's contribution, there never would have been a first edition to follow.

Some Surprises

Workflow Modeling was published in February 2001, at which point it was still a surprise to us that we had even *finished* the book. The real shocker came a little later, with the reception the book received. Sales were very good almost immediately, driven in large part by word-of-mouth referrals and Web searches on the topic, indicating an unmet need. Lucky timing was also part of it—as we explain in Chapter 2, interest in business processes was reignited in 2001, so we benefitted from a desire for up-to-date literature on the subject. Many readers e-mailed to thank us for providing it and let us know exactly why they liked the book. The words or phrases that came up most often were "practical," "clear," "step-by-step," and "real world." Our stated goal was to provide a practical guide, by practitioners for practitioners, so this feedback was especially gratifying.

Later, the book was picked up by universities as a text for both undergraduate and MBA courses, which was another nice surprise. (I have to confess it was a real thrill the first time a participant in one of my workshops introduced themselves by saying "I signed up for this course because your book was a text in my MBA program.") We even heard from employees at the major management consulting firms and ERP[3] software vendors that the book was being used internally as a consulting guide. A final bonus was that the book led to some very interesting consulting assignments during which we were able to work with the methods in new environments and refine and extend them.

The first edition had been a lot of work, but at this point it certainly seemed to have been worth it!

How the *Second* Edition Came to Be

In mid-2005, Wayne Yuhasz, our acquisitions editor at Artech House, burst the bubble of complacency by suggesting that it was time for a second edition of *Workflow Modeling*. Sensing that work would be involved, I resisted. Laziness isn't an impressive excuse, so I took a different tack and pointed out that even though there had been major developments in the technologies supporting business processes, in particular the appearance of Business Process Management Systems (BPMS), our book was focused on methods, not the supporting technologies. We were still getting positive feedback on the first edition, and besides, there was nothing actually *wrong* with it—the methods were still sound, since we hadn't included anything that didn't work in real life. I think I even (another embarrassing admission) suggested that it was "sort of timeless."

Wayne, however, is a good guy and a persuasive guy, which is a tough combination to deal with. And persist he did. He pointed out that sales would inevitably decline, if for no other reason than the 2001 publication date. I had to agree that the world was a very different place than it was in early 2001, and a book published then would seem to have come from a different era. I ran this reasoning past my friend Roger Burlton, whose book *Business Process Management*[4] was also published in 2001. Like a good friend, he gave clear advice that wasn't necessarily what I wanted to hear. He agreed with Wayne that in our field, no matter how "timeless" I thought it was, a book published five or six years ago was going to be viewed suspiciously.

Evidently, I needed to rethink my arguments, so I had a closer look at the first edition, my workshop materials, and the stacks of notes on methods and techniques that I had accumulated from consulting jobs, developing conference presentations,

---

3.   Enterprise Resource Planning is the umbrella term used to describe large, multimodule, commercial software packages that integrate and automate the core functions of an enterprise, such as product planning, purchasing, material management, manufacturing planning, order fulfillment, human resources, customer relations, finance and accounting, and so on.
4.   Burlton, Roger, *Business Process Management,* Indianapolis, IN: SAMS, 2001.

and the questions and comments of thousands of workshop participants. Sure enough, even though the overall methodology was largely the same, many refinements had been made over the intervening six or seven years, and I had a host of new how-to tips and techniques that were working well for me and for others. It turned out Wayne was right, and there was more than enough new material to justify a new edition, so I agreed to get to work on it.

Once again, I found out how much work it is! In fact, it was much harder the second time around. As my friends have pointed out, being a bit ADD and a bit of a perfectionist is a bad combination. Without a writing partner to keep me on track, it was that much worse. Patrick's participation would have been a wonderful help this time around, but my travel schedule just didn't permit it.

Do We Really *Need* a Second Edition?

When we wrote the first edition, we had the luxury of a wide open field. No books had appeared in the business process arena for quite some time, although there were terrific works in progress concurrent with our first edition. Roger's book *Business Process Management*, as noted earlier, was published shortly after ours, in 2001. Paul Harmon's book *Business Process Change*[5] was published a couple of years later, in December 2002. Within a year or two of that, many more process-oriented books were appearing on the market. Ours had a different emphasis than the others, being aimed more at the "in the trenches" analyst, but in the larger scheme of things, all were "process books." This was apparently a field that was gathering interest.

Now, in 2008, the field is quite a bit more crowded, especially if you're looking for titles on Business Process Management, Lean methods, or Six Sigma. That being the case, a reasonable question is "Aren't there already many books covering what yours does?" Surprisingly, the answer is no. Let's explain that by first establishing what this second edition *doesn't* cover.

For starters, this is *not* a book on Business Process Management, Lean, Six Sigma, Lean Six Sigma, or any other widely used methodology. Practitioners in those areas told us they found the first edition useful, and I hope this one is as well, but if you want coverage of those topics there are already several fine titles to choose from. What else isn't it? Well, it's not a collection of case studies, nor is it a call to action exhorting you to get serious about business processes, nor is it a book on the necessary standards and supporting technologies such as BPMS, BAM, BPMN, BPEL, XPDL,[6] or any others.

So, what's left? Is there a market segment for business process books that *isn't* getting crowded? Yes, and it turns out to be the same one we set out to address over 10 years ago—anyone who has to undertake a process-oriented project, whether it's focused on business process redesign, information system implementation, or both. We still get feedback that *Workflow Modeling* is the only book that explains, in step-by-step fashion, how to carry out a complete project, from process discovery, scoping, and assessment, through modeling, analysis, and redesign, and on to cap-

5.   Harmon, Paul, *Business Process Change,* San Francisco, CA: Morgan Kaufmann, 2002.
6.   Respectively, Business Process Management System, Business Activity Monitoring, Business Process Modeling Notation, Business Process Execution Language, and XML Process Definition Language.

turing information systems requirements with use cases, services, and data models. Messing with that would be a thoroughly bad idea, so the purpose of the second edition is to provide an updated work that is even *more* useful and *more* practical than the first edition for people who are trying to get the job done on real projects. Sounds good, but what will the specific differences be?

What's Different This Time?

The first difference that a reader of the first edition is likely to notice is that the second edition has much more content than the first and is almost twice as large. That's because a substantial amount of additional material is included to address the issues that seem to bedevil people everywhere when they work on business processes:

- How to identify a true business process and convincingly demonstrate where one process ends and another begins;
- How to maintain focus on what a workflow model is really for and avoid the "deep dive into excruciating detail";
- How to separate "business modeling" from "implementation modeling";
- How to prepare for and facilitate a process modeling session;
- How to assess a process, before and after mapping it, without casting blame or building resentment;
- How to generate "out of the box" ideas for the to-be process;
- How to assess those brilliant ideas so the process isn't inadvertently made worse than it was before;
- How to transition from the to-be process model to information systems requirements.

Questions like these arise again and again, on projects in every sort of commercial or government enterprise, so they have received particular attention. The overall changes that readers of the first edition will notice include:

- The book is even more practical and how-to than the original; that's what people liked before, so now there's more emphasis on techniques, tips, tricks, traps, and advice.
- There's a refined overall structure that supports a clearer, three-phase methodology reflecting how successful projects are structured.
- It provides useful materials and samples to educate others on the key concepts and issues for business processes, which is necessary because "business process" is a widely used but misunderstood phrase.
- Timeframes are tighter and sessions are harder to organize than ever before, so there is greater emphasis on techniques for preparation and facilitation of highly productive sessions; specific methods are provided for process discovery, assessment, and mapping sessions.

- The refined techniques are supported by better and more (over 110) illustrations.
- An integrated example, included as an appendix, provides a sample of each key deliverable from a process-oriented project.

Regarding that last point, we were surprised after the first edition that we never received any comments that a single integrated case study should have been used throughout the book. Perhaps readers felt, as we did, that one case study couldn't cover the range of situations that had to be demonstrated. We were also reluctant to take a single client's project, "dirty laundry" and all, and share it with the world. Still, it seemed like a good idea to be able to demonstrate, all in one place, each of the key deliverables from a typical project. That has been accomplished with the help of my friends Brianna Knox and Dennis Korevitski, both of whom work in the BPM practice at Covestic, Inc. (www.covestic.com). Brianna and Dennis have a wealth of experience working with business processes, and all of us have completed assignments in the workplace safety and health field for various national and state or provincial agencies. We've used our experiences at these and similar regulatory agencies to create a realistic, composite example that studies the Inspect Employer process. We hope it will give you a better sense of the activities you'll go through as a project unfolds.

We'll look more closely at some of the updates in Chapter 1, but that summarizes what's different, which is substantial. In fact, the book has been almost completely rewritten, and we're optimistic that readers of the first edition will find this a worthwhile update. What hasn't changed are the intended audience and the goal. The book is still directed at the needs of business analysts and process analysts for whom process modeling and analysis is a core responsibility. It is also meant to be useful for others, such as business managers and project team members, whose interest in business processes might temporary but who nonetheless need clear explanations and practical techniques comprehensible to mere mortals. The goal is still to provide a set of methods and techniques that actually work in the real world, written by practitioners for practitioners, but augmented by close to a decade of additional experience.

So, for new and returning readers, I hope this book hits the mark. Either way, I look forward to hearing from you.

PART I

Background, Principles, Overview

CHAPTER 1

Business Processes—More Important Than Ever

Plus ça change, plus c'est la même chose.
(The more things change, the more it's all the same.)

Fosdick's Thesis

The first edition of this book began with the sentence: "Just when process orientation has become mainstream thinking for business people and systems people alike, it seems that the flow of process-oriented literature has pretty well stopped." That is hardly the case now, with a barrage of process-oriented books, articles, and conferences upon us. However, the comment is still relevant, so let us continue with what we wrote in 2000, which seems an eternity ago:

> So here we are, thousands of us, up to our necks in process improvement and information systems projects, finding that there is a real shortage of practical, how-to information. The irony of this situation was described in Howard Fosdick's terrific 1992 article, "The Sociology of Technology Adaptation" [1]. Our book isn't a book about technology, but there is a connection—the article dealt with the adoption of new technologies, and this book deals with the adoption of new methods and approaches for solving business problems.
>
> The article begins with the observation that when any significant new technology appears on the scene, it receives widespread publicity in the information technology (IT) arena. This attention could be displayed graphically [see Figure 1.1] in a publicity vector measured by such attributes as the number of articles on the technology in the trade press, the frequency of conferences on the topic, how many industry analysts discuss the technology, to what degree vendor sales pieces and ads employ the technology's terminology, and similar measurements. This curve initially rises steeply, but the high degree of publicity received by the technology is completely disproportionate to the usability of the technology and the number of people and organizations doing anything more than just talking about it. However, if the new technology takes hold and becomes widely used, as depicted by the rising usability curve, it seems to fall off the collective radar screen of the various publicity machines, and the publicity vector moves back toward zero.
>
> This happens, of course, because it's no longer a hot, new topic. Bluntly put, once the technology is widely installed, it is evidently time to focus on the next big thing—the consultants and IT advisory services have made their money, and the

vendors have a revenue stream in place. The consequence is that just at the point when the most people need practical information on the technology, the attention paid to it in publications becomes negligible. We always, it seems, are provided with a glut of material on the *next* big thing and not enough on how to make the *last* big thing actually work. Or, as Fosdick put it, "Ironically, once the technologies achieve full maturity, supporting hundreds or even thousands of shops on a daily basis, they receive much less attention in the media and other publicity forums."

Fosdick made his case using examples such as relational databases and expert systems, but the relevant example in our case is, of course, the emergence of business processes and business process reengineering (BPR) as important topics. The first references to cross-functional business processes appeared in the mid-1980s, and, by the early 1990s, BPR was without question the next big thing. It was attracting the attention of executives, managers, consultants, pundits, academics, IS professionals, and, of course, writers of books and articles from both business and IS orientations. These first publications covered the problems encountered by functionally oriented organizations, the justification for becoming process-oriented, a few soon-to-be-familiar examples, some introductory process concepts and terminology, and, if we were lucky, some actual how-to advice. Some of this how-to-do-it material was really just an attempt—sometimes sincere, sometimes a bit cynical—to capitalize on BPR by recasting older methods such as business systems planning or information engineering with a process-oriented spin. This was a familiar pattern, and, as usual, the results were not terribly useful. The other how-to material really tried to describe the new BPx[1] approach, but in the end provided little more than a high-level or broad-brush outline. The focus was on what had to be done, but the method was unproven and there was precious little guidance on how to actually do it. Practitioners the world over read about identifying the core business processes, mapping the as-is process, or creatively rethinking the process, but when they tried to put this guidance into practice, all manner of issues and problems arose.

However, those early works did serve a purpose. In fact, they were invaluable. They paved the way for widespread adoption by promoting process orientation with a key audience of early adopters—executives and other decision makers—and making it familiar and acceptable to the rest of us. Besides, how much practical advice could we realistically expect? At that point, there simply wasn't a large enough base of experience to draw on, and, without those books and articles to promote the concepts, there might never have been.

And Now?

On the surface, it seems that the situation is very different now. We can hardly say that the flow of information has dried up, because "business process" currently has a very high profile. Countless organizations have adopted business process management (BPM), which is supported by myriad books, courses, consulting organizations, and conferences. And of course, process improvement approaches that have their roots in manufacturing, like Lean and Six Sigma, have entered the daily business vocabulary and are backed up by books, courses, consulting organizations, and conferences.

---

1.   There are several variations of the term "business process reengineering." We like the one given in a presentation by Jerry Huchzermeier of ProForma Corp. He refers to *BPx* where "x" is "management," "engineering," "reengineering," "design," "redesign," "improvement," "innovation," and so forth.

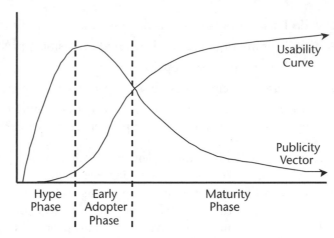

Figure 1.1 Usability versus publicity for new technologies. (*After:* [1].)

And real work is being done. Enterprises of all sizes and types—commercial, government, and not-for-profit—realize that business processes are the mechanism by which they deliver value, externally to the marketplace and their partners, and internally to their own organizations. Second, with the reality of the extended enterprise, the complexity and visibility of processes are rising because they now do not just span functional boundaries within an enterprise, they cross the boundaries between enterprises. In supply chain management, it's not unusual to see a business process with activities performed by the customer's customer, the customer, the enterprise, the supplier, and the supplier's supplier. In the face of this reality, organizations have made major investments of time and resources in the redesign of their processes and in the implementation of information systems to support them. Frequently, the order is reversed—an enterprise purchases an information system, often an enterprise resource planning (ERP) application, and then adapts its processes to take the best advantage of it. Either way, "process" is the focus of attention.

These developments mean that thousands of professionals from both business and information systems (IS) disciplines are engaged in the design and implementation of new business processes and systems. In spite of all this, we are regularly reminded that people and organizations need practical guidance in how to work with their business processes. That is where Mr. Fosdick's observation again proves to be true—there is a lot of literature available, but still very little to guide professionals through the day-to-day work of completing a project focused on business processes.

The Need for Practical Guidance

The need has been demonstrated in two ways. First, in our consulting and education assignments, we are continually asked by professionals working on process redesign and system implementation projects to suggest a reference book that will get past the theory of processes, or the management of processes, and into the practical matters they are struggling with. They want answers to questions such as the following:

- How do I discover my business processes?
- How do I get my organization interested in business processes?
- How do I clarify process scope?
- How do I assess them and establish appropriate goals and objectives?
- How do I model business processes in a way that is understandable to my business partners but is useful to my implementation teams?

Yes, BPM texts will advise on implementing and managing processes, Six Sigma texts will advise you on precisely how to analyze an activity within a business process, and the Lean literature provides marvelous techniques on eliminating waste and expediting flow within a process, but there is still precious little that really explains how to figure out what those end-to-end processes are and how to make them visible and vital to the enterprise.

What people look for is a book that addresses the issues they encounter when studying a complete business process and then makes the transition into the business analysis techniques that are the next step. We've heard repeatedly that the first edition of this book is the only one that focuses on these needs. In fact, one of our favorite reviews from Amazon.com begins simply, "At last, a how-to." It seems strange, though, that there aren't more books available offering a practical methodology.

The second kind of evidence of the need for this book comes from troubled projects. Many of our consulting engagements come about because a project has run into problems, often verging on outright failure. Our assignment, should we decide to accept it, is to determine what's gone wrong and set it right. The same issues show up so often that we have to conclude that people aren't getting the advice they need to help avoid these recurring problems. How could this be, given the number of people and organizations promoting business process management? This situation became so commonplace that Alec, somewhat in frustration, developed a conference presentation entitled "Getting Traction for Process—What the Experts Forget." The motivation was reading the literature and sitting in presentations that demonstrated that many business process experts had lost touch with the basic problems faced by professionals in the field. The first delivery of the presentation, at a BPM conference in San Diego, was very well received, and has since been delivered in various forms several times on three continents. The reaction has consistently been "Yes! Those are the issues I'm dealing with. Thanks for some ideas on how to move forward." Ironically, the issues addressed in the presentation were largely the same ones we cited in the first edition of the book:

1. Right from the earliest stages of a project, the wrong body of work is identified as a business process. This is common to virtually every troubled project we encounter. The "process" might be some activities that are actually just a piece of a process, the work performed by a specific department, or what we call a "process area" such as customer relationship management that comprises many processes. The result is that the scope balloons, the project drifts, and the potential benefits associated with improving a specific, complete business process are never realized. The alternative is that a single activity within a process is optimized without regard to other activities, and the entire process performs worse.

2. The complications that inevitably arise with a true, cross-functional business process are not addressed. Because the typical business process crosses many organizational and enterprise boundaries, issues around ownership, control, and objectives have to be expected and dealt with from the outset. The most important factor is that the goals and objectives of the process have to be put in context with the goals and objectives of the organizations involved, and they must be aligned. At a higher level, the goal of the process must match the goals of the enterprise. By default, it is usually assumed that the goal is to make the process more efficient (faster and cheaper) but this is not always, or even usually, a good assumption. Every organization doesn't choose to compete as the faster, cheaper provider, and every process customer doesn't choose the faster, cheaper alternative. We have a host of case studies where speed and cost were not the important variables, and new processes that met the fast and cheap criteria ended up failing.

3. Once the team begins to map or model the current ("as-is") process, the work gets bogged down in excruciating detail while, ironically, missing important participants and steps. Modeling leaps ahead from scope (which might not be all that clearly specified, either) directly to implementation issues, bypassing a business-oriented view. In extreme cases, so much time is wasted on excessively detailed as-is modeling that the project is canceled before any improvements can be identified, much less implemented. In any case, the true dynamics of the business process are not revealed, as they are buried in models depicting detailed rules and logic. An additional downside is that the organization learns that studying a process means engaging in a "death march" of sorts, and "process" gets a bad name.

4. Business processes and information systems are treated as two different worlds. This is becoming less common, but we still see major applications or technologies implemented without regard to the impact on end-to-end business processes, and new processes are designed and redesigned without taking into account how innovative use of IT could transform them. The result: the system impedes rather than supports the process, the wrong activities are automated, or a system that supports individual tasks as they are currently understood is developed but doesn't expedite the entire process.

5. The assessment of the current process and the design of the new process don't take a holistic view. The most common issue is that all of the factors that constitute a successful business process—the six enablers that we introduce in Chapter 4—aren't considered. Another issue is that the needs of individual stakeholders, including customers, performers, and owners, aren't addressed. This leads to incorrect assumptions about what aspects of the process are causing problems and need to be changed, which in turn leads to process "improvements" that are, unbelievably, detrimental to the overall process.

Obviously, there was a need when the first edition was written, and many people, projects, and organizations are still using and presumably benefiting from it. We've worked with a number of groups that refer to it simply as "the bible" (or "the green book") and have seen many copies that positively bristled with Post-it notes where someone had marked key points. We hope that a new edition, incorporating even more practical guidelines and techniques, with a shiny new 2008 publication date, will attract new and returning readers.

Building Methods to Meet the Need

At this point, you might well ask, "How did *you* figure this out?" Probably much the same way that you would—we had to piece techniques together ourselves, drawing on multiple sources, experimenting on the job, and learning from colleagues and clients. For example, when we wrote the first edition, there was no Business Process Modeling Notation (BPMN) standard for swimlane diagramming, and not a single text provided any guidelines for the techniques; they provided just a few examples. In fact, there still isn't a text that provides guidelines—the closest we've seen are descriptions of the standards, but nothing that answers many of the questions people have when they draw their first workflow model. We had no choice but to "make it up." This has continued over the almost 10 years since the first edition, and many new techniques and lessons have been incorporated.

As before, we are grateful to our clients and associates for helping us develop our methods, by trial and error, on real projects. In return, we will preserve their anonymity. Much of our experience comes from dealing with projects that have gone off the rails, so we refer to these cases throughout the book because people learn just as much from the stories of what *not* to do as from advice about what *to* do. However, we will not refer to any organizations by name, and in some cases we will even disguise the industry or build an example that is an amalgam. We do not want a client to read this and suddenly realize in horror, "Oh, no! They're talking about my project!" If you were worried, you can breathe a sigh of relief and get back to reading the book!

Another important factor has been the two-day "Workflow Process Modeling" workshop that Alec conducts globally for business and IT participants and was the basis for the first edition of this book. During the initial development, almost 15 years ago, it provided the incentive to look back over past projects and document what had worked well and what hadn't. Sometimes, it was a surprise—it's amazing what can be learned by looking objectively at your own experience! Since then, the workshop has been a great vehicle for keeping our methods up to date. First, it motivates us to constantly keep an eye out for what is working in practice so it can be reflected in the workshop, as well as watch for methods that used to work well but are less effective now. Obvious factors that have changed the business environment include outsourcing, globalization, and time pressures, each of which has led to changes in our approach. Second, it puts us in direct contact with hundreds of professionals per year who tell us exactly what issues they face, what works and doesn't work for them, and, if they're already using our techniques, what their organization's experience has been. Their questions are a great source of insight into the problems faced in the field. Sometimes we wonder who is teaching whom.

What to Expect

As we noted in the preface, the goal of this book was, and remains, to provide a practical exposition of methods that actually work in the real world, written by practitioners for practitioners. Alec still remembers how useful the classic textbook *Structured Systems Analysis* [2] was in 1979 when he was coping with his first major analysis assignment. He'd go through a chapter or two in the evening and put the material to work the very next day. The next night, another chapter, and the day after that, more progress on his project. And, wonder of wonders, the project was very successful. We have heard many times, from readers around the world, that the first edition met that goal, so we have tried to make that aspect even stronger by having the core three parts of the book organized around the three phases of our methodology:

- Part I—Background, Principles, Overview;
- Part II—Phase 1: Establish Process Context, Scope, and Goals;
- Part III—Phase 2: Understand the As-Is Process;
- Part IV—Phase 3: Design the To-Be Process;
- Part V—Related Requirements Definition Techniques.

Part I provides the necessary underpinnings; Parts II, III, and IV cover our three-phase, project-oriented methodology; and Part V introduces the requirements modeling techniques you will employ if you carry on into specifying information systems requirements.

Whatever you do, please don't leap immediately into Part II. Chapter 3 answers the question "what is a business process?" and is essential reading. It lays the groundwork of terms, definitions, and methods that will be critical when you undertake the discovery of processes using the techniques in Chapter 5. The entire approach is summarized in Chapter 4, "The Approach in a Nutshell," which provides context for individual phases and steps. After you read those two chapters, you will be able to read a later chapter and immediately apply it to your project, read the next chapter or two, apply them, and so on.

Who Are "You"?

We have tried to make the book suitable for a broad audience that includes business people responsible for improving their business processes and systems personnel working on a development or implementation project with a process focus. The book has to address both perspectives, because successful process redesign projects usually involve major information systems efforts, and the implementation of a significant information system usually involves redesigned processes.

The three specific audiences we aim to satisfy are as follows:

- Process analysts or study/implementation team members whose job or project responsibilities include process improvement. This is the primary audience, the people "in the trenches," and we aim to provide a toolkit for discovering, modeling, analyzing, and improving business processes. This group includes those whose ongoing job is process analysis and those with a temporary assignment to a process improvement project.

• Business analysts, systems analysts, and project leaders who have responsibility for requirements definition, possibly associated with purchased software selection and configuration. We will demonstrate how to work with business processes, how to use "process" as a means for getting the attention of the business, and how to use it as framework for requirements definition, whether the intent is system development or system selection and configuration.

• Business executives and managers who have been given responsibility for process improvement. In addition to showing how to work with processes, we'll show how to link business strategy and business processes.

In closing, a caveat—we describe an overall methodology and the details of specific steps, but this isn't a cookbook. It's close, but not quite. Every project we have worked on has unique issues, and yours will be no different. Use these methods and techniques as a starting point, but please adjust and experiment as you see fit—that is how we developed many of our methods and continue to evolve them. Remember, though, that experience shows unequivocally that if you skip steps like "framing the process" or "characterizing the to-be process," you will regret it—"adjust and experiment" does not imply "short-circuit and eliminate."

That point about not skipping steps, strangely enough, brings us back to Howard Fosdick, whose description of the publicity vector introduced this chapter. While writing this chapter, it seemed appropriate to do a Web search to see what Mr. Fosdick was up to these days. We found an article he had written on "Reincarnating a Discarded Laptop with Linux" [3], which is interesting in its own right but also included an observation that perfectly backed up the point about not skipping steps. Late in the process of making a discarded laptop useable, probably anxious to see the fruits of his labors rewarded, Mr. Fosdick skipped a small step in the installation of new memory. Just as it is on a process improvement project, skipping a simple but vital step caused no end of grief. He wrote, "This one error cost me two days of mystery and consternation (as much time as the entire planning and install process). I had proved the hard way that jumping ahead too quickly—instead of patiently working through procedures one step at a time—is often the most costly error you can make." That is profoundly true in the world of process improvement, so once again Mr. Fosdick provides a touchstone for our book.

Before moving on to the methods, the next chapter offers a brief history lesson of how enterprises have come to be process oriented. This will set the stage for Chapter 3, which clarifies what we mean by "business process," which in turn sets the stage for Chapter 4's overview of our methodology for working with business processes.

References

[1]   Fosdick, H., "The Sociology of Technology Adaptation," *Enterprise Systems Journal*, September 1992.

[2]   Gane, C., and T. Sarson, *Structured Systems Analysis: Tools and Techniques*, New York: Improved Systems Technologies, 1977.

[3]   Fosdick, H., "Reincarnating a Discarded Laptop with Linux," http://www.desktoplinux .com/articles/AT6185716632.html, August 1, 2006.

CHAPTER 2

A Brief History—How the Enterprise Came to Be Process Oriented

Those who are ignorant of history are condemned to repeat it.
—George Santayana

Learning from the Past

Within less than 20 years, the improvement of enterprise performance through the identification, assessment, and improvement of the enterprise's business processes has become standard practice at organizations all over the world. More than standard practice, it has become a recognized discipline, known less formally as process orientation and more formally as business process management. You can even get a master's degree in it. Now, "process" seems so intrinsic to the management of corporations, government agencies, and other institutions that it's easy to forget that it's still a relatively new field. In fact, for most of the twentieth century, until about 1990, there was virtually no discussion of the concept of business processes. Deming is a notable exception, but his seminal work on quality was largely ignored (except in Japan) for decades. At the dawn of the century, the scientific management revolution[1] began the quest to find the best way to design manufacturing processes, but the focus was on individual tasks, not on improving what we have come to know as an end-to-end business process. This focus on individual tasks remained in place for most of the century, and didn't start to change until the mid-1980s, when references to "cross-functional work" first started to appear widely. Then, in the early 1990s, BPR burst onto the scene with an explosion of interest in business processes. This was accompanied by a massive transfer of wealth from large enterprises to BPR consulting firms, which played no small part in our interest in the field.

And then, almost as quickly as it had arrived, BPR went from "silver bullet" to "pariah" status. By the mid-1990s, apologetic books and articles were common, explaining what had gone wrong and even how misguided the notion of BPR had been. Reengineering fell off the list of hot topics. At many organizations, reengineering went from badge of honor to forbidden term, and consultants moved on to greener pastures (ERP and Y2K,[2] anyone?).

---

1. By Frederick Taylor and others. See Robert Kanigel, *The One Best Way: Frederick Winslow Taylor and the Enigma of Efficiency* (New York: Penguin Books, 1997), for a good story about the dawn of management consulting. Although he is often criticized for a focus on tasks, Taylor clearly understood the principles of end-to-end processes and may have been the first reengineer.
2. As the Year 2000 crisis was popularly known.

Fast forward to the present, and we see another surprising about-face—"business process" is again very much a hot topic, and even the term *reengineering* has been rehabilitated and is serving a useful, albeit fringe, role in business. What brought about this roller coaster ride? How can a concept like "business process" go from silver bullet to pariah to fact of life? To understand this, we first have to recognize that "business process" has taken on a specific meaning—a complete end-to-end set of activities that provide value, through the delivery of a product or service, to the customer of the process. End-to-end means that the process is wide—it crosses organizational and functional boundaries (a critical aspect of most true business processes!), encompassing activities all the way from the triggering event right through to the end result expected by the customer.[3]

So what's the big deal? To take the most common example, wasn't it obvious that there was a Fulfill Order process that began when a customer placed an order, and ended when it was delivered and paid for? How could this simple discovery have been a breakthrough in the organization of work and the cause of a virtual revolution in management thinking? To understand, we need to take a brief, simplified look at the history and forces that led to the reengineering revolution, and what has happened since then. This certainly won't be an exhaustive account, and probably not even a linear account, but that's not our purpose—we just want to help put the current state of affairs in context by illustrating the themes, phases, and trends that got us here. With apologies to Stephen Hawking, author of *A Brief History of Time*, let's start our Brief History of Process by going back to a time before we worried about functions and processes—before the Industrial Revolution.

The Multiskilled Craftsworker

Prior to the Industrial Revolution of the mid-1700s, most products were produced by individuals we'll call craftsworkers—highly skilled people like weavers, blacksmiths, or jewelers who were responsible for all phases of making a complete, finished product. To them, you might say that process and product were the same thing. It was possible to stand at one spot in their workshops and observe the construction of a product in its entirety. In fact, one person often accomplished the entire process—and not just the manufacturing, but the marketing, sales, design, and service as well. Today, a small proportion of workers are directly involved in making the products or delivering the services their companies provide, and those few typically see only a small part of the process. For many products and services today, you would have to visit multiple locations, on two or more continents, to view the complete process of building or providing it, unlike the process that had been visible from one spot in the craftsworker's shop.

The age of the craftsworker was characterized by an expert individual performing most or all of the activities comprising a central production process, and exhibited the following:

---

3. When discussing business processes, "customer" isn't restricted to its usual interpretation as an external, paying (usually) client of the enterprise. Customer can be any internal or external stakeholder expecting a result from a process.

- Positives:
  - It was clearly understood who the customer was, what the product or service was, and what needed to be measured—the output of the finished product.
  - The craftsworker, who knew the whole process from beginning to end, was the single point of contact for the customer.
  - Products and services could be customized relatively easily.
  - With a single contact, there could be no miscommunication or handoffs between specialties.
- Negatives:
  - There was very limited output, and scaling up was extremely difficult.
  - The work essentially stopped during the transitions from one task to another, resulting in high overhead.
  - There was no entry-level workforce available, as a new craftsworker required an extended apprenticeship.
  - There was a single point of failure with no backup or synergies.
  - Quality could be erratic, because the individual was not necessarily expert in all aspects of the process.

Many of the negatives (and positives) were swept away with the Industrial Revolution and the advent of factories.

The Advent of the Specialist

In 1776, Adam Smith heralded the Industrial Revolution in *The Wealth of Nations* [1]. James Watt's invention of the steam engine provided power that only a new industrial organization could harness. To be supported by newly available mechanical power, this new organization called for the division of labor into specialized tasks. The simple pin provides a classic example of the power of specialization. Before this advance, pins were made individually by craftsworkers. This made them such expensive luxuries that money for frivolities was called "pin money," since only people with money to squander bought pins. Smith describes in detail how this changed when the manufacture of pins was divided among many workers, each performing a specialized task: "One man draws out the wire, another straightens it, a third cuts it, a fourth points it, a fifth grinds it at the top for receiving the head; to make the head requires three distinct operations; to put it on is a peculiar business, to whiten the pins another; it is even a trade unto itself to put them into the paper." This specialization allowed a fantastic increase in the number of pins produced, making pins readily available to anyone. Smith notes how 10 men, who, individually, could not make even 20 pins in a day, were collectively able to make 48,000 pins in a day by dividing the labor and specializing.

Popularly, the Industrial Revolution is associated with the arrival of the steam engine, but its real legacy was the division of complex work into simpler tasks. The success of this approach during the age of the factory gave rise to further division and narrower specialties, leading to the emergence of large organizations structured around functional specialties.

The Rise of Functional Specialties

As the successes arising from the Industrial Revolution took hold, organizations grew and required personnel not just in manufacturing, but in such diverse areas as finance, accounting, legal, human resources, and facilities. More sophisticated products and customers necessitated growth in other areas as well, among them marketing, research and development, engineering, purchasing, stores, logistics, manufacturing planning, and sales. Equally important was the emergence of professional managers to "plan, organize, and control" all those various activities. Since specialization worked spectacularly well in the factories, it seemed likely to apply equally well in the growing field of office work. Consequently, white-collar (professional, technical, and managerial) employment levels rose steeply, with a corresponding decrease in the proportion of employees actually doing the work that produced the product. A cynic might argue that many, if not most, white-collar workers were concerned with increasing the efficiency of the few remaining blue-collar workers, but that misses the point. While the resulting bureaucracy has often been criticized, it was the glue that allowed large organizations to come into existence and thrive.[4]

It is fair to ask how this new breed of professional manager was to manage all of the additional work. Well, for one thing, it's easier to manage people and their activities if they are grouped into specialized fields such as finance, engineering, and manufacturing, each with its own skills, language, tools, and outlook. The strengths of specialization were already well known, so the path of least resistance led to further specialization and the "functionally oriented" organization that dominated most of the twentieth century. While this specialization has been widely condemned, it has certain advantages, and the large enterprises of the twentieth century simply would not have emerged without this style of organization.

Positives of specialization include:

- Vastly increased output and economies of scale, often with a consistent and surprisingly high level of quality;
- Easier management of personnel, as they were doing a specific kind of work ("birds of a feather");
- Development of very high skill levels that were constantly increasing;
- Ability to scale up or down relatively easily (add, subtract, or reassign specialists);
- Building around recognized fields allowing educational institutions to supply entry-level recruits who then have a career path.

---

4.   Although our discussion so far has centered on manufacturing organizations, the same happened in service-providing organizations—banks, insurance companies, hospitals, utilities, government agencies, and so on.

All in all, the functionally oriented organization was a spectacular success, although obviously not without its problems. Otherwise, reengineering would never have had any reason to emerge. Before looking at the downsides, however, we need to clarify a common point of confusion, which is that function and organization are the same thing.

Function and Organization—What's the Difference?

The distinction between function and organization can be subtle. Take a moment to think about the functions of your company—what are the specialties that make up the whole? You would probably list the major divisions or departments comprising the higher reaches of your organizational chart. The functions of an organization are usually so similar to the structure of the organization that most people think organization and function are synonymous, with the manufacturing function being carried out by the manufacturing organization, the logistics function carried out by the logistics organization, the customer care function carried out by the customer service organization, and so on. However, as noted, function and organization are actually different concepts. An organization is a mechanism for grouping people and other resources to achieve a common purpose. The purpose could be to provide not only a function, but also to support a particular customer segment or product line or geography, or even to carry out a complete process. A function, on the other hand, is a specialized field of endeavor involving work of a similar nature, employing particular skills and knowledge. They're often treated interchangeably because it's so common for major organizational units to be defined along functional lines. These definitions provide an important clue to the central problem with organizations based on functional specialties—what *was* the common purpose that these functional organizations sought to achieve? Not surprisingly, it turns out that common purpose was to provide a function, which can be quite a different orientation than to provide some end product or service.

Losing the Process in the Functions

In general, workers and departments in a healthy organization do the best they can to contribute to the organization's success, so they optimize the work they do. But optimizing the individual parts does not optimize the whole. For one thing, if you can't see the whole, you might inadvertently be damaging the end result when optimizing a piece of the process. What's good for sales might not be best for the entire company. Immediate considerations, such as getting the order, might conflict with financial considerations, such as "collect all necessary information to cost and bill the transaction." Consider the steps of the process to fill an order for a customized widget, illustrated in Figure 2.1.

Take Order should collect all the information to make, ship, and collect payment for the widget, even if it slows down taking the order. If manufacturing must be tracked in sufficient detail to bill costs to the customer and to analyze the process for improvement, wouldn't that also introduce delays? While the billing and ship-

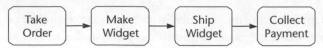

Figure 2.1   Main steps in the Fulfill Order process.

ping functions might prefer to batch transactions for efficiency, that might not be best for the customer or the enterprise. So the limited perspective of each part might lose us the opportunity to improve the whole. We'll explore this phenomenon much more closely later on, beginning in Chapter 3.

In many cases, the measurements underpinning the reward system further exacerbate this situation. A manufacturing function trying to maximize equipment utilization by minimizing setup or changeover time might schedule production runs in a way that meets these targets. The problem is that the schedule might not take into account the dollar value or profitability of the order, the importance of the customer, or any number of other factors that are ultimately just as, or more, important than equipment utilization.

To summarize, while specialization yielded huge efficiency gains, it introduced problems as well. Many have been documented, but they are usually variations of the following:

- The overall process became so fragmented that it was no longer visible and thus couldn't be measured or improved. Remember, the process was always there, it was just hidden by a focus on functions and specialties. No one could see the big (end-to-end) picture, and narrow specialization often led to inadvertent narrow-mindedness. The terminology introduced with business process reengineering to describe functional departments—the *functional silo* or *functional stovepipe*—graphically conveys an image of a vertical structure that you can't see into or out of.

- Activities and methods optimized the function to the detriment of the overall process and the customer. The common purpose driving organizational units (divisions, departments, and so on) became inwardly focused. If they were doing well, it was assumed that so was the entire enterprise. Similarly, "customer" became such a distant concept as to be irrelevant to many groups.

- There was a lack of communication, and sometimes there was even outright conflict, between functions, and these cross-functional disputes were difficult to resolve, typically requiring executive involvement.

- As a work item or transaction winds its way through the fragmented process, the handoffs between specialized individuals and groups cause delay, errors, expense, and frustration. Two common examples that made the function more efficient but had a negative impact on the overall process:

  1. For the function to handle a specific work item as efficiently as possible, it was common to batch several items up before work was started so that many similar pieces of work could be done at once.

  2. To further improve processing efficiency, the item was transformed in some way—for instance, by translating, formatting, and reentering data into another system.

As none of this is intended to imply that these problems were the product of some deliberate malfeasance, we'll take a moment to address a couple of important points:

1. In practice, we avoid the use of the term *functional silo* because it has such negative connotations. There's nothing inherently wrong with a functionally based organization, and using the term can alienate the people who manage or work within them. As we'll start to explore in Chapter 3, it's arguably the best way to organize resources.
2. The people that were optimizing their functions at the expense of the overall process were not lazy, stupid, malicious, or anything of the sort. As previously noted, everyone in a healthy organization is typically doing their best, usually within in the constraints of a structure they had no part in designing.

What was becoming apparent by the mid-1980s, however, and is still happening in many enterprises, was that over two centuries the pendulum had swung too far from generalization toward specialization. This led, not surprisingly, to a reaction, which was, of course, business process reengineering. Just as the age of the craftsworker gave rise to the age of the factory, the rise of functional specialties led to the reengineering revolution.

Enter Reengineering: 1990–1993

The insight of reengineering, profound at the time, was that by identifying, making visible, understanding, rethinking, and then radically redesigning *end-to-end* business processes, they could be dramatically improved. The process-centered organization would focus on the whole and see accumulated inefficiencies and irrationalities eliminated. Measurement would shift from individual tasks, such as checking the most forms or stamping the greatest number of fenders, to the achievement of value, such as the acquisition of a desirable new customer or the timely delivery of a high-quality product or service. The innovative use of information technology was a crucial factor, but so was rethinking the flow of work, the measurements that motivated performance, the underlying policies of the enterprise, and other enabling (or disabling!) factors.

The "shot heard 'round the world" of the reengineering revolution was the late Michael Hammer's article, "Reengineering Work: Don't Automate, Obliterate" [2]. Hammer introduced BPR and called it "undoing the Industrial Revolution," because it undid overspecialization and reunified tasks into coherent, visible processes. Actually, reengineering was well under way before the term was coined by Hammer and then promoted by newly minted BPR consulting organizations. For example:

- The auto industry was using concurrent engineering and team-based assembly well before BPR burst onto the stage.
- Financial services organizations had learned to completely transform excruciatingly sequential and fragmented processes such as granting a loan along lines we'd later describe as "end-to-end business processes."

- Deming had for many years stressed that "everyone doing their best is not the answer; rather, the system must be changed." In other words, understand and improve your business processes.

- By the mid-1980s, Michael Porter had introduced *value chains*, and Tom Peters, famous for coauthoring "In Search of Excellence," had predicted that the coming decade would see a focus on *cross-functional work*.

Michael Hammer, though, performed the invaluable service of identifying the approach, describing it, and, possibly most important, giving it a great name—*business process reengineering*. That name instantly appealed to the frustrated engineer in many of us. The credit given to Hammer seems to drive some observers crazy, because they feel that Porter, Deming, Rummler and Brache, and others deserve wider recognition for their contributions in the area. This is true, but it was Hammer who moved the concept of "reengineering end-to-end cross-functional business processes" into the limelight. After that, the improved performance of some early adopters drove home the point that process orientation was the way to go.

It's hard to convey, almost 20 years later, the impact this had. The concept of looking at end-to-end processes made so much sense—it was so "intuitively obvious"—and there was so much shared frustration from working *in* or *with* the oft-cited functional silos that BPR just *had* to take off. And take off it did. Reengineering took the management world by storm in a way no trend before it had. And in that rapid rise were the beginnings of its downfall a few short years later.

Exit Reengineering: 1994–1995

By the mid-1990s, so many organizations were claiming to be "doing BPR" that a 1995 "Devil's Dictionary" in *Fortune* magazine defined reengineering as "the principal slogan of the '90s, used to describe any and all corporate strategies." And therein lay the root cause of BPR's demise—it became a buzzword, subject to misuse, as buzzwords always are. Consider some statements we actually heard at the time:

- "I *reengineered* my department by putting our forms on an imaging-based workflow system."

- "We *reengineered* our customer service operation by laying off 30 percent of the staff."

- "Our logistics process was *reengineered* by outsourcing it to a low-cost provider."

Reengineering became a euphemism for the thoughtless application of IT, for slash-and-burn downsizing, restructuring, and outsourcing. Reengineer went from something you *do*, to something that's done *to* you, as in "I was reengineered out of my job."

On top of outright misuse of the term, the principles at the heart of true reengineering proved to be difficult to implement and widely misunderstood. This isn't all that surprising, given that we now know how complex it can be. Most of the literature and education that began appearing after Hammer's article didn't really describe *how* to work with business processes. Instead, it breathlessly explained the theory and recirculated the popular case studies, all the while ignoring the motivational, human resource, and other factors that, as we'll see, are so important. In many cases, advice was given that was just plain bad. The classic example—"don't worry about analyzing the as-is process, because you're just going to abandon it anyway." Another common problem (which Hammer had explicitly warned against!)[5] was "reengineering" something that wasn't actually a process. It's astounding how many reengineering efforts applied to a "business process" that, strangely, exactly fit within the boundaries of a department or function. Of course, this only exacerbated the problems of isolation and specialization.

The Wonder Years: 1996–2000

On the heels of the reengineering backlash, the mid- to late 1990s saw focus on information technology to an extent that caused us to wonder just *what* everyone could have been thinking (hence the term *the wonder years*). Attention shifted from the silver bullet of reengineering processes through IT to IT itself as a silver bullet. "Process" as a discipline fell by the wayside, along with other skills and practices. Some of the IT topics getting the most attention and money included the following:

- All things Internet-related, such as *e*-business, *e*-commerce, *e*-procurement, and *e*-recruiting, to name but a few. We've somewhat uncharitably referred to this as the "*e*-whatever" phenomenon—take any struggling project, put "*e*-" in front of its name, and suddenly it's revived.

- Y2K remediation, with which, unlike some post-2000 commentators, we have no problem. At many organizations, we saw these efforts head off serious problems. Of course, the fact that the problems then failed to occur was grist for the cynic's mill. Our interest, for this discussion, is that it did divert a lot of time and resources, and the avenue chosen by many firms was to implement an ERP package, as per the next point.

- ERP applications from providers like SAP, Oracle, and PeopleSoft (before its acquisition by Oracle). ERP was the name given to families of very large, commercial software packages intended to integrate mainstream business data and functions (e.g., sales, human resources, finance, and manufacturing) across the enterprise, which likely has a familiar ring to it.

Unfortunately, many of these initiatives weren't any more successful than the previous BPR initiatives, such as the following:

- A manufacturer's e-business project receives a chilly reception from its intended beneficiaries—clients who would use the facility to submit design

5.   Hammer was on record as saying "Reengineering a department is an oxymoron." The upshot was that reengineering efforts worked out much less well than hoped, and within a few short years of the ascendancy of BPR, reports of high-profile failures spread. There was shock in reengineering circles when articles appeared [3] citing a failure rate among BPR projects of 70 to 80 percent! BPR began fading from the consciousness of the enterprise, and interest shifted to other bright and shiny objects.

validation requests. The process required substantially more effort on the manufacturer's part than anticipated and didn't fit well with its development process.

- At an engineering firm specializing in oil exploration, an expensive intranet-based program combines best practices from the disciplines of data management and knowledge management, but the firm finds the results unused.

- A beer distributor decides that typical development practices such as business analysis and systems architecture were anachronistic and trusts the development of a major new distribution application to a hot-shot Web design company. When we were called in to look at the unfolding disaster, we were stunned to find that the developers thought they were going to prototype their way to a successful implementation across a complex supply chain and that they really (really!) didn't know what a database was.

- The costs of an ERP implementation at a global retailer spiral ever-upward, with configuration becoming increasingly complex; the results are met with hostility by the primary users, and no net benefit is realized.

A common denominator in all of these examples was that they failed in large part because they didn't adequately take "business process" into account, a realization that was soon to take hold.

Business Process Rides Again!: 2000–Present

Readers of the first edition of this book might wonder at this point if we've engaged in a little revisionist history. In that edition our timeline went directly from "Exit Reengineering: 1994–1995" to "The Reengineering Aftermath: 1996–Present," in which we offered the rosy view that we'd seen the merging of continuous improvement and reengineering into what we called *process management*. But what about "the wonder years"? Well, we wrote our process history in 1999, and, in hindsight, we were a little optimistic about that post-1995 period. Being heads-down at organizations that had embraced a process perspective, we weren't paying a lot of attention to some of the "wonder years" hysteria or IT disasters unfolding throughout the economy. The dot-com meltdown of 2000 and the subsequent economic contraction were followed by a flood of analysts' reports and "true confessions" articles about what had really been going on, which led us to look at the preceding years more critically.

A consequence of the "dot-bomb" bust was that money was no longer falling from the skies, and many companies suddenly had to pay intense attention to expenditures. Some individuals found that "after years of being asked to do more with *more*, [they were] being asked in a serious way to do more with less," as Richard Hunter, a research fellow at Gartner, Inc., so aptly put it. Boards of directors started asking about previous expenditures, and a common avenue of inquiry was "What was the return on investment for our ERP implementation?" Bear in mind that these projects had price tags that extended into the tens and even hundreds of millions of dollars! Perhaps these execs had been listening to John Parkinson, VP and chief technologist at Cap Gemini Ernst & Young. In an April 2003 Fast Company article he said, "Between 1997 and 2000, the North American economy bought 40% more technology than it needed. It wasn't entirely irrational, but it wasn't all that smart either." He continued: "I believe the $300 billion we spent on ERP systems was the biggest waste of money in the last century."

Much of the executive curiosity about ROI was driven by our old friend Michael Hammer, who concluded in a significant and widely publicized study that implementations of a certain large ERP application fell into either the "winners" or "losers" category. That is, the enterprise either did really well, or not very well at all, with little middle ground. What accounted for the difference? Of course, it seems self-serving, but it turned out that the winners treated their ERP implementation as primarily a business process improvement undertaking, supported in part by new technology but with due attention to the other important factors. The losers, on the other hand, treated it primarily as a technology undertaking, without regard for the all-important business process issues. Observations such as this one spread and, together with regulatory developments like Sarbanes-Oxley and BASEL II, highlighted the need for organizations to understand and control their business processes. As Ed Yourdon, the longtime IT leader and commentator pointed out at a conference around this time, "You process folks just got a whole new lease on life." Figure 2.2 summarizes the path process orientation has taken.

From Fad to Business as Usual

Process orientation is part of the organizational landscape, and part of the reason for this is that best practices and a balanced perspective with some middle ground have emerged—the focus on business processes is less faddish and more reasoned

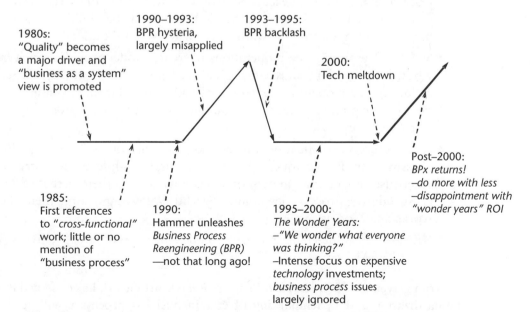

Figure 2.2 The rise and fall and rise again of continuous process improvement.

and pragmatic than it was in the reengineering era. Rather than proclaiming that they are "doing reengineering," organizations understand that dealing with their business processes is normal behavior. We'll now touch on some of the evidence that "process is normal" but please (please!) bear in mind that this is by no means intended to be a compete survey of "the state of business process"—it's just a quick overview of the current environment with some references for readers interested in following up on specific topics.

Process-Oriented Products

Products and services are available in a growing number of process-oriented areas, such as the following:

- Supply chain management (SCM) and reverse SCM for dealing with returns;
- Customer relationship management (CRM);
- Product lifecycle management (PLM).

Note that each of these is an example of what we'll later define as a "process area," a named collection of interrelated business processes. A quick Web search will uncover a wealth of information on these and other areas.

Process Frameworks

Vendor-neutral bodies have made available a number of process frameworks that provide a variety of resources, including standard process descriptions and terminology, benchmarks, and best practices. The best-known are probably the following:

- ITIL—The Information Technology Infrastructure Library, which was originally developed under the leadership of the U.K.'s Office of Government Commerce (OGC) but is now used globally as a baseline for IT service management. See http://www.itil.co.uk or www.itsmf.org.
- SCOR—The supply-chain operations reference model provides a rich framework, covering plan, source, make, deliver, and return process types. See also the design-chain operations reference (DCOR) model from the same organization, covering plan, research, design, integrate, and amend process types. See http://www.supply-chain.org.
- APQC process classification framework—quoting from it, "the APQC Process Classification Framework[SM] (PCF) serves as a high-level, industry-neutral enterprise model that allows organizations to see their activities from a cross-industry process viewpoint." See http://www.apqc.org, then "Frameworks and Models."
- VRM—The value-chain reference model. See www.value-chain.org, then select "VRM."

Tom Davenport, in a *Harvard Business Review* article [4], has observed that the standardization and benchmarking of certain business processes will accelerate. Standard process definitions and performance measures will in turn allow businesses to choose more objectively among alternate business process outsourcing service providers. And this, as the title implies, will lead to the commoditization of outsourced business processes, which surely demonstrates how much process orientation is part of the landscape.

Less Polarization

Currently, we see much less tension between perspectives previously at odds with one another:

1. Process and function;
2. Continuous improvement and radical redesign;
3. Systems development and process reengineering.

Let's take a look, in turn, at the rapprochement that's occurred in each of these.

Process and function: In the rush to embrace the new, writers and consultants often fail to take note of the benefits of whatever they want to leave behind. This was certainly true during the heyday of reengineering, when there was a steady stream of commentary about the flaws of functional orientation and the virtues of process orientation. However, if functional orientation did not have some benefits, it would not have prevailed for most of the twentieth century. The benefits became evident, belatedly, at some companies that took process orientation to the extreme of implementing organization structures based on processes rather than functional specialties. It seemed like a great idea at the time, but, in most cases, didn't work out very well. The new structures were hard to manage and inefficient in sharing skilled resources. Worst of all, skill levels in functional specialties declined. More recently, there is general awareness that functional specialties are a great way to develop high levels of skill in a pool of resources that can be used efficiently across multiple processes. The processes, of course, must be designed to flow smoothly through the functions and focus effort around the end result.

Continuous improvement and radical redesign: Continuous process improvement (CPI), and its cousin total quality management (TQM), are outgrowths of Deming's work, especially in Japan, where the term *kaizen* originates. Kaizen [5] is the concept of continuous improvement, its central tenet being that you must continuously improve your processes to keep a quality product in production. When reengineering first emerged, there was considerable tension between the reengineering and kaizen (or CPI or TQM) communities. The reengineers wondered why their kaizen-oriented counterparts were improving processes that ought to have been scrapped. Those who espoused kaizen found the reengineers to be rash and destructive, often throwing out the baby with the bathwater. Eventually, the two were brought together under the milder terms *process orientation* or *process management*, with the recognition that reengineering a process is done once (or periodically), and improving it (kaizen) goes on forever (see Figure 2.3). Kaizen and BPR have become less state of the art and more standard practice, even though the terms are not used as widely as they once were. In recent years, the "official" term has become business process management (BPM), which is the subject of numerous books, service offerings, conferences, and courses. A quick Web search will reveal

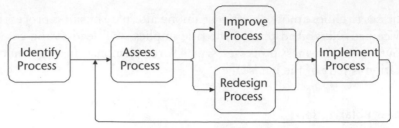

Figure 2.3   Merging of process reengineering and continuous process improvement.

many sources of information, or you could go directly to the always excellent www.bptrends.com, www.bpminstitute.org, or www.bpm.com. When supported by an appropriate business process management system (BPMS), BPM extends to controlling the execution of processes and the active monitoring of and intervention in executing processes. As noted earlier, this is a book on process modeling and analysis, not BPM or BPMS, so we won't try to explain the field. There are many other books available, and a visit to either of the aforementioned Web sites or Amazon.com will uncover them.

Systems development and process reengineering: Just as BPR proponents were at loggerheads with kaizen aficionados, they also ran into conflict with IT professionals. In many cases, the reengineers clearly felt that the systems people were uncommunicative and insensitive to business issues, while the IT staff was convinced that the BPR consultants had some clever slogans (and nice suits!) but never had, and never would, actually implement anything. Now they're inseparable. In fact, often they are no longer identified as separate "process redesign" or "application development" initiatives. In an effort to improve business operations, both aspects will be combined and referred to simply as "the project." After years of being treated as a support organization, IT is frequently a full partner in developing business strategy and implementing new processes. In fact, we've seen many successful projects originally formulated within IT, probably because their role gives them a view across the organization and they have the necessary analysis skills. (Or, perhaps they were just fed up with stitching together disparate applications and trying to reconcile conflicting goals.) So, the design or redesign of business processes is no longer the exclusive purview of consultants and specialists: everyone is involved. Successful efforts invariably involve a variety of disciplines, including management, performers, consultants, and specialists from IT, human resources, training, facilities, and other areas.

A Predictable Complaint

We know from experience that, at this point, some of our readers may be somewhat annoyed because we've chosen not to make this a book on business process management. Proponents of specific methodologies like Lean or Six Sigma (or Lean Six Sigma, or Lean Six Sigma for Services, or…) might be disappointed that we haven't paid more attention to their preferred approach. Our combined 50-plus years of professional experience have shown us that this is a fact of life whenever named methodologies are involved. In fact, it seems that when a methodology is named and popularized, you can predict that three things will happen:

1. Some people will become single-minded in the belief that their chosen method is the *one true path*. This group usually includes those with little or no prior experience in the field, and so their first exposure to a documented methodology will be a revelation of sorts. This proves what Alec's mother, Barbara Sharp, told him as a teenager: "The most recent convert is the most zealous."
2. Many people will misapply the method or apply it slavishly, in ways that will make the original creators shudder.
3. If, as a relative layperson, you try to describe or characterize the field, you'll be met with a chorus of criticism that will range from "you didn't get it quite right" to "the field has evolved since then" to "you've missed the point entirely."

We've seen this happen in business with strong approaches like activity-based costing or balanced scorecards and in the IT field with methods such as object-oriented analysis and design or, more recently, with agile or extreme methods. Given these examples, we're a little nervous about even commenting on the most popular of the current methods, but here goes:

- Six Sigma has its roots in continuous improvement and tends to focus at what we'd call the activity, or step, level, bringing to bear a variety of tools and methods that emphasize minimizing variance and defects in the output of that step.
- Lean, or lean manufacturing, has its roots in the Toyota Production System (TPS), which emphasizes looking at significant parts of the entire process with an eye toward the elimination of waste and the maximization of speed and efficiency through "pull" and a smooth flow.

To summarize, you could say that Six Sigma emphasizes individual activities and the consistency of their outputs, while Lean emphasizes the connection between activities and the smooth flow of the end-to-end process. Both are the subject of many books, articles, conferences, courses, and so on, with Lean Six Sigma adding even more. We won't try to augment the wealth of resources already there. If you want to draw comparisons, our method is philosophically closer to Lean's emphasis on flow, and we enjoy the excellent newsletters produced by the Lean Enterprise Institute (www.lean.org). Both Lean and Six Sigma offer a great many techniques that will be valuable additions to your business process toolkit, and vice versa. During recent engagements at manufacturing companies, we have been gratified when internal experts observe that our methods are valuable additions to *their* toolkits, providing an approach for situations where their methods had "hit the wall." One observed: "Your methods are stronger in the psychology of processes, while ours are stronger in the physics," which struck us as an apt distinction.

Process Orientation—The Best of All Worlds?

A process is a way to organize work, and over time different approaches to organizing work have prevailed. In the age of the craftsworker, work was organized around a multiskilled individual who accomplished the entire process and was focused on delivery of the end product to the customer. In the eras of the factory and functional specialization, work was divided among individual and organizational specialties, which internally became highly efficient and skilled, but often disconnected. Finally, the reengineering era and the current process-oriented era have seen work organized to expedite alignment among the various specialties participating in the overall process, with a focus (again) on the end result for the customer. Each of these was an advance over the previous era, and each had strengths and weaknesses. At organizations that have embraced a process-driven approach, we see that strengths from each of the eras we've cited are in place:

- Appropriate focus is on the customer and on outcomes.
- Defined, repeatable processes can be measured, improved, and compared against industry benchmarks. They can also be explicitly aligned with enterprise goals, which are not necessarily pure efficiency but might instead be flexibility or innovation.
- There is much greater overall efficiency through streamlined flow and elimination of unnecessary, redundant, or counterproductive work.
- Functionally specialized organizations and individuals provide high levels of expertise, but with their efforts aligned with the goals of the business processes they participate in.
- We've moved away from excessively narrow job definitions, so jobs tend to be richer and more satisfying. However, there's no avoiding the fact that everyone has to work very hard these days.
- Greater awareness of the whole leads to a healthier organizational ecology and greater opportunities for employees to move into new areas.

That's not to say everything's perfect in the process-driven company, but, all in all, it's a pretty good state of affairs. Achieving this state depends on multiple factors, but certainly one of the most fundamental is a clear and shared understanding of what a business process really is. That's what we'll look at in Chapter 3.

References

[1]   Smith, A., *An Inquiry into the Nature and Causes of the Wealth of Nations*, London: W. Strahan and T. Cadell in the Strand, 1776.

[2]   Hammer, M., "Reengineering Work: Don't Automate, Obliterate," *Harvard Business Review,* July–August 1990. At the same time, Tom Davenport and James Short published the other seminal article, "The New Industrial Engineering: IT and Business Process Redesign," *Sloan Management Review,* Summer 1990. In 1993, Hammer's article was expanded with James Champy into the now classic book *Reengineering the Corporation: A Manifesto for Business Revolution* (New York: HarperCollins, 1993), and Davenport published *Pro-*

cess Innovation: Reengineering Work Through Information Technology (Boston: Harvard Business School Press, 1992).

[3] Hall, G., J. Rosenthal, and J. Wade, "How to Make Reengineering Really Work," *Harvard Business Review*, November–December 1993.

[4] Davenport, T. H., "The Coming Commoditization of Processes," *Harvard Business Review*, June 2005.

[5] Imai, M., *Kaizen: The Key to Japan's Competitive Success*, New York: McGraw-Hill, 1989.

CHAPTER 3

Business Processes—What *Are* They, Anyway?

The trouble with "process" at this company is that everybody has one.
—New employee at global corporation

The Trouble with "Process"—Why We Need a Clear Definition

No Definitions, but Lots of Opinions

This whole business of process improvement can be very frustrating for the people who actually work in the processes we're trying to study—the executives, managers, performers, and other subject matter experts. Among the various frustrations, like the negative connotations that go with process improvement or being taken away from their process in order to study it, is the problem of vastly different understandings of what constitutes a business process. Consider two extremes:

- A participant in a recent workshop introduced himself by offering that he spent his days "writing processes."
- An executive wanted assistance in improving her organization's product lifecycle management process. Note the singular "process."

Both were quite correct in their use of the term "process" but were using it to describe work of very different scale or granularity:

- The "process writer" was talking about what we call a procedure—instructions for completing a specific task—and it's perfectly reasonable for someone to spend their days writing procedures.
- The executive was talking about what we call a process area—a collection of several related business processes—and, of course, it's perfectly reasonable to want to actively manage a product through its entire lifecycle.

Somewhere in between these two is what we define as a *business process*. For instance, within the process area Product Life-Cycle Management are multiple business processes such as Develop Product Plan, Develop Product, Launch Product, Revise Product, and Retire Product. In turn, the business process Revise Product might at some point involve a procedure to record the receipt of a field engineering request.

So, it appears that "process" is a very useful word because it can mean just about anything, from the procedure for completing a single task through to an enterprise-wide set of activities. And we've looked at only a few examples from a business setting. Factor in the ways the term can be used in daily life—"due process," "the courtship process," "the respiratory process," "the educational process," "a stochastic process," and so on, and you can see that there is ample room for confusion when we embark on a process improvement project.

At this point, two questions might have occurred to you:

1. Aren't distinctions such as "process area" versus "business process" completely arbitrary? Wouldn't we, if pressed, be unable to deal with objections that a body of work we call a process area could just as well be called a business process, or that what we call a business process could just as well be called a subprocess?

2. Does it really matter that "process" has so many different meanings to the people who will participate in process improvement? Will the confusion amount to any more than a minor annoyance?

Is "Business Process" an Arbitrary Concept?

The answer to the first question is "no, the distinction isn't arbitrary at all." In this chapter, we'll provide repeatable, unambiguous, and defensible guidelines for distinguishing among the different kinds of work that fall under the general label of "process." We'll clearly describe how we make the distinction between what we call business processes, the process areas they belong to, and the subprocesses they contain. (Along the way we'll clarify related terms such as function, activity, task, procedure, use case, result, and objective, as well as introducing techniques for identifying *your* organization's business processes—these will be expanded on in Chapter 5.) *Specific* differences will be illustrated between, for example, a process area and a business process, as we define them. That said, you could certainly argue that there is some arbitrariness in the specific names we use, so you might choose not to adopt our exact terminology. For instance, you might prefer to call our *process area* a "level 0 process," our *business process* a "level 1 process," and our *subprocess* a "level 2 process." Or instead call our *process area* a business process, our *business process* a subprocess, and our *subprocess* an activity. Or...well, we could go on and on, because the possibilities go on and on. Whatever you call them, we'll demonstrate that these have significantly different characteristics, and you must be able to unambiguously identify which is which. The important thing is that you can clearly and consistently make the necessary distinctions on *your* projects at *your* organization, no matter what terminology you have chosen for what we call process areas, (end-to-end) business processes, and subprocesses.

Does It Matter?

That's important because the answer to the second question is, emphatically, "yes, it matters a great deal that *process* means different things to different people." Making the distinction and eliminating the confusion right at the outset of an undertaking is vital to avoiding a variety of problems.

Frustration for Participants

If you don't begin with clear definitions and guidelines, some problems will show up early, when you begin interviews and facilitate sessions to explore questions like:

- What's wrong with the current process?
- What should the process look like?
- What specific changes should we make?
- What systems or tools do we need?

These, of course, require an answer to the question "what *is* the business process we're looking at?" There will be differences of opinion of the sort we described earlier—"that's not a process, it's a procedure!"—which soon lead to the question "what actually *is* a business process?" The ensuing discussions will be circular, frustrating, time consuming, and possibly acrimonious. Hardly a good way to start a project!

Trouble Controlling Scope and Producing Useful Deliverables

Other problems can arise later on. Without clarity on what a process is, it will prove very difficult to control scope because in any organization, all activities are ultimately related somehow—by being part of the same process, but also by using the same data, or being done by the same people or organizations, or by serving the same customers, or using the same system, or some other reason. Inability to control scope is perennially cited as one of the top few reasons projects fail. For the same reasons, it will also be very difficult to construct a useful workflow model. Either you'll have a multitude of smaller models, which individually don't provide much insight, or you'll end up with something that grows and grows until it becomes impossible to follow and progress ceases. Trust us, we've seen both situations.

These problems are bad enough, impacting the progress of a project, but if you get past them, the most serious problems of all might not arise until a new process is implemented, and performance turns out to be worse instead of better. This is a distressingly common occurrence.

Improvements That Make Things Worse

Identifying the wrong collection of activities as a process is one of the most common and serious problems we encounter. As we just described, if your process is too "big," and you can't get a grip on it, modeling and analysis quickly become an exercise in frustration. More commonly, though, processes are defined too "small," leading to the sin of "local optimization causing global suboptimization," as described by Eliyahu Goldratt.[1] That's what happens when a fragment of a business

---

1. See *The Goal* by Eliyahu Goldratt, which describes this and other important process improvement concepts in the context of an entertaining novel.

process (e.g., a subprocess or activity) is improved in a way that actually causes the overall process to behave worse than it did before. An example is provided in the third of the three examples coming up next.

Problems Caused by Improperly Defined Processes

Nothing gets the point across like an example, so let's look at three real-life cases of projects that failed because of a lack of clarity around the definition of "business process." In all three cases, that lack of clarity led to improperly scoped process improvement efforts, with serious consequences.

1. We've seen many variations on this example since the mid-1990s, when organizations began committing to ERP implementations. Senior management at a manufacturing company specifically instructed a project team to develop cross-functional business processes during a major ERP implementation. After a month's work, the team sensed that all was not well, and we were called in to provide some assistance. Early on, we had the team use our guidelines and methods to identify a set of processes, which was completed in under an hour. It was a very plausible-looking set of processes, so we were feeling rather pleased until one of the participants said, "But those aren't our processes!" We were baffled until we got a little more background. It turned out that with the assistance of one of the largest international consulting firms, the team had *already* identified their processes, and difficulty in modeling them was what led to our visit. We asked what those processes were, wrote them on the whiteboard, and immediately saw that they didn't look right. Alec suggested cross-referencing the processes to the organizations that participated in them, which made it clear that the processes the team had been working with for the past month were anything but cross-functional. In fact, there was a 1:1 relationship between organizational units and the supposed business processes—the processes had *exactly the same boundaries as the existing functionally specialized organization structures*. We advised the team that they were not going to achieve the benefits their executives were expecting unless they proceeded with true, cross-functional processes like the ones they had just identified in our session. The project managers, however, opted to "stay the course" and continue with the original processes because of the work that had already been done (and, no doubt, the consulting fees that had been spent!). A year later, the problems from this decision were apparent to everyone, spanning everything from trying to draw a *process* model of a *department* to configuring the ERP to support the conflicting views of the various organizations. In the end, the team had to go back and redo most of the work of the past year using the "real" cross-functional processes. The costs were tremendous in terms of lowered morale, wasted resources, and lost opportunities. Moral: *Don't confuse process and organization.* Alternate moral: *"Functional" processes yield dysfunctional results.*

2. A project team attempted to model the workflow for a major area they had improperly described as a single process—supply chain management. Eventually, the effort collapsed amid finger pointing, frustration, and missed

deadlines because their process model became too confusing to follow (or complete!). The reason was clear—their scope was actually what we call a "process area," comprising five related business processes, so it was impossible to express in a single diagram. There was no clear beginning point—there were many—and there was no clear ending point—there were many. It was impossible to trace a path (a workflow) through all of the included activities, especially because of timing issues. Some tasks were part of transaction-oriented processes that happened hundreds of times per day, others were part of ad hoc processes that occurred several times a month, and still others were monthly or quarterly. Try getting all that on one diagram and then improving it! Moral: *Don't confuse individual processes with families of processes*.

3. One organization enthusiastically embraced process improvement, with good reason: customers, suppliers, and employees found the company's processes slow, inconsistent, and error prone. Unfortunately, they were so enthusiastic that each team defined the work of their small group or department as a complete process. Of course, each of these was in fact the contribution of a specialized functional group to some larger, but unidentified, processes. Each of these "processes" was "improved" independently, and you can guess what happened. Within the boundaries of each process, improvements were implemented that made work more efficient from the perspective of the performer. However, these mini-processes were efficient largely because they had front-end constraints that made work easier for the performer but imposed a burden on the customer or the preceding process. The attendant delay and effort meant that the true business processes behaved *even more poorly than they had before*. This is a common outcome when processes are defined too "small." Moral: *Don't confuse subprocesses or activities with business processes*.

Let's restate the lessons from these examples:

- Don't confuse process and organization.
- Don't confuse individual processes with families of processes.
- Don't confuse subprocesses or activities with business processes.

We can conclude from these examples that failure often begins with not identifying business processes properly. Time and again, when we are called in to look at a process improvement project that is in trouble, we find this is the root cause, even in organizations that are sure they are "process oriented." But does this mean that the only correct scope is one, complete business process? No, it doesn't.

Your Scope Will Often Be Smaller Than a Business Process

Our goal is to be sure your project gets off to a good start and avoids problems by defining a project scope with respect to complete business processes. It's best to work on an entire business process, because your scope is clear and the potential benefits are maximized. If your organization has an enterprise architecture that includes process architecture, and projects are defined in process terms, where appropriate, then gaps and overlaps will be apparent and more easily avoided.

However, your intent or authority may not be to work with a complete business process or processes. Instead, because you lack the sponsorship or resources to take on the whole thing, your scope may be some other set of activities, like a subprocess or the work done by a particular job function. That's fine, and will be the most common situation, but *understanding* what constitutes a complete business process is still important. That allows you to unambiguously describe project scope and put it in context with the business process(es) it touches. And that in turn will greatly reduce the chance that you'll make things worse through local optimization without regard for the whole.

A related consideration is that you want to understand how the scope of the process work you want to undertake relates to sponsorship. Taking on a body of work with a scope wider than your sponsor's span of authority is not an exercise for the inexperienced or fainthearted—it will generally fail. That's not to say you shouldn't *point out* the scope that should be undertaken; you *should*—because, as we'll see, that's part of lining up the sponsorship you need. Identifying business processes and mapping (cross-referencing) them to organizations will help you determine the sponsorship you require to before starting a process improvement project.

Hasn't This Problem Been Solved Already?

One other question might be bothering you—why are we spending so much time on this point? Surely it's been dealt with elsewhere. Couldn't we just quote one of the other books on business processes, or go to the dictionary, and use their definitions of function, process, task, and activity? Perhaps not surprisingly, the answer is "no," because of multiple and overlapping meanings.

What Do Books in the "Business Process" Field Say?

A survey of all the major books on BPx reveals that none actually provide a definition of "business process" that is unambiguous enough to deal with objections such as "that's a process fragment, not a process!"—there's essentially nothing said that clarifies how big or small a business process is. All titles contain some variation of the idea that "a process is a set of activities that deliver value to the customer of the process." Some go on to say that "a typical organization has between ten and twenty business processes" or "major processes." Others, and often the same book, refer to typical organizations having "thousands and thousands of business processes." And we encountered the always helpful "processes can be subdivided into smaller processes almost infinitely." We know from experience that statements like "a process can be decomposed into a hierarchy of processes," while true, are deeply unsatisfying for business people brought together to improve processes. They clearly dislike the ambiguity surrounding discussions such as "is this a process or a subprocess or what?"

The terminology even depends on what type of book you read, because within the process improvement community there is a range of uses of the word "process."

Six Sigma texts, for instance, generally use "process" to describe *any* repeated activity that transforms the object of the activity in some way, corresponding to what we might call a step *within* a production process. A book on reengineering, on the other hand, is more likely to treat "process" as something larger, including the notion that it is "end to end," although we won't be treated to a concrete definition.

If the books written for business process professionals don't have the answers we need, how about the dictionary?

What Does the Dictionary Say?

Dictionaries will provide fine definitions for understanding the terms as generally used, but that doesn't mean they'll be helpful on a process-oriented project. Let's look at a few examples.

Except where noted, definitions are from [1].

- *Process*: a particular course of action intended to achieve a result (synonym: procedure) [2]; a series of actions or operations conducing to an end; especially: a continuous operation or treatment especially in manufacture;
- *Function*: a professional or official position: Occupation;
- *Activity*: a natural or normal function: as a process (as digestion) that an organism carries on or participates in by virtue of being alive; a similar process actually or potentially involving mental function; an organizational unit for performing a specific function; also: its function or duties;
- *Task*: a usually assigned piece of work often to be finished within a certain time; something hard or unpleasant that has to be done; a duty or function;
- *Procedure*: a particular way of accomplishing something or of acting: a step in a procedure; a series of steps followed in a regular definite order.

So a process includes actions, which we can take to be activities, and an activity can be a process or a function. A task can also be a function, and a procedure is a way to complete something, which seems to take us back to the definition of a process. Yikes! About the only thing we can conclude is that it might be unpleasant and some work (or is that activity?) is involved. It also helps to explain why a top-notch participant in a recent workshop, who had an English degree, saw a "procedure" as a very large body of work, encompassing many "processes," which caused considerable confusion until we compared our definitions. Again we'll point out that the dictionary definitions are, of course, correct and appropriate, but they don't really help us in a business setting to answer the question "what is a business process?"

The English terms can be confusing, but things get downright contradictory when we look at how the same words are used the IS field.

What Do Information Systems Dictionaries Say?

Years ago, a phrase that commonly appeared on coffee mugs and posters was "To err is human, but to really foul things up, you need a computer." And the usual definitions for terms like "process" and "function" in the computer field can really foul things up when they're added to the already ambiguous mix of definitions from general usage. This might happen early in your project, because people with an IS background (e.g., many business analysts) will be involved, or it might happen later in the project, when we focus on the systems that will support the process. Either way, we need to be aware of the potential confusion. Let's look at some "computerese."

- *Process*: the sequence of states of an executing program. A process consists of the program code (which may be shared with other processes which are executing the same program), private data, and the state of the processor, particularly the values in its registers [3].

- *Function*: a computer subroutine; *specifically*: one that performs a calculation with variables provided by a program and supplies the program with a single result [1]; or a set sequence of steps, part of larger computer program: (synonym: subprogram, procedure) [2].

- *Procedure*: a function which returns no value but has only side effects; a sequence of instructions for performing a particular task [3].

So processes are programs, which may incorporate functions. But the terminology for the information engineering methodology introduces another scheme: functions are composed of processes, and an activity is either a function or a process [4]. In another scheme, functions are composed of processes, which are composed of activities, which are composed of tasks. In yet another, activities are composed of processes. A process can even be "a generic term that may include compute, assemble, compile, interpret, generate, etc." [5]. On Alec's first teaching trip to Bangalore, India, he was teaching business process concepts to a very talented group of IS professionals. There was some unexplained confusion until Alec realized that to everyone in the room, a process was quite specifically an executing program, per the first definition stated earlier.

Similar conflicting definitions can be given for the other terms: tasks can compose, or be composed of, processes, and if we cared to bring in an event, operation, or, worse yet, a system, we could easily construct a huge circular definition that would require a computer to process—and you can be sure things would get fouled up in the process.

The point in going through this isn't to confuse you further or to suggest that there's anything wrong with all the different uses of the term we've covered. The point is that when you assemble a group of people to carry out (we hate to say it) a process like identifying processes, they will all arrive with the baggage of multiple, conflicting assumptions about what the various terms mean.

So What, Finally, *Is* a Business Process?

From the definitions in the preceding section, we conclude that a process is a collection of activities (or steps or tasks or whatever) that is a way to get something done. The problem is that this covers any repeatable body of work, from low-level tasks and procedures up to and beyond enterprise-level processes. What is missing are concrete tests or guidelines to determine if one collection of activities qualifies as a business process and another doesn't. We need to establish our own set of terms, definitions, and guidelines if we're going to eliminate confusion, make progress, and improve the situation. Let's get started on that.

The Approach We'll Take

We'll build up the definitions progressively by going through the typical examples and guidelines that we employ at the beginning of projects. The approach we've developed makes sense to the participants and provides some comfort that things aren't arbitrary or ambiguous. In short—it works! What we'll go through in the remainder of this chapter is:

- Some examples of what could be considered to be business processes.
- What is a *process*, in general? Tests to check that you have a "well-formed" process.
- What is a *business* process, in particular? Tests to check that you have one.
- How *big* is a business process? An objective test to determine the size (boundaries) of a true business process.
- Summary of main points, cautionary reminders.

Although we've taken some time to get to this point, the actual guidelines can be covered quickly, but don't let that make you think they're trivial or unimportant!

Defining "Process" in General

The first column of Table 3.1 illustrates some of the suggestions we received when we started identifying the processes within a company's Customer Relationship Management area. You can see immediately that the suggestions are, to put it mildly, all over the map. This is typical. Some (the last three) aren't even bodies of work—they're organizational or technological areas. The others vary wildly in size or granularity, by a factor of thousands. What we'll cover in the rest of this chapter is our rationale, with guidelines and tests, for deciding what is and what isn't a business process.

Involves Work

It goes without saying that a process involves work. That work can be described as a set of activities or as a sequence of steps and decisions, and can be completed by a person or a machine or both. It might surprise you that the work is initially the least important aspect of the process, so we won't say anything else about it just yet. That's because a process is a defined method to achieve some *result*, and that *result* is far more important to the definition of a business process than the work that goes into it.

Named in Verb-Noun Form

The first step in deciding whether or not you have a process is to name it and apply two exceedingly simple and exceedingly useful guidelines:

Table 3.1 Examples of Potential Processes

Suggested Process	What We Call It	If Not a Process, Why Not?
Customer Relationship Management	Process area	Doesn't deliver a single, specific result; a set of related business processes meeting an overall objective.
Acquire New Customer	Business process	Delivers a single, specific result, and meets all other criteria in this section. An "end-to-end business process."
Assess Prospect Financial Status or Set Up Customer	Subprocess	Too small—both deliver specific results, but are intermediate results in an end-to-end business process.
Calculate Customer Credit Limit or Create Customer Account	Activity, step, task, … (no specific term)	Much too small—a part of a subprocess. Possibly described in a procedure, or use case and service.
Determine Customer Credit Limit or Set Customer Account Type	Activity, step, task, … (no specific term)	Much, much too small—a single step or instruction. Possibly one line in a procedure, or step in a use case.
"The Inside Sales process"	Function	Doesn't deliver a single, specific result; an organizational unit that participates in multiple business processes.
"Our Oracle CRM process"	System	Doesn't deliver a single, specific result; a system that supports multiple business processes.
"Our e-business process"	Technology	Doesn't deliver a single, specific result; a technology employed by multiple business processes.

1. The process name, at its simplest, must be in the form *verb-noun* (e.g. Assign Inspector). It might be in the form verb-qualifier-noun (e.g., Assign Backup Inspector) or verb-noun-noun (e.g., Assign Inspector to Route). Note that processes are almost always defined in the singular! Not Handle Orders but Fill Order, as in fill *an* order or Fill *a specific* Order. By the way, a widely used alternate naming format is "from-state to to-state" (e.g., order to cash, requisition to settlement, or posting to hire). We use this informally in discussions, but not as the backbone of our approach.

2. Here's where it gets interesting—the verb-noun name must indicate the result of the process, as follows. If you flip the terms around into *noun is verbed* form, the phrase should indicate the intended result of the process. For instance, the result of Assign Inspector is Inspector is Assigned. It sounds unbelievable, but people find this a very clear and satisfying guideline, especially when we add the following, which quickly weeds out vague processes.

Delivers a Specific, Essential Result

And now it gets *really* interesting. The result of the process, in "noun is verbed" form, must meet three criteria:

1. The result is *discrete and identifiable*. That is, you can differentiate individual instances of the result, and it makes sense to talk about "one of them." For instance, for the result Inspector Is Assigned, you can identify each individual case of an inspector being assigned, and it makes sense in a business context to talk about a particular assignment, as in "when was Joe Bloggs assigned to the midtown route?"

2. The result is *countable*. That is, you can count how many of that result you've produced in an hour, a day, or a week. Certainly you can count how many inspector assignments were completed this week. This second criteria is really a corollary of the first, but it provides a useful test.

3. The result is *essential*. That is, it is fundamentally necessary to the operation of the enterprise, not just a consequence of the current implementation. For instance, if Fax Inspector Assignment or Mail Assignment to Inspector were suggested, we'd say the essence of the process hadn't been reached yet, as it isn't essential that a fax or a telephone be the means of notification. All that really matters—the essence—is that we Notify Inspector of Assignment.[2] Another way of saying this is that the process must focus on "what, not who or how"—we don't care *who* assigns the inspector, or *how* they do it, just that it is done, and *what* it does is necessary to the operation of the business.

Figure 3.1 summarizes these points, using the symbol that we think of as a "bulls-eye," which is commonly used to indicate an end point or result in a process. Properly named processes meet two additional guidelines:

1. They are named in the singular, to focus attention on a single, specific, countable result.

2. They are named to indicate not just an essential result, but the result the customer of the process wants.

Figure 3.2 shows an example for each guideline.

Results Versus Objectives

Although the terms are often used interchangeably, we distinguish between result and objective. A *result* is the output of a single execution of a process. It could be "employee is hired" from the process Hire Employee, or "service is activated" from the process Activate Service. An *objective* is some desired state or performance target. Related to hiring employees, that might be "hired employees will go on to have

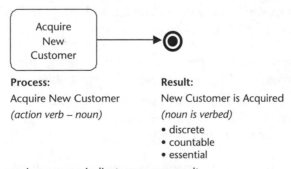

Process:
Acquire New Customer
(action verb – noun)

Result:
New Customer is Acquired
(noun is verbed)
• discrete
• countable
• essential

Figure 3.1 Process naming—name indicates process result.

---

2. This use of the term "essential" to describe activity without reference to implementation can be traced back to McMenamin, Steve, and John Palmer, *Essential Systems Analysis*, New York: Yourdon Press, 1984.

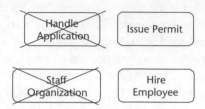

Figure 3.2   Process naming—singular, customer perspective.

an average tenure of greater than five years" or "fewer than 10 percent of newly hired employees will leave the company within the first year." A result is specific to a single instance of the process, while an objective generally measures performance over many instances.

The point about "what versus who or how" is worth expanding on. One of the most important skills for any kind of business analysis, including process analysis, is the ability to separate the *what* from the *who* and *how*. While discovering and defining business processes, *who* and *how* will certainly come up, but you must get at *what* is being accomplished. As we've seen already, if *who* does the work is brought into the definition of a process, problems will arise, such as confusing functions (who) with processes (what). Earlier, we discussed how damaging this can be. Likewise, if *how* is brought into the mix, you end up defining processes that that are tied to the current implementation, which leads to identifying multiple processes when there is really just one, raising the likelihood of inefficiencies and conflicting objectives. Worse, it makes it more difficult to get at what *really* needs to be done, hindering redesign.

What tends to be relatively stable over time, while *who* and *how* change much more often, and are the main focus of redesign. For example, a company's Fill Order process may in the past have been carried out using faxed or telephoned orders and a dedicated fleet of delivery trucks, while after redesign, orders are submitted over the Web and delivery is outsourced to a logistics company. What (Fill Order) is the same, but who and how are very different. You'll begin to factor in *who* and *how* later in analysis—*who* by cross-referencing the process to the organizations and actors that are involved, and *who* and *how* by developing swimlane diagrams.

This distinction will arise in the other types of analysis that are introduced in the next chapter, which summarizes the methodology, and in Chapter 15 (data modeling) and Chapter 16 (use cases and services).

- In data modeling, the focus is on *what* things the business needs to maintain information about, regardless of *how* (e.g., files, databases, or paper records).
- In requirements modeling, services describe *what* the application must do, and use cases describe *who* needs access to a service and *how* they will interact with a system to receive it.

To summarize, whether or not something is a process is independent of who does it or how it's done. A process should be defined in terms of the essence of what it does—the result it delivers—not the technologies used to support it or the organizations and roles that carry it out.

Name with Action Verbs, Not Mushy Verbs

Consider the first suggested process in Table 3.1, Customer Relationship Management. If we flip that around into verb-noun format, we get Manage Customer Relationship. If we now try to determine the result by putting this in "noun is verbed" format, we arrive at Customer Relationship Is Managed. And what, precisely, does this mean in terms of a result? Nothing! As indicated in Figure 3.3, that is neither discrete, countable, nor an essential result. That's because manage is a *mushy verb*, along with maintain, administer, monitor, handle, and many others. Only action verbs should be used in naming processes.

An *action verb* indicates a *single* activity that happens at a particular *point in time* and helps us to visualize a result. Examples are count, evaluate, print, attach, return, prioritize, sort, and provide. Allocate Service Rep, Calculate Stock Index, Retrieve Sample, Issue Refund, and Translate Document all use action verbs, and it's easy to visualize a specific result from each.

A *mushy verb*, on the other hand, tends to indicate an activity or *multiple* activities that happen *over time*. While they might indicate some overall objective, they don't help us visualize a single, specific result. Maintain Inventory, Administer Refunds, Monitor Prices, and Handle Request all use mushy verbs and don't help us visualize a result.

In December 2005, David Letterman might have made the first mushy verb joke on late night television when he said, "The post office today handled 500 million pieces of mail. They didn't deliver them—just handled them." That is as good an example as any of the problem with mushy verbs—they sound good until you realize that there might not be anything useful happening. It might sound okay for the post office to handle mail, but what we really want is for them to Deliver Mail.

When we introduce this guideline on an assignment, people take to it immediately and gleefully start checking their organization's published processes and procedures for mushy verbs. At one company, somebody said, "Oh, you mean résumé verbs!" a reference to the fact that they're often used in résumés because they sound good but don't actually say very much. At another company, someone called them "360 verbs," a reference to the company's annual 360-degree employee performance evaluation process. The reasoning was the same—they sound good, but often say little about what was actually accomplished.

This isn't to say mushy verbs are all bad. You'll need to use them if you're discussing a collection of processes (a process area such as Supply Chain Management)

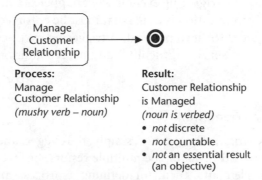

Process:
Manage
Customer Relationship
(mushy verb – noun)

Result:
Customer Relationship
is Managed
(noun is verbed)
- *not* discrete
- *not* countable
- *not* an essential result
  (an objective)

Figure 3.3 Process naming—no mushy verbs.

or an organization's responsibilities ("We manage risk."). If you use one in a process name, though, you aren't yet specific enough about what is actually being done. Often times, if a mushy verb has initially been used in naming a process, subprocess, or process step, they can be translated. For instance, "review" can usually be replaced with some variation of decide, assess, or route—"review application" could become "decide if application is complete," "assess application," or "route application." Examples of good action verbs and suitable translations for mushy verbs will be explored further in Chapters 5 and 8.

Initiated by a Specific Event

We know that the process ends with a result, discrete and countable, but what makes it begin? It's necessary when describing a process to be able to identify the event—the *triggering* event—that starts it. Initiating event is an equivalent term. Events fall into one of three categories:

1. *Action event*: These happen when a person or an organization decides to do something, for whatever reason. Examples include a customer deciding to place an order, a manager deciding the company needs a new employee, and a regulator deciding to issue a new guideline. You can't predict in advance exactly when a particular action event will occur.
2. *Temporal event*: These happen when some predetermined date or time is reached at which some activity must begin. Many processes in an organization are triggered by temporal events—time to run the payroll, time to close the books, time to take inventory, and so on. Unlike action events or conditional events, you always know exactly when a particular temporal event will next happen, because it will be recorded somewhere within the business system.
3. *Condition or rule event*: These happen when a monitoring activity detects some exception condition, like a smoke alarm being set off or a stock price hitting some predetermined limit. The smoke alarm might trigger an emergency response process, and the stock price might trigger a buy or sell process. You can't predict in advance exactly when a particular condition event will occur.

It isn't uncommon for analysts to confuse the concepts of triggering events and preconditions. The triggering event is what happens to make the process (or activity) start, while a precondition is a rule that must be enforced after the process (or activity) starts in order for it to proceed. A triggering event could be "customer initiates contact to report service difficulty" and a precondition could be "customer is in active status."

The Organizing Framework

At one end is a triggering event or, simply, the trigger, and at the other end is a result. Actually, there will probably be multiple results, but we'll get to that soon enough. The essential elements, then, for defining a process are the triggering event, the named action being carried out, and the result. This is illustrated in Figure 3.4, which introduces the "solid circle" symbol commonly used to depict a triggering or initiating event.

More commonly, the input-process-output framework is used to describe the core elements of a process, but we don't for two reasons:

1. Business people respond more favorably to the trigger-result or event-result idea than input-output, which sounds a little mechanical.
2. It doesn't help to define a process as the middle part in an input-process-output triad—using a term to define itself is never very satisfying.

Instead, we use the idea that what's in the middle is a defined sequence of steps and decisions or, if you prefer, a related set of activities. Then the overall framework is trigger-steps and decisions-result or trigger-activities-result. Either is appropriate. If the process is a predictable, transaction-handling process, we'll say it is a defined sequence of steps and decisions. If the process is less predictable, like a collaborative or creative process, we'll use the phrase "set of related activities."

Another framework is inputs-guides-outputs-enablers (IGOE), although this is used less widely than it was several years ago. It adds the guides that govern a process and the enablers that support it. This can be useful when taking a broad look at an overall process during scoping, but we prefer to use a framework we'll introduce in the next chapter that looks at six distinct enablers. IDEF0[3] process flow diagrams take it further and explicitly show the guides and enablers for each step, in addition to the usual inputs and outputs. We stopped using that style of diagram many years ago because it so often led to painful arguments like "this isn't an input, it's a guide." The technique works well enough in expert hands, but mere mortals more often have difficulty and find it confusing.

Summary of Criteria for a Well-Formed Process

We now have a few guidelines that a process must meet if it's going to be suitable for further analysis:

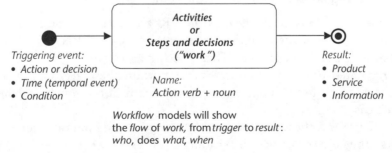

Figure 3.4 Essential components of a process.

---

3.   IDEF, the integration definition language, was developed under the sponsorship of the U.S. Air Force. IDEF0 is a technique for function or process modeling, and IDEF1 is a technique for information or data modeling.

- The process comprises an identified body of work that can be characterized as a set of related activities or a defined sequence of steps and decisions.
- The process name is (essentially) in action verb–noun format, although it might have a qualifier or another noun.
- The name is in the singular.
- The name, if put in "noun is verbed" format, will indicate the intended result (output) of the process.
- The result must be discrete and countable. If a mushy verb is used, these criteria will not be met.
- The result is what the *customer* of the process wants.
- The process is initiated by a triggering event that could be action, time, or a condition.

You won't always be able to meet the guidelines for process naming, but you should strive for them.

So far, our focus has been the result—no result, no process. We haven't yet put any emphasis on the work—the steps, tasks, activities, and so on that make up the process—or the people and organizations that carry them out. That's because one of the biggest mistakes when discovering processes is to focus too soon on the work being done, or who does it, rather than the result that is achieved. Too often, analysts see an identifiable body of work, no matter how big or small, and call it a process. As you'll see, our approach depends on first identifying necessary results, then working toward identifying the processes that delivers them.

Defining *Business* Process in Particular

At this point, an excellent question would be "is any set of activities with a trigger and a result a *business* process?" We would say, "no," because we attach specific meaning to the term "business process." Let's build up to a definition of a business process as an end-to-end, cross-functional process that meets definite criteria.

Introducing an Example to Make the Point (Telco)

In the mid-1990s, in the heyday of BPR, a large telephone company (hereafter the "telco") went to its regulator, a federal agency, with a request to raise the rates charged to their subscribers. This is known as a "rate case," and if you've worked in a regulated utility, you know how important these are. In fact, it has sometimes seemed to us that every activity in these organizations revolves around justifying the rate case.

This time, the regulator denied the application for a rate increase on the grounds that the telco's Service Provisioning processes were generating too many complaints—it simply took too long for the telco to respond to the three types of service orders handled by Service Provisioning:

1. *In*: the connection of a new telephone service, typically when a subscriber moves into the service area;

2. *Out*: the disconnection of telephone service, typically when a subscriber moves out of the service area;

3. *Move*: the relocation of telephone service, typically when a subscriber moves to a new address within the service area.

Collectively, these were referred to as "ins, outs, and moves."

Having a rate case denied was a serious situation, so a task force was struck immediately. The regulator had told the telco to improve their processes, so the task force sensibly started by figuring what those processes were. The five processes they identified are shown in Figure 3.5. The caption indicates that they didn't get this step quite right.

A separate team started analysis and improvement on each of the five processes, all with considerable success. The Facilities Management process is an excellent example. The engineers in this area were responsible for assigning the network facilities, such as cable pairs and network addresses, which would deliver service to the subscriber's premises. The team studying the process conducted detailed task analysis, getting right down to time and motion studies. They discovered that the engineers spent a large proportion of their work day retrieving large "network maps" from the map cabinets, updating them, and then replacing them—a cycle that was repeated for almost every order. The network maps showed what facilities were available in a particular neighborhood and were updated by hand when facilities were assigned or freed up. (Updates were recorded in pencil, and the maps were printed on a specially coated, heavy paper that could withstand repeated erasing.) Because in, out, and move orders were handled on a first-come, first-served basis, an order would require the network map for one neighborhood, and it was almost certain that the next order would require the map for a different neighborhood. Because of the retrieval and refiling time, an order typically took around 10 minutes to complete.

The team came up with a solution that was brilliant in its simplicity—they sorted the orders by neighborhood and within each neighborhood they were sorted into outs, ins, and moves, in that sequence—outs first because they freed up facilities, ins next because new customers were the priority, and finally moves. Each neighborhood was typically handled once a week—Green Acres on Monday morning, Shady Acres on Monday afternoon, Vistaview on Tuesday morning, and so on.

The improvement in time-per-order was amazing—the time went from around 10 minutes per order down to 1 to 2 minutes per order! Management was thrilled, and the team was treated to an evening of beer and pizza. Other teams did just as well. Within the installation process, installers drove to subscriber premises to complete wiring and install equipment as necessary. A lot of time was spent driving around, so a route scheduling system was implemented that ensured that each installer was given a schedule of orders that were for nearby premises. This didn't mean that the installer arrived when the customer wanted them to, but it certainly

Figure 3.5 Demonstrating flawed business process identification.

raised the installer's performance as measured in visits per day. Beer and pizza for the team!

Everyone was thrilled with the improvements that had been made, until the regulator denied the subsequent rate case—it turned out that it now took *longer* to complete service orders than previously, and complaints were rising. How could this be?

What Went Wrong—Three Problems

It's probably obvious to you what went wrong, but remember, each team was working within the confines of a particular (we hate to say it) silo, so it was a surprising outcome for them. Let's work through the three errors that led to this outcome.

1. The processes weren't named correctly, at least according to our guidelines. This isn't the most important problem, but it contributed. Facilities Management, like the others, is a classic case of "mushy verb fuzziness" that ultimately prevented them from seeing the specific, individual result that they were providing for *each* customer. Assign Network Facilities is much more specific, especially when you think of it as Assign Network Facilities for one particular Order.
2. They confused process with functional organizations. When we came in later to help the telco determine what had gone wrong, it was easy to see why they had identified the processes they did. Each one was, in fact, the work provided by a single functional area. This further emphasized the focus on the functions rather than the needs of the customer. These first two points are illustrated in Figure 3.6.
3. They focused on achieving local, task-based efficiency rather than on delivering the result the customer ultimately wanted.

Collectively, what this all added up to was that each individual service order spent a lot of its time waiting to be "handled." If a customer moving to Shady Acres placed their order on Tuesday morning, it wouldn't be dealt with for almost a week! But it would certainly be handled efficiently! That happened throughout the process, as it so often does when the focus is on efficiency instead of quality or service. The customer doesn't really care how efficiently an engineer assigns facilities, or

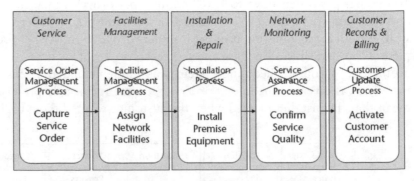

Figure 3.6   Problems—improper naming, confusing function and process.

how efficiently the network monitoring specialist determines signal-to-noise ratio on their line; they care how quickly their new telephone service is working or how dependably their existing telephone service is moved on the desired date.

What the Process Should Have Been

If the approach had been to focus primarily on delivering the result the *customer* wanted, rather than *functional* efficiencies, the outcome would have been quite different. When a customer places a move order, they are effectively saying "I want my telephone service moved." That's almost a perfect "noun is verbed" statement of the desired result—"telephone service is moved." That means that the process, in verb-noun form, is Move Telephone Service, which isn't completed until all five of the processes have been completed. And what did the telco actually want? Of course, they ultimately wanted an efficient process and a rate increase, but from each customer request they wanted a receivable in the customer's account and an active customer service that will generate ongoing revenue. As in the customer's case, that result isn't delivered until the triggering event, the order from the customer, has worked its way through all five processes.

That's why we say that a *business process* is the end-to-end chain from the initial (earliest) triggering event (the customer placing the order) through to the final results (the customer has service, and the telco has a receivable) that stem from *that* event. The five activities the teams identified are what we call subprocesses of this process. The true business process, together with the trigger and results, is illustrated in Figure 3.7.

A Test for Business Processes Boundaries

An Objection

During a recent workshop, Alec worked through the telco example and felt that he'd done a particularly good job of illustrating the idea that a business process spans all of the activities in a chain that begins with the earliest event in the chain through to the final result. Evidently, the old proverb "pride goes before a fall" holds true. At a financial services company, a vice president (of "process," no less) objected. "That's just semantics!" he said. He contended that the definition of business process was completely arbitrary and lacking in any quantifiable, repeatable

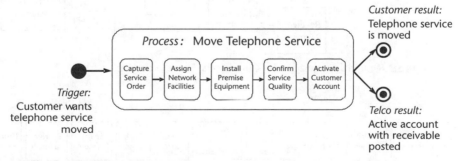

Figure 3.7 The actual business process.

guidelines. Assign Network Facilities had an event at one end and a result at the other, with a chain of activities in between, so why wasn't it a "business process" instead of a subprocess, as we claimed? At the other extreme, the arrival of a new customer could be seen as an event that led to a long chain of activities, possibly extending over years or decades, ending with the result that the customer ceased to be active. Along the way, there might have been many service orders filled, but wasn't this ultimately one event-result chain and therefore just one (albeit large) business process? Ouch!

When a situation like this arises, it is unlikely that further arm-waving is going to help, so it is best to take a deep breath and venture out onto thin ice. That means making the point using the questioner's own example, which isn't guaranteed to work out the way you hope it will. If you're confident in your methods, though, it usually will, and you'll have made your point in convincing fashion. Just don't gloat—after all, pride does go before a fall.

Our Response—Collecting Suggested Processes

Alec decided to demonstrate one final guideline by using one of the projects the VP's team was working on, which involved analyzing the processes within the Commercial Loans Management area. The first step was to write down, on Post-it notes, the processes that the VP could immediately think of. Other team members were present, and they fleshed out the list, and a total of 12 processes were listed, each on a Post-it. Initially, many of them had incomplete names, like Booking or Qualification. This is the usual case, but we soon had them in action verb–noun format. The 12 processes are illustrated in Figure 3.8.

The next step was to put the processes into their typical sequence, as shown in Figure 3.9. It's amazing how much you learn while doing this simple activity. The participants are fully engaged, because they're the ones moving the Post-its around, and at the same time are usually explaining the rationale for the sequence and inter-

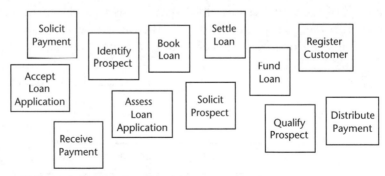

Figure 3.8   Initial suggestions for Commercial Loans processes.

Identify Prospect	Qualify Prospect	Solicit Prospect	Register Customer	Accept Loan Application	Assess Loan Application	Fund Loan	Book Loan	Solicit Payment	Receive Payment	Distribute Payment	Settle Loan

Figure 3.9   Suggested processes put in typical sequence.

esting facts about each process. For example, we found out that in commercial loans, the prospects are qualified (financial health, industry standing, anticipated developments, current lenders, and so on) before they are contacted in the Solicit Prospect process. By coincidence, we went through a similar example the next week at a consumer lender, and found that they always solicited first, checking for any sign of life, and then qualified the prospect.

Analyzing the Suggested Processes

The next step was to apply a guideline that first occurred to us several years ago, more or less out of the blue, on the 12 processes. For each link (a sequential flow from one process to the next) we would look at the ratio of one process to the next, and the ratio of that next process back to the previous one. It's more confusing to describe than to do! Starting at the beginning, one instance of identify prospect is followed by one instance of qualify prospect. And looking "backward," one instance of Qualify Prospect is preceded by exactly one instance of Identify Prospect. Thinking in terms of the "token" or work item that is moving through the process, it can add clarity to instead say one identified prospect becomes one qualified prospect. Either way, we say then that the ratio from Identify Prospect to Qualify Prospect is one to one (1:1).

Moving along, one instance or execution of Qualify Prospect leads to one instance of Solicit Prospect. At this point, two wrinkles show up:

1. If Qualify Prospect determines that the prospect isn't desirable, then it is followed by zero instances of Solicit Prospect, meaning that the ratio could be 1:0. Don't worry about these cases—the "dropouts" that don't continue—focus on the "happy path," which is the 1:1 case.
2. Solicit Prospect, in all likelihood, will "loop back" on itself. The bank will probably have to engage in multiple solicitation meetings before the prospect (or the bank) makes a go/no-go decision. That means the ratio from qualify prospect to solicit prospect is actually one to many, or 1:M, This is another case we don't worry about—if "looping" means that a ratio becomes 1:M, we focus on the "going forward" case, which is 1:1.

Eventually, we will hit a true 1:M or M:1 ratio. For instance, once a customer is registered, the bank hopes that over time they will apply for many loans, hence the 1:M ratio from Register Customer to Accept Loan Application. Similarly, one loan will be followed by many payment cycles, and many payment cycles will eventually lead to one instance of the loan being settled. Figure 3.10 illustrates the results of this analysis. As it is with sequencing the processes, it's amazing how much you learn about the fundamentals of a business while analyzing the linkages.

The Outcome

Here's where it all comes together, and in a surprisingly simple way. If processes are connected on a 1:1 basis, then we say that they are part of a single, end-to-end, business process. Those "processes" you are linking might be what we call subprocesses,

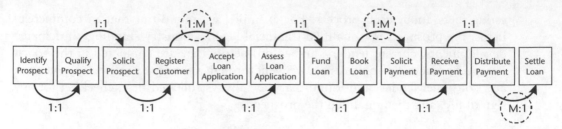

Figure 3.10   Analyzing relationships between processes.

or they might be activities or tasks or steps, depending on how big or small the suggestions made by your group are, but they are *part of* a complete business process. Figure 3.11 illustrates this. We'll look at subprocesses more carefully in Chapters 5 and 6, but two good guidelines are:

1. A business process generally has 5 ± 2 subprocesses.
2. A subprocess achieves a significant milestone along the way to the achievement of the final result of the business process and is often something that the organization would like to count or measure.

If there is a 1:M, a M:1, or a M:M linkage, that almost always indicates the boundary between two separate business processes. To understand why, we'll introduce another useful test, which is that within a single, end-to-end business process, it is the same "token" or "work item" that is moving through the process, although its state is being changed. For instance, through the first four processes, the same person or organization is being acted on, with their state changing from prospect to customer. In the next set of activities, it is a loan application that is moving through the processes, changing from an application to a booked loan. Later, it is a payment request that is being acted on. Ultimately, the reason the 1:1 ratio works is because it is the same token moving along. Whenever you hit a 1:M or an M:M connection, you will find that a different token is the focus of the process.

Applying the guideline in the commercial loans example, we arrive at four business processes, each containing probable subprocesses, which were the processes originally identified by the VP and his team. Note that we don't, at this point, have confidence that the subprocesses are complete or well defined, because they came out of a brainstorming exercise—a means to an end, which was to discover business processes. Settle Loan has been identified as a business process, but as yet has no identified subprocesses. In Chapter 6 we'll get more precise about defining subprocesses. In our terminology, the set of processes we just identified comprises a *process area*, Commercial Loans Management. These three levels are depicted in Figure 3.12. By the way, further work with the team uncovered a fifth process that

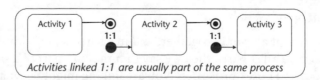

Activities linked 1:1 are usually part of the same process

Figure 3.11   Guideline for "assembling" activities into business processes.

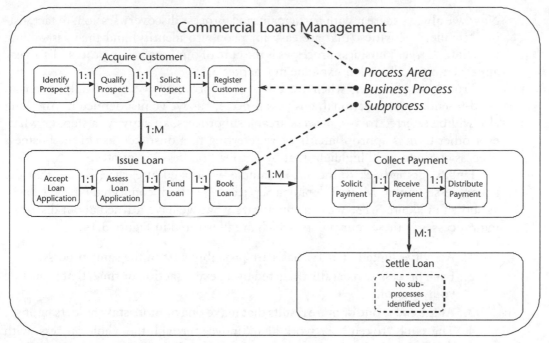

Figure 3.12 Process area, business processes, and subprocesses.

had initially been missed, Resolve Loan Service Issue. The missing business process and the missing subprocesses indicate a fact of life—discovering and defining business processes is an iterative effort.

At this point, you might be wondering what the "objector"—the VP—thought about this approach and the results. "That works for me!" was his response. He felt that the guideline was clear, objective, explainable, and defensible, which probably explains why we've had such good luck with it.

Applying the Guideline

We first stumbled across this approach over beer and sushi while trying to figure out how to explain to a client why their process boundaries had turned out to be what they were. They were happy with the processes a team had identified (they were true business processes) but they wondered if there wasn't more science to it. It was at a newspaper, and they were journalists, so they were probably digging for the truth! For some reason, while sketching out the processes and subprocesses on the proverbial napkin, we applied a data modeling technique and determined the *cardinality* of the relationships among the various elements. Lo and behold, we saw that within a process, subprocesses were connected on a 1:1 basis, and the connections between processes invariably had an M on them—they were 1:M, M:1, or M:M. A guideline was born!

For several years, other than at the newspaper, we kept the guideline "private" and didn't expose clients to it. When we first brought it out, at a hospital where we were working, the clients loved it! To them, it made a repeatable undertaking of something that had been a bit of a black art, fraught with subjectivity and intuition.

Now, we always share it with participants in a process discovery session. In fact, listing "smaller" activities (that are easy for people to identify) and then assembling them into "larger" business processes is the core of our bottom-up process discovery approach, as we'll further examine in Chapter 5.

From this point on, when we refer to a "process" we specifically mean an "end-to-end, cross-functional, business process," as we've just defined it. Anything else will be referred to as a process area, a subprocess, an activity, a step, or whatever other term is appropriate. If we're referring to a mistaken use of the business process concept, we'll highlight that by putting "process" in quotes.

Finally, going back to the telco example we looked at earlier, we see that the subprocesses within Move Telephone Service are, indeed, connected on a 1:1 basis, as shown in Figure 3.13. We can summarize what we have learned about discovering processes in these four points, which are illustrated in Figure 3.14:

1. Activities linked on a 1:1 basis are probably part of the same process.
2. Each process is generally triggered by an event (action or time) that is outside your control.
3. At the end is one or more results that make one or more stakeholders happy.
4. The same "token" or "work item" moves through the whole process, with the process typically transforming it (e.g., the loan application moves all the way through the process, eventually becoming a booked loan).

These clear and repeatable guidelines are very useful in practice.

Linked subprocesses assemble into business processes, and related business processes assemble into process areas. Process areas such as Customer Relationship Management, Supply Chain Management, and Demand Chain Management are widely discussed, and are often referred to as processes, as in "our CRM process."

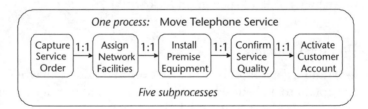

Figure 3.13   Guideline applied to the telco process and subprocesses.

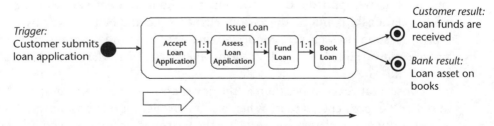

Figure 3.14   Four criteria for business processes.

This calls for a certain amount of caution. They *are* cross-functional, the way a business process should be, but they are not countable, so they behave more like a function. You cannot say how many Customer Relationship Managements you did yesterday. And if you try to map, assess, and improve Customer Relationship Management all at once, you'll find it to be a very frustrating endeavor, following all the events, paths, and results. When working on a process area such as CRM, it is essential to break it down into individual business processes, such as Secure New Customer, Resolve Customer Inquiry, and Complete Customer Communication. Each of these can then be modeled and analyzed separately.

So What?

It might occur to you that these definitions and guidelines are self-evident, which occurs to us on a regular basis, too. Most companies already know they need to focus on their business processes, and they know that these processes transcend specialties and organizational structures. Certainly many experts in BPx feel that this is familiar territory for everyone, and can be treated as a given.

This is a dangerous mindset on the job—even after all the exposure process orientation has received, many businesses cannot state what a business process really is or what their major processes are, much less describe how they should, or even do, operate. How can this be? The answer is that the concepts of organizational structure and functional specialization are so embedded in the organizational psyche that it is amazingly difficult to break out of functional orientation. You might be fully comfortable with the distinction between process and function, but *never* assume that the business or IT professionals you're working with are.

Is Everything a Process?

All of the activity in an organization can't be expressed as processes, with a definite trigger-activity-result structure. There's simply no point in trying to reduce the work that your C-level or CxO[4] executives perform to repeatable processes; if you could, then they wouldn't deserve the compensation they earn for constantly dealing with a shifting environment. That said, more activities than you might think are suitable for looking at as processes. We had a workshop participant in Malaysia who objected that what his team did was "raise community awareness" but "awareness is raised" was hardly discrete or countable, therefore their work couldn't be looked at as business processes. With some probing about the work they did, we were able to uncover some repeatable processes—Develop Awareness Campaign, Conduct Awareness Event, and Measure Community Awareness, all of which met the criteria. Our friend was satisfied that his team's work could, indeed, be studied as business processes. However, another question soon arose.

---

4. C-level or CxO executives—chief executive officer (CEO), chief operating officer (COO), chief financial officer (CFO), chief administrative officer (CAO), chief technical officer (CTO), and others, including, at some organizations, the chief process officer (CPO).

Can All Processes Be Modeled?

While discussing the Develop Awareness Campaign process, it became clear that some parts of the process were a defined sequence of steps and decisions, notably the "gating" parts when a campaign under development was seeking approval for further development. These parts of the process were very suitable for workflow modeling. Other parts of the process, especially the more creative and free-flowing parts, were better characterized as a set of activities that didn't follow any set sequence or interactions, and therefore weren't suitable for workflow modeling. The question that came up was whether or not develop awareness campaign was in fact a business process, given that some parts of it defied process workflow modeling. The answer was definitely "yes," and it highlights an important point—you can have a well-defined business process, with a clear event and result, but it might not be possible to model the entire process in a flow model. This can be summarized by identifying three kinds of processes and their characteristics:

1. *Executive or strategic processes*: Much of the work done by your CxO can't be reduced to a defined set of activities, so modeling it as a process is generally not worthwhile. It's more useful to look at information needs and analytics than steps or activities.
2. *Creative or collaborative processes*: Like executive processes, much of the work in one of these processes, like Develop Product or Create Marketing Campaign, defies workflow analysis. However, there are parts that are eminently suitable. We'll touch on how to model these kinds of processes in Chapter 10. The key is recognizing what can be modeled and what can't.
3. *Transactional processes*: Highly repetitive work that falls into the "defined sequence of steps and decisions" category is probably an example of a transactional process, like Open Account or Fill Order. These processes are generally highly suitable for workflow modeling.

Summary

Criteria for Business Processes

Essentially, a process is a way for an enterprise to organize work and resources (people, equipment, information, and so forth) to accomplish its aims. Historically, an enterprise would organize its work and resources into specialties or functions. Nowadays, an enterprise will still organize *resources* into functions, but will try to organize *work* to contribute to the achievement of a specific output—a result—for a specific customer. This is process orientation and gives rise to this definition:

> A business process *is a collection of interrelated activities, initiated in response to a triggering event, which achieves a specific, discrete result for the customer and other stakeholders of the process.*

In this context, "activity" is a generic term encompassing anything from the five or so subprocesses that comprise the process all the way down to individual procedures and the work steps they contain. There just isn't any value (or satisfaction) in trying to rigorously define a hierarchy of terms for work below the subprocess level. Instead, we use the generic term *activity* when we refer to work that might be named as a single unit but can involve multiple actors, each separately making a contribution, and the generic term *step* when referring to work that is typical done by one (or cooperating) actors at a point in time.

We will now look at each phrase in that definition of a business process, but not in the order they appear. As we noted earlier, even though the first reference is to activities, they are the least important aspect of a process in terms of discovering them and understanding what they should achieve. Far more important are the result, the customer, and the event. Let's take Stephen Covey's sage advice, and "begin with the end in mind":

…That Achieves a Specific, Discrete Result…

The only reason a business process exists is to deliver a specific result. That result might be goods, such as the products requested on an order, or services, such as information in response to a query. The all-important guideline is that the result must be individually identifiable and countable. The processes Develop New Product, Resolve Service Problem, Fulfill Order, and Hire Employee all conform to this guideline. You can identify the specific new products that are developed and count them. In other words, it is possible to count how many times the process Develop New Product was completed. Similarly, it would be possible to identify and count the service problems that were resolved, the orders that were fulfilled, and the employees that were hired. However, you cannot count how many research and developments, help desks, telemarketings, or human resources were completed because those are departments or functions, but not processes. A good process name clearly indicates the result or end state of the process—new product is developed, service problem is resolved, and so on.

…For the Customer and Other Stakeholders…

This is critical: A customer is the recipient or beneficiary of the result produced by the business process. This customer may be a person, an organization, or even a broad marketplace, but the customer can be identified and can pass judgment on how satisfactory the result and the process are. The customer might be internal to the organization, such as the employee whose service problem was resolved or the department that receives the newly hired employee.

Taking the customer's perspective helps identify and name processes accurately. At a government motor vehicle licensing agency, a process called Handle Application form would not pass the customer perspective test, because the application form is not what the customer cares about. Would you be satisfied knowing that your form had been handled—taken, copied, sorted, sent, filed, retrieved, bent, folded, spindled, stapled, and mutilated? No, you expect some result like a driver's license issued or a vehicle registered, so the appropriate processes are Issue Driver's License and Register Vehicle. Also note that while the business process must provide a result to the customer, it likely has to provide a result to other stakeholders, notably the organization itself. The classic example: most customers would probably be happier if you did not bill them for the result they receive, but since you would go out of business if you did that for long, the process result includes collecting the payment, the result expected by the organization itself.

...Initiated in Response to a Triggering Event...

You must be able to trace a process back to the earliest event that triggers or initiates it. Think of the process as a machine that is inactive until the on switch is flipped. The triggering event is the processes' on switch that makes it go. The event is often a specific request for the result the process produces. Develop New Product begins in response to the event "market opportunity is confirmed," which is a request for a new product that will satisfy the market opportunity. Resolve Service Problem begins in response to the event "customer reports service problem," which is a request for the service problem to be resolved. Identifying the earliest event is not always easy. Does Fulfill Customer Order begin in response to the organization's receipt of an order, or a customer initiating an order, or a customer realizing they have a need? Sometimes, there are multiple events that can initiate a process. Taking inventory (Determine Stock Level) can be initiated by a temporal event, because it is done twice a year, but can also be initiated by a conditional event (e.g., when a significant discrepancy is discovered). In any case, the effort in determining the event(s) is worth it—once you have an event and a result, it is far easier to trace the flow of work that transforms the former into the latter.

...Activities...

The business process is a collection of activities, steps, tasks, actions, or whatever you want to call them. Whether we are discussing the five or so subprocesses that comprise a business process, the dozens of activities we brainstormed during process discovery, or the potentially hundreds of individual steps between trigger and result, they all collectively comprise the process. During process discovery, we will typically refer to *activities*, during framing we will identify the *subprocesses*, and, later still, when we start to draw workflow models, the term will be *step* because workflow models show the process steps completed by the actors. Even then, a step in the initial workflow model will likely divide into more and finer steps during development of more detailed models. During this discussion, and others when the precise granularity doesn't matter or we don't know if one or multiple actors are involved, we'll use the term *activities*. The point of all of this is that a process is made up of defined work, whatever granularity you are breaking that work into.

...A Collection of Interrelated...

The activities in the process must interrelate—they are not just an arbitrary collection of work. For instance, we do not want to end up analyzing Joe's job or the human resources (HR) department. Joe does a variety of tasks, from taking orders to handling customers' problems. The HR department does a variety of things, from recruiting and retiring employees to administering their benefits and reimbursing training costs. In both cases, the only relationship among the activities is that the same organization does them all. That may be interesting, but it is not a single process—Joe probably participates in many processes, and the HR department certainly does. In a process, the steps are interrelated through sequence and dependency—in simple terms, the completion of one step leads to (flows into) the initiation of the next step, in sequence. Sometimes the sequence is arbitrary, and other times there is a true dependency—step B cannot take place until step A has completed. Another important point—the steps are interrelated by dealing with the same token or work item, such as a specific employee retirement, or benefit enrollment, or whatever the process deals with. Further, all of the steps are interrelated by being traceable back to the same initiating event. For example, when Joe finishes taking one employee's benefit program enrollment order, he may return to resolving another employee's reassignment problem, but in process terms the two are unrelated—they deal with completely different work items and are part of the response to completely different events.

...A Business Process Is...

Throughout this book, the terms *process* and *business process* refer to this definition, which ultimately looks at a business process as the chain of activities that establish a 1:1 relationship from the earliest triggering event through to the final result.

Other Business Process Characteristics

So, we have established that a business process begins in response to an event, proceeds through a sequence of activities (or steps and decisions), and ultimately yields a result for the customer of the process and the other stakeholders. Let's add a few more characteristics to the definition.

Measurable

We must be able to measure the business process in whatever way is important to the stakeholders. Customers may care about the effort they have to invest and the total time until they receive the result. The organization's performers may care more about training time or the impact on their own productivity statistics. The owner or manager will want to track cost, overall customer satisfaction, and other variables. A well-defined and well-designed business process should satisfy the demands of all stakeholders, and the appropriate measures will help to determine if it does. Caution! As we'll see in the Chapter 5, inappropriate measures are the most common cause of poor process performance.

Automation

In looking at individual tasks within a process, automation may or may not play a role. A task could be totally manual (e.g., Interview Client). However, nowadays almost all processes are at least partially automated, and with widespread use of straight-through processing (STP), many processes, such as executing a trade order on a stock exchange, may be completely automated. In that example, the initiating event could be the detection of a particular condition, such as a preset stock price "sell" threshold being reached, and the result could be the deposit of proceeds from the sale into the client's account. The entire, end-to-end process can be completed with no human intervention at all. This means that automation is a nonissue when deciding whether or not a step belongs within a process—a step could be totally manual, partially manual with automated support, or fully automated. We mention this because it emerges as an issue. Unbelievably, we were once told by a group of reengineering consultants that process models should only include steps that involved people and by another "guru" that process models should only include automated steps.

Levels of Detail

A business process can be described at progressive levels of detail. Early in a project, when we are clarifying scope and context, we use a three-level decomposition, as shown in Figure 3.12—process area, business processes, and subprocesses. Later, we'll model the workflow of each process using swimlane diagrams to two or three levels of detail, as described in Chapter 9. Eventually, we'll describe individual tasks with "out of context" depictions like flowcharts, decision trees, procedures in various forms, and use cases.

Customers: Internal and External

Every process has a customer, the person or organization expecting the primary result that the process delivers. Obviously, customers must be identified so we can obtain their assessment and ensure that a redesigned process meets their expectations. Another reason to focus on the customer is that in many processes, there is no overall responsibility—no one in the organization makes sure the process is completed. So we must focus on the customer because the customer is the "human glue" that holds the process together and must retrigger the process periodically to keep it moving along. An example is that one of us had a major appliance fail, and had to "walk" the warranty claim from the dealer to the manufacturer, then to the local service organization, then to the appliance repair agency to which they subcontracted the job, and finally back to the manufacturer to obtain reimbursement for the repair charges! The moral: sometimes only the customer sees the entire process from beginning to end, so identifying the customer is essential to understanding process behavior.

We sometimes distinguish processes depending on whether the customer of the process is internal or external to the organization. Figure 3.15 shows an example of each type of process.

Processes that serve *external* customers are typically why the business exists, so they are often referred to as *core processes*. Most businesses have only about 7 to 10 core process areas in total, such as Market Research, Customer Relationship Management, Product Life Cycle Management, Supply Chain Management, Demand Chain Management (which includes filling orders and manufacturing in a build-to-order environment), Workforce Management, and Regulatory Compli-

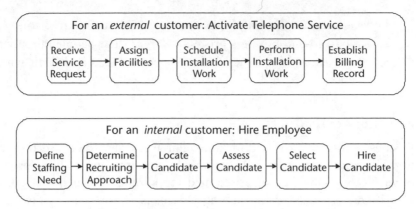

Figure 3.15 Processes with external and internal customers.

ance. These areas are useful for high-level presentations and to get people "into the ballpark," but are not specific enough to analyze and improve. When it gets down to actual workflow process modeling, you have to get down to real processes.

A process focused on an external customer is ideal for a project, because it's so much easier to demonstrate that the bottom-line performance of the company is being improved. But for some business processes, the customer is internal. HR-oriented processes such as Enroll in Benefit Program or Resolve Contract Issue are definitely internal. Some experts say to focus only on the external customer—we disagree. How you treat your internal resources inevitably translates into how your customers are treated. It's been demonstrated time and again that an organization can't, over the long haul, treat its customers any better than it treats its employees. And in time of labor shortage, if you treat your employees poorly you may soon lose them all and go out of business. Just be sure you don't arbitrarily redefine the process to use an internal customer when there really is an external customer.

Processes that serve *internal* customers are sometimes referred to as *supporting processes,* and within this category we have seen them further subdivided into *technical supporting* and *social supporting processes.* Technical supporting processes provide or enhance infrastructure, and they almost always serve other business processes. Examples include Provide Facility, Deploy Application, and Develop Business Process. Social supporting processes provide or enhance people (e.g., Hire Employee, Assess Employee Performance, and Provide Employee Benefits).

All processes matter, so don't use this as a way to decide which processes are more or less important, as some experts do. This classification scheme is useful because it helps avoid drifting out of a process's natural boundaries. For instance, if you are mapping a process within Product Development (core), and you find yourself including training activities (social supporting), you may be mixing two different processes, which can get very confusing.

Closing Advice

Keep three key points about the nature of business processes in mind when defining process boundaries:

1. Processes are *hidden* within your organization.
2. An end-to-end business process is *larger* than people initially think.
3. There are hidden issues that must be surfaced and dealt with, or failure is likely.

Processes Are Hidden

Business processes are seldom immediately evident, because they are hidden by organizational structure, job definitions, systems, geography, product lines, and other factors. Don't be surprised or disappointed if your organization has trouble identifying its processes and gaining consensus. In some cases, it is easier for customers to define the business process because they are the only ones who see it all. Remember our telco example, where the process improvement team initially identified processes that corresponded exactly to organizational divisions. The customers, of course, did not care about the organizational structure of the phone company—they just wanted their telephone service moved, and the real process was eventually identified as Move Telephone Service. Remember, even if the organization doesn't recognize it, the process is there—somehow, the initiating event eventually makes its way to a result. Even though process orientation is mainstream thinking, it's still hard for companies to identify their processes because of years of looking at things organizationally.

They're Bigger Than You Think

Business processes coordinate their elements: people, resources, systems, and work. Without business processes, everything would be done on an ad hoc (and probably uncoordinated) basis. In a well-designed process, all of the elements are well coordinated, including the individual work steps.

You should walk the process backward from any point in the process until you find the event, often with a customer (internal or external) attached, that kicked off the work. Then, walk forward until all of the final results from that triggering event have been produced for the customer and other stakeholders. Except for processes triggered by temporal or conditional events, you'll have a customer on each end.

If you take a single "natural" process, like our Move Telephone Service example, it will virtually always perform better if designed as a single end-to-end business process than if the same result was achieved through five smaller processes. Remember what happened at the telco when they first looked at Move Telephone Service as five smaller processes—service got worse! But why should this be so, especially if each of the small processes is well designed? Let's go back to the notion of coordination to answer that.

In an ideal process, the inputs and outputs of the individual steps are well coordinated. That is, the output from one step flows smoothly and uninterrupted to become the input of the next step in the process. The Lean methodology uses lovely words such as flow, pull, cadence, and rhythm to describe how a well-designed process operates. That is the whole notion of an ideal workflow. This is often accomplished within the boundaries of a subprocess, but it is often not achieved between subprocesses. That is because there is a strong tendency, when trying to achieve optimization within their area, for designers to put constraints on work entering and leaving. Rekeying of data, batching of inputs, transport to a separate location, and fixed processing schedules are some obvious examples. Processes designed this way often require the process that precedes them in the flow to reenter data into a format that is optimized for the receiving process. This makes the receiving process internally optimal, but the overall (natural, end-to-end, business) process is slowed by the additional work. Worse yet, errors will be introduced during the rekeying of data that will ultimately cause even longer delays. Batching introduces similar problems. The idea behind batching is that a process will handle individual work items most efficiently when they are grouped into batches of like items. The process performers can then get set up to handle that type of item most efficiently. It appears that the process is very efficient, but *only within that process for those performers*—the natural process is less effective. Individual work items might spend a lot of time waiting for their batch to get big enough, or for their turn to come.

As noted earlier, this phenomenon was described by Eliyahu Goldratt, and it leads to this conclusion: processes should be defined as large as possible, because multiple small processes each tend to strive for internal efficiency, resulting in local optimization causing overall suboptimization. This really is not surprising, because it is essentially the same problem as functional organizations putting constraints on the entry and exit of work.

Well-meaning process improvement teams can unwittingly make a large process less effective by locally optimizing a subprocess. This leads to an important corollary: if you know that your project scope is less than a complete business process, *be sure to focus attention on expediting the flow of work into and out of your process.*

Hidden Issues

Discovering and modeling processes is enough of an issue technically, and to make things even more challenging, difficult issues—politics, conflict, and emotions—will all arise. Some of the main ones are as follows:

- Who "owns" the process, and how can they influence the various functional areas?
- There may be conflicting performance targets for the participating organizations and individuals.
- The blame game may arise—participants often feel that they are blamed for poor process performance.
- Process improvements can have unanticipated consequences, and they'll usually be bad.

Have no fear—strategies for dealing with these, and others, will be covered, starting with Chapter 5, when we look at discovering business processes.

What's Next?

In this chapter, we've given some very specific guidelines on what constitutes a business process, that chain of activities that links the earliest triggering event to the delivery of the final result to the customer and other stakeholders. We looked at how important it is to define business processes properly: not too small (by activity), not too big (an entire area), not by specialty (a function), not by organizational structure (such as a division or department,) not by technology (e-commerce or social networking or Web 2.0), not by system (the CRM application), and not by any other convenient grouping of effort.

In Chapter 4, we'll get an overview of the complete methodology, and in Chapter 5, we will put the guidelines we've just covered to work with specific techniques for discovering business processes and dealing with the issues they raise. Chapter 6 will show you how to clarify the scope—the boundaries and contents—of an individual business process, and Chapter 7 will show you how to assess current process performance and set objectives for improved performance. All of this is essential before getting into modeling process workflow, but don't worry—it can actually be done fairly quickly! That's good, because we want to remember the advice from Chapter 1—don't skip any of the steps!

References

[1]   By permission. From WWWebster Dictionary, copyright © 1999 (based on *Merriam-Webster's Collegiate® Dictionary, Tenth Edition*) at Web site http://www.m-w.com by Merriam-Webster, Incorporated. These have been checked against the current version: Merriam-Webster Online, copyright © 2008 (based on *MerriamWebster's Collegiate® Dictionary, Eleventh Edition*, © 2005) at Web site http://www.m-w.com by Merriam-Webster, Incorporated.

[2]   WordNet 1.6, copyright © 1997 by Princeton University. All rights reserved. Checked against the current version: WordNet 3.0, copyright © 2006 by Princeton University.

[3]   The Free Online Dictionary of Computing, http://wombat.doc.ic.ac.uk/, Denis Howe (ed.), copyright © Denis Howe, 1993–1999. These have been checked against the current version: The Free Online Dictionary of Computing (FOLDOC), http://foldoc.org, Denis Howe (ed.), copyright © Denis Howe, 1993–2008.

[4]   Texas Instruments, *A Guide to Information Engineering Using the IEF: Computer-Aided Planning, Analysis, Design*, Plano, TX: Texas Instruments, Inc., 1988, pp. 14–15.

[5]   Sippl, C. J., and R. J. Sippl, *Computer Dictionary and Handbook*, Indianapolis, IN: Howard W. Sams & Co., Inc., 1980, p. 402.

CHAPTER 4

The Approach in a Nutshell

This Chapter and Beyond...

This chapter summarizes the methodology we've employed on many successful process improvement and application development projects. Readers from around the world have also reported success following this approach, because it gave them concrete activities, deliverables, and guidelines. This approach—a process for process improvement—is organized into three phases:

1. *Establish process context, scope, and goals*—includes identifying a set of related business processes, and for each, clarifying its boundaries, contents, and some aspects of the current implementation, performing an initial assessment, and setting to-be goals.
2. *Understand the current (as-is) process*—includes modeling its workflow and making initial observations on factors impacting process performance;
3. *Design the new (to-be) process*—includes finalizing an assessment of the process, devising and assessing potential improvements, selecting which changes (improvements) will be made, defining the important characteristics of the to-be process required to implement the changes, and designing the new workflow.

In the first edition of this book, we included a fourth phase, "Develop use case scenarios—makes the transition into system requirements analysis by describing how process actors would interact with a system to complete tasks." We'll still introduce use cases and use case scenarios at the end of this book, in Chapter 15, but no longer treat developing use cases as a phase in the process improvement methodology. Rather, that is one aspect of a methodology for defining information system requirements, along with developing service specifications, finalizing the data model, and defining reporting and information needs.

The reason for this change is that we now treat characterization of the to-be process (part of phase 3) much more explicitly than we did in the first edition's phase 3, and it now includes defining initial system requirements (e.g., the main services and use cases that will need to be developed). However, we also define initial requirements for each of the other key factors. These are known as the "enablers"—they'll be discussed shortly—but include factors such as human resources, and policies and rules, along with information systems. Addressing each is almost its own project, so it no longer felt right to treat IT requirements differently and make them a phase of the methodology and not the other enablers.

This chapter also introduces the various modeling techniques and frameworks that are employed by this approach. Process workflow modeling is the central technique, but others are necessary to establish context and visibility for the process and to ensure that critical factors in addition to workflow are addressed.

This is your guide to the rest of the book—a one-chapter summary of everything else we will cover, intended to clarify how the individual parts make up the whole. After some brief notes on the method and the intended audience, we will get into the specifics.

Why It Works

This methodology works because it uses modeling techniques, frameworks, guidelines, phases, and steps that make it complete, repeatable, and learnable. Just as important, it is a practical response to where projects *actually* go wrong rather than a theoretical exploration of how things *ought* to be done. Many process improvement projects stumble badly or fail outright, and key lessons from these experiences have been incorporated in this approach and verified in practice. The methodology is conceptually similar to many others, but it differs substantially in five important ways:

1. It includes frameworks, specific techniques, and guidelines to ensure that real business processes are identified with clearly delineated boundaries—failure to do so is a common denominator of troubled projects.

2. It initially uses one process modeling technique—a form of decomposition—to make process scope and context clearly visible, and then later uses another technique—a particular form of workflow model—to depict the flow of work. (That's not surprising, given the title of this book!) This form of workflow model stresses diagrams that are simple to read, make the overall flow visible rather than hiding it in rules and detail, and highlight the role played by individual participants. These factors increase participation, buy in, and accuracy. That's an especially important point because complex and rigorous modeling techniques have arisen in recent years that are excellent for *technical* modeling—configuring automated workflow engines—but don't work at all well when they are employed for *business* modeling with process participants and subject matter experts.

3. It includes methods for addressing all of the factors (enablers) that support a process and the environmental factors that constrain it—otherwise, projects tend to zero in on the obvious enablers, workflow and information technology.

4. It shows how process-oriented and IT-oriented efforts can be integrated by including techniques such as use case modeling that support the transition from process improvement to requirements definition activities.

5. Most important, it provides a clear, step-by-step guide to carrying out a process-oriented project, covering identification, modeling, analysis, and improvement. The points most commonly raised in feedback we get from readers are that they appreciate the explanation of things that other experts often assume "everyone knows" (like "what actually *is* a business process?")

and the clearly defined activities and products. Every project is unique, but this provides a solid foundation.

Whom It's For

We developed and organized this material specifically for people working on or responsible for a process improvement project, including the following:

- Business analysts, consultants, and project leaders, whether internal to the organization or employed by a consulting firm;
- Systems analysts defining IT requirements;
- Business managers with a mandate to fix their processes;
- Other professionals with an interest in the topic, especially those participating in executive M.B.A. or continuing education programs. (The book is now widely used as a university text.)

Many of the examples are drawn from medium to large enterprises, but there is nothing in the material that prevents using it in smaller organizations—we've had success with this approach in companies as small as 40 people. On the topic of examples, we have avoided relying solely on one main case study and have drawn upon a variety experiences to illustrate key points. We did this because a single example cannot represent the range of issues encountered in practice and tends to encourage a focus on the specific example rather than the general message. Instead, we've used a variety of examples throughout the book and have provided a single, complete example in the appendix.

The book concentrates more on how-to and less on justification, case studies, or management issues. The book will not, however, cover everything that goes into the full design and implementation of a redesigned process. Issues such as the design of organization structures, developing compensation schemes, and managing change are beyond our scope, and others have already done a fine job of covering subjects like those.[1]

This chapter, once again, is an overview of the rest of the book. It introduces various concepts, methods, frameworks, and tools, but at the core is the business process, so we will begin by recapping the definition.

Processes—Results, Not Work

As we illustrated in the previous chapter, the term *business process*, or simply *process*, is used in many contexts, with varying meaning. Here, we'll recap some of the key points we have made about business processes. The definition we gave is "a *business process* is a collection of interrelated activities, initiated in response to a triggering event, which achieves a specific, discrete result for the customer and other

---

1. One book that does an excellent job of addressing some of these issues is *Improving Performance* by Rummler and Brache (Rummler, Geary A., and Alan P. Brache, *Improving Performance: How to Manage the White Space on the Organizational Chart*, San Francisco: Jossey-Bass Publishers, 1995). It's an essential title in the library of anyone interested in improving business processes.

stakeholders of the process." It's awkward, but it includes the main elements in establishing the scope of a process—the event at one end, and at the other, the result and the customer expecting it. Do not be confused by the term *customer*—it doesn't just refer to a customer purchasing goods or services. The customer of a process could be a regulatory agency, a supplier, an employee, a trade association, or any internal or external person or organization expecting a result from a process.

The result is the most important part of the definition—without a result or output, what reason is there for a process to exist? And the result is not a vaguely defined service or condition—individual results must be specifically identifiable and countable. For instance, a client called to report problems with his company's process improvement project. The team was having trouble controlling scope, and could not seem to get all of the activities into a single process model. The root of the problem was that the scope was "the logistics process," which violates the rule about specific, countable results—it is impossible to identify specific occurrences of "logistics," or answer a question like "How many logistics did we do today?" That's because logistics isn't a process, but a function that provides resources and expertise to multiple processes. Deliver Shipment, however, is a manageable process because you can identify each specific shipment delivered, count how many have happened, and identify the process's customer.

Without a clearly defined process or subprocess as its scope, a project will suffer "scope creep," or implement improvements that do more harm than good. A more complete definition of business process was in Chapter 3, and techniques for process identification are in Chapter 5. The essence, though, is a triggering event, work of some sort, and a discrete, countable result for the primary customer and each of the process's other stakeholders. For some processes, those that are repetitive or transactional in nature, it makes sense to replace the word *work* with the phrase *a defined sequence of steps and decisions*. For other processes, especially those that are less linear and more creative or collaborative in nature, it's reasonable to replace *work* with *a collection of interrelated activities* because there may not be a "defined sequence of steps and decisions." Either way, there is value-added work in between the triggering event and the final result.

Trigger—activities (or steps and decisions)—results is a framework for defining a process, one of several frameworks employed in this methodology.

Frameworks in General

A framework is a structure for discovering, organizing, and presenting ideas or information. They are as simple as the two-by-two matrices loved by consulting organizations for categorizing products, or as complex as a multidimensional structure for financial analysis. Ours are typically straightforward—a set of categories to be filled in or questions to be answered. For example, the simple framework we use to state clear and actionable objectives is the three Ts—topic, target, and time frame. Improving customer service is a fine overall goal, but it is vague, until the framework is used to break it into measurable objectives:

• Topic: telephone hold time for calls to the customer service line;

- Target: 60 seconds or less 98 percent of the time;
- Time frame: within 45 days.

Frameworks manage complexity by reducing vague or complex topics to a set of simpler questions. They organize work, maintain focus during interviews or facilitated sessions, ensure coverage of all aspects of a topic, and provide a standard format to document the findings. One of the most important frameworks is the one we use to consider all dimensions of a process.

A Framework for Process Enablers

We defined a process as a set of steps or activities, but there is more to it than that, specifically the important concept of enablers. An enabler is a factor that can be adjusted to impact process performance. Much of the work of process modeling and analysis is directed at finding the cases where the enablers are hindering the process, so they can be adjusted appropriately. That's the essence of process redesign. Ideally, then, in a redesigned process, the enablers will be adjusted in such a way that they help the process to deliver its intended results and achieve performance targets within the applicable constraints. The two enablers that we are most concerned with are workflow design and IT support, but the complete framework includes a total of six, as illustrated in Figure 4.1:

1. Workflow design;
2. Information systems;
3. Motivation and measurement;
4. Human resources;

Figure 4.1 A process is supported by six enablers.

5. Policies and rules;
6. Facilities design (or some other category appropriate to your situation).

Collectively, enablers are how we make the process work, and no process will work optimally until all of the enablers are acting in concert. Even though this is a book on workflow modeling, and later provides an overview of IT requirements definition, we stress that these are *not* the only factors that matter and in fact are often less important than other enablers. For instance, improvements in workflow and information systems will have little impact if personnel are untrained (an aspect of the HR enabler) or are motivated by inappropriate measures and rewards to behave in ways that are ultimately destructive to the process (an aspect of the motivation and measurement enabler). Successful process redesign involves adjusting all of the enablers such that they support one another and support the goals of the process. Each enabler addresses a specific aspect of the total process.

Workflow Design

The process workflow design is the work plan for responding to a triggering event. It shows the sequence of steps, decisions, and handoffs carried out by the process's actors between the initial event and the final result. The terms participants or roles are often used instead of actors. Whatever you call them, as we'll explore later, a participant could be a person, an organization, an information system, a piece of machinery, or anything else that "holds the work." Having a workflow model can certainly uncover problems in the design of the workflow, but just as or even more important, it allows you to assess the other enablers in an organized fashion, step by step and actor by actor.

Information Systems

Information systems could also be referred to more generically as information technology (IT), which includes systems, information, computers and other devices, telecommunications equipment, and the networks they comprise. Our focus is on information systems—platforms, applications, and databases that provide specific capabilities and that are managed and referred to as a whole, such as the Booking System or the Reverse Logistics System. Information systems enable a process by automating or supporting steps, capturing or presenting information, or managing and expediting the workflow. Increasingly important is the role of a business process management system (BPMS), which provides many capabilities that enable the execution, monitoring, and management of business processes as they flow through multiple systems.

Later in this chapter, we will look at a framework for breaking systems down into their main components as a way to make requirements definition more manageable.

Motivation and Measurement

Motivation and measurement encompass the explicit and implicit reward systems of the organization. Their concern is how people, organizations, and processes are measured and assessed, and the associated consequences—be they reward or punishment. Experience shows that people do what they are measured on and rewarded for, and if the measures do not align with the goals of a redesigned process, failure is virtually certain. Without question, the most common problem we see when analyzing business processes is that performance targets encourage people and organizations to behave in ways that work against the goals of the process. The program manager for the redesign of processes in a national justice system coined a wonderful phrase to describe performance targets like that—*perverse incentives*. An especially common reason for a redesign effort failing is carrying yesterday's performance measures and metrics into tomorrow's process.

Human Resources

The human resource enabler covers the knowledge, skills, and experience of the workforce, how they are recruited, trained, and assigned within the organization, the design of the organization and individual jobs, and so on. A process requires the right people with the right skills in the right job. After inappropriate motivation and measurement, the most common problem we see is the wrong people having responsibility for certain tasks. The worst cases occur when poorly considered cost-cutting and downsizing have resulted in expensive professional staff doing work that could be performed better, at lower cost, by clerical, administrative, or support staff.

Policies and Rules

This includes the rules and policies established by the enterprise to guide or constrain business processes, as well as applicable laws and regulations. In practice, many processes include work and workflow to enforce rules or regulations that are obsolete, contradictory, or overly complex. So, before investing effort to implement a policy such as "any requisition over $2,000 requires approval from a vice president," which will have a substantial impact, the analyst must determine what the rules really are. Surprisingly often, they turn out not to be documented policy at all—they're simply assumptions that have been perpetuated over time and codified in practice. During redesign, these will be challenged and either revised or eliminated. We can't revise or eliminate laws and regulations very easily, although in some famous cases organizations have tried to ignore them, so these might be considered more of a constraint than an enabler.

Facilities

Facilities are the workplace design and physical infrastructure such as equipment, furnishings, machinery, lighting, air quality, and ambient noise. There is a growing trend to recognize the importance of facilities as enablers to effectiveness, productivity, and well being. Facilities may not be of concern in your process, and might be replaced by other, more relevant, enablers. In Chapter 12, we'll provide an example where a process analyst determined that documents were a significant concern, so a "document enabler" was added to the list.

All too commonly, we see new processes with well-designed workflow and information systems fail because other enablers, especially motivation and measurement and human resources, were not adequately considered.

A Framework for Putting Processes and Systems in Context

One of the enablers, information systems, is of particular interest in this book, and we use a framework for putting the analysis of business processes in context with analysis of information systems requirements. We will build this framework up progressively, beginning by recognizing that neither processes nor systems exist in isolation—their sole purpose is to support the aims of the enterprise. Once the enterprise has clarified its mission, strategy, goals, and objectives, business processes that support them can be developed. In turn, information systems can be developed or acquired that support the aims of the business processes. Thus, we arrive at the following three-layer framework, illustrated in Figure 4.2, for organizing analysis and design activities:

- Mission, strategy, goals, and objectives;
- Business processes;
- Information systems.

One Person's Mission Is Another Person's Objective

Conversations about the top layer are often ambiguous because the most commonly used terms—mission, strategy, goals, and objectives—take on multiple definitions. We'll attempt to attach a specific meaning to each:

Mission

The mission articulates the essential nature and overarching goal of the business—it clearly states why the enterprise exists in terms of the products or services provided and the markets or customers served. It's a clear statement of "what we do and who we do it for." Generally, there is also an indication of the "style" of the

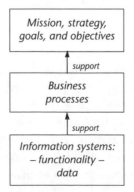

Figure 4.2   Context for processes and systems.

enterprise—how it wishes to be perceived by stakeholders such as customers, employees, investors, and the community.

Strategy

This term is used to describe everything from a specific action plan through to the competitive space the enterprise wishes to occupy. We use a definition closer to the latter, in which strategy describes how an enterprise differentiates its products and services (e.g., low price, customization, leading-edge products, and so forth), and, therefore, why a customer would choose it over competing alternatives. It can be seen as a refinement, or even part of, the mission statement, in that it will provide more specific answers to the following questions:

- What do we do?
- Who do we do it for?
- Most importantly, why do they choose us?

As we will see, this concept is just as applicable in government agencies or internal services where there doesn't appear to be a choice.

Goals and Objectives

The overall improvement directions and destinations established by an enterprise are its goals, backed up by performance targets, which are the objectives it needs to reach along the way. Think of objectives as measurable, intermediate destinations, and the goals as end states. That said, goals often reflect a shifting or ever-changing target—"being the industry's undisputed leader in customer service" is a goal that will mean different things, requiring different objectives, as the competitive landscape changes. For example, once an objective to bring telephone wait time on the customer support line down to a certain level has been reached, it might be necessary to formulate another objective specifying that customers from certain geographies will be connected to a customer service rep who will use the caller's local accent and idioms. Individual processes have their own goals and objectives, which must align with their enterprise counterparts and must be clearly articulated because they provide important guidance when making design decisions. Without them, there is a tendency to assume that the intent of the process is to make things more efficient or comfortable for individual functional areas, which might not support enterprise goals at all.

Expanding the Framework

We started this discussion with a three-layer framework, but in practice we use a five-layer framework, which we arrive at by expanding on the information system layer. Information systems are not monolithic, but are themselves made up of layers (tiers) of interacting components. In the three-tier information systems architecture, these layers are named according to the service they provide—presentation or user interface, business rules and logic, and data management. This is illustrated in Figure 4.3:

- Presentation services;
- Business services;
- Data management services.

This is one of the most widely used frameworks in the world of systems analysis and design. If we take this three-tier framework and use it in place of the simpler information systems layer in the preceding framework, we end up with the five-tier framework illustrated in Figure 4.4:

1. Mission, strategy, goals, and objectives;
2. Business process;
3. Presentation services;
4. Business services;
5. Data management services.

This five-tier approach is at the heart of the methodology we employ for studying business processes and information systems requirements. Our focus in this book is on the top two layers, but because our process improvement methodology will typically be followed by a systems requirements definition phase, we'll further explain each tier in the three-tier systems architecture to provide context and separation.

A Closer Look at the Three-Tier Architecture

Presentation Services

A system (or any automated device) requires mechanisms to capture data and instructions from a person (e.g., for an ATM, "Withdraw $200 from the checking

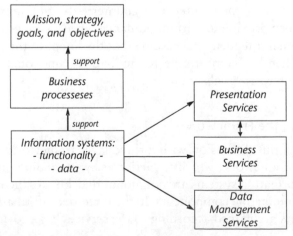

Figure 4.3   The three-tier information systems architecture.

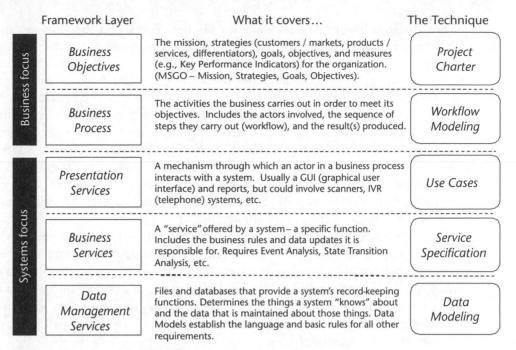

Framework Layer	What it covers…	The Technique
Business focus		
Business Objectives	The mission, strategies (customers / markets, products / services, differentiators), goals, objectives, and measures (e.g., Key Performance Indicators) for the organization. (MSGO – Mission, Strategies, Goals, Objectives).	*Project Charter*
Business Process	The activities the business carries out in order to meet its objectives. Includes the actors involved, the sequence of steps they carry out (workflow), and the result(s) produced.	*Workflow Modeling*
Systems focus		
Presentation Services	A mechanism through which an actor in a business process interacts with a system. Usually a GUI (graphical user interface) and reports, but could involve scanners, IVR (telephone) systems, etc.	*Use Cases*
Business Services	A "service" offered by a system – a specific function. Includes the business rules and data updates it is responsible for. Requires Event Analysis, State Transition Analysis, etc.	*Service Specification*
Data Management Services	Files and databases that provide a system's record-keeping functions. Determines the things a system "knows" about and the data that is maintained about those things. Data Models establish the language and basic rules for all other requirements.	*Data Modeling*

Figure 4.4 A five-tier framework for business analysis.

account for this customer/password combination") and a way to convey information back to that person (e.g., "Sorry, insufficient funds in account."). This mechanism is provided by the presentation services layer, also known as the user interface (UI). It includes any mechanisms by which people (or other systems) interact with an automated system.

In our context, the user interface is usually a graphical use interface (GUI) running on a desktop, like the familiar Windows, Macintosh, or Web browser interfaces. However, it could be just about anything—a character-based computer terminal, an interactive voice response (IVR) system, a kiosk's touchscreen, a bar code scanner, a badge reader, a mobile phone, one of the increasingly common biometric devices (e.g., scanners for hand geometry, fingerprint, or retina), or some new device technology just over the horizon. We can also consider it to include printed output, such as receipts or reports. The presentation services layer for an ATM includes a variety of mechanisms—a touch screen display, selection buttons, a numeric keypad, a card reader, an envelope taker, a cash dispenser, a receipt printer, and a security camera.

Business Services

Everyone seems to have a different name for this layer—process logic, application, application logic, business logic, business rules, and modules, among others. Whatever the name, the concept is the same—programmed modules containing logic to enforce the rules of the business and properly update files and databases. These are defined in such a way that they have relevance from both business and IT perspectives—for the business, each service represents an essential, all-or-nothing unit of work that has business value, while for IT they represent a function or capability that must be packaged in such a way that it can be accessed as a service from different business processes and presentation services.

Continuing the previous example, the Withdraw Funds business service receives a message from the presentation layer and then checks that the personal identification number (PIN) is valid for the account number, verifies that the account has adequate funds, determines applicable service charges, and so on. It also coordinates updates to the data management layer, updating the account balance and logging details of the transaction. Depending on the technology, the programmer might implement the logic in programs called stored procedures, methods, components, modules, transactions, or (this year!) services. As analysts, our concern is only with defining the business rules and data updates.

A major strength of the three-tier architecture is that the same business service might be invoked by different presentation mechanisms. For instance, the same transfer cash functionality may be accessible via an ATM, via a terminal at a teller's workstation, over the telephone via an IVR system, or over the Internet via a Web browser. This gives us the flexibility to add or modify user interfaces without reprogramming business services or to change the rules of a service without having to change all of the user interfaces.

Data Management

In a business setting, most computers are relied on for the computing they perform, but even more so for their ability to store and retrieve data. The data management layer provides this service, maintaining the records of people, places, things, events, and so on that are necessary for an enterprise to operate. Commonly, a relational database management system (DBMS or RDBMS) is used, but any of a number of database or file system technologies could be employed. Since business computers are primarily data processors, and since processes act on things that are represented as stored data, data is considered throughout our analysis. Even though much of this is accomplished by data modeling, in a business setting we speak less about "data," and more about what the data represents—things, objects, or entities are common terms.

Each of these three tiers, as well as business processes, is analyzed and documented using specific modeling techniques. Before introducing these, we offer a few observations about models in general.

Models in General

A model is a representation of some subject matter and is one of two types. An aircraft mockup used for wind tunnel testing, like an architect's model of a building, is an *iconic model*—it resembles the physical object it represents, except that it is smaller and simplified. A mathematical model of the economy is a *symbolic model*—a representation of some physical (e.g., the weather) or conceptual (e.g., a budget or a project plan) subject matter that isn't intended to look like that subject. Symbolic models often represent concepts that can't actually be observed. For example, our workflow models are symbolic—they are made up of boxes, lines, and text that bear no resemblance to the people, documents, and inboxes that they represent. All of the various models we build must be developed with the full participation of business subject matter experts, who are probably not experts in our modeling disciplines. So, to be successful, the modeling techniques we employ must meet the following criteria:

- They're an abstraction of something (like the flow of work through a process) that otherwise can't be directly observed or can't be observed all at once.
- They highlight particular facets of the subject that are of interest while masking unnecessary detail.
- They employ conventions for adding detail and precision progressively.
- They typically have an obvious starting point and direction.
- They use the minimum number of graphic elements that is feasible, such that mere mortals can comprehend them without continual reference to a legend.

Generally, it is more convenient, less expensive, and safer to manipulate a model than it is to manipulate the corresponding real-world objects. In our case, a process workflow model supports understanding and assessing a process design without actually implementing and then observing it.

Modeling is not an end in itself, and people frequently need to be reminded to stop modeling when the purpose has been achieved. In our method, an as-is workflow process model is used to understand why the current process behaves the way it does, and modeling stops as soon as that understanding has been reached. In other situations, of course, you'll want to carry on with modeling to a greater level of detail and precision. For instance, you will do more modeling if your purpose is to fully document the as-is state or if you are preparing for more detailed, statistical analysis such as you would do in Lean or Six Sigma. We prefer to save our effort for the to-be workflow model. The model of the to-be process is used to guide implementation and will continue to be maintained through implementation and revision—and therefore requires more detail and precision.

The Modeling Techniques We Employ

As noted, there are associated modeling techniques for each of the lower four tiers of the five-tier framework. These are introduced in Figure 4.5.

Business Process: Process Workflow Models

Process workflow models (or workflow process models) as illustrated in Figure 4.6 are known by many names, but because of their appearance they are most commonly referred to as *swimlane diagrams*. A swimming pool might be divided lengthwise into swimlanes for racing or swimming laps. Just as each swimmer is expected to stay in his or her swimlane, each participant or actor in the process has their own swimlane. A box represents a step in the process, and is placed in the swimlane of the responsible actor. Arrows connecting the boxes indicate the sequence and flow of the steps. This type of diagram can be used to show both current (as-is) and

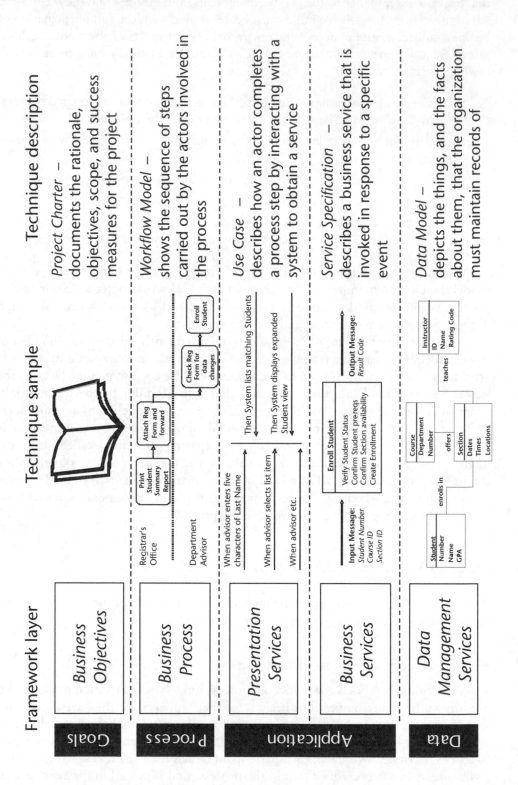

Figure 4.5 The business analysis framework and corresponding modeling techniques.

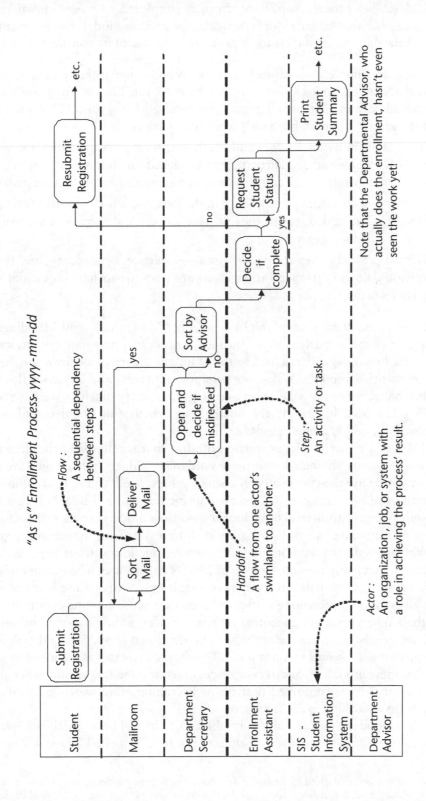

Figure 4.6 A workflow process model or *swimlane diagram*.

proposed (to-be) process workflow, from a simplified overview down to very detailed steps. This particular form of workflow process model[2] has become the de facto standard for depicting business processes because of its merits:

- They are simple and self-explanatory. While other techniques may require considerable training before they can be read, this form of swimlane diagram should be immediately understandable by almost everyone. (That's not to say they're easy to build, but that's what this book is for.)
- They show individual actors and emphasize their responsibilities and interactions with other actors. Participants can identify with the model, so it's easier for them to validate it, leading to more complete and accurate representations.
- They show *all* actors participating in the process, whether or not their activities are value-added, and so they provide a realistic depiction of the workflow that is not sugar coated.
- Drawn properly, they are highly visual—sequence, dependency, and time are obvious, flowing from left to right, as are patterns such as sequential versus parallel activities.

At this point, some readers might be saying "Wait, that's a BPMN diagram!" referring to the widely used business process modeling notation (see http://www.bpmn.org). That's true, as the swimlane diagrams we draw use the same core symbols that the BPMN describes—lanes, activities, and sequence flows. On the other hand, we're drawing swimlane diagrams pretty much as we have for the past 15 years, long before BPMN emerged, so whether or not that makes them "BPMN diagrams" is a moot point.

BPMN is a rigorous and powerful notation that standardizes the drawing of swimlane diagrams but includes far more symbols ("widgets") than you'll see in this book—we only use the core symbols, a small subset. We'll run the risk of invoking the wrath of BPMN fans everywhere by pointing out that full BPMN is best suited for drawing specification level or technical workflow models in preparation for configuring an automated workflow facility or business process management system. We wholeheartedly endorse it for that purpose but know from experience and observation that using the entire range of BPMN capabilities when communicating with business professionals can leave them goggle-eyed and confused—there are far more symbols for representing different kinds of events, activities, gateways, and flows than are necessary to document the main concepts and flow of a business process. They are, however, necessary when you get down to specifying detailed rules and logic that will execute in a computer. We characterize this as technical modeling versus business modeling, and recent discussions at conferences and other professional meetings have confirmed that this is becoming more widely acknowledged among people working in the field.

We're optimistic that at some point the BPx field will have widely accepted terminology that differentiates the two kinds of models.[3] With luck, there will also be a

---

2. This modeling style was popularized by Rummler and Brache in *Improving Performance*.
3. In the data modeling field, for instance, there is a distinction between conceptual and logical data models (although there isn't universal agreement on what each contains).

formally identified subset of BPMN that will be used for business modeling, and the rest of it will be reserved for technical- or specification-level modeling. Experienced practitioners do this anyway, but less experienced people will use the symbols "because they're there." If you doubt that, consider how many fonts (and colors, weights, sizes, and styles) are used by amateur designers in Web sites or documents for no better reason than "because they can." So, we'll describe workflow models using the basic conventions we've employed since the mid-1990s. If you want to look at this in BPMN terms, we are using a modified subset of the BPMN. We'll get into the specifics of this later—several chapters are devoted to process workflow models, beginning with Chapter 8. As well, related to the topic of business versus technical modeling, we'll describe three specific levels of detail, each supporting a particular perspective and need, that all of our models go through—scope, concept (or overview), and specification (or detail). The concept level is the business modeling we just referred to and is our focus.

Presentation Services: Use Cases and Use Case Scenarios

Eventually, while we are designing the to-be process, we begin considering how information systems will help an actor complete a task. Swimlane diagrams are not appropriate for this kind of detail, so we switch gears and employ our own variant of the popular "use case" technique. In fact, everyone seems to use their own variant, which is one of the difficulties inherent in use cases.[4] Essentially, a use case models a generalized dialogue—the back and forth—between an actor and a system that enables the actor to complete some task or obtain a service that is of value to them. In addition to the normal flow, the use case also describes extension flows illustrating how errors and exceptions will be handled. A use case scenario is like a single test case, with defined actors, conditions, data values, and outcomes. In some environments, such as on extreme programming (XP) projects, this same concept is implemented with acceptance test (or fitness test) dialogues.

Why is this necessary? Well, think of all the times you've used a system and wondered, "What in the world were they thinking?"—Web sites with torturous navigation, interactive voice response systems that never get where you want to go, and ATMs that take you through 15 steps before concluding that you made a mistake in the second step and must start over. By depicting the interaction between actor and machine before the system is designed and developed, use cases help us avoid this sort of problem by identifying the real requirements and constraints. Later, they will be used in various stages of testing and are often even used in training materials.

Use cases are introduced in Chapter 15, along with information on how they relate to their "neighbors" in the framework—business processes and business services.

---

4. A note to avoid potential confusion for those of you who have seen use case diagrams as drawn in the unified modeling language (UML)—those aren't actually the use cases, they are a visual catalog or directory of the use cases and their interrelationships, much the way the catalog at a library isn't the actual books. Somewhere else, the use cases themselves must be documented, and it is here that we see a wide range of styles and perspectives.

Business Services: Service Specification and Supporting Techniques

This is a complex area, requiring considerable discipline and a number of techniques including event identification, state transition modeling, and, finally, service specifications. The key point is that service specifications describe "what" a system must do without reference to "who and how," which is what use cases accomplish. The "what" might be a business service such as Withdraw Funds, which can be accessed by different use cases such as Customer Withdraws Funds via ATM and Teller Withdraws Funds via Teller Workstation. Business services are covered in Chapter 15, along with use cases.

Data Management: Data Models

A data model represents the things about which an organization must maintain records. More to the point, these are the things that business processes act on, and information systems maintain and manipulate. Data models have both a narrative component and a graphic component, with the latter being an entity-relationship diagram (ERD). This in turn is made up of three types of components:

1. *Entities:* The distinct things about which information is needed (e.g., Order, Customer, Facility, Product, Part, Supplier, and so forth);
2. *Relationships:* The associations among those entities (e.g., Part is used in Product, Product is requested on Order, and Order is placed by Customer);
3. *Attributes:* The facts about each entity that must be recorded (e.g., the attributes of Part include Part Number, Description, Unit Weight, and Unit Price).

The most important part of the narrative component is the entity definitions. A definition is produced for each entity, to ensure consistent interpretation by all project team members. The first time you go through this step, you might feel a little silly—"I'm asking the obvious"—but you'll be amazed at the different interpretations for common terms like Product or Customer. In one memorable example, even we were surprised by how differently justice system professionals defined Case, depending on whether their perspective was policing, prosecution, or probation. And the number of different interpretations of Customer at a globally known provider of credit cards made one's head swim. This makes data models a powerful tool early in a process-oriented project—they improve communication and consistency, because the entity names and definitions provide a standard vocabulary for the things the process deals with. Later in the project, data models are essential for database design and for describing system requirements such as user interface behavior (use cases) or program logic (business services) in a consistent way.

Examples can be seen in Chapter 14, which is an overview of data modeling.

Five-Tier Thinking

To summarize, this framework encapsulates the essence of our approach—it organizes the analytic techniques we employ on all process improvement and application development projects. It lets us look at a business, including the processes and systems that support it, as a whole. As we have noted before, processes and information systems are inseparable, and both exist to support the aims of the enterprise.

We have found this five-tier approach very useful for explaining the analysis steps that a project will undertake. Often, during a project kickoff, we will present a variation on Figure 4.4, and review each layer while making the following points:

1. An enterprise has a mission, strategies, goals, and objectives...
2. ...which are supported by business processes. Actors in a business process are in turn supported by information systems that they interact with via...
3. ...the presentation services layer, which communicates events to the...
4. ...business services layer, which enforces business rules and coordinates updates to the...
5. ...stored records in the data management services layer.

Participants, from senior executives to technical specialists, consistently express support for this framework because it shows the interrelationships between their respective areas of interest.

A Workflow-Driven Methodology—The Process of Studying Processes

Finally, let's review the methodology we will explore in the remainder of the book. We describe it as a starting point, because there are unique aspects to every project—the world of business processes is filled with politics, intrigue, sensitivities, conflicting goals, old habits, seemingly unshakable paradigms, resource constraints, and a host of other pitfalls, so you'll probably have to tailor the approach to your environment.

As outlined earlier, the approach proceeds through three phases:

1. Frame the process.
2. Understand the current (as-is) process.
3. Design the new (to-be) process.

The key elements of this approach are summarized in Figure 4.7.

This is followed by a detailed requirements definition, design, and implementation phase for each of the six enablers—workflow, information systems, motivation and measurement, human resources, policies and rules, and facilities. For instance, on one recent project, after we'd completed the third phase and characterized the key elements of the new process, the HR manager headed up a project to address design and implementation of changes in his area, the facilities manager, with her team of architects, started work on the design of a new workplace, and the IT department began the development of detailed requirements for a new supporting system. All of them worked within the overall specifications ("characteristics") that came out of phase 3, but bringing to bear their particular focus and expertise. We'll have more to say about IS requirements in Chapters 14 and 15, but this isn't to diminish the importance of the areas—it's just a reflection of where our expertise lies.

1) Establish process context, scope, and goals	2) Understand as-is process-workflow and other enablers	3) Define to-be process characteristics and requirements

• *Identify related processes*
  • identify and link activities
  • 1:1 links are in same process
  • draw Overall Process Map
• *Clarify target process' scope*
  • triggering event, ~5+/–2 sub-processes, result for each stakeholder, cases/variations
• *Clarify as-is process elements*
  • functional areas
  • actors and responsibilities
  • systems and mechanisms
• *Assess as-is process by stakeholder* (initial)
  • also specify context and consequences of inaction
• *Specify to-be process goals*
  • subjective and objective
• *Specify performance metrics*
  • customer-focused outcomes, not internal task efficiency
	• *Organize and initiate session*
	  • staff and management plus external stakeholders
	  • review scope, issues, goals
	  • review ground rules
	• *Build as-is swimlane diagram*
	  • one case and path at a time
	  • 1) "Who gets it next?"
	     2) "How does it get there?"
	     3) "Who *really* gets it next?"
	• *Check each step - 5 questions*
	  1) again "How does it get there?"
	  2) "No mushy verbs?"
	  3) "All triggers shown?"
	  4) "All participant actors shown?"
	  5) "All outputs shown?"
	• *Model other process cases*
	  • create new diagram, or use original case as a starting point
	• *Add additional levels of detail*
	  • *only if necessary*
		• *Assess as-is process by enabler* (final assessment)
		  • using as-is diagram as a guide
		  • helps us take a *holistic view*
		• *Decide on approach*
		  (abandon, outsource, leave as-is, improve, or redesign)
		• *Conduct challenge session*
		  • challenges hidden assumptions, generates creative ideas
		  • helps us "*think out of the box*"
		• *Eliminate infeasible ideas*
		  (cost, legal, resources, impact, ...)
		• *Assess improvement ideas by enabler*
		  • helps us *avoid unanticipated consequences*
		  • builds requirements document
		• *Lay out to-be workflow*
		  • handoff level first, then milestone and task levels

Figure 4.7   Three-phase project methodology.

Establish Process Context, Scope, and Goals

This is arguably the most important phase, because, while quick, it prevents many common problems later. When we are called in to assist with a project that is in trouble, we invariably find a lack of clarity in context, scope, and objectives. We then have to take the team right back to the beginning and work through "framing the process," as this phrase is also known. The key steps include:

- Identify and name a set of related processes by developing an overall process map or process landscape. This clarifies what's in and what's out of scope by showing each process to be studied, one at a time, plus touch points to other processes.
- Establish the scope of the "target process" to be studied, using a framework for clarifying a process's boundaries and contents:
    - *What*—Triggering event, result for the customer and other stakeholders, approximately five plus or minus two subprocesses ("milestones") within the process, and the primary cases or variations of the process;
    - *Who*—organizations currently participating in the process, plus individual actors and their main responsibilities;
    - *How*—systems and mechanisms currently supporting the process.
- Review or document relevant enterprise mission, strategy, goals, and objectives.
- Perform an initial process assessment:
    - Stakeholder based (customer, performer, owner/manager, and if necessary, consider other stakeholders—supplier, regulator, and so forth);

- Summarize in the initial process assessment (or "case for action").[5]
- Determine process goals and performance objectives:
  - Describe subjectively how different stakeholders will perceive the new process, determine the overall differentiator or "improvement dimension" for the to-be process, and, finally, establish objective performance metrics and targets for the to be process;
  - Summarize in the process goals (or "vision").
- Develop glossary of terms and definitions (the start of the data model): As you'll see in the next chapter, on identifying processes, we actually start with development of terms and definitions, even if we don't finalize it as a glossary until this point.
- Summarize—construct and distribute a poster or some such summary;
- Optionally, begin documenting noteworthy observations of culture, core competencies, and management systems.

Understand the As-Is Process

Now that the goals for the process are clarified, you will need to understand why, *really,* those goals are not being met—many so-called "improvements" are implemented that don't actually improve anything because other factors are the root cause. The key here is not to exhaustively document the current process in excruciating detail, but to document it well enough that it can be assessed and understood:

- Map the current process workflow to show who, does what, when:
  - Develop swimlane diagrams, focusing on overall flow;
  - Refine swimlane diagrams, adding alternatives, exceptions, errors, and so on;
  - Use progressive levels of detail (we will define them later), stopping when process behavior is understood—don't get bogged down in detail!
- Document important observations about all other enablers (current use of IT, motivation and measurement, and so forth) as well as observations about culture, core competencies, and management systems;
- Record initial thoughts on strengths and weaknesses of the current process, especially leverage points where significant improvement is possible.

Design the To-Be Process

We divide this part into two stages. The first, "characterize the to-be process," conducts a detailed assessment of the as-is and uses this to aid in determining a set of improvements or design characteristics that will work in concert to achieve process goals. We do this stage specifically because teams often leap into the design of a new workflow that incorporates "improvements" that actually work at cross-purposes

---

5. This phrase was introduced in Hammer and Champy's book.

or are inconsistent with other enablers. Once the team is satisfied that it has identified a cohesive, effective set of characteristics for the new process, the second stage begins—"design the to-be workflow."

Characterize the To-Be Process

- Perform an enabler-based final assessment of the as-is process:
    - These are enablers: workflow, IT, motivation and measurement, human resources, policies and rules, facilities (or other).
    - At this point, you will also start to collect ideas for the to-be process. Because this step involves assessing the as-is to help generate ideas for the to-be, it's really almost a separate phase between understanding the as-is and designing the to-be.
- Decide on direction—abandon, stay as-is, improve, redesign, or outsource.
- Optionally, assess each individual step (e.g., is it necessary, is it done by the right performer, and so forth).
- Develop additional ideas for characteristics or features of the new process, to augment those identified during final assessment of the as-is. Techniques include:
    - Identify improvements that would address leverage points.
    - Challenge assumptions underlying process steps.
    - Brainstorm by enabler (this may, in effect, have been done during assessment).
- Reject some ideas because they are infeasible, illegal, conflict with culture or direction, and so on.
- Assess promising ideas in context (with respect to other enablers) using a matrix format (e.g., a change in workflow may require a change in job definition that may in turn require changes to recruiting and training, as well as changes in compensation and performance measurement).
- Based on the assessment, select the key characteristics of the to-be process and document them.
- Develop/revise conceptual data model.

Design the To-Be Process Workflow

This is actually quite straightforward if all the previous steps have been worked through, because the core elements of the new workflow will have been identified while assessing and documenting key characteristics of the to-be, or they will be carried over from the as-is:

- Draw the to-be workflow.
- Progress through the different levels of detail.
- Assess and check viability at each level.
- Revise, or move on to the next level of detail.

- Iterate.
- Review with a wider audience.

After the Three-Phase Method

While other specialists look at enablers such as human resources or facilities, business and systems analysts will make the transition to looking more specifically at how information systems can support the process. This is highly iterative, but the main activities are:

- Identify the business services that must be provided, by considering:
    - Business events or essential results;
    - The needs of specific actors;
    - Steps in the process workflow.
- Document each business service using the templates and defined levels of detail we'll cover later on.
- Identify use cases by considering:
    - Each business service in turn, and determining which actor(s) need to access it;
    - Other cases where an actor requires access to a service (to ensure that exception or error conditions that may not be shown on workflow models are identified);
    - Specific steps in the workflow where an actor will need to access a service;
- Document each use case using the template for each defined level of detail.
- Identify use case scenarios:
    - Identify a set of process scenarios (usually around 5 to 10) that will exercise the main paths through the new workflow. (A process scenario is a single test case that works its way through the entire business process and therefore spans many use cases.)
    - For each process scenario, identify the individual use case scenarios (typically 7 to 15) and document the situation, actors, major decisions, and outcomes for each.
- Develop individual use case scenarios:
    - Focus on the dialogue for each scenario.
    - Refine use cases as necessary.
- Throughout the work on use cases and scenarios, revise the business services and data model as necessary.

More information is provided in Chapter 15, but a detailed treatment of information systems requirements definition is beyond the scope of this book—we just hope to introduce the main concepts and put them in context with process modeling and improvement.

Applications of the Approach

Our approach could be characterized as process focused and workflow driven, but should you always use a process-focused, workflow-driven approach? Here's a short answer—a tautology, in fact. If work flows at all, you should consider using workflow, and if it flows far, you must use workflow. Let's clarify that.

Anytime the application or business improvement project under consideration involves multiple actors (e.g., job titles or organizational units), and the handling of an event flows between them, workflow should be considered. It may not be essential until at least four or five actors are involved, but you can always give it a try. If you are able to develop a good workflow process model easily, without any significant discoveries or major issues arising, it may not have been necessary, but you won't have wasted much time.

In other cases, the problem at hand is entirely transactional—an event is handled almost completely by one or two actors in a single transaction. These types of projects are becoming less common, but in those cases a workflow-driven approach may not make sense. An example is an application to automate the basic transactions of a library—reserve a title, initiate a loan, return a copy, and so forth. None of these are complex, multistep, multiactor processes, so we'd define the scope and objectives and then jump right into data modeling, business services, and use cases. Note though that other aspects of running a library, such as the process to acquire a new title, would definitely require a workflow because multiple actors and multiple activities are involved, from receiving the request from a patron, through assessing it, ordering it, cataloging it, receiving it, stocking it, and so on.

Finally, there are other cases that we have not alluded to where elements of this approach have proven to be extremely useful. So far, we have described a method in which a new process is designed and then a supporting information system is developed. Often, this is not the sequence of events. Instead, a major information system is acquired, such as a customer relationship management or supply chain management application from a vendor such as SAP, Oracle, or i2.

Experience shows that when these implementations don't take a business process orientation, the result is often disastrous. One approach is to develop process workflow models for your desired (to-be) business processes to use in selecting and configuring a purchased application. Alternatively, many commercial applications are designed around an ideal (best practices) business process. If the necessary expertise (usually from the vendor or a consulting firm) is available, a model of the process the application supports can be developed. This will clarify whether a particular offering supports your goals and objectives, and assist you in identifying the changes necessary to implement it.

We have also used these techniques when integrating enterprise applications with preexisting legacy and custom applications. This is one of the major strengths of the BPMS offerings we mentioned earlier, which had their roots in the enterprise application integration (EAI) systems of the 1990s. In fact, in the late 1990s we observed that EAI vendors and consultants would achieve far greater success if they coupled their products and services with process-oriented approaches and suggested that the field should have been named "enterprise process integration." That didn't stick, but the idea emerged anyway, and the field morphed into BPMS.

One of the hallmarks of a powerful tool, technique, or approach is that it proves itself useful in a wide variety of situations, some of them quite unexpected by the originators. The process-oriented approach and the techniques that come with it fall into this category. Armed with this overview, let's dive into the details and see how it can work for you, beginning with the most important step of all—correctly identifying your business processes.

PART II

Phase 1: Establish Process Context, Scope, and Goals

CHAPTER 5

Discover Business Processes

Process Discovery—What, Why, and How

The success of process-oriented initiatives depends on this vital step, which precedes one or more individual process improvement or redesign projects, because of the following:

- A clearly articulated project scope is a vital element of project success, and identifying true business processes provides a perfect framework for establishing project scope.
- Those processes must have been identified in such a way that people will agree, "Yes, those are our business processes."

It is especially true that process improvement projects require a clear scope—it's all too easy to drift into related processes or to drift into other activities performed by the participating functions. The consequences are never good when a project team skips these upfront activities and jumps in and starts drawing swimlane diagrams and proposing process changes right off the mark. Modeling will spiral aimlessly, there will be endless discussions and recrimination in a belated search for scope and/or meaning, and if the team gets that far, they might just implement "improvements" that actually make things worse. You might end up in this situation in different ways:

- You are legitimately trying to improve processes, but find yourself saying, "I know what a business process is, and I know what one isn't, but the theory and rules aren't helping. I need some step-by-step techniques to help me identify my business processes."
- You were handed a "process improvement" project that was defined from on high before you even heard about it. Probably, almost certainly, the boundaries won't correspond to a proper business process. You'll start with something like "Fix our logistics processes" or "Move our customer-facing processes to the Web." You need to scope or cope—adjust project scope, or adjust to the situation.
- The focus is on installing a purchased software application, perhaps even one large enough to qualify as "enterprise software." You know the track record—failing to address business process issues is a prescription for fail-

ure—but you aren't sure how to shift the focus away from the software to the business processes the software is intended to support.

All of these require a method for getting through the cloud and identifying relevant business processes. Then, for each of these, you must accurately specify its boundaries and contents, problems and goals, and some important facts about the context in which you will be studying it. We refer to this as "framing the process," and it is the first of the three phases in our method—phase 1: establish process context, scope, and goals. The three phases are illustrated in Figure 4.7. Per its name, this phase in turn has three main steps:

1. Discover a related set (a "family") of business processes that ensures context when studying individual processes (this chapter).
2. Establish the scope of each business process you will study (Chapter 6).
3. Establish as-is process issues and to-be process goals (Chapter 7).

Step 1, discover business processes, is done once per process area. Steps 2 and 3, scoping and assessment, will be done for each individual business process. If your process area has five business processes, you'll go through these steps five times, assuming each process becomes the subject of a project.

Process discovery and the subsequent two steps are totally interdependent. First, you need to discover a set of related processes so you can start studying an individual process with an understanding of what it *doesn't* include. Knowing an overall set of processes, you can more easily complete the framing activities for each individual process, which includes establishing its boundaries; contents and participants; and its issues, goals, and particular style (differentiator) in meeting the goals of the enterprise.

Because part of it is done once, and part of it multiple times, some people find it clearer to think of process discovery (this chapter) as distinct from framing; that way, process framing is an activity that you do for each process, including the scoping, assessment, and goal setting (Chapters 6 and 7). Either way, you have to have completed process discovery first. Increasingly, this is done separately at the enterprise level by a group responsible for process architecture or a business architecture group. Framing will then be done for each process by the team responsible for it.

By the way, we often call it "process discovery" rather than "process identification" because the latter makes it sound like they're immediately evident and just need to be identified. The fact is, they're pretty well hidden in the structure and systems of an enterprise, so it is really more a voyage of discovery, requiring a mix of archaeology and anthropology, than it is a surveying expedition over visible terrain.

A Few More Notes on Discovering Processes

More often than not, when we see a process analysis or redesign effort that has gone off the rails, it is because little or no attention was given to the upfront steps of unambiguously defining the business process, rigorously establishing its scope and putting it in context with "related" business processes, and establishing goals that make sense for the process and its role within the enterprise. In our terms, the process was not "framed." Often times, the team thought this had been done properly, but it emerged (painfully) later on just how unclear and incomplete the initial effort was. In *The Reengineering Revolution*, Michael Hammer identified process identification and analysis as the second and third top mistakes in reengineering, summing it up with the statement "Moral: Only (business) processes can be reengineered. Before you can reengineer processes you must identify them" [1]. With the benefit of many years of study at The School of Hard Knocks, we're able to be quite precise about what needs to be included in this upfront identification and analysis.

Your scope will clarify exactly what a project will include, and, just as important, what you'll exclude. This can be a tricky area, because your scope should be small enough to master, yet large enough to make a difference. If you include too little—a subset of a process—the project might not address enough of the problem to make any real difference. Unless you've been very careful with this situation, you can easily find that your project suffers scope creep, slowly and steadily expanding backward and forward through the process and into the participating functions. This can easily happen when you undertake workflow modeling without clear scope, because the team will follow workflows into other areas. Even if you do keep the scope small, if you established it without adequate context, your "improvements" might even make the overall process *worse* through the phenomenon of local optimization.

Two clarifications are in order before we proceed:

- It is perfectly reasonable to have project boundaries that are smaller than business processes—you just have to make sure you don't damage any processes and don't expect the benefits that come from improving a complete cross-functional process. Scoping in this case means knowing what the whole is (the next layer of activities around your scope), what pieces it comprises, and which of those are in your scope. This means that your overall process map might look more like what we cover in the next chapter, on scoping an individual process—a picture showing the subprocesses or major activities within a single process, with an indication of which are in your scope.

- We're not saying that every project has to be process-oriented, or that process modeling is always the right approach. It just happens to be the focus of this book. There are all sorts of other projects that have value, such as those that focus on infrastructure or a job-related productivity tool.

The Goal: An Overall Process Map

The overall process map or process landscape is a simple, graphical depiction of a set of related processes, usually five to seven. By related, we mean that they deal with the same topic and overall goal (e.g., all involve maintaining a supply of spare parts, managing a customer relationship, or managing a product through its entire life cycle), and there are significant information flows and dependencies between them. These flows are typically information, but could be goods or other items. We refer to the set of business processes as a process area, process family, or process domain. Some of these are widely recognized, such as customer relationship management or supply chain management, but it is essential that they be broken down into the specific processes they comprise at your organization. Figure 3.12 showed a bank's Commercial Loans Management process domain, with an additional level of detail, the subprocesses that comprise some of the business processes. Figure 5.1 shows a simple example for Supply Management process area.

The value of the overall process map is that it clarifies what is out of scope as well as what is in. In the process Procure Item, stakeholders might assume that establishing an ongoing supply contract for the item, or paying the vendor, is part of the process scope. However, the example shows that Establish Supply Agreement and Pay Vendor are specifically out of scope—they are separate processes. If you don't make it clear to all actual and potential stakeholders what you are excluding, you will inevitably face the wrath or disappointment of those who assumed you were going to help them. Alas, the need for an overall process map is clearest in hindsight, after suffering the delays and conflicts arising from unclear scope. More than once, we have been called on to assist a project that started without one. They have usually done a fair bit of as-is modeling, and even some to-be models, before the problems start to mount up. Then, there is very strong agreement from everyone—from senior managers to junior analysts—that they need to go back and build a map putting their project in context. Typically, they also feel that they could have avoided slipping into other processes, and could have made their processes big enough to make a real impact.

Even if your project scope is less than a full process, you should use this technique. Just show other related process "chunks" of about the same size as your project, and you will at least have visually clarified what is out of scope (and possibly where some important flows or interfaces have to be accommodated).

Ideally, an organization should have a business process architecture showing the major process areas and their business processes cross-referenced to the organizational units that participate and enterprise goals and objectives. A growing number of organizations have one, as well as a data architecture, application architecture, and technology architecture. Cross-referencing these yields valuable insights for planning and scoping initiatives, and managing the organization's assets. Unfortunately, we often find that the process architecture actually depicts their major functions—accounting, human resources, sales, manufacturing, logistics, marketing, and so on—which doesn't support a cross-functional view. This is evident when the process architecture is cross-referenced to the organizational structure, and a lot of 1:1 relationships emerge.

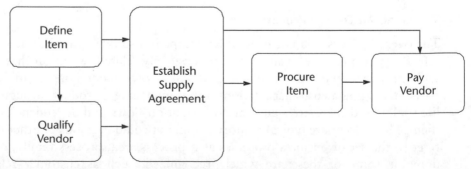

Figure 5.1   Overall process map for the Supply Management area.

The Approach

Rationale

This chapter relies extensively on what we learned earlier about business processes. If you skipped Chapter 3 (Business Processes—What *Are* They, Anyway?), perhaps because you were sure you already knew what a business process was, your assignment is to go back and read that chapter now! It laid a foundation of definitions and techniques that is essential to understanding this one. Three key lessons from Chapter 3 are applied throughout this phase:

1. A process has a triggering (or initiating) event at the front end, ultimately leading, on a 1:1 basis, to a discrete, countable result at the other end, produced for the process' customer. That customer could be internal or external to the organization, and will often have triggered the initiating event. Almost always, there will also be a result for the owner of the process (the enterprise that operates it) and other stakeholders. Some analysts refer to the owner as the service provider, and the customer and other stakeholders as the service recipient. Typically, the same token moves through the process, being transformed along the way (e.g., from a prospect to an approved prospect, to a committed prospect, and finally to a registered customer).
2. Almost all business processes turn out to be larger than people expect; they include more activities, they involve more actors, they cross more functional or departmental lines, and, increasingly, they cross enterprise boundaries.
3. You must have terms, definitions, and techniques, as we provided, to differentiate collections of business processes (process areas), individual business processes, and parts of business processes (subprocesses or activities).

The approach we'll illustrate embodies two principles:

1. In most cases, it is most effective to identify processes in "bottom-up" fashion.
2. Identifying processes is best done in a group session, and that group should include people who will participate in subsequent process improvement projects.

It is often surprising (especially to the experts!) that we identify processes in a "bottom-up" fashion, given that the goals and objectives (and therefore what processes need to achieve) is established top down. Further, the analysis of individual processes proceeds top down, from identification through scoping and on to modeling, which in turn proceeds top down through progressive layers of detail. It seems to be a top-down world!

In practice, though, a bottom-up approach works best most of the time. That is, identify a whole bunch of individual activities or milestones that have to be achieved and then string them together into processes. But what about the top-down approach many authorities suggest? That is, from the top (operate enterprise), you should identify the major processes through progressive decomposition. It sounds easy, but in practice, it is quite difficult, because of the intense gravitational pull of the current enterprise structure. What happens is that the only top-down view that is available is based on the organizational (functional) structure of the company, so that is what is played back as the company's business processes. We end up with the all-too-common phenomenon of the business process that looks suspiciously like an organizational unit. That is why experienced analysts have learned that top-down analysis usually starts with a significant bottom-up component: you gather more detail than you need, and then synthesize it into the higher-level abstraction you were seeking. Other than just being easier, three advantages of this approach are (a) the clients always give you more detail than you want anyway, (b) it's easier to start by capturing detail than anything else, and (c) people like to see where the processes came from with respect to activities they recognize. Once processes have been discovered, the rest of the modeling and analysis takes place in a traditional top-down fashion, working through well-defined, progressive levels of detail.

That takes care of why we do it bottom up, which also mostly answers why it has to be done in a group. First, a facilitated session is a great way to generate those activities that our bottom-up method depends on, because synergies (piggybacking and leapfrogging) from the group dynamic simply generate a richer base of material to work with. Related to that, everyone hears firsthand other perspectives and terminology, vastly accelerating group learning and paying off major dividends later on. When you try to discover processes by conducting a series of one-on-one interviews, you soon find yourself going back and forth between people you've interviewed, playing "he said, she said."

We have included material in this chapter to help you prepare for your process discovery and framing sessions, get them started in a productive fashion, and facilitate them to a successful outcome.

The Steps

Discovering processes proceeds through seven steps:

1. Get started—gather background material on the organization and meet with the sponsor to get their take on the overall strategy and business model, issues, goals and objectives, and suggested participants.
2. Conduct pre-session interviews—meet with functional area representatives to understand their responsibilities and issues, and to identify terms and activities for later analysis.
3. Prepare for first session—consolidate the findings from the interviews (issues, terms, activities), prepare materials for use in the discovery sessions, and develop a session agenda.
4. Initiate first session—have a quick introduction from the sponsor, describe business processes and the important issues, show sample process landscape, describe approach, and review session behaviors.
5. Analyze terms and find the nouns—present the terms collected during the interviews, collect more suggestions, determine the core nouns, and again collect suggestions.
6. Identify activities—present the activities collected during the interviews, collect additional suggestions, add verbs to the core nouns to identify additional activities, and confirm that all are real, essential activities.

7. Link the activities and determine business processes—arrange activities in sequence, analyze links (1:1, 1:M, and so on) to determine process boundaries, verify and name processes.

The steps in this phase, and the next, are a completed in a mix of one-on-one interviews and facilitated sessions. Figure 5.2 provides a broad outline.

Before we describe each step more fully, we will answer some questions that usually arise.

Questions You'll Probably Have

If you are like most individuals and groups we deal with, some or all of these three questions will have occurred to you:

1. Are we identifying as-is or to-be processes?
2. Why aren't we using published process frameworks?
3. Why aren't we starting with a problem statement?

Let's look at each in turn:

Identifying As-Is or To-Be Processes?

In most cases, the answer is neither. We are identifying the essential processes (the "what") for some part of the enterprise, and this is usually independent of as-is or to-be. For example, you might determine that your company has processes called Define Item and Qualify Vendor as shown on the sample process landscape. Those are simply what your company does, now and in the future. When you start to analyze one of those processes, you will get into the current "who and how" by drawing as-is swimlane diagrams and later the future "who and how" when you design the

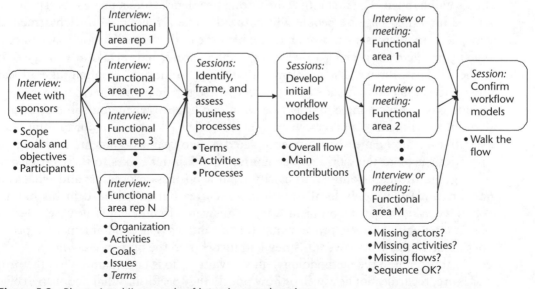

Figure 5.2 Phases I and II are a mix of interviews and sessions.

to-be process. Sometimes, however, the process landscape does take on a to-be flavor because it must include processes that the company isn't currently performing but feels it should. In one recent engagement, a manufacturer shifted from a modified built-to-inventory process process to a build-to-order process, which significantly changed their processes. This situation comes up less often than you might expect.

Why Not Start with a Published Process Framework?

As we mentioned earlier, there are a number of widely available frameworks such as IT Infrastructure Library (ITIL), Supply-Chain Operations Reference-Model (SCOR) and the APQC Process Classification Framework. These are often, however, not at the level of end-to-end business processes as we have defined them; instead, they are at a higher (process area) level or a more granular (activity) level. That isn't to say they aren't useful resources, because they are. We refer to them to understand what kind of work an area typically involves and as a checklist of sorts after process discovery, but we don't recommend taking them into a session and saying, "Let's start with this." People will buy in to the processes much more strongly if they can see that they discovered them for themselves, by using their own activities.

On that last point, always bear in mind that what companies in the same industry, or even across industries, do is fairly consistent; what distinguishes them is how they do it, which begins to emerge from the activities we work with during discovery.

Why Not Start with a Problem Statement?

The simple answer is that we've been burned often enough by starting with a problem statement that we try to avoid it, although that isn't always possible. We try to first identify the enterprise's business processes, and only then focus on problems so they can be put into a process context. If you focus on problems prematurely, two things will happen. The first is that the wrong problems, from a process perspective, will be identified because people will naturally take a functional or departmental view. Second, there is an almost unavoidable urge to dive into solution space once a specific problem has been identified—it's human nature, and we take advantage of it in the final assessment. The problem is that these "solutions" so often take a local perspective and end up making the process worse rather than better.

Here is a real example to illustrate what can happen when you solve problems without the context of a process viewpoint. A while back, at one of our briefings, an executive in attendance had just completed a two-year assignment, traveling to operations around the world implementing "quick hitter" fixes to their problems. After going through examples to clarify what a business process is, and what can happen when you apply local fixes, this executive buried his head in his hands. When we asked what the problem was, he answered that he could now see clearly that at least half of the "improvements" (in "air quotes") he had implemented probably made things worse overall—they had just shifted the burden elsewhere.

At this point in the methodology, all we want to do is understand what the processes are, regardless of how well or how poorly they perform. What people perceive as problems changes when they see complete business processes and they understand much more clearly what the real problems are.

Now, let's look at a bottom-up, brainstorm-based approach for discovering business processes and for organizing them into an overall process map. We'll start with some advice on interviewing prior to, and then preparing for, the facilitated sessions in which the actual process discovery will take place. Much more emphasis will be placed on steps 1–3, which cover preparation for the project and for your facilitated session. That is because if you invest the time in preparation, the sessions will be surprisingly straightforward, and Chapter 3 has already introduced the essentials of the bottom-up approach to process discovery.

Step 1: Get Started

Gathering Background Information

This step is primarily about meeting with the sponsor of the project or program. You'll want to discover or confirm the same sorts of things you would for any project, including the overall purpose of the project, the current situation, objectives or deliverables, success measures, and so on. You might assume that the purpose of the project is process improvement, and it often will be, but just as often there is simply a problem to solve or a solution to deliver. If it's the right thing to do, you might finesse the project scope and objectives into being more process oriented. However, that isn't necessarily what the sponsor has in mind, and you shouldn't push a process perspective too soon. Regardless, you will certainly be able to use the techniques in this book on all sorts of projects

Know the Business

Before you meet with the sponsor and if you're new to the enterprise, invest some time in learning about the organization—both the sponsor's and the overall enterprise. It's not that you want to prejudge what the issues, solutions, and strategies are, but you want to appear as if you've done your homework. Whether it's a private corporation or a government agency, you'll want to know the obvious things like mission or mandate, organization structure, key personnel, operating locations, major product or service lines, customers and markets served, and so on. This information is readily available from annual reports, training materials, published reports, Web sites, and so on. When a company has one, we find the corporate library/librarian to be a gold mine of information.

Business Mission, Strategy, Goals

In general, what you need to know is why the business exists, what it hopes to achieve, and what it will do in order to hit those targets. This is a broad area, and many terms and concepts arise: mission, mandate, values, vision, goals and objectives, strategy and tactics, critical success factors, differentiation, stakeholder analysis, shareholder value, and so on. We will just provide an indication of the main questions that need to be considered, for two reasons:

1. The project team must share a clear understanding of the mission, strategy, and goals of the enterprise that the improved process must support.
2. Each individual process has its own mission, strategy, and goals, which also must be articulated, clearly understood, and aligned with those of the enterprise.

Now, let's get a little more specific with our terminology.

Mission

The mission articulates why the business exists in a more specific way than make money, fulfill legislative mandate, or promote special interests. In their Articles of Incorporation, corporations claim their purpose is "to engage in any lawful act or activity for which a corporation may be organized under the law," but whether stated explicitly or not, every organization exists to do some things, and, just as importantly, not others. The essence of the enterprise's mission is a statement of "what we do and who we do it for"—specifically, the products and services provided and the markets and customers served. There may also be an indication of the style in which the enterprise conducts business, or there might be a specific statement of style for each stakeholder group: customers, employees, owners, investors, communities, and so forth.

Strategy

Closely related to the mission is the way we define strategy, which is the specific competitive space the enterprise intends to occupy. Any enterprise should ask itself the following questions: Why would a customer choose us in the face of similar offerings? What strategic discipline do we use to differentiate our products and services? Is it low price, convenience, flexibility, innovative products, or what? Without knowing the answers, how can you focus your business processes? Surprisingly, we can also apply this concept in monopolies and government organizations where there doesn't appear to be a choice. We also use it in specifying the improvement dimension or philosophy for individual processes.

Goals

In order to focus its efforts and gauge its progress, an organization will establish goals (overriding performance targets) and objectives (intermediate targets). Try to make these as specific as possible, using the topic, target, timeframe framework mentioned earlier.

Working with Mission, Strategy, and Goals

Your organization may have a well-formulated mission statement, one that is too ambiguous to be useful, or none at all. The actual mission statement is not as important as knowing what your enterprise is all about and what differentiates it from others. Using whatever resources are available, your team has to be able to answer the following questions:

1. "Which customers or markets do we—or should we—serve?"
2. "Which products or services do we—or should we—serve them with?"
3. "What differentiates us?" or, more clearly, "Why choose us over competitors or alternative providers?"

Given that there is probably no confusion over services and customers, our interest is primarily in the third question, "Why choose us?" which is the essence of strategy. Different strategies call for entirely different processes, with very different characteristics. The underlying information systems will also require different characteristics. Consider a couple of examples:

1. Two organizations were each in the business of providing corporate training, and many individuals have attended workshops and seminars from both. However, they were highly differentiated. One was a mass marketer of $129-a-day seminars for administrative and support staff, while the other specialized in developing and delivering customized training for high-tech sales forces.
2. Two transportation companies were headquartered in the same West Coast city, and other than ostensibly being in the same industry, that was where the similarity ended. One specialized in cross-border trucking of agricultural products. The other specialized in "secure, discreet, worldwide" handling of small shipments—not necessarily fast, but secure from the prying eyes of competitors.

In both cases, the organizations were in the same industry but they certainly weren't in the same business. And of course, they had totally different business processes operating with totally different styles.

Understanding the Current Situation

To dive a little deeper, we still use a list that appeared in the December 2, 1996, issue of *Computerworld* in a sidebar by Efrem Mallach titled "Do you *really* understand your business?" It provided a list of questions that IS professionals within an organization ought to be able to answer if they really understand the business they are supporting. They are also excellent questions for external consultants to use when getting up to speed on a new client. The questions are aimed at a senior level and have a distinctly "marketing" orientation, but we like the thinking and have found it easy to adapt them to public service organizations. The article had some additional commentary and scoring instructions, but here we have only reproduced the questions posed by Professor Mallach:

1. What must your firm accomplish this year to be considered successful?
2. What competitive factors have affected it most strongly in the past two years?

3. What are its three most important product lines?
4. What are the annual sales of the top three product lines in dollars (within 20 percent)? In general terms, how is this expected to change in two years?
5. When and, approximately, what is the next major change in each of the top three product lines?
6. What is the major market for each of the top three product lines (type of customer, geographic area, and so on, as appropriate)?
7. What are your firm's market shares in these markets? How do these shares compare with those of the leader? Are your shares growing or shrinking?
8. Who are your firm's top two competitors in each of these markets? How do your market shares compare with theirs?
9. What is your firm's strategy for each of its key lines? Does it stress low cost, high quality, range of options, or does it focus on a niche market, customer service, or superior technology?
10. How does one of your competitors use IS in a way you don't? (This doesn't necessarily mean you should copy them.)

You might not be able to find answers to all of these, but that means you'll have some excellent questions for the sponsor.

Know the Real Business Model

A little more difficult to uncover is the real strategy, business model, or differentiator of the enterprise, which is not necessarily the same as how the organization promotes itself. This is essential, because if you leap into process redesign without this knowledge, you could optimize your way right out of profitability.

A workshop participant told us about a reengineering project at his firm, a health insurance company, which eventually had to be undone because it was losing the company money. A well-intentioned reengineering team had sped up the claim settlement and payment process and greatly reduced the time between when the insurer received money on one end and when they paid the claimant at the other end. Unfortunately, this float was where the money was actually made. Fairly quickly, the process had to be de-reengineered and slowed down.

At a motorcycle dealership we were at recently, it was a surprise to learn that it doesn't actually make much profit on sales of bikes or service, although the accessories make a good contribution. The profit keeps staff employed, but mostly pays the mortgage on the carefully selected land the dealership is located on. The real payoff for the ownership team comes years later when they sell the property. And it may be apocryphal, but we've heard many times that the profit in the rental car business comes not from rental operations, but from turning new cars into used cars and selling them.

Examples abound of companies that make sophisticated products in fields such as printing, or cutting and welding, but actually make their money on low-tech consumables like the ink and cutting tips that their products require. The point is that you need to know where the money comes from, or you might make things worse instead of better.

Another factor to begin investigating is the differentiator, which is covered extensively in Chapter 7 when we look at conducting the as-is process assessment. Briefly, the differentiator is why a company's customers choose them. It's the way in which a company seeks to differentiate itself from the competition and better serve its customers. It boils down to three choices:

1. Operational excellence—the company values consistent, error-free, low-cost operations with savings that are either passed on to the customer or increase profitability;
2. Product leadership—the company values the creation of innovative products and services, or the ability to rapidly adapt its products or services, or the mix;
3. Customer intimacy—the company values the ability to adapt itself to the needs of individual customers, so that customers view the company as an extension of their own.

A not-uncommon error is to focus on operational excellence (op ex) in an organization that competes on one of the other two differentiators. We saw this recently in the hospitality industry, where a team introduced systems and processes to improve op ex, with serious negative impacts on the product leadership that the chain was known for. You might not be able to find out what the differentiator is, and many organizations don't know, but it's never too early to start looking for clues about what they value most. If you suspect this is going to be an issue, jump ahead to Chapter 7 and read more about this topic.

Meeting with the Sponsor

Purpose

From your perspective, the sponsor has three primary responsibilities:

1. To determine project issues and objectives;
2. To set and control scope;
3. To select and recruit project participants.

The essence of the interview with the sponsor is "what do you want?" or "how can I help?" but having slightly more insightful questions will make you look more professional. As you go through the following list of questions, remember that you can't treat it as a script. You have your own style, as do the sponsor and the company, so adjust accordingly. In the same vein, you won't usually be able to go through the questions in sequence—it will be more parallel and iterative. You might want to start with background, but the sponsor will leap ahead to the solution they visualize. And remember that the sponsor might not be thinking in process terms, even if it's already clear to you that is where the problem lies. As a professional, you're obligated to give your honest assessment of the situation, but perhaps not in the first meeting.

Interviewing the Sponsor

For many years, we've used the following list as a guide or starting point for these sorts of interviews. Some of the questions are oriented to IT development projects, so if they're not appropriate, don't use them. Remember, this isn't a script, the order varies with the situation, and it is *always* iterative.

1. What is the overall purpose of this project or initiative we're discussing?
   - In broad terms, projects are usually aimed at either achieving some significant improvement (efficiency, effectiveness, flexibility, innovation, timeliness, quality, service, ...) or achieving compliance (legal, regulatory, industry standards, ...).
   - Try to probe enough that you could boil it down to a single sentence in a form such as "Overall, the purpose of this project is to improve _____ by _____." Here's a sample: "This initiative intends to improve order throughput time by implementing process and application improvements that will reduce exceptions and human intervention. We hope to have more than 80 percent of orders handled entirely by our suppliers and logistics partners without being touched at all by our employees."

2. What is the current situation?
   - Is there a particular problem or factor that motivated this project?
   - In general terms, how does the operation currently work?
   - Why isn't that good enough anymore? What's changed in the environment? This is the "context" item that we'll look at later during as-is process assessment.

3. What is the primary business objective driving this project?
   - How will benefits be measured (using "topic, target, timeframe" method, such as "throughput time will be reduced 25 percent in the first six months")?
   - If possible, look into the overall strategy of the organization or process you're dealing with; we generally define "strategy" as having three components:
     - Customers or markets—who are you serving?
     - Products or services—what are you providing, what do customers pay for?
     - Differentiator—as discussed earlier, what is the unique strength of your product or service, or how you'll deliver it? In other words, "why choose us?" This could be price, features, quality, flexibility, and so on.
   - Note: organizations can be incredibly mealy-mouthed about this, tossing around phrases like "operational excellence" and "customer focus" without clarifying what they actually mean.

4. What is the scope, or "What's in and what's out?" A simple framework for expressing this is process – organization – application – data.

- If this is a process-oriented project, which processes are in or out of scope (see question 5)?

- Organizationally, who will be impacted by this, including specific departments, job functions, or operating locations?

- Which existing applications or new applications are involved? See further points in question 6 (deliverables) and question 8 (links and dependencies).

- Which business data will or won't be involved?

- What are the business data areas ("topics," independent of current files or databases)?

- What specific files or databases are associated with particular systems?

5. Is this is essentially a business process improvement project? If so…

- Which cross-functional business process or processes will or won't be in scope?

- What marks the start of the business process, and what is the result?

- How would each stakeholder group (especially customers, performers, and owners/managers) assess the current process for both weaknesses and strengths (areas to consider include cycle time, quality, employee satisfaction, flexibility, consistency, or whatever other variable may be important)?

- Are there areas that clearly need improvement, including workflow design, use of IT, job definition, training, tools and facilities, or performance measures?

- What would be the main characteristics of the improved process, and what would differentiate it from a similar process at another organization?

- How would success be measured? Try to use the "topic, target, timeframe" format.

6. What are the technical or project objectives and deliverables?

- For systems development projects, *who* do you expect to use the application to do *what*? This could include obtaining a service, processing a transaction, obtaining information via queries or reports, or any other use. This is essentially a preliminary list of use cases. Note that what is eventually implemented might be very different, but this is a starting point. This simple but *critical* question lets people get ideas off their chest and gets expectations out on the table.

- Is a new application to be developed, existing ones enhanced or integrated, a commercial-off-the-shelf (COTS) application selected and installed, or an application service provider (ASP) used, or what?

7. Who is the sponsor?

- Possibly the most important question of all is *"Who is the sponsor?"* If you are already dealing with that sponsor you must carefully determine "Are you *really* the sponsor," and "Do you have the final say on scope, resources, acceptance, and so on?" You need to determine, without being too blunt, whether they have the necessary authority, given the scope of the undertaking.

- What is the relative priority of this project compared to other initiatives? How important is it to you?

8. What are the links and dependencies?

- What areas or systems outside of the scope will require interfaces?
  - Sources—where will data or work arrive from?
  - Sinks—where will data or work be passed to? Note that the earlier you can determine how much integration (interfacing) and conversion work is needed, the better. Experience shows that these two areas can account for 70 to 80 percent (and even more!) of the development effort. If you don't budget for this, you'll end up in trouble!
- Are there other initiatives we should be aware of?
  - Are there related projects, perhaps with dependencies?
  - Has this been attempted previously, and, if so, why didn't it succeed the first time? Is there existing material we can utilize?

9. What are the known issues and constraints?

- Have any significant issues or difficulties arisen, such as conflict, a policy decision required, or technical difficulty?
- Are there any constraints we need to take into account, such as deadlines, regulations, strategy, security, audit, control, and resources, including staff, space, equipment, and budgets?
- Of the three main variables—scope, timeframe, and resources—which are fixed and which are elastic?
- Have any important decisions already been made, such as approach, hardware or software platform, consulting firm, or industry framework?

10. Do you have any advice for us on how to succeed with this project? Similarly, are there things we could do that would substantially increase the chances of failure?

Pushing Back on Scope

What can emerge at this stage is a case we have all seen many times—an initiative has been formulated, but you recognize that the overall process is being ignored and only a piece of it is under consideration. You recognize it as a pattern that spells trouble, but the sponsor doesn't see it as a complete process. The classic examples were "Webifying" or "e-ing" transactions during the e-whatever (e-business, e-commerce, e-cruitment, e-whatever) era of the late 1990s. In other words, putting up a Web front end without an integrated business process behind it. This often raised customer expectations so they could fall even farther.

How you handle this depends on your comfort level and credibility with the sponsor. You have an obligation to point out that if the complete process isn't integrated, the results are almost certain to be negative. You can sometimes determine and demonstrate what needs to be included by "nibbling at the edges." For instance, in an online ordering initiative, ask, "What has to happen to get current customer, account, and product information to the site, along with the customer's previous order activity? What has to happen to complete the interaction that the customer has initiated? When is it fully completed, and what else can happen along the way (out of stock situation, order changes, and so on)?" This is usually enough to get the scope reconsidered. If not, do what you can to expedite inputs and outputs and then run.

Once you have gone through "scope-stretching" phase, you can wrap up with any unanswered questions from your earlier research and then on to getting the sponsor's thoughts on team organization.

Team Organization

One key role for the sponsor is to help to identify and secure participants, because you probably won't have the pull on your own to obtain the necessary time commitment. Generally, a project is organized into the "core team" which is dedicated to the project and is responsible for all aspects of running the sessions, including preparation, facilitation, and documentation. The core team usually includes a project leader plus one or two people acting as process analysts, and one or two people with broad subject matter expertise.

Of course, you'll also need participants to represent all the relevant organizational units or areas, which might be defined by organizational structure or functional area, by geography, by product line, or by customer or market. "Relevant" means they play a role in a process you and the sponsor believe will be in scope or directly depend on it in a significant way. In the simple case, you'll have representative from each org unit that participates in the process and won't have to worry about factoring in geography, product line, market segment, and so on. Good luck!

Four points to keep in mind:

1. You need the right people, not just whoever is available. You need to stress up front that they need to be appropriate, not convenient. More than once, we've had trainees assigned as project representatives because "It'll be a great way for them to learn the business!" It's awkward when we have to go back to their manager or the sponsor and request someone else.

2. If it is at all possible, try to have a range of personalities and styles represented. That's a tall order, given how difficult it is just to get participants with the necessary expertise. What you want to avoid is situations we've ended up in, where you have a session where almost all the participants are free-wheeling, creative types, or where they are all heads-down, analytic types. Neither leads to the best results.

3. People love to warn us in advance that a selected participant knows their area but is a "difficult person" who needs to be managed carefully. The interesting thing is that the supposed troublemaker never is, and usually turns out to be a valuable participant, so don't be discouraged when you're warned about somebody.

4. If you have trouble securing participation, that's a bad sign for the success of your project. They might not be able to participate because they're too busy,

or perhaps their area is just not interested. Either way, if you can't secure the involvement of an important internal area, what does that say about the project's chances of success? Expertise and participation are critical for buy-in, and buy-in is critical for a smooth implementation, so insufficient participation is a good predictor of trouble ahead. This is an issue for the sponsor, so you will have to go back to them and have them apply some pressure in getting the necessary groups involved. Along with setting scope and objectives, this is the sponsor's main responsibility.

Step 2: Conduct Pre-Session Interviews

Purpose

Business process discovery is best done in groups, using facilitated sessions, but preparing for those sessions is best done with one-on-one interviews. As a colleague observed, you always get the juiciest information in one-on-one interviews.

The purpose of the pre-session interview is not the same as the purpose of the sessions. In the pre-session interviews we're preparing for the sessions, not trying to accomplish work that is planned for the sessions. Too often people try to accomplish in the interviews what is best left for the sessions. What you want to accomplish in the interview is as follows:

- Build a relationship with the interviewee.
- Understand the current operating model, including organizations, mandates, roles, and responsibilities.
- Understand issues, pain points, sensitivities, cultural dynamics, history, and other factors that will impact your project. You want to demonstrate to the interviewee that their issues are important but stay out of problem-solving mode.
- Gather the raw material for process discovery, in particular business terms (the nouns) and business activities (the verb-noun pairs).

After you read the rest of this chapter, you'll have a better idea of what sort of business terms you'll be listening for, but for now it's anything that is referred to by a name, including things, facts, metrics, organizations, roles, processes, activities, systems, tools, reports, forms, and so on.

The purpose of the interview is *not* to try to accomplish the things that we'll address in the sessions, such as the following:

- Clarifying terminology;
- Identifying processes;
- Scoping ("framing") the processes;
- Assessing the processes;
- Mapping the processes.

Interviewing Basics

Everybody we work with seems to want advice on interviewing and suggestions for interview questions, so we will devote some time to both. Organizations and individuals have their own style, so as we have advised with earlier lists, you will want to adapt these to your situation and not use them verbatim as a script.

Our style is to conduct interviews in an informal, conversational manner beginning with background and some direct questions (e.g., about job title and organizational structure) and then work toward more open-ended questions (e.g., "What would you change if you could?") We don't generally arrive with a cheat sheet of questions, because the basics are burned into muscle memory. If you have, or appear to have, a prepared laundry list of questions, then the interviewee can rightly wonder, "Why didn't you just send me a list of questions to deal with at my convenience rather than wasting my time with an interview?" To respect their time, we schedule interviews for no more than one hour, and aim to wrap up within 45–50 minutes.

Here are a few guidelines to keep in mind for maintaining the engagement of the interviewee:

- Don't be afraid to smile, and if this doesn't come naturally, practice. Really. We encounter many people who think this is all *very serious business*, and seem to think smiling is inappropriate or unnatural.
- Speak only 25 percent as much as the interviewee, if that.
- Regularly paraphrase their answers for confirmation and to show that you're listening.
- If there are two interviewers, one should take the lead with the other filling in as needed.
- No matter how much you know about a field, don't show off your knowledge.
- Remember that the interviewee may have passionate feelings and strongly held convictions, but that doesn't mean they're correct.
- Always allow time for the interviewee to ask questions or "vent" about issues.
- Always thank them for their time and invite them to contact you with any further ideas that come up.

A common failing among interviewers (and analysts in general) is the inability to stay at the appropriate level of detail and not dive in prematurely. We raise this as an issue because so many interviews and sessions are derailed by this weakness. We watched in amazement once while an analyst, seemingly without even pausing for breath, took a discussion into the problems with a *single* tool used for *one* activity by a *narrowly focused* group when they had not yet established even the basics of the organizational structure. It is hard to dig yourself out of a hole that deep, especially if you don't stop digging. To ensure maximum value from the allotted time, you need to avoid this "deep dive for detail" and instead follow a "breadth first, detail later" approach. That is, your questioning should lead *across* the hierarchy of detail before going *down* to the next level of detail. For instance, in this list of questions, you want to cover each as thoroughly as time permits before going down to the next question on the list.

1. What is the primary service or mandate of your organization?
2. How is it structured or subdivided?
3. What is the purpose of each group (subdivision)?
4. What are the main activities of each?
5. What is the result or outcome of each activity?
6. Who is involved in each activity; what tools or supporting mechanisms are used?
7. And so on.

Conducting the Interview

Begin with the usual points:

- Introduce yourself and exchange business cards (and clarify how they would like to be addressed if there is any doubt), confirm the time available for the interview, and thank them for taking the time.
- Recap the purpose of the interview in a 30-second sound bite, for instance:
  - "Process" participants: to understand the responsibilities of you and your area, and the issues you currently face;
  - Other "process" stakeholders: to learn what you get from the process, and how well the process and the product work for you.
- Ask if they have any questions before beginning the interview.

Presession interviews boil down to three basic questions:

1. What does your organization do, and what is your role?
2. What issues are you currently facing?
3. What cultural or historical factors will impact the success of this undertaking?

You might take a more conversational tone, and instead say, "Tell me about the issues…" If time is limited, you can simply ask each of those three questions. Typically, though, we use them as a starting point and then experience and intuition take over. Depending on what the interviewee is saying, the interviewer will go where it seems most valuable. For each of those three questions, here are some of the likely supplementary questions:

"What does your organization do, and what is your role?" will lead to these questions:

- What is the mandate or overarching responsibility of your group?
- What is the organizational structure and reporting lines? These are the "up and down" relationships.

- What is the role you play within your organization? What are the other major roles?

- What do you do on a daily basis? What five activities take up the most time? How much time?

- Where does work come from ("sources") and where does it go to ("sinks")? Who do you work with, either as coworkers, or as internal suppliers or customers? These are the "side-to-side" relationships, and understanding them will help determine if the right participants are lined up for the sessions.

- Specifics about the work:
  - What is produced and where does it go?
  - If there's time, ask about volume, frequency, percentage of different cases.
  - What other groups do you work with to carry out your roles and responsibilities?
  - This is tricky, but it's a good idea to find out if someone *actually wants* what the group does, or if *on the other hand* they are providing some sort of oversight or control.

- What goals and objectives are you working toward, and how do you and your customers measure success (i.e., what measurements or metrics affect you)?

- How do they think all stakeholders (customers, managers, performers, and others) assess the current methods and services? Try not to use the word "process" yet, only because you are probably not there yet.

- Are there any geographic, cultural, or language issues?

- Other than your ongoing responsibilities, what specific projects are your business area currently working on, what are their goals, and what are the timeframes?

"What issues are you currently facing?" will lead to these questions:

- What are your pain points or sources of frustration?

- Is there currently a particular issue or set of issues that is commanding attention?

- Has anything recently become particularly better or worse?

- Are there changes you can identify right now that would make your life easier or enable you to deliver more or better service? This can include practices, policies, tools, information, or other process enablers.

- What one thing would you change right now if you could?

"What cultural or historical factors will impact the success of this undertaking?" will lead to these questions:

- Have there been any significant changes, internal or external, in the environment you're working in that affect what you do, how you do it, how it's received, and so on?

- Have there been any notable successes or failures that we should be aware of?
- Can you tell us anything about the corporate culture that will impact the success of this undertaking?
    - Beliefs, stories, and mythology;
    - Guiding principles and behavioral norms;
    - Specific behaviors that are rewarded (or punished);
    - Factors that continually "get in the way" (e.g., the pace of decision making, political interference, the motivation and reward system, fear of change).
- Do you have any advice for us on this effort?

You'll never get through all these questions in a one-hour interview, but they should provide an idea of other avenues you can follow. Don't forget that you don't have to learn it all now—you haven't even started the sessions yet and still have more time for process modeling and analysis ahead of you. However, having gone through these questions in interviews, you will have a really good idea how things hang together, and running the sessions will be less intimidating.

Be sure to leave some time for their questions and concerns. We like to close by asking "Is there anything I've missed or should have asked?" and also try to enlist their help by asking "Do you have any advice on making this a successful project?"

Finally, thank them for their time, invite them to contact you with any further ideas that come up, and get out *on time or early* unless they've specifically asked to extend their time.

Step 3: Prepare for First Session

Purpose

We'll begin with a common observation from session participants—"It's great to see someone actually *use* the interviews to prepare for a session!" In the same vein, we often hear during a subsequent session "It's so nice that you actually worked with what we did at the last session so we have something clean to work with at this session." Actually, the wording is more like "Wow, you guys actually *did* something with all that!" but it's the thought that counts. People like to see that effort has gone into preparation so their time in the session is used effectively. When it comes to running sessions, preparation = productivity. That doesn't mean you will develop answers and conclusions for them; the preparation can be as simple as writing terms on Post-it notes prior to the session.

So, our purpose here is to prepare for a productive series of sessions, especially the first one, at which impressions will be formed. We will do three main things:

1. Extract terms, activities, and issues from the interview findings, and prepare these for use in the session.
2. Confirm participants and develop the session agenda.
3. Arrange facilities and supplies.

If you are tight for time, and got good results from the interviews, you can use the terms and activities to build a "strawman" glossary and overall process map to bring to the session for validation. In the approach we'll describe, you will clean them up but leave the development of products for the session.

Terms, Activities, and Issues

This step is vital for a productive session, but is so straightforward there is very little to say. First, you want to find and highlight every piece of terminology—every noun—that came up during your interviews. In the first session, these will be sorted according to the criteria described ahead in "Step 5: Analyze Terms…" Read that step before attempting this one so you know what sort of terms you'll be looking for. Sometimes we enter the terms into a spreadsheet or table, and then sort them so we can easily spot and eliminate minor variations, but other than that, don't worry about cleaning them up too much. Now, simply print (neatly!) each term onto a large (4 × 6-inch) Post-it note, using a flipchart marker so they'll be clearly visible. The 3 × 3-inch Post-it notes can be used if you have a lot of terms or a small group, but they will be hard to read from any distance. It isn't unusual to have 60, 80, or more terms. Arrange the Post-its onto sheets of flipchart paper, as few as possible, so they will be easy to move around and then tape or pin up during your session. Notes are coming up in the section on facilities and supplies on the pens, paper, and Post-its to use.

Now that you've started on sorting out the core nouns, you can get started on collecting the activities—the verb-noun pairs—that will be the basis of process discovery. Sometimes there aren't many specific activities mentioned in the interviews. If that is the case, you can skip this step and not collect any activities until the session. Otherwise, as with the terms, write each activity on a large Post-it and arrange them on flipchart sheets. Don't try to standardize the terms, and accept that many of these will have to be changed later because the group will settle on different nouns and verbs. The activity that you record now as "register client" might end up as "enroll customer."

Finally, if there were issues that came up repeatedly during the interviews, or if there were recurring themes, you can summarize these on flipcharts. You only want to call out the common issues at this point and avoid those that you think will be contentious, sensitive, or clearly came from one specific area. You want people to know they have been heard, but not raise anxiety in the first session.

Participants and Agenda

This is another straightforward step. First, confirm that you have the right attendees lined up for the upcoming work sessions. During the interviews, there might have been individuals or groups that were mentioned regularly and seemed to play a key role but were not included in the list of interviewees/participants you prepared with your sponsor. If so, you should have your sponsor confirm the need for their participation and arrange it. Try to interview them before the session so they arrive on an equal footing.

Next, you'll need to prepare an agenda or session plan, which of course will lead to the question "How long will this take?" We've found that estimation is a mug's game, and there just isn't any formula that will take in all the factors that you've uncovered, such as the number of organizations, activities, terms, and so on, and then produce an estimate of how much session time will be needed. Instead, we assume that two to three half-day sessions will be sufficient to clarify terminology, discover a related set of processes, and possibly prioritize those processes for subsequent analysis and improvement. Sometimes you will produce a more detailed and refined product, sometimes one that is less so, but either way, you'll have a better grasp of the size and complexity of the area to use in future scheduling.

We specifically advise against scheduling all-day sessions, because productivity dips so much after 2:00 or 2:30 pm. We would rather work hard from 8:30 am until noon and then let people get back to their other commitments. If people have traveled to attend the sessions, we still don't conduct all-day sessions. Instead, we have a light lunch brought into the room with a half-hour break starting at about noon, and then we'll continue for another 90 minutes or so. These sessions can be very effective, with interesting points arising during the break and with people still having a few hours to take care of business.

Here are the items we typically aim to include on the plan for the first session:

- Introductory presentation by the sponsor on overall project goals (10 minutes);
- Introductions (5 minutes):
    - Facilitator;
    - Participants.
- Brief presentation by the facilitator (10 minutes);
    - What is a business process and what are the issues?
    - State the key elements in defining a business process.
- Objectives for scheduled sessions and today's session, plus today's session plan and ground rules (5 minutes);
- "Venting" ("What's on your mind?") (15–30 minutes):
    - Key issues to address;
    - Specific outcomes or expectations for the session.
- Clarify terminology (90 minutes);
- Identify significant activities (30 minutes).

We don't produce an agenda for the second session until after the first has been completed, because you don't know exactly how far you will get. Generally, the second session will be devoted to gathering additional activities, linking the activities and discovering business processes, and naming and refining the business processes. Straightforward transactional processes will be dealt with in a little less time, creative and collaborative processes will take longer.

Facilities and Supplies

We encounter as many problems with facilities as any other factor, so we'll provide more information on this point. People who are not in the business of running facilitated session usually have no idea how large an impact the facilities have on the productivity of sessions. Cramped rooms produce cramped results. It is essential that you inspect a room before agreeing to use it for your sessions, and, if someone else is arranging the facilities, you must make it clear what the requirements are. The easiest way to cover this topic will be to provide an extract of the note we send to people who are arranging facilities on our behalf:

- The primary requirement is for a bright, well-ventilated room with lots of "plain" wall space. During a single session, we often end up posting 30 to 40 flipcharts of "group memory," so meeting rooms of the sort found in many hotels, with lots of windows, pillars, artwork, and so on, don't work at all well. The nature of these sessions will require working on the walls with rolls of paper posted that can extend to 20 to 30 feet long, so, again, an area of plain wall space that everyone can stand around is important.

- Seating in a "wide U" configuration. Note that a "wide U" is greatly preferable to a "narrow U" (boardroom setup) because it puts all participants as close to the facilitator as possible, which has a large, positive impact on the dynamics of the session. It is also preferable to a "classroom" setup (tables in rows), which prevents participants from seeing each other face to face. If there are too many participants for a "wide U" to be feasible, then a "chevron" setup is the next best solution—that's like a classroom style, but the there's an aisle down the middle and the rows of tables are angled in. Please ensure that sessions are not conducted in a room equipped with PCs, because many people end up "hidden" behind the machine and distracted by e-mail or the Internet.

- Lighting is an extremely important factor. In many training or meeting rooms, the lighting has been set to a low level or the lighting at the front of the room has been disabled, either because older data projectors were not bright enough to work well in a normally lit room or someone thought that would make the room more comfortable. The simple fact is that dim lighting makes people sleepy, so it is probably the most negative environmental factor we encounter; anything you can do to avoid this problem will be appreciated. That might involve inspecting the room well ahead of time, and, if necessary, asking facilities staff to replace any light bulbs or fluorescent tubes that have previously been removed to bring light levels down.

- A table large enough (at least 4 feet wide by 2 feet deep) to accommodate the facilitator's supplies—notes, handouts, pens, and so on.

- A large whiteboard, or, better yet, a wall of whiteboards. If this isn't possible, the need for plain wall space is even greater.

- Two sturdy flipchart stands with full pads of white bond paper. Our preference is for bright white paper, with a perforated tear line and faint lines or a grid on it. The large office supply companies carry excellent house brands that aren't expensive. Self-stick flipcharts don't work as well because they can't easily be rolled up and moved, and because (ironically) Post-it notes don't stick well to Post-it flipcharts. (A *lot* of the session work involves Post-it notes.) The inexpensive pads of rough "scrap paper" don't work well either—they're too small, harder to read because of the beige color, and ink tends to bleed through.

A final note on facilities—allow no "energy holes," which is the facilitator's term for empty seats. You want participants seated comfortably close to one another, with no gaps. We aren't sure what the psychology is, but this point makes a big difference.

In addition, you will want a good supply of bullet-tip whiteboard and flipchart markers. Try to find markers specifically for use on flipcharts, like the Staedtler flipchart markers we use. If you aren't careful and get regular permanent markers, you can end up with pens that have an overpowering odor and bleed through almost any paper. A variety of colors (black, blue, green, violet, and red) will add visual interest. Masking tape for posting flipcharts will be needed, and you should try to get a lower-adhesion variety that won't harm the walls. Finally, stock up on Post-its in 3 × 3-inch and 4 × 6-inch sizes. We use the Super Sticky Neon Post-its, because they are so much more visible than the customary "yellow stickies." They also just seem to liven up a session.

Step 4: Initiate First Session

Purpose

The initiation sets the stage for a productive session by giving everyone a common understanding of what's ahead and why it's important, and defusing some of the common concerns.

Getting Started

How you start makes a difference. Start on time, have a pep talk from the sponsor to establish rationale and direction, and then provide background on business processes and an overview of what's to come. Then get on with it! Don't bore them—do it fast and get them started on "venting" as quickly as possible, ideally within 30 minutes.

The ideal session kickoff has the sponsor describe the overall goals for what you hope by now is a process-oriented project. There can't be a set script for this, as it has to be authentic and unexaggerated, but there are a few themes that are helpful:

- Something in the environment has changed, so we have no choice but to improve and adapt.
- Everyone is already working hard, so having everyone work even harder isn't the answer.
- *How* we accomplish *what* we do must be improved, and that is the focus of these sessions.

If they are egoless enough to state that some of the policies, rules, procedures, and metrics imposed by management are the problem, and will eventually be up for challenge, all the better.

After that, have a quick round-table introduction by everyone (name, organization, brief description of role) and then a quick review of the session plan.

All of the preceding are important, but the most important points often turn out to be the following:

1. Ensuring that everyone really understands what a business process is, what the typical issues are, and that processes can perform badly even when everyone is working their hardest;
2. Providing an opportunity for everyone to "vent" about what's on their mind.

In dealing with the first point, you must bear in mind that people and organizations often:

1. Do not know what a "business process" really is;
2. Do not know how their activities fit into the bigger picture;
3. Are sensitive or take offense to the idea that their process needs to be improved.

Therefore, in turn, the process consultant and facilitator must:

1. Make it clear what a "business process" really is;
2. Make it visible what the processes are, and how their activities fit;
3. Make it blame-free.

Then, as the sessions unfold, you will let the facts speak for themselves.

That, in a nutshell, is our "process consulting philosophy," and it has served us well. During the introduction, you will deal with points 1 and 3, starting with explaining what a business process is.

Explaining "Business Process"

In order to accomplish this, you need to have one or two prepared examples to walk through. The telephone company example we went through in Chapter 3 works very well for explaining what a business process is, and why a business process must be managed as a whole. We often use another example to demonstrate that individuals and groups can be working hard and meeting their targets, yet process performance still suffers. Feel free to adapt either example to your needs and use it or create your own. A cautionary note—do not use one of the processes that you expect to be studying as your example, or people will argue with the details and miss the point. It must be an example that is not from their industry.

In this second example, for a global manufacturer of sophisticated electronic products, their "fulfill order" process crossed four major organizations, as illustrated in Figure 5.3. As it emerged, however, the process was not managed as a

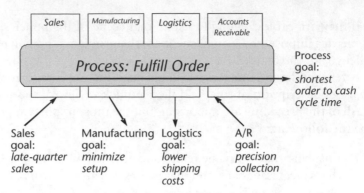

Figure 5.3   Process versus organization chart for Fulfill Order.

whole, with all functional areas striving for the same goal, which is the point of the example.

This was a "build to order" operation that involved custom marking and labeling, so for each order there was a separate production run (lot) scheduled. We explain the involvement of each organization as follows:

- Sales negotiated the terms of the order and booked it.

- Manufacturing planned the order, and determined which production stages would take place at which manufacturing facility.

- Manufacturing completed the first stage of the manufacturing process for the lot and turned it over to Logistics for movement to the next stage.

- Logistics moved the lot to the next stage, which was often on another continent.

- The next manufacturing stage was completed, and Logistics was then involved, for a total of two or three stages.

- When Manufacturing was complete, the lot was turned over to Logistics for delivery to the customer site.

- Accounts Receivable invoiced, collected, and applied the payment for the order.

Next, we explain that each organization had performance targets that seemed reasonable until they were compared to the target for the process. In this case, the process target was rapid fulfillment, because the sooner the client got their order, the sooner payment could be collected. As it turned out, the goals of the individual organizations worked against the goals of the process, proving that having the pieces working well doesn't mean the whole is working well:

- Logistics, because of a cost-cutting program many years ago, strives for lowest unit costs for shipping. Accordingly, they consolidate shipments and choose lower-cost carriers, both of which lower shipping costs. Of course, that also negatively impacts the process, but who is looking out for that?

- Manufacturing measures itself in equipment utilization, and so it schedules orders in a way that optimizes this measure. Of course, some high-value orders move to the back of the queue.

- Accounts Receivable is focused on a new "precision collections" program and spends a great deal of time ensuring that the invoice is accurate to the decimal point.

- Of course, we have to close with Sales, because the incentive programs that Sales works under leads to some strange results. In this case, sales reps received a cash bonus for any order received in the closing days of a fiscal quarter. Predictably, there was a surge in orders in that final two weeks, because reps would delay finalizing or submitting their orders until they were in the bonus period. Not only did this introduce delays, but the glut of orders caused a "pig in a python" effect and gummed up the works for Manufacturing.

This example always goes a long way toward illustrating why process must be managed as a whole. It also is invaluable in making process improvement blame free, because it shows that all areas can be meeting their targets, but if no "higher authority" has coordinated those targets, process performance will suffer. You should then make the point that business processes are fundamentally about coordination and alignment around the end result, which sounds much "friendlier" than the assumptions people have that it's all about efficiency. Later in the framing process, you can come back to this process versus organization chart and update it to show their process, organizations, and targets. This can be a compelling demonstration of internal misalignment.

A brief interlude on this type of chart: We will use process versus organization charts throughout a project. We always find it to be the most useful diagram for clarifying the essence of process versus organization or function and often hear, "Oh, I guess we knew that, but we've never seen it put quite that way before." One of our clients stressed their experience that "consistency and repetition" are fundamental to getting traction and momentum for process orientation, and this is one diagram that we consistently repeat! Later we'll use it to highlight different aspects of the situation by listing different factors under the functions—measures and metrics (versus those for the process), ownership (versus for the process), systems used by each function, actors and responsibilities by function, and duplicated activities, among others.

Returning to your session kickoff, you will explain whatever else you think is important about business processes, including the idea of a triggering event, discrete results for one or more stakeholders, action verb–noun naming, and subprocesses. Also reinforce the distinction between process and organization, that a business process is almost always cross-organizational or cross-functional, and that alignment is the goal. Finally, let people know that processes come in "families" and show the group a sample overall process map or process landscape, whichever term you've chosen. You can adapt the Commercial Loans Management example from Figure 3.12, use the Supply Management example in Figure 5.1, or use the example in Figure 5.4. This example is from a supplier of bulk fuel and lubricants to the transportation industry (shipping, trucking, and airlines) and will be used throughout the text

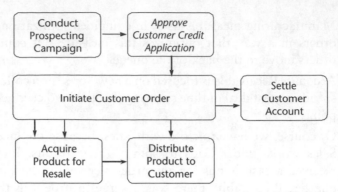

Figure 5.4 Overall process map for Customer Acquisition and Order Fulfillment.

as an example. Let the group know that the purpose of these two or three sessions is primarily to discover a related set of processes within the target area, and depict them in this form. Provide an overview of the session plan, and then it's time for some participation with one of our favorite parts of running sessions, "venting."

Venting

We include this activity in almost all of the facilitation jobs we take on. Most people arrive with some concern, question, or point that they need to get off their chest, and if you don't provide the opportunity, they'll be distracted while they look for an opportunity to make their point. Set aside a short time for this early in the session to gets gripes and worries off of participants' minds. Then they can concentrate better on the task at hand, and it often uncovers some truly useful points. But a caution! You must strictly control this, or it will spiral into unfocused details. You really do only want first impressions of what's on people's minds, so we allow 15 to 30 minutes of session time. Tell the group you want to know "What's on your mind?" and explain this is a chance for them to raise questions or concerns, highlight an issue they want addressed, state an expectation for the sessions or the project, or whatever else might be relevant to the project. Then, start brainstorming. After everyone has had two or three turns, you can answer any outstanding questions or address some concerns, but don't try to solve the deeper issues! Just say, "Thanks, that's going to help," and move on.

If you summarized some common issues during session preparation, you can review those with the group now, or you could have done that before the venting. The advantage of doing it before is that it lets everyone know what issues have already been raised, but the disadvantage is that it can turn the venting into a discussion of those issues, which isn't the intent.

We make a lot of use of brainstorming, so we offer a few guidelines to keep in mind.

Brainstorming in General

Brainstorming is a simple but powerful technique for two reasons. Properly handled, it gives everyone a chance to participate and gets them used to it. We always include some brainstorming early in a session to help establish the group dynamics. Second, it can generate a lot of raw material to work with in a short time. This turns out to be far more productive than agonizingly trying to get it right immediately. Most of you are probably familiar with the brainstorming technique, so we'll just provide a brief recap:

- The intent of any brainstorming session is to generate a *lot* of suggestions on whatever the topic or question is.

- It works because judgment is specifically held until later. Without the fear of immediate criticism, participants are more likely to join in and make suggestions. Many believe that brainstorming works because the human brain can't effectively be creative and critical at the same time.

- The guidelines are simple:
  - Each participant makes one suggestion during their turn or says "pass."
  - The facilitator (or a scribe) records the idea without editing, except perhaps to have the participant restate it more briefly.
  - There must be no criticism or negative comments.

We always try to have the group arranged in a wide "U" or semicircle and go around the group clockwise with each participant taking a turn in sequence. This may seem slower than "random" brainstorming, but it encourages participation from everyone and prevents anyone from taking over. The change in dynamics can be invaluable, with shy people becoming more participative, and others becoming less overbearing than they might otherwise be. This only works if you stress and enforce the primary rule of brainstorming: no criticism or evaluation of any kind is allowed during the brainstorming session, and your job as the facilitator is to ensure this. When we use this technique later to generate ideas for the new process, even absurd and impossible ideas are encouraged. You are after quantity, not quality, and people are encouraged to piggyback, or take another idea and modify or extend it.

On the topic of getting people involved, we've become disenchanted with inclusion activities and mind expanders. Everyone is so busy nowadays these activities are often greeted with eye rolling, so we'll suggest that you avoid the parlor games unless you're already quite skilled in that sort of training and facilitation technique.

Now, we can get into the heart of the session, working with terminology and then process discovery. We've covered the harder parts, including interviews, preparation, and initiating the session, and the groundwork of those activities makes the upcoming steps much easier. Also, they make use of techniques you've already seen earlier in the book (e.g., Chapter 3's illustration of bottom-up process discovery).

Step 5: Analyze Terms and Find the Nouns

Purpose

It is much easier to identify and work with your processes if you have agreement on the things your process acts on and needs information about. These are the nouns in the verb-noun pairs that make up process and activity names. Eventually, you need agreement on what each of these things will be called, how each of them is defined, how they interrelate, and what information is needed about each. That is what a data model does—it depicts the things that a business needs to maintain records (data) about as an entity-relationship diagram (ERD) and ensures everyone is on the same wavelength about terminology and meaning before getting into the details of process and system design. We introduced data models in Chapter 4, and Chapter 14 provides an introduction to the technique, should you wish to look ahead at that.

The heart of the data model, and the starting point for building one, is an agreed-upon list of core things or nouns, which are the entities. We are about to start building that list, which is effectively a project glossary, and later in the project you will deal with other components, such as the ERD and the attributes. Our interest now is on exploring the terms that people use, highlighting potential sources of confusion, and agreeing on standard terms. For instance, it might emerge that your participants have different terms and definitions for product, customer, and order, such as item, account, and purchase. That will certainly impact what they assume is meant by the process Fulfill Order. Having the list of terms will also be an excellent aid to process identification. Each of the major terms or entities just mentioned will likely have at least one significant corresponding business process—Acquire Customer, Introduce New Product, or Fulfill Order.

The Steps

1. Using the preceding paragraphs as a resource, introduce the idea that processes work on things, and we need to get some agreement on what those things are and what to call them.
2. If you haven't done so already, post the flipchart sheets that hold the Post-its of terms on a section of plain wall with lots of room around it. We usually have this up from the beginning of the session so people can look it over.
3. Invite the group to spend 5 or 10 minutes thinking about the most important terms in their area and checking that they are on the list. Hand out more large Post-its and let people add any terms they'd like. Stress that all ideas are good ideas, and anything that is referred to by a name can be added—we'll sort them out in the next step. It's a good idea to use the same color of Post-its that you used for the terms, so nobody's ideas stand out. (We learned this the hard way, when a participant was unhappy that most of their terms ended up in an "other" category.)
4. Explain that each term will probably fit into one of the following eight categories. Review the list "criteria to be a thing" with the group as well and point out the things are what we are really after. Also, some roles (customer, service rep, and so on) will become things if they meet the criteria.
   a. Things (guidelines to follow);
   b. Facts about things (add new "thing" if it's not there already);
   c. Metrics;
   d. Organizations, departments, jobs, roles, …;
   e. Processes, functions, activities, tasks, …;

f. Systems, tools, equipment, mechanisms, ...;

g. Reports, forms, screens, queries, ...;

h. Other: too vague ("the competition"), only a single instance ("the company itself"), or not in scope.

Have a flipchart prepared labeled "criteria to be a thing," or sometimes simply "thinginess." People often just "get" the idea of "a thing" but this will help. Here's the text of that flipchart:

Generally, is a specific thing the business needs to know about that meets these criteria:

- A singular noun that implies a single instance:
    - We can discuss "one of them";
    - Not a plural or collective noun, list, set, collection, report, and so on;
    - Common categories: person, place, thing, event, organization, or concept.
- Has *multiple* occurrences;
- Need to keep track of *each* occurrence and can tell one from another ("uniquely identifiable");
- Has *facts* that must be recorded and maintained;
- Processes *act* on them, so they make sense in a *verb-noun* pair;
- Refers to the *essence*, not the implementation ("what, not how") so it is not a report, form, list, query, screen, metric, or other depiction of things and facts.

You can also provide some examples, such as the Customer, Product, and Order we just referred to.

5. Then, have the group come up and sort the terms into the eight categories. We have at least two flipcharts labeled "things," and then other flipcharts labeled so each flipchart can take terms for two categories. The labels are on Post-its (like everything!) so if one category fills up, it's easy to adjust the flipcharts. For example, there are often many suggestions in "metrics." Sometimes, there will be a term that could go under two categories, such as "sales," which is both a metric and an organization, so create a duplicate Post-it. We would be fine with not worrying about it and placing it under one or the other, but this will upset some participants. As the facilitator, your job is to have participants explain their rationale for placing terms, and to stimulate discussion. Encourage them to move the Post-its themselves, because there's nothing like physical involvement to stimulate interest and encourage buy in. (No, if you were thinking about it, it's not a good idea to do this with a spreadsheet and a data projector!)

6. Within the things, there will be many synonyms. If you didn't do it while sorting the terms, arrange the Post-its now so that synonyms are in a row across the flipchart. You'll probably need additional flipcharts for this. Some terms will end up in a row of one, with no synonyms.

7. Finally, have the group select the term that will be the standard one to use and move it to the left side of the row. Sometimes this goes smoothly, and

other times there is disagreement. Figures 5.5 and 5.6 illustrate the outcome. Dealing with this disagreement could be the subject of an entire chapter in a book on data modeling, so our short advice for now is to remind people that there are only so many good words to go around, so flexibility is important, and that they should strive for the term that will be clearest or most intuitive to the widest range of people.

Congratulations! You now have some terms that you'll be able to use throughout the process analysis and redesign effort, and right into subsequent requirements modeling. They will be the target of many important activities, as will some of the

Selected nouns	Synonyms
Survey	
Market segment	Market need
Product	Section, feature
Issue plan	Editorial calendar
Editorial item	Article, story, interview, wire item, copy
Writer	Reporter, freelancer, columnist, contributor
Issue	Edition
Page	Flat
Customer	Prospect, account, client, advertiser
Display ad order	Order, ad order, retail ad order
Display ad	Ad, retail ad, proof, artwork
Classified ad order	
Classified ad	Classified
Invoice	Bill, receivable
Payment	Receipt, cheque
Commission	

Figure 5.5   Terms chosen as "things" arranged into selected nouns and synonyms.

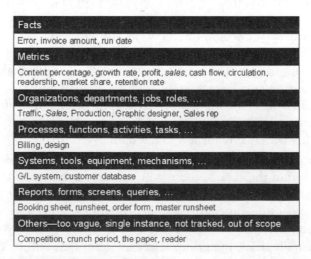

Facts
Error, invoice amount, run date
Metrics
Content percentage, growth rate, profit, *sales*, cash flow, circulation, readership, market share, retention rate
Organizations, departments, jobs, roles, …
Traffic, *Sales*, Production, Graphic designer, Sales rep
Processes, functions, activities, tasks, …
Billing, design
Systems, tools, equipment, mechanisms, …
G/L system, customer database
Reports, forms, screens, queries, …
Booking sheet, runsheet, order form, master runsheet
Others—too vague, single instance, not tracked, out of scope
Competition, crunch period, the paper, reader

Figure 5.6   Terms other than "things."

facts and metrics. If your experience is like ours, both you and the participants will find this an interesting and even fascinating activity. The number of different interpretations for the same term and the number of different terms that are used to describe the same thing always surprises people. You will also find that when people explain the meaning, or their meaning, for a term, you learn more about the business in a shorter period of time than with any other analysis technique we know.

You'll get some use out of those nouns in the upcoming step, identifying the activities that will be the raw material for process discovery.

Step 6: Identify Activities

Purpose

In this step, you will identify the activities that in step 7 will be sequenced and clustered into business processes. This is the "bottom" part of our bottom-up method for process discovery, as in Chapter 3's Commercial Loans Management example. Even in an organization that is heavily functionally oriented, people have little difficulty identifying individual activities, which is one reason this step usually goes very smoothly.

An important piece of advice right up front—whatever you do, don't get into all the exceptions, variations, and rainy day cases, or you'll never finish. That comes later with cases, and much later with scenarios. For now, the focus is on normal, mainstream, sunny day activities. Similarly, don't get into all the management and control activities that sit over the process. These are typically supported by information, not workflows.

The Steps

1. It usually helps to first have the group go through an example, such as Commercial Loans Management from Chapter 3. Have the 12 activities from Figure 3.8 already on Post-its, invite the group to sort them (hands-on!) just as we did in Figure 3.9, and then lead them through the analysis of the linkages per Figure 3.10, arriving at the processes from Figure 3.12. A recap of the guidelines from Figure 3.14 should be reviewed and posted on a flipchart. This will help them visualize what will be accomplished in this step and in step 7.

2. If you prepared any in advance, place the flipchart sheets of activity Post-its on the wall. Then, invite everyone to brainstorm for activities, or additional activities, that are within the area of interest. You can have blank Post-its mounted on flipchart sheets and treat this as a group brainstorm or organize the session into breakout groups and have each identify as many activities as they can within 10 or 15 minutes. Give each group a pad or two of Post-its, again, all the same color. Once we inadvertently gave each of four teams a different color, and then were terrified that one team would produce all the selected activities and another team none. Yikes! Later, we were immensely relieved to find that all colors were represented in the final set of activities we selected. Here are some guidelines to share with the group:

- Don't think too hard—you're doing discovery, not analysis.
- You don't have to get every single activity.
- They don't all have to be the same granularity, but a good guideline is that each is "large" enough that counting them could be part of a statistical measure. One way we have explained it is that somebody might get a raise if they could do more of them.
- Focus on what, not who or how (no actor names or technologies).
- Focus on the sunny day case, not everything that can go wrong.
- They don't have to be named properly while you're collecting them.

3. Next, you will use the selected nouns as a tool to uncover additional activities. Simply take each noun and ask the group to identify activities by thinking of which verbs go with it. Any activity that hasn't already been identified can be recorded and added to the collection. As with initial collection, this can be done as a group brainstorm or in breakout groups.

4. The last task is to clean up the brainstormed activities. This will not necessarily go strictly in this sequence:

   - Clean up the activity names so they use an action verb and one or more nouns. During brainstorming on our newspaper project, the suggestions "designing," "writing," and "billing" became "design ad," "write editorial item," and "issue invoice." At the same time, generalize any that refer to specific actors or technologies unless those references are key to understanding the activity.
   - Eliminate duplicates, and if there are some that are essentially the same, choose (or create) one that uses the proper noun and the most appropriate verb.
   - Confirm that the activity produces a real (discrete, countable, and necessary) result by putting the name into "noun is verbed" form. You might need to remind people of the distinction between a result or output and a goal or objective.

Regarding that last point, in the first edition we recommended brainstorming for results in noun-is-verbed form and later transcribing them into verb-noun form. That is still our preference, because it produces a higher proportion of real activities. However, we now work directly in verb-noun form because participants often objected to the time it took to transcribe the activities into a new form, and some also found it confusing—"Why are we doing this?" As long as you check each name with the noun-is-verbed test for results, this method works just fine:

- Reserve product leads to product is reserved, which passes the test.
- Pack shipment leads to shipment is packed, which passes the test.
- Replenish inventory leads to inventory is replenished, which passes the test.
- Accept order leads to order is accepted, which passes the test.
- Submit order leads to order is submitted, which passes the test.

Figure 5.7 shows a subset of activities that were brainstormed when we were helping the telephone company from Chapter 3 discover their real processes. In your case, there could easily be 50 to 100 activities, but it all depends on the area and the group.

Step 7: Link the Activities and Determine Business Processes

Purpose

The name of this step pretty well says it all—the purpose is to uncover a set of related business processes by linking the activities from step 6 into sequences or "result-trigger" chains, analyzing the linkages, and determining business process boundaries. After all that preparation, this can seem like an anticlimax, but the benefits of the preparation will sustain you through the project, and you'll have identified other useful products such as a standard set of terms and some issues.

The Steps

As you saw earlier, the trick in this approach is that a cluster of activities with 1:1 links generally constitutes a well-formed business process. If a work item (the object of a process) is intended to flow from one step into the next on a 1:1 basis, then we should try to synchronize or coordinate these steps within a single business process. On the other hand, 1:M and M:1 connections cannot generally be coordinated because some other event must happen. These types of links usually signify flows between processes that have quite different timing cycles. In the case of 1:M connections, there must typically be some other event that occurs before the next set of activities can begin. In the case of M:1 connections, the many often build up waiting for some temporal event like month end or close of business.

This technique doesn't work all the time, but it has a very high success rate compared to attempts to define processes top down. It's simple, and it works. As an added bonus, it also gives you the major activities or subprocesses within a process, one of the key parts of framing it.

You've seen this often enough to only require a brief recap, which we'll follow with some guidelines.

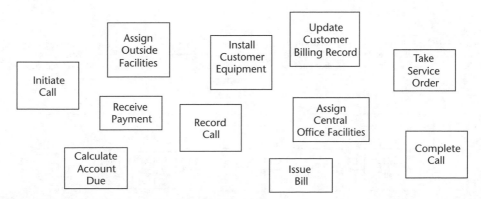

Figure 5.7   Partial results from activity identification.

1. On long sheets of plotter paper, possibly two sheets wide, have the group begin placing the activities in sequence. Simply ask the group to identify cases when an activity is generally preceded or followed by another activity. Stringing them together has another important advantage: it makes activities that were missed earlier more evident. One approach to sequencing is to have the participants select an activity that is early in the business cycle and then trace through subsequent activities. Alternatively, they can just start picking any pair of activities where the result of one is the trigger for the next or where they just happen in sequence. Sometimes a group will notice that the nouns in a set of sequenced activities are the same, or strongly related, so they'll first cluster the activities that way. Our examples have typically formed one long chain of activities, but it is more common in practice for there to be parallel streams in there as well.

2. Once you are happy with the layout, identify the ratio for each link, which will be one to one (1:1), one to many (1:M), or many to one (M:1). The example in Figure 5.8 includes each. M:M linkages are possible too, but are uncommon. Remember not to worry about looping, or instances (1:0) where there is a "dropout" and the sequence doesn't continue—you are looking forward, and focusing on the "happy path."

3. Identify the business process boundaries and contents using the guidelines that activities linked 1:1 are within a business process and linkages that are not 1:1 usually indicate a process boundary.

4. Name the business processes, per the guidelines coming up. Figure 5.9 shows the outcome.

Patterns to Watch For

There are a few common patterns that can cause confusion during process identification:

- A chain of 1:1 activities is followed by an M:1 link to a chain of activities that is followed by a 1:M link to a another chain of activities. It sounds like three distinct processes, but might be only two—the initial chain of activities was the front end of a process, and the final chain of activities was the back end of the same process, and they were temporarily interrupted by another process.

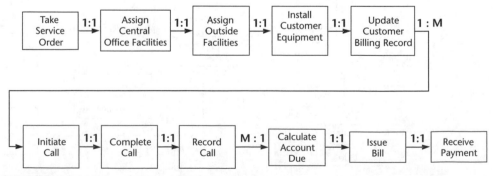

Figure 5.8 Sequence activities and analyze linkages.

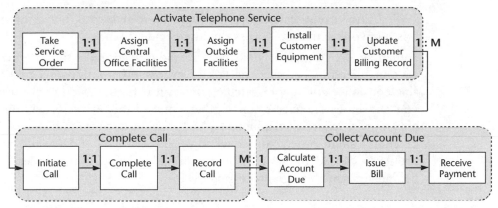

Figure 5.9 Identify business processes.

What has happened in these cases is that multiple instances of a process handoff (M:1) to a single instance of a process that provides some shared service, which in turn hands back (1:M) to the individual instances of the first process, which then "start up" and proceed. In some cases, this other shared service process might even deliver the result the customer expects from the process. Figure 5.10 illustrates an example from a marine bulk terminal—multiple ship-loading orders flow into a separate process that assigns and schedules resources, after which the individual order processes start up again. We see this pattern all the time.

• The reverse situation occurs when a chain of activities splits on a 1:M basis into parallel activities that eventually rejoin on a 1:M basis a chain of activities corresponding 1:1 with the original triggering event. In this case, it is not three processes; it is all one process. A good example is a process that does point-of-experience research at major events, such as a championship football game. At the front end of the process is interview and survey design, then multiple (1:M) field workers collect survey data, which they all upload (M:1), and the process continues with data crunching and report preparation. So, it's a 1:M (where all the "manys" are the same thing) followed by 1:M and the orig-

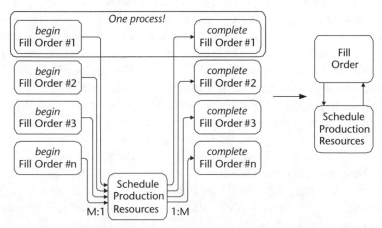

Figure 5.10 A process "interrupted" by another process that provides a shared service.

inal "1" (the event) carries on. The wording is awkward, but if the situation arises in your activities it is usually quite evident.

- Sometimes batching (M:1) has been introduced to make things efficient but isn't an inherently necessary part of the process. We want people to focus on a single instance and ignore batching unless it is fundamental to the process. If you remember the telco example, they batched the service orders for facility assignment, so it looked a bit like a M:1, but the key was to focus on the path taken by a single order, from triggering event through to final result. Resolving problems caused by systems built around batching is the underlying idea behind straight-through processing (STP).

Using a Top-Down Approach

Occasionally, you'll want to use a top-down approach, as we do roughly one time out of ten. We choose a top-down approach when we know we're dealing with conceptual thinkers who are conversant with business process concepts. A group like this will often be frustrated by wading through the details of the bottom-up approach and be quite sure they can get directly to business processes.

With such a group, simply ask what they believe the business processes are. You will of course enforce all the usual guidelines about naming and results. The interesting thing is that in these cases, it still ends up being somewhat bottom up, because people will identify "processes" that are legitimate activities but are smaller than a complete business process. In the end, you will still need to put the suggested processes on Post-its, analyze the links, and then determine the business processes. Remember, this is essentially what happened in the commercial loans management example.

Naming the Business Processes

Naming processes in a tightly structured way makes a real difference. It tightens up everyone's thinking and focuses attention on the essence of the process or activity and the result it achieves. Business processes, *and the individual subprocesses, activities, and steps within them*, should be named in action verb–optional qualifier–noun format that clearly identifies the intended result. As we've seen, the noun will be the grammatical object of the verb and describe an important business object or entity (e.g., Pay Invoice, Receive Shipment, or Load Ship). Occasionally the noun will be a fact about an entity, as in Record Customer Address, or a metric. Note that the process name is usually treated as a proper noun and capitalized to make it clear we are referring to a defined process, which is the convention we follow.

In all cases, flipping the order of the action verb–noun pair indicates the result we expect from the process. For example, the result "order is taken" is achieved through the activity Take Order, "new product is developed" is achieved through the business process Develop New Product, and "distributor is acquired" is achieved through Acquire Distributor. Other examples include Pay Invoice, Hire Worker, Fire Worker, Settle Claim, or Receive Payment. This works as long as you don't use mushy verbs.

Mushy verbs are easy to use, so they give the illusion that progress is being made, but they really don't tell us anything. For instance, what is actually achieved by the processes Monitor Shipment, Administer Application, and Track Project? Exactly what are single instances of "shipment is monitored," "application is administered," and "project is tracked"? Determine Current Shipment Location, Accept Application, and Record Project Task Completion all use active instead of mushy verbs and convey much more information.

Following is a list of mushy verbs you should avoid using, except when naming process areas or other broad groups of activities:

- Maintain;
- Manage;
- Administer;
- Handle;
- Process;
- Do;
- Improve;
- Support;
- Facilitate;
- Drive;
- Track;
- Review;
- Analyze;
- Monitor;
- Coordinate.

Once, during one of our workshops, a participant who had brought a swimlane diagram for us to look at said, "Oh, no! All of my steps have mushy verbs!" We took a look, and sure enough, that was the case. And sure enough, the process map really did not tell us what was going on except in a very general way. By the way, the class clown then congratulated the participant on having produced a highly reusable process model—it could mean anything to anybody!

Choose the First Process Project

You would like to use an objective, analytic approach to defining your project, but in reality the road is fraught with politics, gut feelings, emotion, negotiation, and compromise. You must explicitly recognize that enterprises are not based on fact and logic, as is often thought, but instead on emotion, habit, untested assumptions, and faith in magic. That being the case, we sometimes choose processes by an analytical approach and in other cases by what we call divine intervention. The latter is the most common, so let's start there.

Divine Intervention

Process improvement and application development projects are often defined in response to a pressing business issue or need, a squeaky wheel, or someone with the checkbook, and so it does not meet the definition of a business process that we have recommended you use. Often your project will be scoped by divine intervention, as in: "Thou shalt fix business process X!" And X is not a business process in any sense of the word. In most companies, budget authority does not equate to business processes, and so the executive with the checkbook is unwilling to spend his or her budget to improve the tasks in another department. Remember, processes have been hidden by decades of organizations, reorganizations, and disorganizations. Business processes cross organizational boundaries—departments, budgets, and authority do not.

New technology or fads drive a surprising proportion of projects. Someone is on an airplane and meets a consultant or reads an article in a magazine, and the next thing you know a project is being formulated—we must have (choose one or some combination) customer and employee blogs, social networking, service-oriented architecture (SOA), user-generated content, e-commerce, and so forth. This tendency is not all bad—first telephones, then computers, then ATMs, then the Web, then Web 2.0 were that way. Probably no pressing business advantage could have been quantitatively shown, but successful implementations proceeded because there was just a gut feeling that this technology could change things for the better.

Some key issues for you are:

- Is this REALLY a business process?
- Is my executive team expecting cross-functional benefits from a project or process that is not cross-functional?
- Is someone really hoping that if they fund a project another department will change their ways?
- Can I repackage this in an appealing way with the boundaries of a true business process?

Confirm your suspicions via the techniques discussed in this chapter. In many of the projects in which we get involved, the team receives some directive, and then iteratively manipulates it to better match a business process. The fact is that many process-driven initiatives start in this fashion, with teams formulating proposals that work their way up the hierarchy and then emerge as a directive. Just as we discover processes in a bottom-up fashion, you can also say that process initiatives are often the result of bottom-up or grassroots efforts. This approach might not be possible, so if you can't get your project redefined, try to keep the whole picture in mind and remember to expedite flow across the boundaries. That is where you can make gains for the overall process. We should note that the situation isn't as bad as we may have made it sound. More companies are undertaking process-oriented projects by design, and many have a business process architecture group to formulate these efforts.

Analytic Approach

Years ago, there was much more use of formalized strategic planning methodologies to direct enterprise initiatives, but these have fallen by the wayside while divine intervention has become the norm. Just as well, they were often a once-a-year blitz that produced some weighty shelfware, after which the organization proceeded on whatever course it was already on. Besides, the truly great ideas, whether they spring from the executive or bubble up through the ranks, are just as likely to come from inspiration as from a formal methodology.

What would you do if you wanted to take a more rigorous approach? Hardaker and Ward [2] described a good approach several years ago, and we have employed it successfully in a number of planning sessions for organizations that wanted a more rigorous and repeatable method. (We suspected they wanted the rigor to back up their hunches, but that's another story.)

The approach begins with identifying your organization's critical success factors (CSFs). A CSF is one of a small number of things that must go exceptionally well in order for your business to meet its objectives. "Completion of the XYZ project on time and on budget" might be an objective. A related CSF could be "Maintain an exceptionally high level of client involvement in requirements definition." See the difference? Rockart, author of the original article on CSFs [3], would say that you have about 5 CSFs, but most organizations identify between 7 and 15. Second, identify your major processes, which we have just done. Again, there might be 7 or so, or sometimes more. Note that depending on your interest and authority, you might be looking at the major process areas that comprise the enterprise or smaller processes within a specific area. Third, build a matrix of processes versus CSFs, and for each cell determine the impact that the process has on the CSF. This could be done numerically from 1 (little impact) to 5 (high impact). Fourth, you will assess the "brokenness" of each process: 1 if it's in good shape; 5 if it's a mess. Finally, you determine where to focus your efforts by building a numerical ranking of each process. What you are looking for is a process that is highly broken and has a high impact on a number of CSFs. In a way, this is like a Lean environment, where you might choose processes for work based on high volume, high cost, and high variation. In the article, they describe a less numerically intensive approach that involves some simple math: for each row (process) in the matrix, add up the number of highly impacted CSFs and multiply by the brokenness. This will identify the process to work on first, but of course there are other issues:

- How difficult will process improvement be?
- Can the process be tied to the needs of customers?
- Is this large, complex, and "dug in," or is it fairly straightforward with some obvious "low-hanging fruit"?
- Are there political support and sponsorship for the process redesign?
- Is there a natural sequence or precedence? Does one process obviously have to be attended to first?
- Are there other issues driving selection of a particular process, such as regulatory concerns or competitive issues?

Although the approach on its own doesn't produce a definitive answer, it does provide some direction. We have seen it yield surprising outcomes, which leave participants slapping their foreheads saying, "Of course!" That's precisely when a rigorous approach such as this is most beneficial.

Now, you have named a set of related processes and determined which one you will start with. However, just naming a process is inadequate for people to fully comprehend what's inside and what's outside of its boundaries. In the next chapter we will begin to "frame the process," employing a framework that includes several other items that help to clarify scope.

References

[1] Hammer, M., and S. A. Stanton, *The Reengineering Revolution*, New York: Harper Business, 1995, p. 19.

[2] Hardaker, M., and B. Ward, "How to Make a Team Work," *Harvard Business Review*, November–December 1987.

[3] Rockart, J., "Chief Executives Define Their Own Data Needs," *Harvard Business Review*, March–April 1979.

CHAPTER 6

Establish Process Scope and Contents

Goals

Good news! This step is quite straightforward, and isn't time consuming. More good news! There is very high payback from this step when we move on to assessing the process and then modeling the as-is process workflow, because the time spent clarifying scope and contents will be paid back many times over in subsequent activities. The best news of all is that we'll be able to cover the material in a straightforward, point-by-point manner, without having to engage in a lot of arm-waving to convey subtle points, because there really aren't many. We'll recap what the benefits are, but first lets look at exactly what we'll accomplish in this step.[1]

Overview

A note to readers of the first edition—this step is now considerably refined, with additional components and more explicit guidelines. We've found these improvements very helpful, especially when we get into workflow modeling.

As a prerequisite to this step, we assume you have the process named in action verb–noun format, and the process's relationship to other (but out of your immediate scope) processes depicted on an overall process map (or process landscape) as described in Chapter 5. When defining scope, whether for a process improvement project or a home improvement project, an important principle is that it is just as important to clarify what is *out* of scope as what is *in* scope. We've heard this idea described as *scope* (in) and *antiscope* (out). If you don't make it clear to all actual and potential stakeholders what is excluded, you will inevitably face the wrath or disappointment of those who assumed you were going to help them. The overall process map is an important tool for avoiding this. The point is, don't dive into framing a particular process without having identified the related processes.

Establishing scope and contents is done in three parts—clarify *what* the process is, clarify *who* is involved (and a bit of *what* they do), and clarify *how* the process is currently supported.

The first four items are the "what" of the process:

1. Triggering event(s)—*what* initiates the process?

---

1. This is our obligatory reminder that if you skipped over Chapter 3 or Chapter 4, please go back and read them, as they establish the foundation for this chapter.

2. Results—*what* are the results expected by the customer and each other stakeholder?

3. Subprocesses—*what* are the main (usually 5 ± 2) stages comprising the process?

4. Cases—*what* are the major variations of the work item that lead to different flows?

The next two items are the "who" of the process:

5. Participating organizations—*who* participates, at the level of major internal and external functions or organizations?

6. Individual actors and responsibilities—*who* are the individual performers and *what* are the main steps they carry out in the process?

The final items are the "how" of the process:

7. Mechanisms—*how* is the process currently supported by systems, equipment, forms or documents, or any other means?

8. Measures—you might optionally describe *how* the process currently behaves in terms of basic statistical measures.

All these items will be refined iteratively within this and subsequent activities. For instance, clarifying the results will often lead to refinement of the triggering event or subprocesses. An example, similar to the one we used earlier: you discover that receiving payment for an individual order is one result of the "customer places order" event, but you had earlier identified Collect Account Due as a separate process that collected payments for all orders in a time period. Now you know that collection is done on an order-by-order basis, so a new subprocess has been identified. This will also require you to revise the processes in your overall process map (process landscape). Conversely, when you identify the subprocesses, one of them might indicate a stakeholder result you hadn't considered yet, and the same will happen when you identify organizations and actors. The message is that you shouldn't approach these eight steps as linear. In practice, we work on multiple steps simultaneously and adjust the order depending on what will be most productive for the group we're working with.

The remaining two components of "framing the process" will be covered in the next chapter when we look at assessing a process and establishing its goals. These activities will help us understand *why* the process must be improved and *what* its future characteristics must be:

1. Assessment of current (as-is) process performance;

2. Determination of future (to-be) process performance objectives.

Not surprisingly, these may again cause you to refine the scope and contents of a process, and that can lead to refinement of your definition of the processes within the process area (i.e., you might refine your overall process map). Iteration is the name of the game during process framing, so don't be disturbed when you have to go back and refine previous work, because that's the norm.

How Specifically Do Scope and Contents Help?

If all of the items in our scope and contents checklist are specified, process scope is far better understood than if the scope statement was simply "our order fulfillment process." It is probably self-evident that clear scope is a good thing, so we won't belabor it—we will just look at two specific ways this helps.

With respect to *assessing the process*, it helps by clarifying what the process actually *is* and what it is intended to *accomplish*, and also *who* is involved, so they can be canvassed during the assessment. Essentially, it sets you up for assessment by clarifying exactly what it is that you're assessing. Otherwise, you can easily find yourself collecting a global laundry list of problems, and drifting out of your target process into other areas the participants are responsible for, raising expectations and angst along the way. The more people there are on your team, the more likely this is to happen.

With respect to *modeling the as-is process*, we think of this step as a bridge between discovery and modeling. You will clarify a number of important issues before you start diagramming the process, including when does it begin, when does it end, what are the main intermediate milestones along the way, what actors are involved, and what are their main responsibilities. This makes diagramming go far more smoothly than it does otherwise, because important (and sometimes contentious) aspects have already been settled. This is very evident when we draw the initial swimlane diagram, making use of the elements from this step—start at the *triggering event*, pick one *case*, take aim at the *result for the customer*, and then draw out a single flow showing the sequence in which the *actors* are involved between the *trigger* and the *result*. The main elements are already determined, so this can be accomplished surprisingly quickly using techniques we'll show you later, after which refining the model is also much easier.

In summary, you will articulate the scope, contents, and core aspects of the current implementation in a way that eliminates many potential misunderstandings in later stages. In some cases, a business analyst who has already been working in the area will be tempted to skip this step, because they feel they "know" already. Whether it is right or wrong, it is almost guaranteed that what they "know" is not the same as what others "know," so failing to complete these steps will surely lead to pain later on. Framing can usually be done within a few hours, so in terms of "benefit per hour" (if there is such a metric), it is among the highest value activities of the entire project.

Step 1: Identify Triggering Event(s)

It came down to a flip of a coin whether this would be step 1 or we should start with what is now in step 2, identifying the results of the process. When we document the conclusions of framing the process (e.g., using the tabular format illustrated in Figure 7.3), this appears "first," on the upper left-hand side, and the result is "last," on the upper right-hand side. People like to see it that way—*from* trigger *to* result, left to right—because that follows the flow of time, from cause to effect. Processes are often named that way—order to cash, requisition to settlement, and posting to hire. That said, we most often start by clarifying the results, because they are why the process exists at all, and then go back to look for the event that started the whole thing off. So, you're welcome to read step 2 first and then come back to this point if that feels more natural to you. Ultimately it doesn't matter, because as we said, *you will iterate!*

To establish a boundary and as a starting point for developing your swimlane diagram, you need to identify the event, or more often events, that initiate each business process. As described in Chapter 3, there are three types of events:

1. *Action events* happen when a person or organization decides to do something, such as a customer registering a complaint, an employee requesting a transfer, or a regulator requesting information. Like results, these are named in noun-is-verbed format (e.g., "transfer is requested"). While you might be able to estimate how many of these will arise, you can't predict in advance when any particular action event will occur.

2. *Temporal events* occur when some predetermined date or time is reached, such as time to remit taxes, time to produce financial statements, time to pay supplier, and so on. As indicated by the examples, these are named in time-to-verb-noun format. We say these are predictable, because you always know exactly when a particular temporal event will next happen. For instance, somewhere within the business system, the date of the next payroll run will be recorded.

3. *Condition or rule events* happen when a monitoring activity detects some exception condition, such as a pressure or temperature sensor signaling an out-of-range condition or an exchange rate reaching a predefined limit. The name is a statement of the condition that has been reached, such as "operating pressure critical threshold reached." The temperature sensor might trigger a shutdown process, and the exchange rate might trigger a buy or sell process. You can't predict in advance exactly when a particular condition event will occur.

A business process can be triggered by any of these and can in some cases be triggered by two or three different types of events. To extend an example used earlier, the process "determine inventory level" could be triggered by a request from the bank (an action event), the annual inventory cycle being reached (a temporal event), and some discrepancy being detected by a monitoring activity (a conditional event). Some business processes have multiple triggering events, all of which must be identified.

Just as we try to focus on the essence of a business process when defining it, we do the same for events. We would say the event was "complaint is registered" or "customer complaint is registered," which is *what* the trigger was. We would not factor in the *who* and *how* of the implementations (e.g., "complaint is registered by the customer over the Internet" or "complaint is registered by customer service rep using CRM system"). These might later lead to different cases or scenarios, but for now we want to focus on the fundamentals, which will prove to be more stable.

A higher percentage of business processes are triggered by action events than by other event types. Generally, an organization's "line of business" processes are triggered by externally generated action events, such as the report of a complaint by a customer. Supporting processes may be initiated by an internally generated action event, such as a request for a system enhancement. Because action events are so common, a problem commonly arises—process analysts fail to identify important temporal or conditional events. Don't fall into this trap—always specifically seek out each type of event, one at a time.

With those cautionary notes, let's get to the key point here—you must devote attention to "working back" to the *real* triggering event. Time and again we encounter situations where a client has identified the triggering event as being, for want of a better phrase, when the work arrived on their doorstep. In other words, the process is assumed to begin when the work arrives at the boundary of their organization. This is a dangerous simplification and can exclude activities that must be understood if the true, end-to-end business process is to be improved. We have actually seen major projects fail specifically because the assumed beginning of the process did not include activities that the customer had to go through to get to that point. A simple example—a project aimed at improving technical support (the help desk) assumed that the Resolve Service Issue process began when a "trouble ticket was completed," and all their improvement efforts focused on activities downstream of that event. The first problem was that this wasn't the "essence" of the event—it was tied to the current procedure of completing a bright blue, cardstock form called a "trouble ticket" which prevented them from seeing other mechanisms for reporting problems, such as customers reporting via the Internet or devices automatically reporting problems using Simple Network Management Protocol (SNMP). The real problem was that the triggering event was actually much earlier, which we uncovered by repeatedly asking "what had to happen before that?" In the tech support example, we found that:

- Before the trouble ticket was completed, the tech support rep ("the tech") had to record a description of the problem.
- Before that, the tech had to determine that they didn't have an immediate solution for the customers.
- Before that, the tech had to get an understanding of the problem and attempt a solution.
- Before that, the tech had to accept the phone call from the customers.
- Before that, the call distribution system had to route the call to the next available support rep.
- Before that, the customers had to phone the tech support line and engage in a dialog with the call handling system.
- Before that, the customers had to find the tech support number to call, which was not easy.
- Before that, and this was ultimately the heart of the problem, the customers realized how hopeless it would be to call tech support, so they tried to fix the problem themselves or with the assistance of well-meaning friends, which typically made the problem worse.
- And finally, before that, the customers realized they had a problem, which in fact was the real triggering event.

Of course, before the customers realized they had a problem, there were other events, going right back to the purchase of the offending computer. However, they weren't part of this specific chain of events. Many things happened after the customers bought their computers, but this process is only concerned with what happened after a specific event—the owners realizing they had a problem. Believe it or not, this is a mild example, and we have seen cases where a huge amount of time and effort was mistakenly excluded from the process.

For completeness, we will describe another interesting type of event—*protocol events*. These are events, other than the initiating one, by which we have the customer reinitiate the flow at various stages. They are only required because it is the process's *protocol* to require them, and almost always purely non-value-added (NVA) Often, they arise when the customer is "walking" the process's work item from one step to another (e.g., when the a customer submits a receipt for a payment to a repairperson in order to obtain repayment from the manufacturer). They represent a major improvement opportunity—any protocol event you can eliminate will probably please the customer. For instance, why not have the repairperson obtain payment or prepayment from the manufacturer? This example illustrates why you should involve selected customers in your process improvement sessions, as they are often the only actors who are aware of these annoyances. Protocol events are action events but they aren't triggering events—they happen along the way, between the initial triggering event and the final results—so we won't worry about them now. We will look at them next when we discover them while modeling the as-is workflow and during the final as-is assessment when we'll decide if they're a problem.

Step 2: Identify Result for Each Stakeholder

The triggering event has established a boundary and a starting point for developing your workflow model, and the results will establish the other boundaries and the ending points for the workflow model. Think of them as the "bookends" for a process, and a workflow model as joining the two by tracing the flow of work from triggering event to result. They are the most critical elements of your scope statement, and the result is arguably the more important of the two—the entire reason a process exists is to provide a result to the customer of the process. Actually, that might not be strictly true—the process ultimately might exist so we can obtain payment for providing a result to a customer, but let's not split hairs. Besides, that payment is also going to be specified as a result for the enterprise itself, along with results for any other stakeholder.

Let's quickly recap some of the key points before specifying individual results.

Results Versus Objectives

A result is what you want the process to produce or accomplish and will be called the output of the process by many analysts. Whatever you call it, you must be able to point to discrete, individual results and count them. Here are some results, each of which meets the discrete and countable guideline:

- Order is filled (we can identify each filled order, and count how many orders have been filled);
- New product is developed;
- Magazine edition is published;
- Payment is received;
- Employee is hired.

The people you are working with, the subject matter experts and performers, will typically equate results and objectives, which is easy given the similarity of the terms. You'll need to ensure that everyone sees the difference. The result is the expected output, while an objective is a performance target that might apply to individual instances of the process or might apply in the aggregate. Compare the results listed earlier with some corresponding objectives:

- Orders will be scheduled into production and a delivery date committed within 12 hours of receipt.
- Sixty percent of revenue will derive from products introduced in the past five years.
- Circulation will be increased to 150,000 by 4Q.
- Advertising revenue will be increased by 10 percent this year.
- Average cost of posting a payment will decrease by 20 percent by year end.
- Turnover will be reduced to 4 percent per annum within 18 months.

These objectives should relate to your organization's key performance indicators (KPIs) but often do not, leading to all sorts of conflict and counterproductive behavior. We will look at this more closely in the next chapter, when we specify performance targets for the to-be process.

Different Stakeholder Groups

We always begin by determining results for each of these three stakeholder groups:

1. Customers—the people or organizations that receive the primary result of the process. Every process delivers a result to a customer that may be external or internal to the enterprise that owns the process. Some analysts specifically name them *external customers* and *internal customers*.
2. Performers—the people and organizations that perform work during the process. Many, even most, processes do not deliver a specific, beneficial result to a performer.
3. Owners—the enterprise itself (its owners and shareholders) and those who represent its interests, including executives, managers, and process owners. Most processes deliver a result to the owner as well as the customer. Some analysts refer to *service provider* and *service recipient* instead of owner and customer.

Other potential stakeholders that might expect a result include:

- Other business processes;
- Suppliers or vendors;
- Partner organizations;
- Government or other regulatory agencies;
- Industry bodies or trade associations;
- The general public, the community, or the marketplace;
- Any other identifiable group impacted by the process.

Customer Result

First and foremost, we must identify the primary result the process is intended to provide, which is the result for the customer. The customer might be external to the organization, like a true paying customer or a regulator expecting financial statements. Or, the customer could be internal to the organization, like an employee expecting to be paid. Often, thinking in terms of a "customer" doesn't make sense, so you would name that stakeholder according to their role in the process. Employee receiving their annual performance evaluations probably don't think of themselves as "customers," so we would just call them "employees" or "reviewees" on the process framing documentation. The defendant at a trial would almost certainly prefer not to be the "customer" of the conduct trial process, and the concept of "owner" and "performer" don't sound quite right either. In this case, we name all of the stakeholders according to their role—the public, the defense, the defendant, the prosecution, and so on.

We already know from process discovery what the basic result for the customer of the process is. For instance, the result of Fill Order is "order is filled," so isn't that an adequate statement of the result? Actually, it isn't—we have looked at order fulfillment in a variety of industries, and find that there can be a wide range of possibilities for when the process is *assumed* to be completed. Here are some real examples of what companies thought "order is filled" meant from the customer perspective:

- The order has been shipped via a courier or registered mail.
- The order has arrived at the customer's loading dock.
- The order has arrived at the loading dock and has been accepted.
- The order has arrived, been accepted, and staged into the customer's inventory.
- The order has arrived, been accepted, has moved to the factory floor (just-in-time inventory), and the materials it contained have been assembled into a product being assembled by the customer, a manufacturer.

The significance of the last example is that the materials were considered to be owned by the supplier up until the point of assembly, at which time payment was due and was issued automatically. Note that these examples don't specify the result for other stakeholders.

To ensure that we have specified the final result for the customer (or any other stakeholder), we always ask, "is there a next step that must be completed?" or "is there another criteria that must be met?" Because of that, our result statements almost always have two parts, the basic result and one or more additional criteria:

- Order is delivered and accepted.
- Product is launched and is available for purchase.
- Edition is printed and turned over to distributors.
- Payment is received and posted to internal accounts.
- Employee is hired, assigned to a position, and has been issued ID.

Some of these are slightly simplified. For instance, in the "employee hire" case, there was a checklist of specific activities that had to be completed, and so the shorthand "onboarding checklist completed" was used.

It's worth noting that sometimes the flow from the trigger to the result ends up back at the same place, because the customer receiving the result is the same actor that triggered the process in the first place.

Other Stakeholder Results

In most processes, the customer is not the only stakeholder to receive a result. The results of a business process must satisfy the customer, but should also satisfy the organization you work for. Put another way, the service recipient and the service provider should both get their expected result. Obviously, the customer's order must be filled, which no doubt makes the customer happy, but it must also be paid for, which makes your shareholders happy, and perhaps a commission must be paid, which makes a sales agent happy. This example highlights the importance of identifying each stakeholder result that can be traced back to the same triggering event—it can substantially change people's understanding of what a business process accomplishes and can even lead to changing process boundaries. In the order fulfillment example, it might have been thought that filling the order, obtaining payment, and paying commission were all the result of *separate* processes, but if each happens on a one-to-one basis with the triggering event, they are all results from the *same* process. There is often an artificial organizational barrier between operations and finance or other supporting organizations, and you must overcome this by considering the after-the-fact paperwork as an integral part of a complete business process.

In addition to asking "What does the customer receive?" we need to consider "What other criteria must be met?" or, more specifically, "Who else must be satisfied?" For each process, ask, "Who are the other stakeholders, and what result do they expect from this process?" Our default is to always consider performers and owners, and we earlier provided a checklist of other possible stakeholders. A useful trick for uncovering stakeholders who might not be immediately obvious is to ask, "Who would be made *unhappy* if they didn't get what they expected from this process?" This might uncover a result that a regulatory agency expects, and, in one case, it reminded the team that their company was obligated to notify a trade association of any orders over a set price threshold.

One project was helped tremendously by the simple technique of asking "who else must be satisfied?" They were providing catering services (running the on-site cafeteria) on a contract basis at various manufacturing facilities. They had correctly identified the people buying meals as customers, but something was missing. Once they identified the other key stakeholder—the organization they were contracting to—they saw that they really had two customers, and both had to be satisfied but in different ways.

This doesn't mean that everyone who receives something from a process has to be identified as a stakeholder expecting a result. A frequent point of confusion is to identify the work going to a performer as a process result. Performers are stakeholders, because they work in the process, but they don't actually receive an end result. A result is one of the end points for a process. For instance, an inside sales agent might take (receive) an order, but that is his or her role in the process, not a result. Taking the order is followed by many other activities, and eventually the inside sales agent might receive a commission payment from a successful sale, which is an actual end result. Don't confuse "a job to do" with "a result to expect," or your process framing will be cluttered by dozens of results.

Now that you have made explicit the "from" and the "to," the question to be asked next is "what happens in between?"

Step 3: Identify Subprocesses

Even though you have clearly identified the business process that you are framing, the major components of the process—the subprocesses—must still be determined. A subprocess meets the criterion we have established for any process, which is that it produces a discrete, countable result. In Chapter 3, we noted that a subprocess achieves a significant milestone along the way to the achievement of the final result of the business process. It is often something that the organization would like to count or measure, it usually achieves an important state change (e.g., from identified prospect to qualified prospect), and most business processes have 5 ± 2 subprocesses. That is a number we set arbitrarily, because if you identify 20 subprocesses, they can't all be grasped at once, so the value is lost. We use these ideas when working with participants to identify the subprocesses within a business process. We ask, "What are the *significant* milestones that must be accomplished between the triggering event and the results? There are usually around five, plus or minus two."

At this point, you don't care *who* does them or *how*—you simply want to list the *what*, which is ideally five or so significant milestones (important, intermediate results) that occur within the overall business process. The body of work following one milestone and leading up to the achievement of the next milestone is a subprocess. Your organization might have chosen to call them phases or activities, but what matters is that they represent the critical milestones, within the process, which must be reached in a successful execution of the process. We don't at this point worry about all the other things that can happen—the focus is on the "sunny day case."

When you assembled activities into processes during process discovery, it is likely that those activities were at a finer granularity than subprocesses. In this case, the emphasis will be on combining activities into subprocesses and filling in the gaps. In other cases, you will decompose the process into subprocesses by asking the question about significant milestones.

You need to complete this step because your process scope will be much clearer if you identify the major subprocesses representing the fundamental work of the process. Two versions of a Fulfill Order process are shown in Figure 6.1, one of which includes manufacturing and collections activities. If all there was to go on was the name Fulfill Order, observers would make different assumptions about what was within scope, so this is a valuable tool for clarifying process scope.

Step 4: Identify Cases

This is an important step, but is also a frequent source of confusion, so we'll devote a little more time to this point than the others. A *case*, or *variation*, of a process is a version of the process that is specific to a particular kind of work item, or token if you prefer that term. Each case is likely to have a substantially different workflow than the other cases. One way to understand this is that if your process is named in action verb–noun form, the case will be named action verb–*adjective or qualifier*– noun. The case will usually be apparent right at the beginning of the process, and, if it isn't, it will become apparent soon afterward. A few examples will clarify the idea of cases.

For the business process Hire Employee, the cases could be:

- Hire *temporary* Employee.
- Hire *regular* Employee.

For the Fill Order process, three cases might be:

- Fill *new* Order.
- Fill *replacement* Order.
- Fill *standing* Order.

For a Receive Shipment process, the cases could be:

- Receive *consumable* Shipment (for fuel, gases, cleaning supplies, and so on).
- Receive *indirect inventory* Shipment (for factory equipment repair or service items).
- Receive *direct inventory* Shipment (for raw materials or product components).

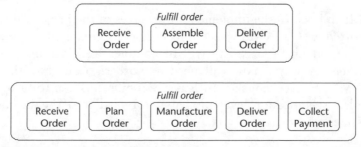

Figure 6.1   Two versions of the Fulfill Order process.

In one of the most extreme cases we have seen, at a logistics company, there were close to 20 cases of the Acquire Customer process.

The reason we identify cases is first that it helps clarify everyone's understanding of what is included within the scope of the process, which is the purpose of framing. Even more important, this will be a great help when you start workflow modeling. You will develop a separate workflow model for each case of your process, or, at a minimum, you will consider each case separately. Usually we build a swimlane diagram for the most common case and then trace through it while considering the next case. It will soon be apparent whether the next case can be added to the initial diagram or if it is different enough to warrant a separate diagram.

Why would you want to have a separate diagram for each case? Most of the time, it will be easier for everyone—you the analyst and the participants in the process—to understand the dynamics of the process when it is possible to see one case at a time. In fact, this may be a better representation of what actually happens. Typically, a decision is made at the front end—"decide what case this is"—and the process flows into one of, say, three separate parallel streams. Often, analysts show all of these streams on one diagram, with a lot of decisions along the way, when in fact the performers aren't making decisions—they know what case they are working on. This makes the swimlane diagram more complex that the process really is, from the perspective of the performers, and it makes it harder to understand and assess the process. The moral—don't put too much on a single swimlane diagram—multiple understandable diagrams are better than one indecipherable one. Another way to put it is don't use decisions to illustrate different cases when there aren't actually decisions being made.

Two points must be addressed to avoid confusion:

1. A case is not something we do when there is a different front end for the process based on *how* the work arrives when the rest of the process is the same. We wouldn't create separate cases for orders that arrived by fax, electronic data interchange (EDI), the Web, or a message from an ERP system. Those are variations on *how*, while a case is determined by *what*. In these cases, we would just draw alternate front ends for the process (or back ends, if that is where the difference arose) as described later in the material on swimlane diagramming.

2. A case is not the same as a scenario, which is a test case that demonstrates a certain set of conditions, with predetermined decisions and outcomes. In practice we often develop separate swimlane diagrams for two or more scenarios for each case of a process.

Much later, in the implementation stages of the project, if the process is being supported with a BPMS you will have to consolidate all of these cases on a single diagram, which by necessity will be complex and include many decision points or other gateways. You will need a more rigorous modeling technique, such as BPMN, to accomplish this. It is a common mistake to bring this rigorous and complex specification-level modeling forward into the business modeling and assessment stages.

Step 5: Identify Participating Organizations

Next, identify the organizations currently participating in the business process. They may include external organizations, such as customers, suppliers, or regulators. *Do not forget them!* They do work and have a role; therefore, they are part of the process. At this point, we are concerned only with organizations directly involved in the process, which means they have some direct contact with the work item as it goes through the process. We are not including stakeholder organizations that receive a result from, or care about the performance of, this process. Occasionally, we might identify an individual role at this point, if they participate but aren't part of a specific organization. An individual person acting as a customer is an example. Organizations in the Fulfill Order process could include:

- Customer;
- Sales;
- Manufacturing;
- Logistics;
- Accounts Receivable.

Be sure to draw a process versus organization chart.

Step 6: Identify Individual Actors and Main Responsibilities

For each participating organization, identify the individual actors. These will typically be roles or job functions. Then, list the main responsibilities of each actor in the process. This must be a clear, action verb–noun pair, not something vague or mushy. What you are looking for is the kind of activity that could show up in a swimlane diagram, although it may not be as detailed as individual, workflow model steps. For example, an actor within the customer organization for the "fulfill order" process could be a purchasing agent, and their responsibilities could include the following:

- Contact sales rep;
- Define needs;
- Negotiate price;
- Confirm order;
- Release invoice for payment.

If it's feasible, we like to list the actors and their responsibilities under their organization on the process versus organization chart, as this provides as terrific snapshot of who is involved and how.

Step 7: Identify Supporting Mechanisms

Just as you identified individual actors, it is also useful to list the supporting mechanisms or tools that currently support the process. This includes applications and data sources, machinery, forms, documents, reports, and so on. This is very tied to the current implementation, but it is safe because we have clearly separated what from how. The reason to do this is simple—people relate to it, so it makes their understanding of the process more concrete.

Step 8: Identify Process Measures (Optional)

You might wish to add an eighth item to the list, covering current operating measures such as how many, how often, how long, and other statistics on process volume, frequency, cycle time, or other basic measures. Think of this as "the numbers." This would cover basic operating measures (counts, percentages, time spans) such as the number of instances of the process per time period (hour, day, month, fiscal quarter, or whatever is appropriate), the percentage of each case, the percentage that end successfully or unsuccessfully, typical cycle times, and so on.

Later, during initial assessment, we might discover additional measures or metrics important to each stakeholder. Note that if you do this, the focus is on measures, which are simple statistical value, not metrics, which are values resulting from a calculation involving multiple measures for the purpose of producing a balanced perspective on performance. You should avoid focusing on these until after the initial assessment (in the next chapter), when we determine what is really important to each stakeholder. Otherwise, you can fall victim to the all-too-common problem of bringing yesterday's metrics into tomorrow's process.

However you arrived at it, you now have the scope of your process unambiguously defined—named and framed. Now let's move on to assessment, so we can describe why your chosen process is getting all the attention.

CHAPTER 7

Conduct Initial As-Is Process Assessment

Establishing Rationale and Direction

Before committing to buying a used car, you would probably have it inspected by a mechanic. A good mechanic won't just stand back and eyeball the car, but will systematically go through the major systems and components—the body and frame, the engine, the rest of the drive train, the suspension, the brakes, and so on. And so it is with a business process—you can't just stand back and eyeball it, asking "What's wrong with it?" That might be a good start, but only by *systematically* inspecting it from a *variety of perspectives* can you make an adequate assessment of what problems it has. Then, before making the commitment, you'll know what must be fixed to make you and other stakeholders (your spouse, the motor vehicle authorities, and so on) happy with the vehicle. The parallel with business processes is that you need to identify early on what the major issues are, and how everyone would like the process to behave in the future. That, likewise, requires a *systematic* approach involving a *variety of perspectives*.

The essence of this chapter is how to carry out a systematic inspection—the *initial process assessment*—so you can answer two questions:

1. What's wrong with the way this process (the as-is) currently behaves?
2. What will be better about it (the to-be) when we're done?

The answers to each of these will be clearly articulated, following specific frameworks, known, respectively, as:

1. The *process case for action*. (What's wrong?)
2. The *process vision*. (What will be better?)

If those terms are a little soft for your liking, there are alternatives:

1. Instead of the process case for action, we sometimes use *as-is process assessment*, *situation assessment*, *current situation*, or *problem statement*.
2. Instead of the process vision, we sometimes use *to-be process goals*, *process objectives*, *future state*, *desired state*, and others.

The primary perspectives taken will be that of the various stakeholders—the customer, owner, and performers, among others.

The case for action begins with an assessment of the process issues or problems perceived by each stakeholder. This assessment will be based more on perceptions than on hard facts, because we have not yet started a detailed study of the as-is process. That does not mean it won't be valuable—it will help us demonstrate that we understand the needs of *all* parties, establish the improvement goals for the process, and identify specific issues that our as-is study (the second phase in our methodology) must watch for. At that time, we can confirm that they are indeed issues, and we can determine causes and impacts.

The process vision also takes a stakeholder perspective when we determine the goals to be articulated for the future state. These goals will be largely based on eliminating the problems uncovered during the stakeholder-based process assessment and, like that assessment, they will be quite subjective. Where possible, though, objective or measurable targets will also be stated.

The third major activity is determining the process' differentiator—what aspect of the process, above all others, will differentiate it from alternatives. For instance, will the primary value be efficiency or flexibility? (If you're wondering "why not both?" you'll find this topic very interesting.)

Later in the initial process assessment, we'll consider the enablers of the process (workflow, IT, motivation and measurement, and so on), some general measures ("the numbers"), and even some overriding factors relating to the enterprise environment, such as mission, culture, and core competencies. These topics will be assessed more thoroughly later on, after the second phase (understand the as-is process), but we will introduce them in this chapter so you'll know what kinds of things to look out for while studying the current process.

To summarize, the core elements of the *initial process assessment* are:

- A stakeholder-based case for action (or as-is process assessment);
- A stakeholder-based process vision (or to-be process goals);
- The process differentiator.

Basic process measures will also be considered, and we'll briefly assess the state of the enablers, the culture, core competencies, and other "big picture" factors. These will be combined with core elements of the *process scope and contents* (from Chapter 6) to produce a "one-pager" or poster summarizing the *initial process assessment*. Publishing, distributing, and continually referring to this will help us explain the project and keep it on track. Note that we call this the *initial* process assessment, because after we've done our workflow modeling and other kinds of analysis, we'll complete the *final* process assessment, based on much more complete information. It's also worth noting that we avoid focusing on measures and metrics until after the case for action and vision have been specified. That's because the current measures are so often task or functionally based and can work to the detriment of a process-oriented view. Instead, we want to first understand how the new process should behave and then determine what measures support that.

The Process Case for Action and Process Vision

The *process case for action* is a concise statement of why the current process cannot be left as is, and the *process vision* articulates the goals for the to-be process. For the most part, we'll just call them the *case for action* and *vision*—we all know we're talking about *process* here. Often, we'll refer to them as a single thing—the *case for action and vision*—as they're always taken together.

The simple format and terms were first described by Hammer and Champy in [1], and it worked so well for us the first time we tried it, way back in the early 1990s, that we've been grateful for it ever since.[1] We employ it on every process improvement assignment without fail, and although we've simplified it a bit, the core elements—the reasons it works—remain. Even though the case for action and vision are simple and short (together, they often fit on a single page), they are extremely useful in uniting people behind the goals of a process improvement project.

Why Bother? Doesn't Everyone Know This Already?

Everyone involved in and affected by such a project needs to know what must change, why it must change, and what it must change to. However, change makes people nervous, and in the absence of credible information, misinformation will fill its place and anxiety will rise. Remember what we covered in Chapter 2—attempts to change business processes will usually face skepticism, mistrust, or outright resistance, spawned by ill-advised BPR efforts, poorly implemented technology, downsizing, outsourcing, offshoring, and a general ratcheting up of on-the-job pressures. These negative experiences may have been real, based on actual events at the organization, or imagined, perhaps stirred up by media reports, but the impact is the same. Or, the reaction could be indifference or puzzlement, because from a departmental or functional perspective, people honestly think things are fine the way they are. Either circumstance can be countered only with clear, compelling, and factual information about the current situation and desired state, and those affected must participate fully in pulling this information together. The larger and more entrenched the process is, the more essential this step, because a good case for action will force an honest appraisal of the current situation. It makes a *case for taking action*, so Hammer and Champy likened it to a wedge, because it helps people get unstuck from where they are—the status quo. Its companion piece, the vision, was likened to a magnet, because it attracts people toward it.

Neither will work unless they are completely factual and unexaggerated. The importance of this cannot be overstated—if they are perceived as bombastic corporate rhetoric rather than "just the facts," especially the problems cited in the case for action, they will lack credibility, be discounted, and undermine the entire effort to the extent you'd be better off not to have produced them at all. That's not to say they should be bland—it must be persuasive, even gripping, but always grounded in fact. They must also be thorough and balanced, addressing multiple perspectives;

---

1. For more information on the process of building the case for change, see the definitive work by John Kotter: Kotter, J., *Leading Change*, Boston: Harvard Business School Press, 1996.

otherwise, important factors will be missed, and you'll arrive at the wrong conclusions and goals.

The case for action and vision frameworks we will look at here have been proven, over and over again, to meet these needs. So, let's see why we're making such a big deal out of them and look at an overview of the components and rationale. You will need this overview so you don't get lost later on when we get into the extensive discussion of the first component, the stakeholder assessment.

The Case for Action

The case must lay out each of the following three points—do not skip any, or change the sequence, because they build up in a specific way. (Normally, we're not so blunt, but it matters in this case.)

Step 1: Stakeholder Assessment

What are the problems cited by *each* of the process stakeholders? What issues face the customer of the process and other *external* stakeholders, such as suppliers or regulators? What frustrations and unmet requirements are described by *internal* stakeholders—the process performers, supervisors and managers, and the owners or executives of the enterprise? Considering the process from the perspective of each distinct stakeholder, one at a time, yields insights that would be missed otherwise. If, instead, a team simply asks, "What's wrong with this process?" they will unintentionally zero in on particular perspectives, and these will often be the needs of the enterprise, as voiced by owners and senior managers, or the needs of individual functional areas. Surprisingly, it is frequently the customers and the performers whose perspective is not actively sought out. The assumption seems to be: "We know what bothers the customer," and as for the performers... well, sometimes we wonder if there isn't a hint of: "it's their job and they should do it without complaining." However, it is *especially* important that the problems felt by the performers—the front-line, individual contributors working in the process—are identified so they can see: "what's in it for me?" That encourages participation from the one group that *really* knows how things are done. Another consideration—you might want to be careful how forcefully you describe shortcomings in the process—today's senior managers might have been the process designers!

There's much more to say about the stakeholder assessment, but we don't want to get too far into the details during this look at the three parts of the case for action. This was just an introduction, and more information is in a section devoted to the topic a little later in this chapter.

After completing the stakeholder assessment, we'll normally sense that some participants are unhappy or uncomfortable with what has emerged. Performers will be thinking: "Hey, things aren't that bad—we're meeting our targets." Or those senior managers we just mentioned will be thinking: "I designed that process, and it's worked fine for years—it's not that bad." Nonetheless, if you're sticking to the facts, you'll certainly have everyone's attention. That is why we characterize this step by saying it *makes it real*. Now, can we keep it real, but take the sting out? That's what step 2 accomplishes when we put the problems in context.

Step 2: Context

What are the changes in the larger environment that make it necessary to change now? More to the point, what changes in the environment, since the current process was implemented, have caused the problems uncovered during stakeholder assessment to arise now? After all, the process probably worked well enough for a long time, so what is different *now*? The *key* point here—the absolutely *critical* point—is that we're focusing attention externally, and asking what factors beyond our control necessitate change. This is crucial because the effect is that you take the blame off the current performers or managers and place it elsewhere, on factors beyond the control of anyone in the process. This sounds like a cheesy consulting trick, or "feel-good" psychology, but processes don't exist in a vacuum so looking at the environment is a fair thing to do. And, in a very high percentage of cases, there really *is* some change in the environment, beyond the control of any of the individuals involved, which is generating the need for change. Obvious examples—a low-cost entrant has upset the balance in a formerly stable industry, new technology is changing a sector's business model, or the regulatory environment has undergone a seismic shift (we've seen a lot of that in the past few years!). Some of the more interesting cases we've seen include the following:

- A manufacturing company was formerly a division of a multinational conglomerate but then was spun off as a separate, publicly traded company, a change that their financial reporting processes were not designed for.

- In a forensic sciences lab, changes in the social environment meant that rather than dealing with a small number of very large and serious crimes, they were now dealing with a very large number of much smaller crimes, which their processes were not geared for.

- A media company underwent a tenfold increase in business, which is a pretty good problem to have, but which their processes were unable to deal with.

The truly surprising point is that in none of these cases had these contextual factors been identified as the reason behind process issues, and participants felt much better about the situation when they realized this. That fact highlights one of the key strengths of the case for action framework. Effectively, what you've done is set the situation up so the people involved can say, "Hooray! The process may be broken, but it's not our fault!" We characterize this step by saying it *makes it blame free*. Everyone's happier, but this isn't a good point to stop—now we have to develop the sense that, blame free or not, there is no choice but to undertake process improvement. That is accomplished in step 3, when we look at what the situation will be if we don't proceed to process improvement.

Step 3: Consequences of Inaction

A simple question—what will happen if no action is taken on the process, and the status quo is maintained? What will the impact be to customers, the performers, and the enterprise itself? An impact on one will inevitably be felt by all, so each perspective must be considered. If, for instance, customer dissatisfaction leads them to go elsewhere, then the enterprise will ultimately fail, and the performers will be out of a job. In a highly competitive world, this has been the answer to the "consequences of inaction" question on many projects, including at government agencies. In each of the three examples cited previously, the result of the case for action analysis was that the company or agency would disappear as a separate entity—the manufacturer through acquisition, the lab through contracting out and absorption into a less prestigious agency, and the media company through shutting down the business. The ultimate result, of course, was that the performers and managers we were working with would eventually lose jobs they really liked at an organization they were proud of. After seeing that, their commitment to process improvement was unequivocal, demonstrating why we say that this step *makes it compelling*.

Arriving at a "burning platform" conclusion like this, one that leaves people no choice but to jump into process redesign, acts as a powerful motivator for getting participants behind a process improvement effort. That's the whole idea, but remember that it must be *credible* in order to be *compelling*. What if there is no compelling outcome in the consequences of inaction? That could well be an indication that the problem isn't really that serious, and perhaps the project should be reconsidered and effort directed elsewhere.

A Note on the Simplified Framework

The case for action carries on the process consulting philosophy of "make it clear, make it visible, and make it blame free." The three components of the case for action, and their impact, are as follows:

1. Stakeholder assessment—*makes it real*.
2. Context—*makes it blame free*.
3. Consequences of inaction—*makes it compelling*.

Careful readers of the first edition of this book, or Hammer and Champy's original work, might recognize that the original case for action framework had five parts to it and was in a different sequence:

1. Business context;
2. External problems;
3. Internal problems;
4. Diagnostics;
5. Consequences of inaction.

The first reason the list is shorter is that we don't separate external and internal problems—they're all stakeholder problems, and we break the analysis down within that. The order changes because we find that it's much more useful to look at the problems first, and then the context—otherwise, the discussion of "what's changed in the environment" gets too open ended.

The really important change, and the other reason the list is shorter, is that we no longer do step 4 (diagnostics), which seeks to identify the root cause of problems. The reason we don't is that too often, because the study of the as-is process has not been conducted yet, we have seen diagnoses based on assumptions and incomplete information. The problem is that people get attached to their initial conclusions and are less likely to be open minded later on, especially if the fault was placed elsewhere. Worse, once a specific cause has been identified, the human mind inevitably starts to identify potential solutions. That's a phenomenon we will take advantage of later, during the *final* process assessment, but it's premature at this point—time and energy will be expended on designing, or even implementing, solutions that haven't been fully thought out. "Diving into solution space," as that is known, always results in *more* time, expense, backtracking, and frustration before an appropriate solution is reached. Of course, sometimes the root cause of a problem will be obvious without explicitly looking for it, and there is no harm in noting it (e.g., "The main reason our approval cycle takes 10 to 14 days is that we have a single-threaded, paper-based workflow, spanning multiple isolated work locations, connected by a slow delivery service"). However, we won't stop here—who knows what else will be discovered during subsequent analysis? In a case just like this "approval cycle" example, it turned out that there were solid legal reasons that the process was paper-based, single threaded, carried out in disparate locations, and supported by a slow (but secure!) delivery service.

The Vision

Now that everyone is galvanized to take action, you need to consolidate a sense of where that action will take them. That's what the vision accomplishes. The case for action says "let's change!" and the vision answers the question "to what?" As Hammer and Champy point out, a great vision will complete the phrase "won't it be great when..." They likened it to a magnet, because it draws people toward it. When we help clients write their process vision statements, we use a similar format, but, like our case for action, it considers each stakeholder individually—"Customers will love the new process because...," "Performers will love the new process because...," and so on. That said, we could just as well have stayed with the original form, and asked, "Won't it be great for customers when...," and "Won't it be great for performers when..."

By its nature, the vision is initially even more subjective than the case for action—we haven't thoroughly analyzed the problems yet, so statements about the future state can't be concrete. That's not a problem, though. As we progress through the project and uncover more specific information, we'll be able to set more specific goals and objectives for the new process. The purpose of the vision is to provide incentive and direction early on and provide a base that can be refined as the project progresses.

On the subjective or qualitative side, the vision will provide an image or feel for what you need to become—the kind of organization you'll be, how you'll operate, and how people will feel about dealing with you or being associated with you. Where possible, we also state an objective or quantitative side that defines how you will measure success. When stating that measurable objective, we use the "topic, target, timeframe" format. For instance, we might have a subjective goal that "We will have the most responsive supplier onboarding process." Sounds good, but it's better if we can make it objective:

- Topic: time from "decision to engage" to "ready to supply";
- Target: 48 hours;
- Timeframe: within 15 days of process launch.

It won't be possible to state a measurable target for every goal, especially at this early stage, and you have to resist the urge to find a specific measure when none is really appropriate or there isn't enough information yet. Think back to our discussions of what happens to business processes when functionally oriented measures are pursued without regard for the outcome; similar problems will arise when a process improvement project pursues measures that are prematurely targeted.

It would be nice to produce, all at once, that fully formed vision, but in practice it doesn't usually work that way. Like process identification, and so many other activities in business analysis for which you'd expect to follow a top-down approach, developing a vision often works best in a bottom-up fashion. It sounds very mechanical, but we often go through the following steps, and it works well:

- Consider each problem identified for a specific stakeholder.
- Describe, subjectively, the future state in which that stakeholder problem was eliminated.
- If possible, state an objective measure for the achievement of that state.
- Synthesize all of the goals for a stakeholder into a single statement that describes their experience with and/or perception of the process.

And finally, don't promise (too much) more than you can deliver—it's supposed to be inspiring, but plausible. The following is a sample from the Approve Customer Credit Request process we mentioned earlier.

An Example

Case for Action

Our credit approval process has become a liability. We are now losing market share to our competitors because they can offer fast, hassle-free credit to new or growing customers. Our credit reps spend most of their time on applications from small customers, who generally pose no credit risk, and little time on large applications, where their expertise is really needed.

The specific failings of the current process are that approval takes far too long (up to seven elapsed days), we can't tell the customers where their application is in the process, we have to go back to the customers for additional information, and our most senior resources aren't used where they are needed most. These deficiencies stem from a paper-based workflow that involves many departments and many stops and starts, policies that force all applications through the same process, and incomplete initial data capture with the initial application.

Two changes beyond our control have caused these problems to surface. First, changes in the transportation industry mean that we now deal with a far higher number of independent owner-operators, whereas we used to deal with a small number of large carriers. Our processes were designed for the high risk associated with large applications, not for the high volume of applications from owner-operators, who individually pose little risk. Second, all of our major competitors have recognized this situation, and implemented solutions to provide instant credit to small operators.

Unless this process is improved, our market share will continue to decline until we are forced to withdraw from the market.

Vision

Small customers will receive instant credit approval, up to a predetermined limit, secured by a bank card. Further credit processing will take place after the customer has been set up to place orders. Applications involving higher credit limits will be handled within two days.

Automated support will be developed to provide improved communication with customers, track current applications, and provide supporting information.

Credit administration clerks will receive additional training to enable them to handle smaller applications in their entirety. Credit representatives will then be free to spend the majority of their time on applications from large customer and other high-value activities. All staff have indicated that they look forward to having more responsibility for and control over their work.

All customers seeking initial or additional credit, whether large and small, will perceive us as the most responsive supplier and the easiest to do business with.

A Closer Look at Assessment by Stakeholder

Now that you know the structure of the case for action and the vision, let's go back and look more carefully at performing the first step in the case for action, the stakeholder assessment.

Everyone's a Critic...

A stakeholder is any identifiable individual or group who is impacted by the business process. Some will receive a specific result from the process (e.g., a customer or the enterprise itself), some will participate in the process (e.g., a performer), and some will have interests that must be protected within the process (e.g., a regulator or the community). It is absolutely crucial that you assess the performance of the current process from the perspective of *each* stakeholder group *individually* and establish process goals for each. We have seen again and again that time spent considering one group at a time uncovers issues that would otherwise have been glossed over. Most of this assessment is usually comprised of subjective concerns and impressions, but some of them you'll be able to back up with objective measures.

Whatever type of process you are studying, there are three stakeholder communities that *must* be accounted for:

1. Customers (internal or external recipients of a result from the process);
2. Performers (typically employees or contractors);
3. Owners (the enterprise itself—its owners and shareholders—and those who represent its interests, including executives, managers, and process owners).

Depending on the process, it will be appropriate to consider other stakeholder groups, most of which you probably discovered during the step covered in Chapter 6:

• Suppliers;
• Government or other regulatory agencies;
• Industry bodies or trade associations;
• The general public or the community;
• The environment—our physical world, which is increasingly identified as a specific stakeholder;
• Any other identifiable group impacted by the process.

Don't Guess—Ask!

Mentally walking a mile in their shoes would be a good start, but don't *assume* you know what each group wants—get out there and *ask!* This is especially true for external customers. There is a tendency to focus exclusively on the expectations of owners, probably because they control budgets and make themselves heard, and on regulators, probably because they control all of us. You'll also hear from the performers, because we have close contact during a project. In fact, you'll probably hear plenty without even having to ask. (That isn't meant to imply that you shouldn't listen—as we've explained, failing to take the performer's view into account is not the way to build support.) Process customers, on the other hand, are often thought to be well understood. "We know what *they* want" is a commonly heard and commonly incorrect phrase.

Consider the example of the insurance company that made large investments in process redesign so they could rapidly implement new options in the auto insurance coverage they offered. These new options would be in response to competition or requests from (vocal) policyholders. It turned out, though, that the vast majority of their customers were irritated by these new offerings. Instead, they wanted cheap, basic, uncomplicated insurance—specifically the "minimum required by law."

One more note before we consider each stakeholder group in turn—when you're surveying or interviewing them, you're likely to get the most interesting information from the most open-ended questions, so start with questions like "What aspect of this process causes you the most problems?" "What do you really like about this process?" and "What is the one thing you would do to improve this process?" You might not even use the word "process." For instance, in determining a customer's issues, you might use a phrase like "dealing with us to get XYZ?" Later, you can get into questions that are more specific to their role in the process.

The Customer

The customer's perspective is obviously of prime importance. That's true whether you are looking at an HR process that serves an internal customer, a government agency's process serving the public, or a corporation's process serving paying customers who have a choice. Surprisingly, many projects don't explicitly survey customers for their perspective, often because there is the assumption that what the customer wants is known—from the sales force, from customer service personnel, from what the competition is doing, or from some hot trend. Or maybe you're not listening to a range of customers, but to a vocal and dissatisfied minority—the "power abusers," if you will. They may even have an Internet forum dedicated to the failings of your organization, which makes research easier, but it is no more representative of the full range of customers than talk radio is of the full range of political views. So, our assumptions are not a good substitute for surveying the frustrations and needs of a representative group of customers.

These often fail to represent what most customers actually want from your process, in terms of both the intended result and what it's like to interact with the process. An overarching factor can even be what the customer expects from your organization above and beyond the product or service. In fact, recent research is challenging long-held assumptions that what customers are looking for is low price, features, or convenience—some groups, such as the oft-mentioned "aging baby boomers" (ouch!) are increasingly making purchasing decisions based not just on those important factors, but on a sense that the company demonstrates respect for them and alignment with their values. None of these are going to be uncovered without asking.

Returning to the product or service, consider the process's effectiveness by first asking if the result—the actual product or service delivered to the customer—is what they really want. This might indicate that the main issues won't be solved by changing *how* the process works, because the issue is with *what* the process delivers. It's not likely that you'll uncover significant issues on this point—if you did, it would be surprising that you're still in business—but we have encountered cases where people in the process were bending themselves all out of shape to compensate for the fact that intended output of the process wasn't what people really wanted. A parallel can be made with a restaurant at which patrons are making substitutions much more often than not, because the basic menu items aren't what people want. Or with an auto manufacturer that compensates for an uncompetitive product with a stream of discounts and rebates.

Related specifically to process improvement, consider the example of a financial services company that invested heavily in redesigning the process for sending transaction confirmation notices (e.g., for stock trades or asset transfers) to their customers, the account holders. They "knew" that the customer wasn't impressed with the three weeks it took for the notices to arrive, and set a goal of getting them in the mail within 24 hours of the transaction. After implementing the new process, it was found that most customers couldn't care less about turnaround time for these documents—in fact, they didn't want paper confirmations at all and were irritated by their arrival. If they thought there was any chance their transaction request hadn't been taken care of, they wouldn't have dealt with this company in the first place. They didn't want all this interaction. Instead, what the customers had wanted all along was a single consolidated statement that reflected all of the activity for all of their accounts. The financial services company dutifully implemented this, but later (after the main competition) and at greater total expense than if they had checked with their customers in the first place.

Once you've confirmed that your process produces, or intends to produce, what the customer wants, check with them for their experiences with the process. Remembering what we said about starting with open-ended questions—don't start by trying to pigeonhole their responses into an exhaustive set of survey questions, just get their stories and impressions, keeping in mind some of the following questions. How much effort is required of the customers? Does the process require too many interactions (protocol events)? Does it appear to the customers that they are the only ones monitoring the process?

To demonstrate that last point, several years ago one of us (Alec) ordered a laptop from one of the top direct-sales computer manufacturers. A trip was coming up that included a lot of time set aside for writing this book! The new laptop was beautiful but unusable on delivery because of a small problem requiring a replacement part, which was (theoretically) ordered after a call to customer service. The small problem soon grew to a serious problem because the manufacturer's problem resolution process was not supported by any mechanism for internal communication (e.g., between sales, customer service, accounting, and shipping), and had no provision for monitoring followup. Other than by the customer, that is. Initially, the replacement was held pending payment arrangements because accounting hadn't been notified that it was a no-charge replacement, and no one knew until Alec called asking "Where is it?" Next, the message wasn't received properly by shipping that they were now supposed to release the part for shipment, so there was no reaction until—you guessed it—Alec eventually called asking, again, "Where is it?" A total of about a dozen problems like these arose while days stretched into weeks and then *months*. Ultimately, weeks of time were lost, which had to be made up during the family vacation. (This, incidentally, led to a promise to the family that "There will be no more writing of books for at least five years!") A process like this does not create customer loyalty. Needless to say, both of us ordered our next laptops (and desktops) from the manufacturer's main competitor.

A similar problem arises when the process requires the customer to walk the "transaction"—which might be the customer themselves—from one part of the organization to another, possibly reciting everything that has happened to date? Most of us have encountered this in health care, for instance, showing up at a lab with a requisition and finding they weren't expecting us, don't know anything about us, and, in any case, don't have the capacity to deal with us. Not today, anyway.

The nature of the business will determine the specific questions you'll ask, but here are some good conversation starters:

- Is it clear how to get started in the process?
- Once underway, are there too many interactions?

- Do the rules and requirements seem reasonable? (Could you explain them, with a straight face, to a customer?)

- Do customer-contact personnel appear to know what they're doing and have appropriate support?

- Do those people appear to care about you, and can they adjust service to suit your needs?

- Is information about you and your transaction available to the people working in the process? In other words, can *your* work be located in the process?

The Performers

Next, we consider the viewpoint of the workers or the performers of the tasks that make up the process. A few years ago, we might have referred to this group as "the employees," but now they are just as likely a contracted organization or temporary staff, which can raise its own issues of information availability, process workflow, and measurement.

But whether they are permanent, temporary, contracted, full time, or part time, why should we discover the performer's point of view on the process? Some answers are obvious—it's the right thing to do, many have direct contact with the customer, and they have the best, first-hand knowledge of how things really operate (as opposed to how they *used to* operate, or how the procedure manuals say they *should* operate, or how you *wish* they operated), and therefore they know what does and does not work. An additional factor is emerging—a growing number of organizations are dealing with a labor shortage and must pay more attention to the needs of their performers if they are going to keep them. This trend is summed up by a newspaper headline that, coincidentally, ran in yesterday's newspaper: "Employers Warned: Adapt or Die—Younger Workers Have Different Values, and Will Leave a Job That Doesn't Satisfy."[2] The article summarizes an address by Professor Linda Duxbury of the Carleton University Sprott School of Business. The point of the article, if that headline wasn't clear enough, is that "Young newcomers to the workforce don't put their priority on money or 'getting ahead.' They want exciting work, free training and, most importantly, lives outside of their jobs. If they're not happy with their work, they'll quit." Later, the article quotes Professor Duxbury as saying "And if you say 'Suck it up and be grateful for your job' you will have no one" and "…three 'saner' young people are needed to take the place of a workaholic baby boomer, yet there is only one waiting in the wings." The summary—"Business success over the next several decades, she says, will depend on how employers deal with workloads, reward and recognition, performance management, recruiting and keeping talent and developing supportive managers." We couldn't agree more—that sounds an awful lot like how we define the two most important enablers of a process—motivation and measurement, and human resources—which we'll look at shortly.

You might start by asking: "Is this how you'd do it if you had a choice?" or "Does this process help you meet your goals, or does it thwart you?" At one organi-

---

2. Hickman, Susan, "Employers Warned: Adapt or Die," *Vancouver Sun*, January 19, 2008, p. H5.

zation, the design of the process ensured, unnecessarily, that an accounting group predictably cycled between total overload and boredom. Customer service was then kept busy resolving errors that had been introduced because of the overload. Other questions that we've found useful include:

- What are your major sources of frustration?
- Are there steps that regularly cause problems or serve no good purpose?
- Are problems for you caused upstream, out of your control, and in areas invisible to you?
- Does your workload vary wildly?
- Do you have sufficient authority to deal with issues that arise?
- Is a resource identified to assist you when you can't deal with an issue?
- Have you been provided with appropriate tools and training?
- Are your performance measures appropriate?
- Is there a documented process?

But remember, the performers are not the customers. If streamlining the work negatively impacts the customer, or improves a step at the expense of the process, it won't make sense to do it. There is always a tradeoff between the interests of different stakeholders, but often on a project the workers are represented while the customers aren't. There can be a danger that we will design the best processes for the workers and managers to no avail since customers desert us.

Owners and Managers

The phrase "owners and managers" refers to the enterprise itself and its representatives. By "managers," we mean the executives, managers, and supervisors who count on business processes to deliver results for which they are accountable. By "owners," we mean the individuals, other companies, shareholders, equity investment firms, and governments that, literally, own the enterprise. In a corporate setting, the owners expect the process to contribute to the reputation, market share, valuation, and, ultimately, profitability of the firm. In a government or not-for-profit setting, profitability may not be the goal, but it is still expected that processes will be fiscally responsible and help the organization meet its mandate. Often, to make this step less abstract, we will refer specifically the enterprise by name (e.g., "What problems does the Department of Social Services have with this process?" or "What issues does this process cause for Amalgamated Enterprises?").

Allocation of capital and resources is a critical issue for any organization, so once we've got past the basic questions, a good one is "Does the process consume resources that would be better allocated elsewhere?" Resources include people, time, money, equipment and facilities, and material and supplies. Answering this requires that opportunity cost be considered as well as the actual cost, where opportunity cost is the gain not realized had you done something else with the resource. For instance, while the sales force is correcting errors, it is not selling, and the lost sales represent an opportunity cost. Other questions for owners and managers are:

- Does the process generate issues for management to deal with that distract from the important goals of the organization?
- Is this process contributing to your personal goals, your department's goals, and the enterprise's goals?
- Is it a net contributor or a source of problems?
- Do issues within the process make it difficult to staff?
- Does the process constrain growth or innovation?
- Does the process provide information for managing it?
- Does anyone understand the whole process?
- Is the process manageable? Do you know how it's performing in aggregate and when specific instances are having difficulty?

Suppliers

Unless you're part of the growing "eat local" movement,[3] a simple lunch involves products from two dozen or more countries, produced, transported, and processed by what amount to literally thousands of people and many interconnected processes. The length of the chain from "farm to fork" is far longer than it used to be, and sometimes a small change in one process can bring unexpected changes elsewhere, like a butterfly in Brazil causing a cyclone in the Indian Ocean. Your organization's processes likewise exist in a web of interdependencies and require the cooperation of suppliers, vendors, contract manufacturers, staffing agencies, subcontractors, and others. You might ask a supplier questions like "How easy is it to do business with us compared to your other customers?" or "What errors or actions on our part cause difficulties for you?" A smooth and predictable flow is essential in today's extended supply chain, so how quickly you and the supplier can establish this is critical.[4] You might even find yourself competing for the services of a supplier, as we saw in a Silicon Valley manufacturer—for them, supplier service became as important as customer service.

Other Groups

The general public has many concerns: ethics, safety, privacy, and, increasingly, the environment. In the end, overlooking these viewpoints can be more costly than addressing them, if only because of public relations and legal considerations. The community may have issues with your involvement in local initiatives. Regulators may seek improvement in how swiftly and accurately your organization responds to information requests or the number of complaints that they handle. Consider the viewpoints of whatever other groups have a legitimate interest in the performance of your process, and above all—don't assume, *ask!*

3. *The 100-Mile Diet* provides an entertaining look at this movement and has implications for processes in that industry. Smith, A., and J. B. Mackinnon, *The 100-Mile Diet: A Year of Local Eating,* Random House Canada, 2007.
4. These ideas are explored in an excellent *Harvard Business Review* article entitled "Lean Consumption," from the authors of the original works on lean production. Womack, J., and D. Jones, "Lean Consumption," *Harvard Business Review,* March 2005.

Process Differentiator

Since we wrote the first edition of this book, two ideas from this chapter have emerged on projects as being more important than ever. The first is the notion of understanding why problems have emerged by looking at *context*—the changes in the business environment since the process was first designed. The second is identifying the *process differentiator*, or *strategic discipline*, which is the subject of this section. The concept was first identified as an enterprise's *strategic discipline*, but we more often use the term *differentiator*. Whatever it's called, what is it?

What Is a Differentiator, Improvement Dimension, or Strategic Discipline?

One way to look at the differentiator is that it answers the question "Why choose us?" Assume that your process customers could select among several competing processes—what would make them select your alternative? Is it because your process is more cost effective, more flexible, more convenient, better able to customize the product or service, or what? The first response is usually "All of those—we can and must do it all!" In fact, you can't, and great companies have figured that out. Ultimately, you can and must be really, really good at the various dimensions of a process, but you can only be great at one. You absolutely must decide, before you get into analyzing and designing a business process, what the most important dimension is—the one that will differentiate your process from the alternatives. You have to know in advance which one you'll consistently turn to when you need to choose between competing improvement ideas. We sometimes refer to this as "the improvement dimension," because it's the dimension or aspect of your process that will always take precedence when designing improvements.

The framework for looking at this issue was provided by Treacy and Wearsma in "The Discipline of Market Leaders" [2]. During reengineering engagements, they studied leading companies and discovered that in each industry or sector there were invariably a small number of top-performing companies (the "market leaders"), and each had specifically chosen to excel in one of three disciplines, whether or not they used the exact terminology and framework described by the authors. The "also rans" had made no such choice or tried to be great at all three. The choices:

1. *Operational excellence* emphasizes consistent, predictable, error-free, and efficient operations. Processes will be more efficient but less flexible in changing direction or meeting the needs of individual customers.
2. *Product leadership* stresses the development of market-leading products that competitors must imitate or the ability to rapidly change the products and services offered. Processes will be less efficient overall, but more flexible in adapting to the needs of new offerings.
3. *Customer intimacy* tailors the delivery of products and services to the needs and processes of individual customers. Processes will be less efficient overall, but more flexible for the customer.

Table 7.1 summarizes key factors in each strategic discipline or differentiator [3]. Figure 7.1 illustrates the three disciplines in the format we use when illustrating the concept on projects—it visually conveys the idea that each differentiator is a choice to move in a specific direction and is becoming a more common way to express the concept.

There's a whole book on the subject, so this is obviously a simplification that misses certain factors and subtleties, but here are some key points.

Operational Excellence

Companies that emphasize operational excellence (op ex) might attract customers either because of low cost and efficient service (Wal-Mart) or because they are a dependable supplier of dependable products (Intel or Toyota). Either way, the lower costs will positively impact their bottom line, and they may also be able to charge a premium for their reliable products, which will flow into the top line. Some companies internally stress the containment of costs through op ex, yet to the marketplace promote themselves on a different basis.

Table 7.1   Strategic Disciplines

| | The Three Disciplines | | |
	Operational Excellence	Product Leadership	Customer Intimacy
Core Business Processes that...	Sharpen distribution systems and provide no-hassle service	Nurture ideas, translate them intor products, and market them successfully	Provide solutions and help customers run their business
Structure that...	Has strong, central authority and a finite level of empowerment	Act in an ad hoc, organic, loosely knit, and ever-changing way	Pushes empowerment close to the point of customer contact
Management Systems that...	Maintain standard operation procedures	Reward individuals' innovative capacity and new product successes	Measures the cost of providing service and of maintaining customer loyalty
Culture that...	Acts predictably and believes one size fits all	Experiments and thinks out of the box	Is flexible and thinks have it your way

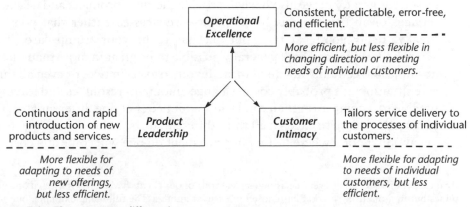

Figure 7.1   Three process differentiators.

Product Leadership

Companies that stress product leadership attract customers because they have the products that no one else offers yet, and because they can rapidly adapt to changing needs. Apple and Starbucks are examples of companies that lead the development and introduction of new products and have incredibly strong brands because of it. Zara, the fashion retailer, has well-tuned design, production, and supply chain processes that allow it to produce relatively small quantities of a new item and then quickly ramp up production of the ones that take off and eliminate those that don't. Thus, it stands out in an industry that traditionally makes bets months (seasons) in advance on which products will sell in what volume. If the product is unexpectedly successful, they can't respond and therefore annoy customers while leaving money on the table, and, if the product fares poorly, they're left with a lot of stock to sell off at greatly reduced prices.

Customer Intimacy

Companies that aim for customer intimacy will build customer loyalty (possibly saving on advertising) and be able to charge a premium because they adapt to the needs of individual customers. Nordstrom is a favorite personal example because they clearly spend time with each customer to ensure they get what they need or want, even when it isn't entirely reasonable, and will tailor the shopping experience to individual customers. Smaller firms can differentiate in this way, holding their own against larger competitors. We came across a boutique on London's Portobello Road called Tonic (www.tonicuk.com) that was a perfect example—they did a good percentage of their business in private openings and visits to the client's location, as well as offering a personal shopping service.

Some organizations and individuals aren't comfortable with the "intimacy" word, in which case we call this "customer flexibility" or "customer focus."

A Common Misconception

Market leaders choose one discipline to concentrate on and build around it.[5] The next point should be written in ALL CAPITAL LETTERS, because this central point is often missed. A frequent objection is "But we can't ignore the other two! Being op ex sounds great, but we also have to provide the right products and decent customer service!" And that's precisely the point—we stressed earlier that you have to be "really, really good" at two, but one has to be your trump card. Treacy and Wiersma found that it isn't generally possible to be great in more than one discipline at a time and certainly not all of them. If you do excel in two, or even all three, a very rare situation, it's probably costing a huge amount of resources and leaving you vulnerable to a competitor than can be just a bit better at one differentiator. Of course, you need to strive to excel in all three differentiators, as far as possible, but you will always hit a point where further improvement on one will come at a cost (or at least

---

5.   By the way, this isn't a "forever" decision—at least one of our clients had clearly mastered one of these disciplines but in a maturing market has chosen to excel at another. The following example, one of dozens we have experience with, demonstrates these points nicely.

prevent further improvement) to the others. If an organization doesn't know what discipline on which they are focusing, redesign will prove to be a painful exercise once the basics have been attended to. That's because an improvement that appeals to some will be anathema to others, because they are striving for different unstated goals, and discussions will go back and forth endlessly. A different outcome is that conflict will be avoided, because everything sounds like a good idea, but the new process will be unsuccessful—it will have no overall "style" and will be in conflict with itself, all the individual improvements canceling each other out. On the other hand, organizations that have decided up front what their process's strategic discipline or improvement dimension will be have a wonderfully clear signpost for decision making.

Differentiators in Action

A large health care organization had embarked on a complete reengineering of its central Deliver Clinical Care process, only to realize after several months that the effort had stalled. All that was moving was large amounts of money to the major consulting firm leading the project. We were called in to help determine what caused the decided lack of progress on the project.[6] The first day, suspecting conflicting goals were a factor, we took the project team through an explanation of the three disciplines and then asked, "Which of the three disciplines was your organization's historical focus?" There was unanimous agreement—product leadership. "Okay, what's the focus now?" Again, there was unanimous agreement the focus had to change as a result of market pressures, the commoditization of health care, and regulatory oversight, and the redesigned core process had to reflect the new focus. However, exactly half the team felt the new concentration should be operational excellence—provide standard health care as consistently and cost effectively as possible. The other half felt it should be customer intimacy—provide the most flexible, personalized health care for each individual group and member within the group. As they say in the consulting business, "Sometimes you earn your pay the first day." Without further prodding, it was obvious to everyone why the project was stalled—every proposed feature of the new process seemed to yield a discussion that went around in circles, back and forth, over and under, but never reaching a decision because there was no overall direction. For instance, a suggestion that efficiencies be improved by opening certain types of clinics at fewer locations on fewer days but for longer hours sounded pretty good to the op ex folks. The customer intimacy side hated the idea. Conversely, the idea that mobile clinics be established that would visit the member's place of work sounded great to the customer intimacy set but utterly profligate to the others. You might find this example hard to believe (and also conclude that consulting must be a pretty easy line of work) but we've seen it again and again and again—if the overall direction (differentiator) isn't explicitly stated, project team members won't have a visible line in the sand to be on one side of or the other. They won't know that they're op ex or customer intimacy or

---

6.   Actually, only Alec was involved, but we will use the royal "we" in this tale, and throughout the book. This was a typical assignment at the time, when a lot of Alec's work involved getting stalled projects moving again or failed projects understood.

product leadership. Once the idea of the differentiator is introduced, it's a real "aha" moment, and disagreements are suddenly put in context and understood.

We used this example in the first edition of the book, and we're using it again because it makes the point, but also because there's a (gasp) sentimental attachment. It was the first time we'd applied the concept of the differentiator to a business process, and since then it has worked so well for us. We didn't tell the whole story, though. One interesting and perhaps embarrassing point is that we'd only read the book on the plane the night before the assignment—to paraphrase what we said before, sometimes a book pays for itself the first day! The other interesting point we didn't cover was what happened to the project. Once the lack of overall direction emerged in our session, one of the senior people excused themselves to report the interim findings to the project's executive sponsor. The sponsor was predictably upset and promptly picked up the phone, called the managing partner of the consulting firm, and ordered all of their consultants off the premises by noon. The project was then canceled, and attention directed to determining what the company was really trying to accomplish. A few years ago, we told this story at a course in Dublin, and a participant said, "they should have gone back to their roots in product leadership." That hadn't occurred to us, but, amazingly, later that same week, one of the online news services ran a story about this same company, and that was exactly what they'd done! They were focusing on introducing innovative services and were winning accolades not just from their customers, but also from regulators and consumer advocacy groups.

The point of all of this? If your team does not agree on how the new process will distinguish itself, some or all of you will be disappointed in the results. If your differences are great enough, the entire project can fail as you tear it apart pulling in opposite directions. That's why the next points are relevant.

The Relevance of the Concept

Let's address two questions that you night have considered: do all processes, including internal and government processes, require a differentiator, and why did we say this concept has become especially important over the past decade?

Is a Differentiator Always Relevant?

For processes that serve internal customers and for processes operated by government agencies, the answer we get to the question "Why choose us?" is often "Because they have to!" In those cases, there are no competing alternatives, so why bother with striving for a particular differentiator? The answer is that even if you aren't operating in a competitive environment, where process customers have choice, your project will suffer all the same tensions as any other project if there is no clear differentiator stated. Otherwise, what will you use as a signpost to guide the decision between competing improvement suggestions? Two other points to keep in mind:

1. You might think there are no competing alternatives for your service, but that can change almost overnight—both governments and corporations are outsourcing services to a degree unimaginable 10 or even 5 years ago. Your

process will have to demonstrate how it excels if you want to keep it (and your job) in house, which has been the focus of a number of our assignments.

2. An effect that you might not anticipate, and that is noteworthy whether or not your process has competitors, is that when a process excels at one differentiator, it also seems to perform better at the other two than organizations that have made no clear choice or are struggling with all three. We're not quite sure why this is so—perhaps excellence breeds excellence, or having a clear focus on one allows improvements to be carefully made on the others in such a way that they don't cancel each other out.

Why Is Differentiation Especially Relevant Now?

As we outlined early in the book, organizations everywhere are focused on improving their performance, whether it's specifically process improvement or some other improvement effort. This has accelerated since the tech meltdown and subsequent recession, for a number of familiar reasons—becoming more efficient during an economic contraction and intense, global competition for customers being the main two. Not all of these improvement efforts are carefully targeted or well coordinated, though, and the particular situation we see most commonly is that senior management wants both substantial efficiency gains along with better flexibility for the customer, with efficiency and competition being the two main driving factors. This leads, predictably, to the kind of conflict we described in the health care example and some terribly angst-ridden project teams. When we put their situation in context by showing that theirs is yet another example of what happens when a differentiator isn't specified, there is almost always one of those "aha!" moments and then a palpable sense of relief. The relief is short lived, as the team soon realizes that they'll have to go back to their executives for direction, but at least it won't be seen (we hope) as whining—they'll be able to put the issue in context with a widely respected framework and some recognizable examples.

We always advise teams that in presentations or meetings with their executive sponsors that they must stress that they are trying to improve as much as possible in all dimensions. Eventually, though, a point will be reached where an improvement in one will compromise another, which must be demonstrated with practical examples. To illustrate, we draw the three arrows from Figure 7.1 with a scale on them and show that once you get to 8 or 9 on all three, there must be a decision on which one you're going to push out to 10. Figure 7.2 illustrates this, and another point we'll get to shortly. This request for direction is usually well received because it's less a complaint that "We can't do this!" and more a request for executive direction when the limits of process improvement are being reached.

If excellence in multiple differentiators is a strategic necessity, perhaps because the enterprise deals with different market segments, sophisticated organizations establish entirely *separate versions* of the *same process*, each working towards a different strategic discipline. They will often have a separate point of entry, and separate staff and facilities, to ensure that work in one doesn't interfere with work in another. In banking, for instance, the average customer deals with op ex versions of the retail banking processes, doing their banking online or at ATMs. High net

Figure 7.2   Different versions of the same process achieving alternative differentiators.

worth individuals, on the other hand, have their own customer intimacy versions of the processes, and the banker will frequently come to them. If you pay for "platinum support" when you buy a new computer, you'll be paying for the privilege of dealing with a different process. A workshop participant in Bangalore with extensive experience as a supply chain consultant pointed out that companies that do this are deliberately seeking to maximize the "area" covered by their processes—more area means higher potential revenue. The area covered by two versions of the same processes is illustrated in Figure 7.2.

Faster, Cheaper, Better, or What?

The previous discussion serves to emphasize one of the most common mistakes we see, because it relates directly to the differentiator or style of a process. That mistake is assuming that the goal is simply to make the process faster and cheaper. Don't assume that your goal is necessarily to lower costs, increase efficiency, and reduce cycle time—like achieving high levels of quality, that's almost a given. It might be the goal, but it isn't the only possible goal. In many competitive environments, simply doing the same thing faster and cheaper will not make anything better. If your competitive environment has changed drastically, you might need to fundamentally rethink what you are doing, not just how you are doing it. A process that does the wrong things faster doesn't really help—as Ghandi said, "There's more to life than increasing its speed."

One of our colleagues encountered two situations where the goal was to *increase* cycle times. Both were in similar areas—legal settlements and arbitration—and both had recently been the subjects of BPR efforts that squeezed the cycle time down to the minimum. Unfortunately, the professionals involved also found out that the think time and cooling-off time had been squeezed out as well. As often as not, this escalated the dispute to the point that it actually took longer than it would have before the redesign, and participants were less satisfied with the outcomes! A classic example of haste makes waste.

As alternatives to faster and cheaper, other process improvement goals that we have seen include:

- More flexible in meeting needs of individual customers;
- Easier for an entry-level workforce to adopt with relatively little training and support;
- Simultaneously support junior staff and provide guidance, while supporting expert staff and staying out of their way;
- Fewer customer interactions;
- Absolute auditability and adherence to applicable regulations;
- Accessible anytime, anywhere, via any medium;
- Easier to standardize and maintain at international locations;
- Less time and effort to integrate new suppliers or customers into the process;
- More suitable for support by COTS software;
- More suitable for implementation using services (service-oriented architecture) and automation using a business process management system.

So, you have to set aside the notion that squeezing time, cost, and effort out of the process is automatically the goal and identified the differentiator or strategic discipline for the process that best fits the enterprise's mission, strategy, goals, and objectives. Then ask, "What specific process characteristics will yield a significant advantage in achieving this differentiation?"

Think about a process you work with. Does it have a clear differentiator? If so, is it appropriate for current conditions, or should a new focus be established? And finally, what process characteristics (think in terms of the six enablers) would be most helpful in achieving the differentiation you need?

Common Questions

Before moving on, let's take a quick look at three questions that often come up.

Differentiator Before or After Assessment?

Why didn't we establish the differentiator *before* doing the case for action? That order seems more logical because the assessment is relative to how well you meet your differentiator. Therefore it would seem logical to first establish your differentiator and then determine how well you're performing against it. That's how it might work in a textbook, but the fact is you often don't *know* what the strategic discipline is, or should be, until you do the assessment. In some cases, you'll be able to establish the differentiator first, but that's not the norm. So, the reality is that after settling on the differentiator, you'll probably have to go back and refine the case for action and vision. Sorry—there's no other way. It's a chicken and egg situation, and they've both come home to roost.

Operational Excellence for Everyone?

Why wouldn't every company strive for operational excellence? Aren't excellent operations the goal of every company? We get this question all the time, and it highlights the fact that "operational excellence" is one of the most misused phrases of the past decade. The most misused phrase two decades ago was simply "excellence," so perhaps this is not surprising. We have worked at many companies that claim to have op ex as their goal, but they usually don't realize that op ex, as the term was originally defined, involves a specific choice among three alternatives. Instead, at these organizations, op ex is a great sounding term that ultimately doesn't mean any more than "doing things right." Unfortunately, it doesn't clarify how rightness is defined. When we ask these organizations what they would aim for it wasn't op ex, we're met with blank stares, meaning that op ex is more slogan than goal. Pardon the interruption, but in the interests of good relationships with our clients, we have to point out that organizations like Intel and Shell are most definitely clear on what they mean by operational excellence. Thank you.

The Same Differentiator Throughout?

Do all the processes in an enterprise have the same differentiator? Definitely not, but let's work our way to that conclusion. When the concept was originally described, it applied to the entire organization, but when we first read it the immediate reaction was that it addressed conflict that we'd seen at the process level. We applied it there, and found it highly effective. With a little more experience, we found that processes in the same enterprise do not all strive for the same differentiator. For instance, in a high-tech company, the processes in their product development area stressed product leadership, which is no surprise. In their human resources processes, however, the goal was customer intimacy, which was necessary to attract and retain scarce technical resources. We've also seen earlier in this section that there can even be different versions of the same process, shooting for a different discipline.

We've now covered the three essential elements (case for action, vision, and differentiator) of the initial process assessment, which is the final step in phase 1 (establish process context, scope, and goals) of a process project. At this point, you could summarize your findings in a "poster," as described at the end of this chapter. However, the material we'll look at next might help you refine your assessment, so let's press on through some other considerations before summarizing your assessment. What we'll look at next are three topics that aren't a focus until the third stage of a project, but we'll introduce them now because you can make a start on them at this point, and they'll inform you of factors to watch for during phase 2 (understand the as-is process).

Look at the Process in Terms of Enablers

In Chapter 3 we introduced the process enablers, six central factors that collectively determine how our process behaves or misbehaves, as the case may be. We don't explicitly focus on the enablers until phase 3 (design the to-be process) when the *final* process assessment is carried out *after* modeling the as-is process. We will give the enablers a more thorough treatment then, in Chapter 13, but here we will provide a little more explanation and some examples of each. This will help you understand what they are and their impacts so you know what to look out for during the upcoming modeling of the as-is process. If there are particularly obvious issues (or strengths) in any of the enablers, you might as well record them now, and possibly even update some elements of the initial assessment. Just don't get carried away and start looking for potential solutions until after the next phase, when you'll know for sure what the issues are.

Now, let's look a *little* more closely at each of the six enablers in turn, beginning with workflow design.

Workflow Design

In Chapter 3, we defined *workflow design*, or simply *workflow*, as "…the sequence of steps, decisions, and handoffs carried out by the process's actors between the initial event and the final result. The terms *participants* or *roles* are often used instead of actors." As well, "…a participant could be a person, an organization, an information system, a piece of machinery, or anything else that 'holds the work.'" Essentially, workflow can be reduced to a simple phrase—it describes *who*, does *what*, *when*. To state the obvious, workflow describes the flow of work.

A key point is that it doesn't matter whether the flow is supported by any or all of the following:

- Technology (e.g., an imaging-based workflow management system or a business process management system);
- Paper (e.g., a form delivered by fax or the postal service and routed through the office mail);
- Human interaction (e.g., one person tapping the next on the shoulder or making a phone call).

It also doesn't matter whether the actors are people, systems, machines, or, as is usually the case, a mix of all of those. We stress this because there are much narrower definitions that specifically mean the automated movement of an electronic document, form, or image through various processing steps that will typically be performed by people. Definitions like this, which have a strong IT slant, were developed by the document management and workflow management industries. The term workflow, which had been in use since the days of Frederick Taylor almost a century ago, was appropriated to mean a particular type of implementation. Our feeling is that *electronic workflow* or *automated workflow* would have been more appropriate in those cases, and the simple term *workflow* used for the general case, which is how we will use the terms. Other authors have made the same point[7] and for the same reason—the limited definition has been shown to constrain people's thinking about what workflow is, and, in turn, what a business process is and which elements of a business process are worth considering.

In the next phase, we'll improve our understanding of a process's workflow by building a visual workflow model (swimlane diagram) that illustrates who, what, and when. Then, we'll look at the steps, sequence, flow, handoffs, and decision

---

7. Notably Peter Keen in his March 2004 article "Business Process Management Is Not Workflow Automation" published at http://www.peterkeen.com.

points to find any bottlenecks, losses, inefficiencies, or other sources of frustration. At this stage, you won't know enough about the workflow to complete a careful analysis, but you can ask questions such as the following:

- Are there steps that you believe are not adding value (i.e., they are NVA)?
- Are there too many approval or inspection steps interfering with the main flow?
- Are the same activities duplicated by different actors throughout the process?
- Does the transport of work or handoff between actors introduce delay, error, or expense?
- Is the flow excessively sequential when steps could just as well be done in parallel?

A quick example: Handling claims at a health insurance provider was completely sequential, to the extent that there was never more than one person working on a claim at a time. That was because the process was based on moving a single, paper-based claim file through the different processing steps. Many of these steps involved redundantly recoding (for different departments) the nature of the disease or injury, completing laborious tracking reports, and checking the work done in previous steps. This was bad enough, but the real tragedy was when "process improvement" led to implementation of an automated workflow system that *perfectly duplicated the workflow of the existing process.* Alec will never forget giving this example at a workshop, and it being met not with laughter, but with nervous glances and shuffling of feet. It turned out that a couple of years before, senior management had given the order to "reengineer" a core process by getting it onto a workflow system, but also ordered "don't change the process or anyone's job!" No wonder "reengineering" often had a bad name. In cases like these, to-be = as-is + new technology. A workshop participant gave us a great formula to express this phenomenon: $OO + NT = EOO$. Old organization plus new technology equals *expensive* old organization.

If there are known workflow problems, identify them now, so you can verify and understand them during workflow modeling. Much of the book discusses workflow, with examples, so we won't spend any more time on this right now.

Information Systems

Information technology is so ubiquitous it goes without thinking—most of us don't even stop to think about the Internet, constantly connected mobile devices, smaller and smaller MP3 players that do more and more, radio frequency identification tags (RFIDs), smarter and smarter smart cards, and other technologies unimagined a decade ago. Many younger readers will think of social networking through Facebook or instant messaging through Messenger not as IT, but as a utility or a fact of life, just as most of us don't think twice about access in our homes to 120 volt AC power. In business and government, systems no longer *support* a manual process that can carry on if the system becomes unavailable: in many cases, the system *is* the business process. No system, no process.

That's why when you consider the information systems enabler, you have to consider not just what's old and clearly does not work, which is easy to identify, but what has been adopted elsewhere and is working, or what is new, and *might* work. The goalposts are always moving—a decade ago it was hard to imagine accessing your company's ERP system except through a hard-wired PC or terminal, and now you can do that from a mobile device while you're sitting on a plane waiting for boarding to finish. And who would have imagined the number of companies using what is effectively a volunteer workforce through company-sponsored support forums. The point? You can't just look at what you have currently installed and what's wrong with it, but also at what technologies and applications you aren't taking advantage of.

Now, that's not to say you shouldn't look at current systems and their short-comings. You should, partly because it will be so satisfying—everyone will be able to help you identify them! Unintelligible error messages, confusing layouts, navigational dead ends, useless features coupled with missing essential functionality, and the capture of multiple data items you *know* will never be used are all distressingly common. In years gone by, misplaced concern with efficiency led to many of these—the greatest programming sins have been committed in the name of computer efficiency or saving programmer time. Now, cheap processing power and even cheaper storage lead to different excesses. And well into the new millennium, we continue to see application development projects that automate the root cause of a problem (e.g., batching transactions, instead of handling them in real or "real enough" time).

As always, it's useful to look at a question from multiple perspectives. In this case, the bottom four tiers of the five-tier framework (introduced in Chapter 3) provide a useful guide. Considering each tier, starting from the bottom:

1. Is the right data maintained in the record-keeping (data management) layer, and is the right information being captured from and presented to each step that receives automated support?
2. Are the right activities automated or receiving automated support? Is important functionality actually in place and available as services?
3. Are user interface designs, including passive reports or queries, appropriate for the task and for the person using them? Are services available through the right user interfaces (browser, mobile phone, kiosk, and so on)?
4. Is the flow of work automated (and instantaneous) wherever possible and appropriate, and is it actively monitored so errors and exceptions are dealt with?

Let's close with a quick example of bad (but well-meaning!) IT and its impact. Nursing staff attached to a major community health program were supported by multiple, dis-integrated applications. Health care management (against the advice of IT professionals) was sure the applications would represent a significant saving because they were provided *free* by various suppliers. The catch was that they were "free" as long as specified supplies were purchased from the supplier. The real impact was that nursing staff spent half of their time manually copying or "cutting and pasting" data between applications. Sadly, this was at a time when nursing shortages were being widely reported in the press.

Motivation and Measurement

This enabler includes how a process is measured, and, more important, how the performers are measured and how those measures motivate people to perform in a particular way. C. R. Luigs, the former CEO of Global Marine Drilling, once wrote something to the effect that people don't pay much attention to what management *says*; they pay attention to what management *measures*. Measurement brings with it reward and punishment, which of course people respond to, and, of course, people will also "game the system" to make measures work for their benefit. That's why we claim that measures and metrics and the associated reward and punishment need to be designed with much more care than many organizations actually invest. Poorly thought out motivation and measurement are the root cause of poor process performance in the majority of cases we study, so we will spend a little extra time on this enabler.

Here are a few real-life examples of how the motivation and measurement schemes affected process performance:

1. At a major metropolitan radio station, sales representatives are measured and rewarded via the commission check, for the number of ad orders that they get. They are not measured (or "punished," via decreased commissions) for errors in the order specs or pricing, nor are they measured on timely submission of ad orders for production. The consequences are predictable: late, incomplete orders. If there were measurements and rewards in place for landing new customers and for timely submission of ad orders, their behavior, and therefore the behavior of the whole process, would be very different. As long as it is adequate, and doesn't distort behavior as it did in this example, nonmonetary measures are usually more important.

2. In one of our all-time favorite examples, seen with minor variations at two different telecommunications corporations, an elaborate new customer service process was implemented, along with supporting information systems. The plan was that this would enable customer service representatives (CSRs) to better deal with the customer's issue, and, more important, to up-sell and cross-sell other service packages or options. Unfortunately, the effort failed, because the company didn't change two key motivation and measurement factors. First, they continued to pay the CSRs a clerical salary, even though they had to go through extensive sales training to meet their new responsibilities and were under substantially higher pressure. Worse, they continued to penalize CSRs who spent more than 120 seconds on a call, even though the added burden of making sales would obviously take longer. In fact, the new systems that were implemented at both companies included the "helpful" feature that when a CSR accepted a call, a countdown timer popped up on their screen! (120, 119, 118, …) In company A, a supervisor would typically show up alongside the desk of any hapless CSR who let a call go on that long. In company B, *a red light started flashing* at the "offending" CSR's desk. (As

they say, "you can't make this stuff up.") To make a long story short, once the projects had failed and we were called in to investigate what had gone wrong (yes, it called for investigation), it emerges that CSRs were abandoning calls abruptly—sometimes in mid-sentence—just before the magic 120-second mark.

3. An internal quality control group was measured on the number of defects they discovered. Naturally, no matter how much the rest of the process improved, this group managed to find an ever-increasing number of defects, each of which introduced delay and expense in dealing with it. This happened in a manufacturing environment, but we've seen it everywhere. It probably exists in some form or other in your organization.

4. An IT executive once complained to one of us about the poor attitude of the company's Computer Services group, who were responsible for installing and tuning new database applications in a large, high-volume, transaction-processing environment. His complaint: "These people seem to be determined to prevent the implementation of new applications that are essential to the corporation's business plans." Their uncooperative attitude became a lot clearer when it was pointed out that these folks were measured on two, and only two, variables: system response time and system up time. Statistics were captured, charted, and distributed to the entire corporation on a daily, weekly, and monthly basis. And what's the surest way to negatively impact response time and up time? You guessed it—install a new application.

Obviously, the issue is whether the measures of the performers support or impede process goals. This doesn't mean that the new process can simply replace individual measures with process measures—designing a new measurement scheme is subtler than this. Deming warned against mixing performance indicators for the process with evaluation measures for the workers. Just about any crude measure can be a good measure and adequate to evaluate a process. The danger is when you start motivating individuals based on it—it skews numbers and ultimately invalidates the measure. People will perform to the measure, not the process, and may even cook the books or game the system. Process performance will inevitably be worse when this happens. A classic example—problems caused when there are incentives to pump up orders close to the end of a financial quarter—too many of them turn out not to be true orders, to have terms bad for the company or are orders stolen from coworkers.

Human Resources

How do organizational structures, job definition, matching of job to task, and skills impact the process? What this enabler boils down to is "are the right people, with the right skills and aptitude, in the right job, assigned to the appropriate activities?" This enabler is second only to poorly considered motivation and measurement as a cause of poor process performance. Consider the following questions:

- Have you ever dealt with a person in a customer-facing role who had no "people skills" whatsoever? Perhaps someone in support or customer service? Or any case where someone had the right skills, but no natural aptitude for the job they were in? Of course you have. That's an HR issue. (By the way, smart organizations "hire for attitude, then train for skills" wherever that's feasible.)

- Have you seen a case where a scarce resource or highly paid employee was doing clerical or support work that (a) they weren't very good at and (b) could have been done better by a clerical or support professional at much lower cost? Of course you have. One of the worst developments of the last 10 or 15 years has been the mindless elimination of support personnel so their work could be done by the very professionals they used to support, at two to three times the cost and not very well.

- Have you seen policies that result in an effective and happy performer (at any level) being promoted to a position they don't like and aren't good at, because that's the only way they can be "rewarded?" Of course you have. It even has a name—"The Peter Principle."

- Have you seen a reorganization that (gasp!) didn't actually improve the situation, but made it worse, possibly by introducing new organizational boundaries and segmentation that led to handoffs and division of responsibility, just the way excessively narrow job definitions can? Of course you have.

We could go on and on with obvious examples, but these are all cases of failures within the HR enabler that are impacting the current process.

Looking ahead to redesign, failure to think through HR issues is a common failing of process redesign efforts. Will the workforce need to change? Sometimes the only way to *change* people is to change *people*. Will new skills, training, and job responsibilities be required? Will selection and placement strategies need to change? Will the organizational structure and physical location of the new process be different from the old? Anything that impacts people's definition of themselves ("I am my job") or their network (peers, customers, suppliers, managers, direct reports) can be amazingly disruptive. If redeployment or layoffs might result from your new process, you might face severe morale and then productivity impacts throughout the organization, not just in the process you're working on. These concerns have to be addressed honestly and compassionately.

You might be in an environment where labor unions are a major influence, and keeping the union involved can be critical. In some airlines and transport companies we've worked in, the work rules were positively Byzantine, impacting the ability to respond to short-term opportunities or temporary changes in conditions. These rules cannot usually be changed without union agreement. You'll need to take into consideration the effect of shifting work from one union to another or changing the work of the individual workers, especially if it reduces total employment of a union's workers.

Anything that impacts the "who" in a process relates to the human resources enabler.

Policies and Rules

Processes are usually guided by business rules and policies, many of which are now obsolete or for which the original rationale is long since forgotten. Some of these business rules are insidious because they are implemented in systems or workflow, but at least they can be uncovered by inspection and questioning. The more insidious ones are those where people assume there is a rule or policy, and act accordingly, when in fact that's all it was—an assumption. "Bad" rules have an effect, because they need to be enforced, making jobs more complex, frustrating customers, and slowing down the process. Policies and rules can be beneficial, but never forget that they all cost money, one way or another, to enforce.

These rules and polices don't exist in isolation—they reflect the bias of the organization, or at least they did at one time, and they impact process workflow, IT, and other enablers. For instance, a retail operation might have a bias toward customer service on one hand or fraud prevention on the other. This will surely lead to different rules and, in turn, different workflows. We'll examine this a little more when we look at the environment in the next chapter, but for now, consider a couple of cases.

In the retail example, there could be a policy that "refunds up to a certain amount can be handled by a sales associate on the retail floor, at their discretion, whether or not the customer has a receipt, and even in cases where we don't carry the product in question." This will have a very different effect than a policy that "all refund requests must be accompanied by a sales receipt and a completed refund reason form; they will be processed by the customer service and AP departments, and a check will be mailed."

Another example would be "requisitions over $1,000 must be approved by a department head, and requisitions over $5,000 must be approved by a department head and a vice president."

Both rules manifest themselves in the process, especially the workflow, and are typical examples of the kinds of rules that are in place. They degrade the process, because the system developers have to know them all, and system changes become a nightmare because the code is increasingly complex. Customers are frustrated because they never get consistent answers, and so on.

Imagine some of the rules in place at your government agencies for taxation, social welfare, and so forth, and imagine the impact on process workflow and the human resources responsible for knowing and enforcing the rules. In some government agencies we're familiar with, no amount of process redesign can improve customer service above a certain level because the rules established over the decades by successive governments are collectively incomprehensible, inconsistent, and incredibly difficult to implement and maintain. We have first-hand experience with cases when government agencies had the software programs in their systems "reverse-engineered" to uncover the rules that were being enforced. (Of course, there was no documentation to refer to.) The reaction, to put it mildly, was shock and awe. In one memorable case, a tax that was supposed to have ended in the 1970s was still being collected!

Facilities

At last, workplace design and physical infrastructure (equipment, furniture, lighting, storage, ventilation, and so forth) is getting more attention. Many offices seem to be designed for anything but getting work done. In fact, for much of the activity in a contemporary organization, you could not design anything worse than a cubicle. There's too much noise and interruption for work requiring intense concentration, yet a one-on-one meeting or telephone conversation requiring privacy is equally hopeless. The cubicle gives the illusion of privacy, but no privacy—everyone can hear your conversation, but since you can't see them, you're worse off than if you were in the open. And in the age of highly collaborative group works, where discussions and meetings take up most of the day, the cubicle is useless. Meanwhile, the universal shortage of properly equipped meeting rooms continues to grow.

DeMarco and Lister talk about the "furniture police" and point out "...for most organizations with productivity problems, there is no more fruitful area for improvement than the workplace. As long as workers are crowded into noisy, sterile disruptive space, it's not worth improving anything but the workplace." They talk of workers who come in early, stay late, or even call in sick in order to get work done [4]. Space, quiet, privacy, and the ability to avoid interruptions are key productivity enablers that are frequently ignored in modern office layouts. Refer to "The Seven Day Weekend"[8] for examples of what a forward-looking Brazilian firm does to accommodate employee needs for a place where they can actually...work.

We've focused here on the office environment, probably reflecting where we spend a lot of time, but the issue clearly extends to manufacturing and public spaces or anywhere work gets done. Practitioners of the Lean methodology will often build flow diagrams that show the progress of a work item (e.g., a person, a part, or a form) through physical space. In some examples, for instance, the movement of a patient through a hospital, it would be almost comic if it wasn't actually so troubling.

All Enablers Matter

From what we've seen, you can design and redesign workflows and information systems until the proverbial cows come home, but if you don't address the other four enablers—motivation and measurement, human resources, policies and rules, and facilities—it's all for naught.

The Environment in Which the Process Operates

We hope the previous section illuminates the six enablers well enough that you can watch for them while modeling the as-is process, even if you won't formally assess them until later. In the same vein, we'll consider the environment within which the process operates, which includes factors beyond the control of the process team—issues such as beliefs, culture, management style, and core competencies. Two points make this a particularly interesting group of topics:

8.   Semler, Ricardo, *The Seven-Day Weekend: Changing the Way Work Works,* Portfolio, 2004.

1. If you try to assess these factors early in an initiative, especially in a new environment, you'll probably get it wrong. Organizations constantly seem to delude themselves about how they really operate and what they're good at, and therefore provide misleading information about what their culture, strengths, and even overriding goals are. Separately, during the discussions that happen while identifying, scoping, assessing, modeling, and analyzing a process, a picture of the actual environment will emerge for the perceptive analyst. (This is a good time to reiterate that the real value of workflow modeling often isn't the workflow model itself, but what emerges while you're building it and what emerges when you walk through each step, decision, flow, and handoff.)

2. If you design a new process that depends on significant change in any of these areas, you're going to be disappointed. These factors are simply not going to change unless the leadership of the organization devotes itself to providing unequivocal support and resources over a multiyear period to the effort. Culture and beliefs are so embedded in the organizational psyche that we have seen companies go through a near-total change of personnel, bringing in a very different group of employees, and yet the culture and attitudes remain the same. The implications for process change are that the as-is process must be understood in light of the environment, and the to-be process must be designed to work within that environment, except in those *very* rare cases where changing it can be seriously considered. These environmental issues are so hard to change, we generally treat them as *fixed* constraints rather than *adjustable* enablers.

With that rather dire warning, we'll try to keep this short, because when the discussion turns to "squishy" topics like culture, beliefs, and style, a few eyes are certain to glaze over. We notice this especially in our more technical or detail-oriented friends, the ones likely to fidget uncomfortably while the earnest HR executive proudly unveils "our latest statement of vision, values, and aspirations." To be sure, too much posterware, shelfware, and meetingware has been produced around topics like these, but the fact is they *do* matter in process improvement. A process that is designed without regard to the skills, attitudes, and behavioral norms of an organization will fail just as surely as one with a poorly designed workflow or information system. A few examples usually have even the hardest-headed technicians nodding in agreement—here is an obvious one that comes to mind.

An Example

A consulting firm spearheaded the development of a new process for resolving disputes at a government licensing organization. Actually, "development" was the wrong word—it was more of a transplant. The firm had just completed the implementation of a similar process at a high tech company, on the opposite coast, in a very different environment. It relied on collaboration, creative thinking, trying to always do what was right for the customer or what it would take to retain the customer, and other factors like that. The bright, young consultants working on the project were inexperienced in the ways of large government organizations but were sure that the process that worked so well at the tech firm would also be a success at the government agency. Of course, that's not how it worked out, because the process was totally at odds with the culture of the agency. People were used to working alone, applying very prescriptive policies in narrowly defined jobs, under close supervision. There was nothing in their background that would prepare them for working collaboratively on creative solutions that do the right thing for all stakeholders. These were all intelligent people who wanted to do a good job, but you can't just sweep away the conditioning that comes with 10, 20, or 30 years of working in a particular environment. Perhaps the change management course the consultants had been on did not make clear just how difficult issues of culture really are. Just as ineffective as processes that don't align with the culture are those that don't align with mission, strategy, and goals, but we will skip further examples for now and get into the heart of the matter.

Topics in "the Environment"

The essence of what went wrong in the previous example is that the consultants ran afoul of factors in the environment that the process operates in—beliefs, culture, management style, and core competencies is our usual list, and those are the factors we will look at now. In the interest of brevity we'll treat the interdependent topics of beliefs, culture, and management style as one. Note that this isn't our first look at environmental factors—we have already covered some important ones when we described mission, strategy, and goals prior to process discovery, and in this chapter when we looked at differentiation for the enterprise and individual processes.

Because there isn't a specific point in our methodology where you will "study the environment," we had trouble placing this topic. Ideally, you would have this information up front, but for the most part, you won't be confident in it until you've seen the organization at work. That reflects how you will use this material on your project—not at a single point, but as factors that you'll keep in mind throughout, recording observations as you go. If you are familiar with the organization (e.g., you work there), you will be able to document the environment earlier in the project. If you are new to the organization (e.g., this is your first consulting assignment there), you will do this later after you have had more exposure to the environment.

And now, the disclaimers. Each topic could span volumes on its own, so our brief treatment will not even be close to the level you'd get in, say, an M.B.A. class on organizational development. And we're not pretending to be experts in these areas—we barely qualify as dilettantes. We can, however, say that the short time spent on these topics has helped immeasurably in guiding us on process improvement, application development, and other consulting assignments, because

- They provide context for establishing process goals.
- They are essential for understanding the current process—a process design feature might be baffling if you observed it in one organization but be the best choice at another.
- They will be critical when you are designing the to-be process—improvement suggestions have to be evaluated in the context of skills, culture, and so on.

Beliefs, Culture, and Management Style

Here is a huge topic we will reduce to a few paragraphs and a list of questions. Let's begin with a definition—French and Bell offer a good one: "By…culture…we mean prevailing patterns of values, attitudes, beliefs, assumptions, expectations, activities, interactions, norms, and sentiments (including feelings) and as embodied in artifacts. By including artifacts we include technology in our definition" [5]. We reduce it to the essence, "behavioral norms." All organizations have a culture, whether it is explicitly stated or unconscious. You might regard it as negative or positive, as did one client who stated, "At our organization, culture is spelled with a K." In any case, you ignore it at your peril.

We have already given an example where a process didn't match the culture or skills of the organization and therefore failed. But cultural misalignment can derail a project well before then. If the methods you employ in a project don't match the culture of the organization, any number of problems will arise. For instance, in one organization, it was a career-limiting move (CLM) to disagree publicly with anyone further up the hierarchy, even if everyone present knew that a statement was patently untrue or sheer fantasy. Clearly, the extensive use of facilitated sessions that we generally rely on was not going to work.

In a similar situation, one of us made a misstep that almost resulted in a project being canceled. A senior vice president of operations was in attendance, and everyone else seemed to be particularly docile. The vice president then made a statement that was so clearly wrong-headed, we thought he must have made it in order to stir up some discussion. We obliged by offering some alternative ideas. Whoops—wrong move. The vice president exploded in anger, and began walking out after noting, in colorful language, that the project ought to be canceled if we couldn't get our heads screwed on straight. Only a brave finance manager, two levels his junior in the organization, was able to calm him down. But in another organization, youthful and high-tech with an almost opposite culture, we were initially startled by the constant challenge of ideas by everyone at a project initiation meeting, no matter whose idea it was. Again, that was just the culture in action—challenge, sometimes for its own sake, was considered the best way to develop the best ideas.

Clearly, culture has a huge impact, and, as noted, it's not going to change without a huge effort championed by the most senior executives. That's why you should take at least a few minutes to describe it. Not a big study—in some cases, a mere 30 minutes of work is all it takes to get real benefits. Sometimes, there's a bit of a chicken-and-egg situation—if you're an outsider, you need to know something about the culture before you can decide how to go about discovering it. If so, observe for a while or arrange a discussion with a few trusted insiders. Then, based on your findings, you might either arrange a session with your project team or conduct a series of private interviews. In either case, don't fall into the trap of believing, without verifying, official statements on the subject. We worked with a company that professed to have "an open, inclusive culture that embraced informed risk-taking and valued the ideas and contributions of all…" As it turned out, it was a risk-averse, exclusionary, command-and-control hierarchy that wanted everyone to keep quiet and do as they were told. That example illustrates a point we'll get to in the summary—your assessment might best be left private, because it will not be flattering.

Everything Stems from Beliefs

Behavior at the aforementioned organization was motivated by a small number of central beliefs, including "management thinks, workers do." We find time and again that organizational behavior—what it does and how it does it—stems from a few basic beliefs, which we can also call assumptions or *paradigms*. Identifying these assumptions is so important that Chapter 1 of a 1991 Peter Drucker book [6] is "Management's New Paradigms." The first paragraph states: "BASIC ASSUMPTIONS ABOUT REALITY are the PARADIGMS of a social science, such as management. They are usually held subconsciously by the scholars, the writers, the teachers, the practitioners in the field. Yet those assumptions largely determine what the discipline—scholars, writers, teachers, practitioners—assumes to be reality." Drucker goes on to explain about paradigms: "They decide what in a given discipline is being paid attention to and what is neglected or ignored." And most important to our point here—"Yet, despite their importance, the assumptions are rarely analyzed, rarely studied, rarely challenged—indeed rarely even made explicit.

Drucker is dealing with the entire discipline of management and outlines seven prevailing assumptions that need to be challenged. Our focus is a little narrower—make explicit whatever beliefs, guiding principles, or paradigms you can at the organization you are working within. This shouldn't be—it *can't* be—a major undertaking that distracts from the purpose at hand. But it will indicate areas of opportunity or constraint. If some of the beliefs are "there's always a better way," "we have a bias toward informed action," and "decision making should be close to the action," then you are looking at an interesting project with many opportunities.

On the other hand, at one organization we ran an executive planning session, and the beliefs that emerged were "our clients are trying to cheat us, the public misunderstands us, and the media is out to get us." Unstated, but evident, was "and our employees couldn't care less." Whew! That certainly constrained the improvement options. At another session, the guiding principle was that above all, process and procedure (in the negative sense) had to be followed. That meant everyone could be engaged in the proverbial death march toward certain failure, and fully aware of it, but that was fine as long as protocol was obeyed. They aren't always negative—"everyone's opinion is valued and should be sought out" is a belief we've seen at some high-tech companies, and "the long-term relationship with the customer is more important than the profitability of any individual deal" was evident at a marketer of high-end properties.

Other Cultural Traits

After you have considered the issue of beliefs, you can ask a short list of questions to identify cultural traits that will impact both the methods you use on your project and the characteristics of the new process.

1. Are there stories or corporate legends that provide instructive examples? These might not be the stuff of Greek mythology—perhaps it's the tale of the

killer product developed in the skunk works, but it just as well could be the story of Ernie working all weekend, writing checks by hand, to get the payroll out after a catastrophic system failure. A quick online search will reveal that corporate storytelling is emerging as a "big thing."

2. What factors continually get in the way? Examples that we have encountered include the slow pace of decision making, political interference, the motivation and reward system, fear of change, a headlong rush to action, or the urge to study every point to death.

3. What factors are seen as expediting progress? This is often a shorter list than the preceding one but might include being free to make the right decision to satisfy a customer, never focusing on the short term at the expense of the long term, or always being given adequate time, resources, and authority to complete a job.

4. How are decisions made? From the top, as in the classic hierarchy, or is there more empowerment? Is there a greater emphasis on intuition or on facts? And are all employees free to offer opinions or challenge decisions made by their managers?

5. Is the orientation toward the individual or the group? This can have a huge impact on the pace of decision making—in some group-oriented organizations and cultures, progress can seem glacial because every decision requires soliciting everybody's input or calling a meeting. On the upside, rash decisions made without critical information can be avoided, and, once a decision is made, it is implemented smoothly.

6. Whose opinion is valued? In one company we worked at, we were reminded daily that "We're a marketing organization," and those who were close to customers and markets were the opinion leaders. At a different, techno-centric organization, we were told, "The geeks shall inherit the earth."

7. Are there any identifiable behaviors that are rewarded or punished? Note that reward (like punishment) can be explicit (positive job evaluations, promotions, raises, and awards) or implicit (praise, attention by management, input solicited for decisions, and plum assignments).

8. Is there a high tolerance for ambiguity? If there is low tolerance, then activities must be tightly scheduled, jobs well defined, lots of facts assembled for decisions, and so on.

9. Does the organization favor results or following procedure?

10. Is the organization cautious or will it take risks? Is it in the nature of the company to set outrageous goals as a way of inspiring people?

11. Is the emphasis on relationships and social interactions or on tasks and getting on with the job?

You do not need to answer all of these, and they are not the only questions. After you get a feel for an organization, use this list as a starting point to develop your own inquiries.

Core Competencies

What Are We Really Good At?

C. K. Prahalad and Gary Hamel introduced a new phrase—core competencies—into the language of business in their landmark *Harvard Business Review* article [7]. In it, the authors demonstrated that world-class organizations had up to five or six core competencies that formed the platform on which their core products and services were based. Interestingly, some of their observations parallel the advantages of process orientation over functional orientation:

- "Core competence is the collective learning in the organization, especially the capacity to coordinate diverse production skills and integrate streams of technologies. It is also a commitment to working across organizational boundaries." And…
- "Organizing around strategic business units is problematic because they under-invest in core competencies, imprison resources, and bind innovation."

A good example is 3M, with products like the tape and Post-its we couldn't work without. All are thin and involve coatings. 3M's core competencies, as described by Hamel and Prahalad, are:

- Substrates;
- Coatings;
- Adhesives.

Canon's core products are based on core competencies in:

- Precision mechanics;
- Fine optics;
- Microelectronics.

Again, we will take a concept that applies at the enterprise level and scale it down to the level of processes or areas within the enterprise. The people, departments, functions, and jobs that will "work" the process have areas of strength—core competencies. We remember the CEO of a manufacturing company bemoaning, "I don't think we *have* any core competencies," but he was wrong. Even in widely criticized government organizations like the one cited earlier at which the consultants tried to implement an unsuitable process, there are areas of real strength. In that case, it was high-volume transaction processing, as long as the right transaction got to the right job function. They were also very good at internal administrative processes. That was not likely to change in our lifetime, so the only sensible path was to design processes that played to the strengths of the performers and minimized the impact of weaknesses.

As in the section on culture, we suggest developing an explicit list of strengths (and weaknesses, if you're feeling brave) for the areas your process will span. This isn't something that will be done all at once—you might develop a draft version based on early observations and refine and extend it based on what you learn during initial assessment, modeling, and final assessment.

Don't let this and your other "environmental assessment" activities become an end in themselves—too much sensitivity might be raised if it became a formal, documented assessment. It could be unflattering or at odds with the prevailing self-image and be interpreted as a public report card on people's performance or aptitude. Although our usual philosophy is to "make it visible," these topics are often better kept to yourself or kept within your core team. A safe approach is to build informal lists of key points that you can refer to during the design of the new process and use (judiciously and with sensitivity!) to drive questions when process design alternatives arise that are at odds with the environment.

Now that we've covered the "squishy" topic of the environment, we'll go to the other end of the spectrum into the "hard" world of numbers. As with our look at the environment, capturing the numbers isn't an activity that's done all at once up front. Some of these you might have captured in the previous step (e.g., identifying the percentage of the total workload represented by each case of the process). Others can't be specified until later, such as the percentage of different types of customer complaints.

Measures

While completing the as-is process assessment, we also collect available information about process statistics—"the numbers"—which covers questions like how many, how often, how long, and so on. These measures, the basic operating statistics, will give us a feel for the dynamics of the process before starting workflow modeling. You might be able to capture baseline figures for some of these now (e.g., percentage of different types of triggering events), while others will have to wait until you have more information (e.g., the total number of participants in a process and the time worked by each). These simple *measures* may be elements that go into the calculation of more sophisticated *metrics* or *key performance indicators* (KPIs), but even fairly simple measures can provide useful guidance to focus our efforts. One of us once got well into as-is analysis without having captured the numbers, only to discover he had wasted time studying a case (a specific type of shipment) that was insignificant in every way—volume, resources consumed, and revenue. If you don't know how many and how much, do you really know if anything needs to change?

Another important reason to collect measures is to evaluate success after you have finished—they will be fundamental to determining critical performance metrics, and you will need this baseline against which to measure the performance of the new process. In some environments, this is crucial—without hard proof, there's no "good job!" and no support for your next initiative. But take care not to overemphasize certain task-based statistics—those that might become "perverse incentives" that encourage local optimization at the expense of overall improvement in the new process, or some other unanticipated consequence. Your organization might be awash in statistics, but readily available statistics generally relate to the performance of individual functions or activities, not the overall process. Staking an assessment on these will eventually cause grief. That also indicates why we always caution that the critical metrics used to monitor performance of the new process shouldn't be designed until goals are clearly stated and you understand how the process will operate. Using yesterday's metrics to monitor and manage tomorrow's process is a frequent cause of poorer-than-expected performance.

For now, collect those statistics that you can, and refine them as you go—you won't necessarily be able to capture certain numbers in the current environment. Often, someone such as a database administrator (DBA)[9] can provide statistics, such as volumes by transaction type. If your organization has a business intelligence (BI) environment with data relevant to your process, all the better. You might be able to develop some queries that provide the measures you need, which will depend at least in part on the process and the issues that come up in the rest of the initial assessment. Use the lists that follow to stimulate your thinking about the measures you'll try to locate.

How Many?

The essence of statistics is not standard deviations and Durbin-Watson coefficients, it's just counting. You must be able to at least count executions of your process at this point, because if you cannot count the process, either you don't understand it or it isn't a process.

The most basic counts involve volume (e.g., 800 per week). Typically, you will want to determine measures such as the following:

- Total volume or frequency (e.g., customer enrollments);
- Proportion of different cases (e.g., new versus reinstatement);
- Proportion of different paths (e.g., straight through versus credit or background check);
- Proportion of different results (e.g., accepted versus rejected).

Got the Time?

How much time does it take to complete your workflow? There are three ways to measure its execution: cycle time, work time, and time worked.

Cycle time is the total elapsed time, end to end, from the time the cycle starts or is triggered until the cycle completes with all results accomplished. It is the time measure most obvious and relevant to the customer. Note that there could be multiple cycle times, one for each stakeholder's result (e.g., cycle time to delivery of order to customer versus cycle time to receipt of payment by the enterprise).

Work time is the time the process is actually being worked on. Most processes have at least some time during which processes are waiting and not being worked on; if all this nonproductive time could be eliminated, cycle time and work time would be the same. This is the goal of straight-through processing. We have seen

---

9. Database administrators: a title commonly used by the people who are responsible for the design and tuning of your database. To tune, they need accurate counts of various record types, although often only at a high level.

cases where the work time was as little as 1 or 2 percent of the cycle time, a dismal statistic indeed.

Time worked counts the actual work hours expended on the process; sometimes more than one person (or other resource) is working on the process at a time: this measure would be the total hours paid for if workers are the resource being measured. If only one person at a time works on the process, work time and time worked are the same. Instead of people work time, you might need to measure work time with another resource, possibly time with a given machine or critical resource, especially if it is a bottleneck in your process.

You might also need to measure peaks and valleys—your critical load. Throughout the calendar cycle (weekday, week, month, year), there are usually times that are busier than others. Statisticians usually call these seasonal variations, because the most obvious variations are those that change with the season of the year. You might want to identify these seasonal variations clearly, and compare the difference between the three execution times (cycle time, work time, and time worked) on the peak versus in the valley. Interesting patterns emerge—in a busy time, time worked can go down significantly because everyone is working so hard, yet cycle times can rise dramatically because of queuing. Peaks and valleys also occur within a single work day. In some environments, the lunch hour gets very busy because clients are on a break from their job and are attending to personal business. In other environment, it gets very quiet over the lunch hour and very busy after.

These patterns will get even more interesting in terms of improvement opportunity when we track the opposite of execution time—wait time. There are four kinds of wait time: idle, transit, queue, and setup.

During *idle time*, the process is just waiting. Perhaps that's because the work is not on a critical path, or because it has not been routed expeditiously, or just because the process is designed that way. It may be that an actor is working on an unrelated but more important task.

Transit time is the time spent in transit between steps. Strictly speaking, when the work is being moved, that is a step in itself, but no other value is being added other than transport.

Queue time is the time an item is lined up before a critical or bottleneck resource: the work item is ready to go on, but is waiting for the resources for the next step to get to it. In a manufacturing environment, partially finished goods will stack up before a bottleneck machine during queue time.

Setup time is time required for a resource to switch from one type of task to another. This is also most obvious in a manufacturing situation—the operator might need to mount a different bit on a milling machine before beginning work on a new lot of a different product type. It is the same in an office environment when an operator sets up for a new type of transaction, possibly by assembling reference material and supplies, and staying within a specific function on the supporting system.

After you have done some as-is modeling, you will want to analyze wait time in the different phases of the process, for instance, trigger to initiation (i.e., how long before you even get started on the process) versus the time lapse between steps, concentrating on known delays at first. And as with all time measures, you will want to look at several measures—not just average or typical, but best and worst.

Who's Involved?

The number of people, organizations, and places involved in your process is a vital concern: for each new involvement, another handoff is required. And each handoff is an opportunity for something to go awry—our standard list is delay, error, and expense, each of which is irritating for customers, performers, owners, or other stakeholders. Some project estimating techniques recommend that you add some percentage, say 25 percent, to your estimate for your project for each new location involved. This reflects the additional complexity added by multiple locations. If applicable, consider the number of different languages and possibly time zones involved. Other factors might be applicable to your process, such as labor unions, countries, and cultures.

You won't have precise information until after as-is modeling (it's amazing how many additional actors will be discovered!), but this will be a start. Try listing and counting the following for your process:

- People;
- Job classifications;
- Departments;
- Total number of known handoffs;
- Labor unions;
- Locations;
- Languages;
- Countries and cultures;
- Whatever else is relevant.

Efficiency

No process is perfect. Typical measures of efficiency and effectiveness include the following:

- What is the percentage of scrap or rework, whether it's a physical or information item?
- What is the percentage of errors?
- How many defects are produced, and where are they produced? The later in the cycle they occur, the more costly they are.
- How soon are defects discovered? Early detection is important as it leads to less waste, since all work done on an item that is going to be scrapped is wasted.
- How much iteration does it take to get it right? In the worst case, it is the customer who discovers it.

- How many customer contacts are there to complete the process? Are you contacting the customer to get information you could have collected (or, even worse, did collect) before?
- How many compliments and complaints are received?

If appropriate, any of these can be further categorized by type, location, or other criteria. A simple tally sheet is often all you need to collect some information on issues or problems ("defects") that arise. After a few days during which performers tally each problem by type, you might be as surprised as we've been at how often the facts were different from perceptions.

Cost

It's not just the financial analysts that should be concerned with cost. Consider Goldratt's concept of true cost as expressed in his book, *The Goal* [8]. If a 5-cent gasket is keeping your most critical machine from running, the cost of that idleness could be millions of dollars, not pennies. If you can, get a rough measure of the cost per execution, and the cost of defects, both in scrap and rework, and in impact on the overall process. Also consider fixed versus variable cost. Fixed costs are those that you will pay even if you produce nothing (e.g., rent and property tax). Variable costs are those that vary with output: materials costs, discretionary labor cost, and so forth.

Note that cost is not a simple measure, but a more complex metric based on many individual measures and assumptions, so we're hesitant about even recommending that you consider it now. Most organizations already have cost figures available, which is why you can consider capturing them at this point, but be aware—until you've modeled the process and discovered the reality of who does what within it, your cost figures are likely to be misleading at best or downright wrong at worst. That's the whole point of activity-based costing (ABC),[10] which determines *true* cost of individual products or services by looking at the activities that are *actually* required, as opposed to relying on percentage-based allocations.

Summary of Measures

Avoid the urge to embark on a crusade for the numbers—the intent is to get a partial indication of process performance, preferably in measures that matter to the stakeholders, and possibly establish baseline as-is measures for comparison with post-implementation to-be measures. Collecting a lot of statistics is seldom helpful at this point—there's so much that you don't yet know about the process, it's quite likely that anything other than the basics will measure the wrong things. Detailed statistical measures will be much more useful after you're designed and implemented a new process and are tuning parts of it with statistical techniques like those employed in Six Sigma methods.

---

10. The original description of the idea is in a 1988 *Harvard Business Review* article. Cooper, R., and R. Kaplan, "Measure Costs Right: Make the Right Decisions," *Harvard Business Review,* September–October 1988

Potential Improvements

"Hey everyone, I have an idea…!"

Those words strike fear into the hearts of experienced process improvement facilitators. But why? Don't we want everyone participating, generating great ideas for the new and improved process? Yes, but not yet. Too often the "improvements" that are suggested early in the game, before the process is really understood, only address symptoms and not root causes, or they create "unanticipated consequences" and problems due to local optimization. Alec will never forget the time a participant in a process modeling session actually started to *code a solution* in Microsoft Access for a perceived problem in one of the process steps. In the new process, the step was eliminated, and the code never saw the light of day.

We deal with the situation by taking a phased approach:

1. When we initiate the process discovery and framing sessions, as described in Chapter 5, we stress in the guidelines that we're not looking for potential solutions at this time—there will be a dedicated time for that once more is known about the process. With luck, that will suffice, but…

2. Because people will naturally generate ideas when problems are identified, and we've just completed an activity in which a *lot* of problems will have been identified, improvement suggestions are going to come up in spite of point 1. When they do, we'll record them on a "parking lot" or "ideas for later consideration" flipchart. This will usually reassure someone that their idea has been recognized, and the session can proceed. We hope. But…

3. If the team insists on discussing a suggestion, or just launches into the usual analysis of how to implement it, we will set aside a time-boxed discussion (5 or 10 minutes) of the suggestion, but with specific rules—the suggestion must be clearly defined, and then (and this is the key point) specific pros and cons of the proposed change must be identified. Sometimes we even put a numeric target on it, (e.g., the group must identify five benefits and five detriments that the suggestion would bring). This is generally enough to demonstrate that more work is needed or that implementation is more involved than it first appeared. (To stress that point, you can have people evaluate the suggestion with respect to each enabler, as we'll do in Chapter 14.)

If you get this far, and it appears that there are real benefits, no significant detriments, and implementation isn't problematic, you can consider moving the idea into the "quick wins" category and hand it off to an operations team for further assessment (we hope) and implementation. Just remember, your responsibility is to keep the group moving toward a thorough yet timely analysis of the process, without getting distracted by "bright and shiny objects" (the proverbial "low hanging fruit") along the way. We're not advocating "paralysis by analysis"—our entire methodology is designed to get you through a process improvement project with no frustration and wasted time. Our reluctance to follow up on quick wins is based on the experience that too many "quick wins" end up being neither "quick" nor "wins"—they undermine the larger effort and have unanticipated consequences. Processes are complex beasts, with many subtle and invisible moving parts, so changes must be made with care. Presumably, you're working on an important process that deserves this care, and Chapter 14 will provide concrete methods. We've worked with people who were responsible for searching out quick wins or doing Six Sigma analysis of activities within a process who realized after working through examples with us that much of what they had accomplished was actually harmful to the end-to-end business process. In one memorable case, we conducted an executive briefing on the most common errors in process improvement. One of the executives became visibly upset (distraught, not angry) and was eager to share the reason with the group. He explained that he had recently completed a two-year global initiative called, ironically, "Quick Wins," and he could now see clearly that at least half of the "wins" his team implemented were actually harmful to the overall process and the company. Think about that unsettling realization when the urge to go for a quick win arises.

One Poster Is Worth a Thousand Words

Summarizing Findings

Now that you know what you are going to do and why, it is time to summarize your findings and direction so everyone can see them at a glance. A useful tool is the process summary poster, which takes the main elements of framing the process—the process scope and contents, and the case for action, vision, and differentiator—and puts them on a single piece of paper or image. The reasons to do so are threefold:

1. A certain percentage of people you need to reach are not going to read more than a one-pager anyway.
2. If you provide contact information, it can encourage valuable feedback.
3. If it's well done, it will be posted in the workplace, the cafeteria, in halls and elevators, in the washrooms, on notice boards, in meeting rooms, on Web pages, or wherever else people might see it.

For people who are directly involved in your project, it will help to keep them on track and in scope. For everyone else, especially those who might be impacted, it will keep them informed and provide a basis for feedback. Prepare your poster in a professional manner, and then distribute it far and wide. Variations on the quadrant format in Figure 7.3 work well. Note that in the lower left, we've listed participants and mechanisms—the systems, forms, reports, and equipment that support the process. Sometimes, we have listed potential enablers (possible improvements) instead, to trigger discussion, but in many environments, it's a bad idea. Along with the other dangers of premature improvement ideas that we've discussed already, it can stir up fear and uncertainty, and give people the idea that the outcome is decided, so there's no point in participating. On balance, we'd stick with actors and mechanisms, or whatever factors are relevant in the situation.

It Matters!

We hope that this chapter has illustrated the importance of carefully articulating process issues and goals from different perspectives. As well, we hope that, although

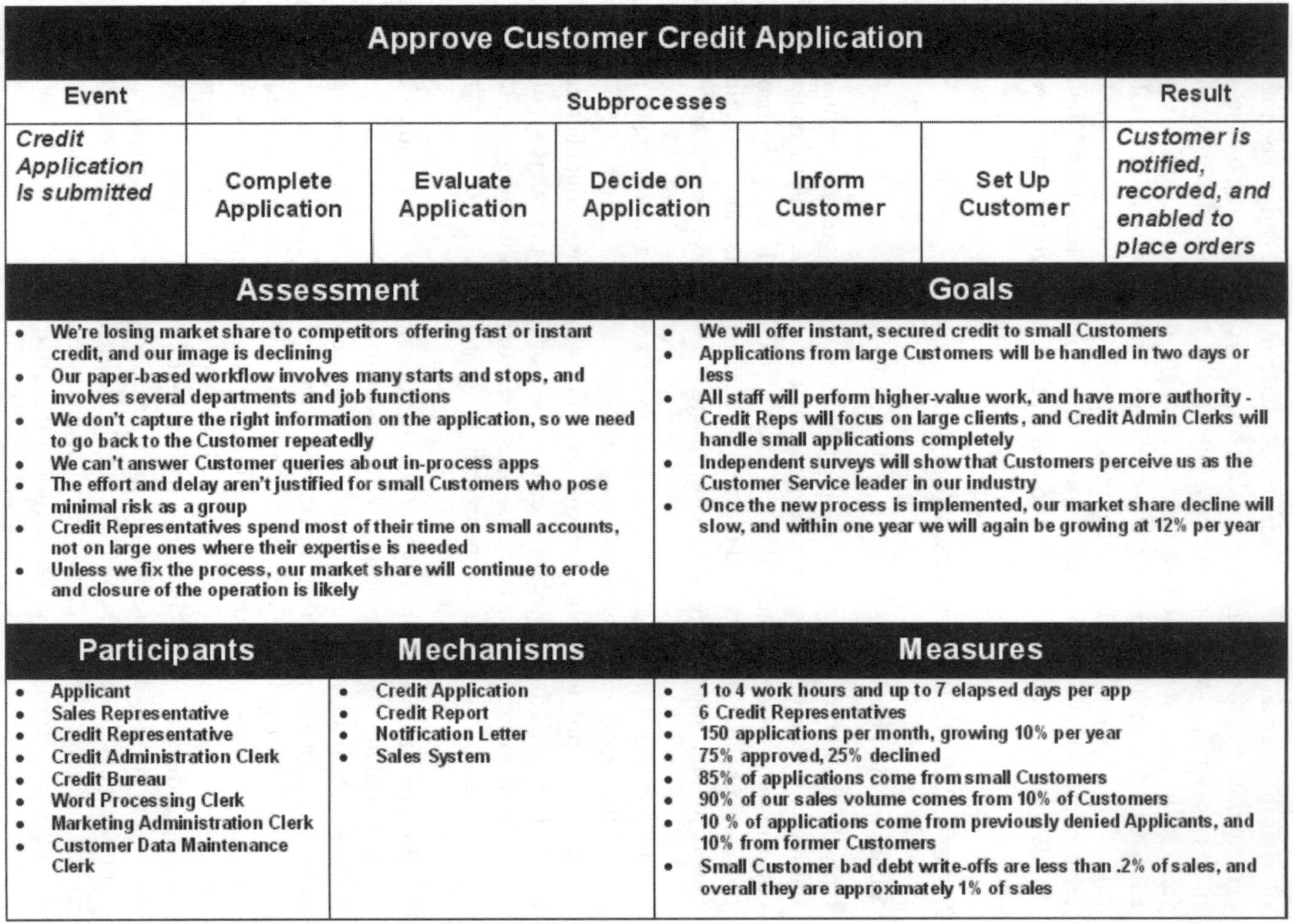

Approve Customer Credit Application

Event	Subprocesses					Result
	Complete Application	Evaluate Application	Decide on Application	Inform Customer	Set Up Customer	
Credit Application Is submitted						*Customer is notified, recorded, and enabled to place orders*

Assessment

- We're losing market share to competitors offering fast or instant credit, and our image is declining
- Our paper-based workflow involves many starts and stops, and involves several departments and job functions
- We don't capture the right information on the application, so we need to go back to the Customer repeatedly
- We can't answer Customer queries about in-process apps
- The effort and delay aren't justified for small Customers who pose minimal risk as a group
- Credit Representatives spend most of their time on small accounts, not on large ones where their expertise is needed
- Unless we fix the process, our market share will continue to erode and closure of the operation is likely

Goals

- We will offer instant, secured credit to small Customers
- Applications from large Customers will be handled in two days or less
- All staff will perform higher-value work, and have more authority - Credit Reps will focus on large clients, and Credit Admin Clerks will handle small applications completely
- Independent surveys will show that Customers perceive us as the Customer Service leader in our industry
- Once the new process is implemented, our market share decline will slow, and within one year we will again be growing at 12% per year

Participants

- Applicant
- Sales Representative
- Credit Representative
- Credit Administration Clerk
- Credit Bureau
- Word Processing Clerk
- Marketing Administration Clerk
- Customer Data Maintenance Clerk

Mechanisms

- Credit Application
- Credit Report
- Notification Letter
- Sales System

Measures

- 1 to 4 work hours and up to 7 elapsed days per app
- 6 Credit Representatives
- 150 applications per month, growing 10% per year
- 75% approved, 25% declined
- 85% of applications come from small Customers
- 90% of our sales volume comes from 10% of Customers
- 10 % of applications come from previously denied Applicants, and 10% from former Customers
- Small Customer bad debt write-offs are less than .2% of sales, and overall they are approximately 1% of sales

Figure 7.3   A "poster" summarizing the results of framing the process.

it was brief, we've provided some tools to clarify the environment your process will be working in, because *it really makes a difference!*

And now, at long last, we've framed the process and can get on to the central topic of modeling the workflow of business processes.

References

[1]   Hammer, M., and J. Champy, *Reengineering the Corporation*, New York: HarperBusiness, 1993.

[2]   Treacy, M., and F. Wiersma, *The Discipline of Market Leaders*, Reading, MA: Addison-Wesley, 1995.

[3]   Table adapted from *Fortune*, February 6, 1995, p. 96.

[4]   DeMarco, T., and T. Lister, *Peopleware: Productive Projects and Teams*, New York: Dorset House, 1987, pp. 40–43.

[5]   French, W. L., and C. H. Bell, Jr., *Organization Development: Behavioral Science Interventions for Organization Improvement*, Englewood Cliffs, NJ: Prentice-Hall, 1984.

[6]   Drucker, P. F., *Management Challenges for the 21st Century*, New York: HarperBusiness, 1999.

[7]   Prahalad, C. K., and G. Hamel, "The Core Competence of the Corporation," *Harvard Business Review*, May–June 1990, pp. 79–91.

[8]   Goldratt, E., *The Goal: A Process of Ongoing Improvement*, Great Barrington, MA: North River Press, 1984.

PART III

Phase 2: Understand the As-Is Process

CHAPTER 8

Process Workflow Models: The Essentials

Overview

The *Real* Purpose of This Section

This chapter—in fact, the whole section—is about the nuts and bolts of swimlane diagrams. Components and conventions, controlling detail, tricky situations, and running a modeling session will all be covered over the next four chapters. But what really matters is that you absorb a philosophy of swimlane diagramming that will help you avoid the three most common problems:

1. Being unclear on the real purpose of a workflow model;
2. Committing the sin of deception by sanitization;
3. Descending into overwhelming detail.

Once you understand point 1, you'll be able to strike what seems to be the difficult balance between points 2 and 3. "Deception by sanitization" is the phrase we coined to describe the situation when a workflow modeler omits some of the actors because "their role isn't significant" or "they don't actually add value to the process." It's a very dangerous thing to do, but avoiding it would seem to push you toward point 3—overwhelming detail. Rest assured, the balance can be struck, especially if you burn these philosophies into your brain, each corresponding to one of the previous problems:

1. The purpose of a workflow model is to show the flow of work.
2. Show *every* actor that holds the work while it flows through the process.
3. Flow first, details later.

Each used the word *flow*, and one of the key lessons of this chapter will be that although the name of the technique includes the words *work* and *flow*, our approach places a priority on *flow*. People get into all sorts of problems by missing the point that you need to focus on the flow before diving into the work.

The Practical Side

As we said, this chapter covers the nuts and bolts—or the boxes and lines—of a process workflow model (PWM), a workflow process model (WPM), or, simply, a "swimlane diagram." It provides the rules and guidelines for using the basic components—actors, steps, and flow—and the next three chapters will preempt any difficulties by addressing the problems that normally arise. Chapter 9 illustrates techniques for managing progressive detail, and Chapter 10 addresses the most common questions and difficulties. Chapter 11 will tell you how to build a workflow model with the participation of content experts. Throughout these chapters, we encourage you to experiment with modeling parts of processes you are already familiar with—"modeling from memory," as it were—to get a feel for the techniques.

Swimlane Diagrams—What and Why

What's the Attraction?

There are several formats for diagramming a business process, but like most people in the business, we opt for the swimlane diagram format. As described in Chapter 3, swimlane diagrams have become very popular because they highlight the relevant variables—who, what, and when—in a simple notation that requires little or no training to understand. Because they specifically show the actors who are involved in the process, a higher level of involvement and buy-in is likely. This is a significant difference with other styles of modeling that concentrate on the essence of the process. The point is that when we ID processes, we have to focus on "what," but when we seek to understand processes, we need to factor in the "who, how, and when" as well. Too many process analysts miss this point and continue to focus on the "essential" activities.

Swimlane diagrams are intended to show an entire business process from beginning to end and can be used both to understand the as-is workflow and to design and depict the to-be workflow. They can show a process at any level, from a very high-level view, depicting only the points of involvement by the actors (participants in the process), down to one showing each individual task. A well-crafted swimlane diagram, one that follows important philosophies and practices that we intend to indoctrinate you in, ensures discussions are grounded in fact. They depict what *really* happens for the as-is or what is *really* proposed for the to-be. This is crucial, because in practice virtually no one understands a complete business process, and most don't even have a full understanding of their "neighborhood" in the process.

What Are They?

These diagrams, with slight variations, go by many names:

- Process workflow model (or workflow process model);
- Swimlane diagram;
- Process map;
- Process responsibility diagram (PRD);
- Responsibility process matrix (RPM);
- Functional deployment chart;
- People-process chart;
- Line of visibility (LOV) chart;

- Activity Diagram in Unified Modeling Language (UML);
- Business Process Diagram (BPD) in Business Process Modeling Notation (BPMN).

In this book we stick with the terms *swimlane diagram* and *process workflow model*, or simply *workflow model*. A reminder—we're using the term "workflow" in its traditional sense, to describe the flow of work, which in no way implies the use of any particular technology, such as a workflow management system, a document management system, or a business process management system. As long as work flows among multiple actors, which might be any combination of people, systems, machines, or other mechanisms, the workflow models we'll describe are appropriate.

Swimlane diagrams show what is done, by whom, in what sequence—"who, does what, when." It is common in the workflow (as a technology) field to say that workflow models depict the three R's—roles, rules, and routes. In line with our "actors, steps, and flow" framework, we prefer to think of the three R's as roles, responsibilities, and routes:

- Roles are the actors who complete steps in the process.
- Responsibilities are the individual steps that each actor performs.
- Routes are the flows and decisions that connect the steps and therefore define the path (or route) that an individual work item will take through the process.

As Figure 8.1 shows, each actor in the process gets their own, labeled swimlane, delineated by solid or dotted lines according to your preference or modeling tool. Each step is represented by a rectangle, usually with rounded corners, placed in the swimlane of the actor that does it. Arrows indicate the flow of work—the sequence and dependency—among the steps.

Compared to other workflow models you have seen, this example might differ by following three important conventions for business-oriented swimlane diagramming that we will return to again and again:

1. Sequence and dependency (time) flow from *left to right*.
2. Use the *simplest* possible set of symbols.
3. Show *every* actor that holds the work.

Figure 8.2 summarizes this.

At this point, you may be wondering, "If these diagrams are so simple and intuitive, why do we need an entire chapter, much less four chapters, to explain them?" The obvious answer is that reading a properly done swimlane diagram is straightforward, but producing one isn't, for a variety of reasons. We're going to begin by looking at three examples, each of which makes a particular point about the philosophy or approach that you need in order to be really successful with the technique. Each example is illustrated in the context of a common problem:

1. Missing the central philosophy—that a model that shows the flow of work and nothing more can be a valuable model indeed;

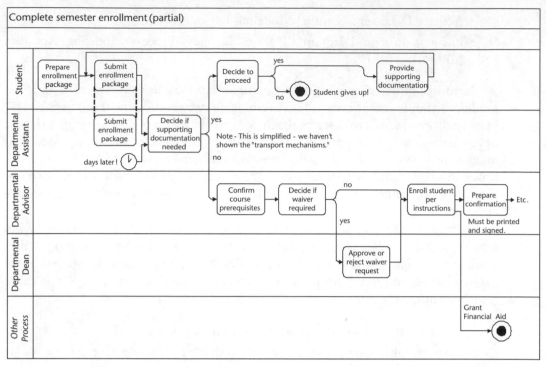

Figure 8.1   A simple swimlane diagram.

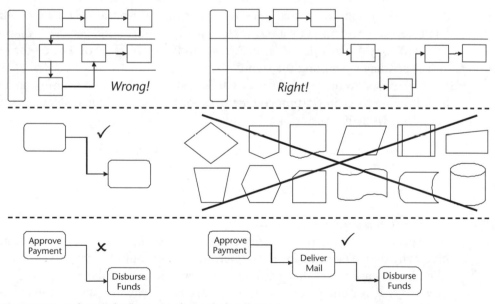

Figure 8.2   Left to right flow, simple symbols, all actors.

2. Not having methods to get through development of a workflow model without getting dragged into the details;

3. Being unable to model certain situations that will invariably arise.

Example 1: The Essence of Workflow Modeling

We were engaged in a process improvement initiative at a major forensic sciences laboratory and had just introduced swimlane diagrams during a facilitated session. The scientist who ran the DNA section was immediately excited about the possibilities afforded by these diagrams, which pleased us no end, so we asked, "Why?" First, she had us confirm some terminology, which was that a flow between actors was referred to as a "handoff." Then, she explained that quality control is immensely important in all forensic testing, especially in DNA testing, and every handoff was a point where things could go wrong—delay, loss, contamination, and so on. A model that showed the sequence of handoffs for various testing processes could therefore be a valuable tool for quality control.

We were impressed at this immediate insight, but were even more impressed ("stunned" was more like it) after the next break during which she and one of her scientists built a workflow model for a core DNA process. It covered the entire process, from submission of a sample by the police through to reporting of the result back to the police, and it took them *less than 10 minutes to complete!* And this was while they enjoyed their tea and biscuits! Figure 8.3 shows a cleaned up version, suitable for inclusion in the book, but we've changed nothing of the content. It's Alec's favorite workflow model ever, because it's such a perfect example of a model that shows *only* the flow of work and, because of that, illustrates a great deal about the behavior of a process. We especially appreciated that they didn't try to draw step boxes, much less put names on them—they just drew a dot to indicate "the work goes here" and then moved on. It's almost a minimalist work of art in the sense that you could take very little away and still have a meaningful drawing.

At conferences and workshops, we like to display a picture of the original diagram alongside a complex, technically oriented process diagram and ask, "Which one actually conveys more information about the process?" There's no doubt that it's the simple one we've shown here, which never fails to raise questions about the reasons behind all the to-ing and fro-ing it illustrates.

This model, which really gets at the essence of the process flow, was produced in less than 10 minutes by two female scientists. We've often wondered, somewhat uncharitably, what two male technologists or engineers would produce in the same time. Once they got past arguing about the right modeling convention to use, that is.

Example 2: Getting to the Essence Without Diving into Detail

You might like the previous example, but think "I could never do that at my company—everyone always dives for the details and the exceptions." Actually, you probably could produce a diagram like this with a minimum of fuss and bother. We have been able to do that repeatedly, and in environments like high tech and health care, where everyone always wants to go for the details or the exceptions. The key is to let a group know, up front, that you're going to trace the flow of work through the process, without details, before coming back to find out what all the participants actually do. Then, you ask these three questions, each time completing one pass through the entire process, from trigger to result:

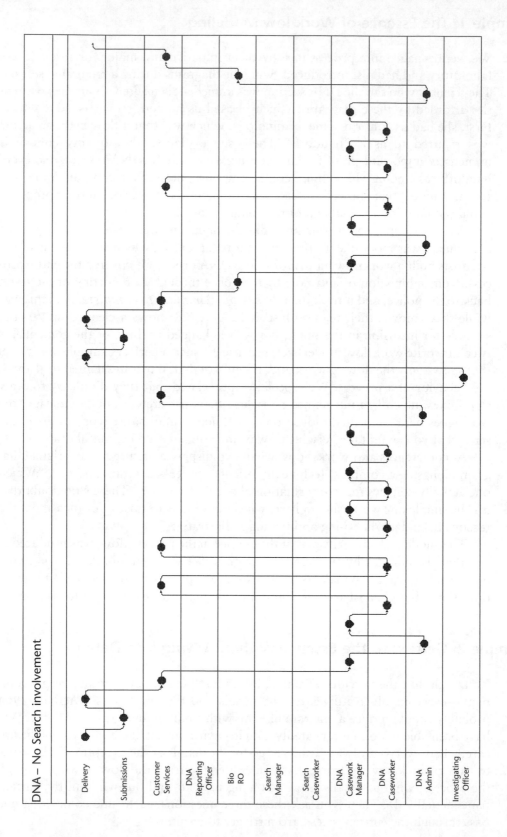

Figure 8.3 The 10-minute swimlane diagram.

1. "Who gets the work next?" Do not, under any circumstances, stop to ask, "What do you do?"
2. "How does it get there?"
3. "Who *really* gets the work next?"

Ideally, there's a little more subtlety and setup involved, but that's the essence. Let's look at a real example.

A mid-sized western municipality knew that it had serious problems in its "issue building permit" process. Issuing a residential building permit could take six months, and a commercial property, multifamily dwelling, or mixed-use project could take up to a year. Complaints were common, but the real problem was that new development had fallen off. This was a particular concern because the downtown business district had been in decline for some time and was shabby enough that even residents of the municipality were increasingly going to malls or business districts in surrounding communities. The municipality desperately wanted to attract the kind of mixed-use developments, with retail space on the ground floor and two or three residential floors above, which had been so successful in revitalizing other areas. The problem was that because it took so long to get a building permit, developers were not inclined to assemble property and arrange financing only to wait for a year for a permit. Among other initiatives to attract development, the municipality undertook to improve their Issue Building Permit process.

The first attempt didn't work out so well. They hired a nationally known consulting firm, reputedly with expertise in process redesign, that produced a stack of diagrams that were indecipherable to all concerned. At that point, we were called in to help out. Much of their budget had already been spent, so we had to dive into process modeling without time for the usual framing. Nonetheless, it went very well. We arranged a session and set about developing a workflow model using our standard three questions. Our intent wasn't to get at the details of everyone's work, but to establish the overall flow as a framework for subsequent analysis. Here's how it unfolded, beginning with the first question:

Question 1: "Who Gets the Work Next?"

The purpose of this question is to force forward motion through the process, toward the result for the customer, without stopping for any discussion of what participants do in the process. Whenever there are flows in multiple directions, or decisions with alternate flows (i.e., a decision point), we always follow the main, sunny-day case that leads toward the result for the customer of the process. In the following, we'll tell you a little more about what each actor does than we let people bring up in the session, because it will help illustrate an important point. The extra information is in parentheses. The following is the essence of how the conversation went, with each numbered point illustrated on Figure 8.4:

1. "What starts the process?" The builder prepares a permit application.
2. "Who gets it next?" There is a meeting of the builder and the permit control clerk (at city hall, during which the application is submitted and fees are collected).

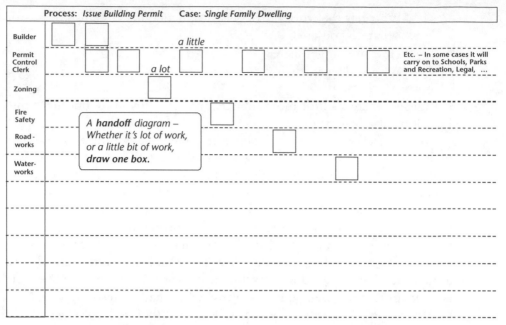

Figure 8.4 The workflow model after question 1: "Who gets the work next?"

3. "Who gets it next?" The permit control clerk (takes the application back to his or her desk and prepares the appropriate routing slip for the application, which in this case is for a single family dwelling, and sends it on to the first stop).

4. "Who gets it next?" The Zoning department (which does a lot of complex work involving checking fit within the official community plan, confirming setbacks, assessing site coverage and floor space area, and completing several arcane calculations such as average roof height, upper floor setback ratio, and even assessment of subterranean volume).

5. "Who gets it next?" The permit control clerk (who ticks off a box on the routing slip and forwards the application to the next stop).

6. "Who gets it next?" Fire Safety (who also do some fairly sophisticated calculations that balance sidewall glass area, roofing and siding materials, and the need for residential sprinklers).

7. "Who gets it next?" The permit control clerk (who ticks off a box on the routing slip and forwards the application to the next stop).

8. "Who gets it next?" Engineering (who consider issues such as road access, curbing, and cutting into existing sidewalks).

9. "Who gets it next?" The permit control clerk (who ticks off a box on the routing slip and forwards the application to the next stop).

10. "Who gets it next?" Waterworks (who confirm the fixture count is within limits, and estimates fresh water consumption and waste water outflow, calculating estimated charges for each—hence the department's unofficial motto "we get you coming and going").

11. "Who gets it next?" The permit control clerk (who ticks off a box on the routing slip and might forward the application to other areas such as Parks

and Recreation, or Education, but we've gone far enough to establish the basic pattern).

Figure 8.4 is hardly a completed workflow model, ready for detailed analysis, but here's the surprise—it actually told the clients more about their process than the excruciatingly detailed diagrams the original reengineers produced. To prove the point, sit down with a coworker, look over the diagram, and see how many questions about policy and practice the diagram raises. We'll come back to this later on.

Another key point—you will have noticed that some of the actors do a little bit of work, while others do a lot of work, yet the diagrams show a single box in either case. Why in the world would we make it appear that Zoning and the permit control clerk do the same amount of work? Answer—because it doesn't matter. All we're trying to accomplish at this point is depict the flow of work—the sequence of handoffs—regardless of how much or how little any actor does. That's why we call the diagram we've just produced a *handoff diagram* (or *level 1 diagram*). The guiding principle is (memorize this!) "whenever an actor holds the work, whether they do a *lot* or a *little*, draw *one* box and *move on*." This is the key to getting through the process before eyes glaze over or you keel over.

Question 2: "How Does It Get There?"

Typically, after using the first question to trace a flow through the process, the core participants have been identified, but there may be many more actors involved. The purpose of the next question is to uncover some of those actors, especially those who help by moving the work along. Every time there is a flow, and especially when it appears to be a handoff between actors, ask how the work gets from one actor to the next. Let's see what happened in our example:

1. There's a flow from the builder to the meeting between the builder and the permit control clerk. "How does it get there?" The builder carries the application to the meeting, so no new actor is involved.
2. There's a flow from the meeting between the builder and the permit control clerk to the permit control clerk. "How does it get there?" The permit control clerk carries the application back to their desk, so no new actor is involved.
3. There's a flow from permit control clerk to zoning. "How does it get there?" Well, now things get interesting. It turns out that:
    a. The application is placed in the permit control clerk's outbox and is picked up by Administrative Services. Even if their next stop is Zoning, they are prohibited by the collective agreement from delivering the application, because that would be "sorting," which can only be done by the folks in the Mailroom. So…
    b. …the application is taken to the Mailroom, where it is logged and sorted into a delivery cart for…
    c. …Administrative Services, who deliver it to Zoning on their scheduled delivery run.

4. There's a flow from Zoning to the permit control clerk. "How does it get there?" Again, the work must go through Administrative Services, the Mailroom, and Administrative Services before it returns to the permit control clerk, who is going to put a tick on the routing slip and turn the application over to Administrative Services... You can see how this is unfolding.

The workflow model to this point is illustrated in Figure 8.5. We now know more about the reality of the process, but there's still more to learn.

Question 3: "Who *Really* Gets the Work Next?"

Even if you did a careful job of framing the process, which we didn't in this example, there will still be other actors in the process you haven't identified yet. The third question helps uncover more of them. Whenever the work has been shown to flow to a particular actor, simply ask if it *really* goes directly to that actor, or if someone or something else (such as systems or other mechanisms) is involved. Here's what happened in our building permit example:

1. At the front end, the work involved the builder and the permit control clerk, so there were no changes to the diagram.
2. We refined the names of the next two actors to administrative services clerk and mailroom technician, but there were no new actors involved.
3. Now it got interesting. We found out that the actor who did the assessment was the zoning compliance officer, but the work didn't go directly there. It first went to the zoning administrative assistant, and then to the zoning manager before going on to the zoning compliance officer, who then completed their assessment. After that, it went directly to the zoning administrative

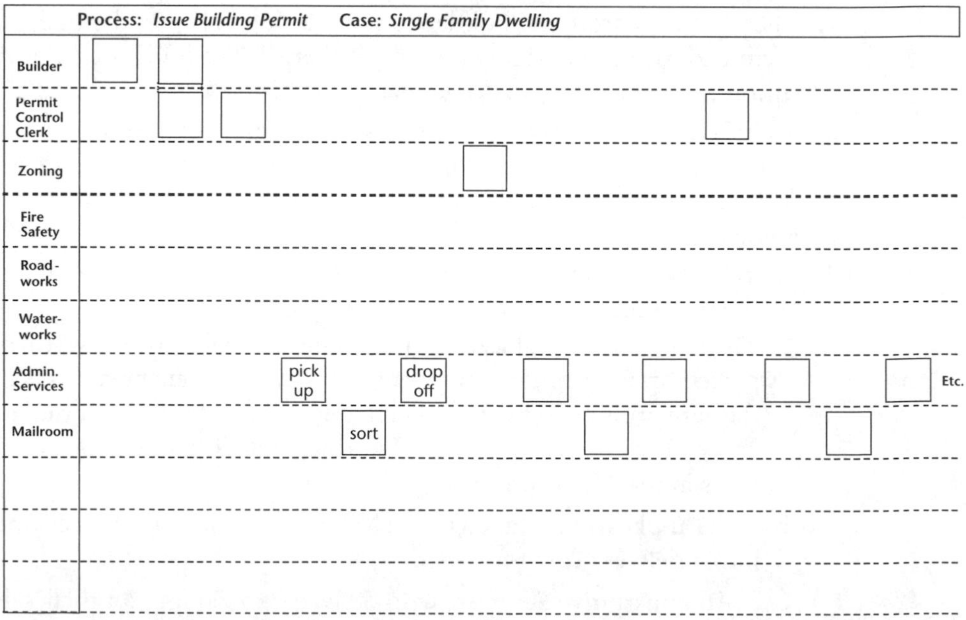

Figure 8.5   The workflow model after question 2: "How does it get there?"

assistant before being picked up by the administrative services clerk and carrying on through the process.

Figure 8.6 shows the emerging workflow model, although there's still more to be done. When this initial pass through the process was completed, after an investment of an hour or two, there were roughly 20 actors identified and the process was much better understood than it had been after many (expensive) hours of detailed modeling by the reengineers. You would be amazed at how often we've been able to complete workflow modeling in a few hours by following this approach. It's not that such a diagram, illustrating the sequence of handoffs, answers all questions, but it's often enough to establish that the workflow is a disaster, or, sometimes, that it's essentially just fine. Either way, it provides a framework that illustrates all actors and their points of involvement and provides a basis for assessing other factors (the enablers) impacting process performance.

What Did We Learn from This Example?

This was a fine example of how a simple workflow model can provide a framework for discovering the real problem, which might not be workflow at all. After the initial pass through the process (after question 1), if you identified questions about policy and practice as we suggested, you might have uncovered the following:

- Are there dependencies among the assessments? For instance, does Fire Safety care what Zoning said about the application? Answer: No, the assessments are totally independent.

- Could the assessments actually be carried out in parallel? Answer: Yes, in fact, they used to be done that way.

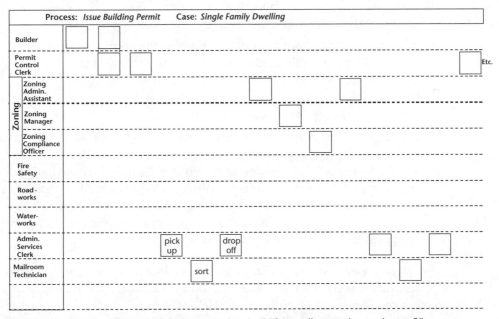

Figure 8.6 The workflow model after question 3: "Who *really* gets the work next?"

- Why, then, are the assessments carried out sequentially? Answer: Because there is only one copy of the plans accompanying the application, so only one department can use it at a time.

- Why aren't multiple copies of the plans submitted by the builder? Answer: Well, actually, we used to get multiple copies of the plans from the builder and send them to all departments at once.

- Okay, why did you stop having the builder submit multiple copies of the plans? Answer: Copying multiple sets of plans used to be quite expensive and could add up to many hundreds of dollars even for a single family dwelling, so when there was a recession several years ago, we waived the requirement for multiple copies as a way of giving the builders a break.

- Well, that explains a few things. Now, why does the application package go back to the permit control clerk after each assessment? Answer: For tracking purposes. When we first implemented the "single copy" process, we had the plans go directly from Zoning to Fire Safety to Engineering and so on. However, builders were forever phoning the permit control clerk and asking where their plans were, so as a service to the builders, we changed the process so the package went back to the permit control clerk after every assessment. That way, the permit control clerk can maintain a log and answer any questions about where the application package is.

- That leads to another question—if the permit application fails an assessment at any point, what happens? Is the builder notified? Answer: No. Back when there were multiple copies of the plans, we waited until all assessments were complete before notifying the builder, and they seemed to prefer it that way. We carried on with that practice after we went to the single copy process.

- So if an application fails an assessment, it just keeps going, without the builder being notified? Answer: Yes.

- And where does an application most commonly fail? Answer: At the first assessment, in Zoning. (And then it just keeps on going...)

- All right, just two more questions. First, if the admin services clerk picks up something that is addressed to one of the later stops on their route, why don't they just deliver it instead of taking it back to the Mailroom? Answer: Because that would constitute "sorting," and according to the collective agreement, only people in the Mailroom can do that.

- Second, does the zoning manager receive the application so they can assign it to the most appropriate compliance officer? Answer: No, the zoning manager simply "reviews" the application to stay "in the loop" with what's going on in the community. Each compliance officer is responsible for certain neighborhoods, so all applications for the same neighborhood will be assessed by the same compliance officer (which results in some compliance officers being very busy, while others have very little to do).

We haven't even started to consider factors like how long the work sits in each step, but, surprisingly, we have derived a lot of value and information from a simple model. Even more surprisingly, the model is "wrong" in the sense that it doesn't show all steps or flow, is still missing actors, and so on. It's a nice illustration of an observation made by Professor George Box[1] that is frequently paraphrased as "all models are wrong, but some are useful." The central point of this example is that a simple workflow model, one that shows only (sorry to be repetitive) the flow of work for a single pass through a process, provides a framework that ensures more comprehensive assessment, and then understanding, of the process. This is illustrated further in Chapter 13 when we look at assessment by enabler. In the building permit example, it was clear that the workflow was excessively sequential, depended a lot on manual transit of work items, with too much tracking and control built into the main flow. That, however, was because it was based on policies and practices that in turn were based on outdated assumptions about what was important to the builder, the customer of the process. They wanted timely assessments, not savings on copying costs. It also helped us uncover one of the central problems, that workload was assigned by neighborhood so it was not balanced across available staff. By the way, we recognize that we're not finished yet. The steps have to be named properly, and there's *another* five questions we'll go through in Chapter 11 to validate and extend the model so it shows all the flows and steps, not just a single path. Often, we'll also need to go to another level of detail, as described in the next chapter.

Example 3: "How Do I Depict...?"

At RB Tel (the Really Big Telephone Company), all sorts of people and departments are involved in customer contact activities. Analysts have determined the responsibilities of various departments, as described in the following paragraphs. You'll get more out of the coming chapters if you take 15 minutes now, as an exercise, to develop a simple swimlane diagram from this information. This is an old example, based on a more paper-oriented process than one would typically see at a telephone company, but the essence of the process remained the same after the paper forms were automated.

Customer Service...

...is primarily responsible for assisting customers who are having difficulty with an RB Tel service. When a customer calls RB Tel's main customer inquiry number, they respond to prompts from an interactive voice response (IVR) unit, and service difficulties are routed to the next available customer service representative (service rep) (other matters—billing, service, disconnect, employment—are routed to the appropriate department). The service rep identifies the customer and enters this information on a call log record (CLR) form. After the customer describes the problem, the call can be handled in a number of ways. If the customer simply doesn't know how to use a particular feature, such as call forwarding, the service rep will assist the customer and record the details in the call log. (If the customer also asks about products or services, that is noted in the call log as well.) The CLR is

---

1.   Professor Box is a preeminent statistician, active in the fields of quality and process improvement. He cofounded the Center for Quality and Productivity Improvement (CQPI) in 1985. See http://www.engr. wisc.edu/centers/cqpi/.

then placed in the rep's "completed" tray. If the rep concludes that the problem is equipment related or requires a software change at the central office switch, the call is transferred to Repair Services, and the CLR is placed in the "pending resolution" tray. If the customer needs phone service connected, disconnected, or changed, the call is routed to a new service specialist, also within Customer Service; CLRs are also placed in the "pending resolution" tray. Note that when a new service specialist deals with a call that was transferred from a service rep, they complete a form describing how the call was resolved and so the service reps can close out their "pending resolution" CLRs.

The CLRs are picked up twice a day, and sent to Marketing Support, which is essentially a data entry department. They are entered into the service tracking system, and any that were "pending resolution" are printed and sent back to Customer Service, to await information from other departments that handled the call.

Repair Service...

...is staffed by inside repair technicians who handle trouble reports from customers who have either called directly or been transferred from another area such as customer service. In either case, the customer describes the problem, and the technician attempts to solve the problem using Xcheck, a sophisticated remote diagnostic system. Eighty percent of the time, they determine that the situation can be resolved by central office technicians working on the switching software, so the diagnosis information is sent to them. The other 20 percent of the time, Outside Repair Services are brought on the line, and an appointment is made for an outside repair technician to visit the customer's premises. In all cases when a call originated with Customer Service, any department that handled the call is expected to complete a form detailing their involvement and send it to Customer Service to record the resolution.

Service Analysis...

...takes the call logs from Customer Service and analyzes them, looking for opportunities to *up-sell* the customer. That is, they look for cases where the customer's inquiry indicates that they would benefit from subscribing to an additional service, such as a billing plan or call alert. Each prospect is written up on a *lead sheet*. If Service Analysis feels more information is needed about the customer, they contact Market Database Research. The additional information provided by Market Database Research is added to the lead sheet if they still feel that the customer warrants an up-selling call. Otherwise, the lead sheet is discarded.

Telemarketing...

...takes the lead sheets produced by Service Analysis and contacts the prospects, trying to sign them up for a new service. They also generate their own lead sheets, using research from a number of sources. If a prospect commits to buying new service, the call is transferred to a new service specialist to finalize the details.

Market Database Research...

...handles a wide variety of queries from other departments that seek information about specific people or organizations (customers or prospects), the marketplace and industry in general, or on specific competitors. They will examine the company's records to obtain further information on a customer, as when a customer has been targeted for up-selling or when someone in the sales force needs additional information. They will often make use of external sources as well, such as government agencies, commercial information providers, or the Internet. A new line of business involves handling queries and research assignments from external customers.

RB Tel—Questions Raised

If you're like most people, you'll encounter many stumbling blocks in trying to turn the preceding narrative into a workflow model. Of course, the first question should have been "what is the process we're looking at, and why are we looking at it?" but we didn't trick you, did we? You know that jumping into workflow modeling without having a clearly framed process is a sure-fire route to difficulties, which this example demonstrates. It also illustrates another sure-fire route to difficulties, which is attempting to build a swimlane diagram from a series of one-on-one interviews. Interviews are a terrific way to prepare for process identification, as covered in Chapter 5, but a terrible way to build a workflow model. You need to bring a group together to identify processes and then to guide you through at least the main flow of each process, after which you could return to interviewing to gather details about each actor's contribution. Even that, however, is a useful group activity for the understanding it provides and the contribution it makes to identifying misplaced, redundant, and conflicting activities. Returning to the example, here are some questions raised by this scenario:

"How do I show..."

- Branching?
- Optional steps?
- The role played by systems or mechanisms such as the IVR:
    - When we hand off control to the system?
    - When the system is used to support an activity, but isn't given control?
- Interaction with other processes?
- The appropriate level of detail?
- Activities such as a conversation that involves multiple actors (activities that span multiple swimlanes)?
- Questions or comments?
- Steps that don't happen in any particular order but must all be completed before a subsequent step can begin?
- Steps that interact continuously, or iterate?
- Steps that are triggered by the clock ("temporal events")?

• Steps carried out by an actor who has a very small, one-time only role in the workflow (i.e., do we show their step, and do they get their own swimlane)?

All of these, and others you may not have thought of, will be dealt with over the next few chapters.

Essential Elements of a Swimlane Diagram

Swimlane diagrams depict the actors involved, the steps they accomplish, and the flow of work between them as per Figure 8.1. The actors are listed down the left side of the diagram, and each is given a swimlane that extends left to right across the page. *Gravity-fed* diagrams can also be drawn, with the swimlanes extending vertically from top to bottom. This is a holdover from drawing flowcharts for software or procedures, which are typically drawn top down. This format quickly gets awkward for modeling a business process, as a longer diagram will spill onto the floor rather than running across a wall. The steps are shown as boxes in the swimlane of the actor who performs them. Arrows show the flow of work from one step to the next. Actually, there's some subtlety here. Technically, the line indicates that the completion of the preceding step is a precondition for the initiation of the subsequent step. Eventually, we'll get more precise and show not just which actor performs a given step, but also what previous steps must be completed before that step can begin. For now, let's keep it simple and just say that the flow arrows indicate sequence. A flow from one actor to another, one that crosses the line between swimlanes, is called a handoff. A key point: a swimlane diagram traces the path of a single token or work item as it flows through the process—it doesn't try to depict multiple simultaneous executions of the process.

In addition to showing *what* gets done, the diagram can show *who*—person, job function, company, organization unit, and so on; *how*—paper forms, information systems, machines, remote sensing, and so on; and *when*—event, sequence, and dependency.

Don't forget a title and date. When you are working furiously on your project you might even need to show the time on the diagram—"Are you looking at the diagram as of 11:15 Monday morning, or the version of 3:15 Monday afternoon?" The title should include the name of the process, the case, and possibly even details about the scenario being shown.

The Details

Actors and Roles

Looking at Figure 8.7, actors are the swimmers actually doing the work shown in the swimlanes. There is seldom a practical reason to differentiate between an "actor" and a "role," so we use the terms interchangeably. Some practitioners of a more academic bent would argue vigorously that there is an important distinction. For instance, the "actor" would be the job title of the person working in the process, whereas the "role" would be the part they played in the process, just like actors and

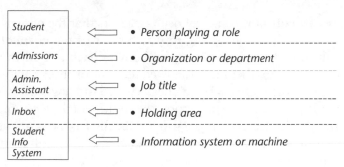

Figure 8.7 Actors.

roles in a play. The actor could be customer service rep but their role might be indicated on a swimlane diagram as order taker. This makes the model more generalized, but it's an example of what a friend calls "genericide"—making a model that is ultimately useless because it is more generic, but also more abstract and difficult for people to relate to. Chapter 10 will look at some cases where the actor-role distinction matters.

Generally, an actor is any identifiable person or group that handles the work (whether or not it is a "value-added" contribution!) between the initial event and the achievement of the process's result. An actor could be a person playing a part, such as an external customer or supplier, or it could be a job function normally assumed by a single person or a job title held by many. Sometimes, the actor is an organization unit such as a company, division, department, or work unit. If multiple actors work in the same organizational unit, you can depict that as was done for the Zoning department in Figure 8.6. This convention can be extended to show any number of layers of an organizational hierarchy. In BPMN, Zoning could be represented with a *pool* and each actor in Zoning with a *lane,* although this isn't the intent of the "pool" construct.

An actor could even be another process. Information systems, other automated devices, machines, and even passive holding areas commonly appear as actors.[2] Again, Chapter 10 expands on this.

All of the work performed by an actor appears in that actor's swimlane. Some swimlanes will be much wider than others, because of complex branching or parallel tasks performed by that actor. Although we haven't seen an automated tool that supports this, sometimes we have to "bulge" a swimlane to make room for a busy period. Actors can appear from top to bottom in any order that makes sense. For years, our default was to initially show the actors in their order of appearance, the way the cast is listed at the end of a movie. Later, we would move the "busier" actors up to the top, because it highlighted the points where the flow left the primary participants. Eventually, we realized that we were adjusting the order to better "tell a story," which might sound manipulative but is actually a reasonable thing to do.

One especially useful variant to tell a story is to lay out the actors according to their physical position, as is often done by Lean practitioners. In a model showing

---

2. But not every system, machine, or holding area that supports a process should appear in its own swimlane, or even appear at all. We'll provide techniques for handling these cases in Chapter 10.

the flow of a patient through a hospital, actors that the patient visited (e.g., various labs) were organized according to which floor of the hospital the patient was on, which illustrated the torturous up and down, back-and-forth path the patient was forced through. Another model showed the flow of checks across the country for settlement processing (e.g., when a check cashed in New York went to a bank in San Francisco for clearing). The actors, the multiple courier companies contracted to move the checks, were arranged geographically from east to west. The flow repeatedly went up and down, telling the story that due to old contracts and patronage, there was definitely not a smooth east to west flow. If you've seen the movie *Catch Me If You Can*, you might remember Tom Hanks's character doing a presentation to his fellow FBI officers on the deficiencies of this process.

Our current default is to list the actors, from top to bottom, in this order:

1. Customer (or customers, if there are multiple customer participants);
2. Core actors;
3. Supporting actors;
4. Other processes;
5. Holding areas, if they are significant;
6. Systems and mechanisms (machinery, equipment, and so on).

Figure 8.8 illustrates this.

Figure 8.8   Default sequence of different types of actors.

Steps and Decisions

A step represents some unit of work performed by an actor. Attempts to develop terminology to formally distinguish among activities, actions, tasks, sets of tasks, steps, work items, and so on are ultimately fruitless. Even if we did develop formal definitions (we have tried, and so have others) experience tells us it's enough to get a group of people to agree on the distinction between function, business process, and subprocess. Arguing about whether a particular piece of work should be called a step, task, or activity only frustrates people, so we keep the terminology fairly loose and generally refer to steps. Occasionally, we will slip and refer to a task or an activity, but the participants never seem to mind. Note that a step on a handoff level diagram might break into multiple steps on a lower level diagram, so the term step provides no information on how large or small the unit of work is. Steps are shown on the swimlane diagram as a labeled box in the lane of the actor performing it. Steps can involve multiple actors—conversations, meetings, and assists are situations in which two or more actors are required. These are referred to as *collaborative steps*. In Figure 8.9, Accept Order is completed entirely by the Order Desk, whereas Develop Production Schedule is completed in a meeting of some sort involving Production Planning and Delivery Logistics—the dotted lines over the order desk's swimlane indicates that they aren't involved. Resolve Order Discrepancy involves all three departments. Be careful not to confuse collaborative work with concurrent (parallel) work. In a collaborative step, the actors are working together on the same step, while in concurrent work, they are working independently on separate tasks. This is also illustrated in Figure 8.9.

Voluntary Simplicity

Tucked away in your desk drawer, some of you still have your trusty green IBM flowcharting template. It was designed for modeling software logic and has shapes for many different types of operations—processing, decision, input, output, sort, merge, and so on—as shown in Figure 8.10.

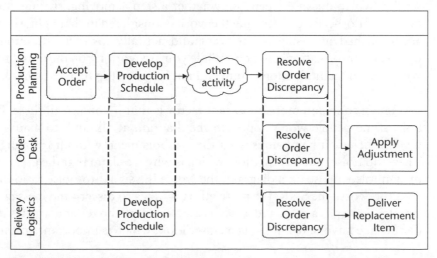

Figure 8.9 Collaborative and concurrent steps.

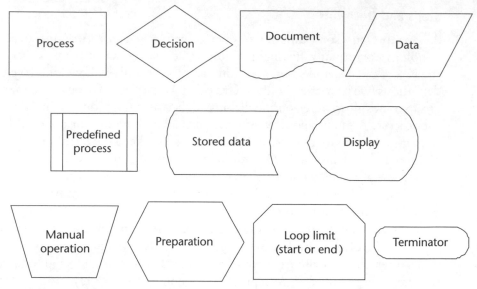

Figure 8.10   Flowcharting symbols.

Some symbologies that were developed specifically for modeling processes also distinguish various types of steps. For instance, the more rigorous approach used by Ben Graham[3] has different symbols for do, originate, add/alter, handle, transport, inspect, storage/delay, and destroy. This is an appropriate tool in many situations, especially those you could characterize as industrial engineering. To the right audience, the symbols are effective at providing a visual cue highlighting the kinds of steps you want to maximize, and those you want to minimize.

On the other hand, in the approach this book describes, every step is a simple box, no matter what kind of work it performs. This gives rise to a frequent question, "Why are these diagrams so simple? Couldn't they carry more information with a richer symbol set?" You would think so, but two factors have to be considered. The first requires a reminder that the purpose of these diagrams is to "show the flow of work," which doesn't depend on whether a step is moving, storing, inputting, outputting, or otherwise processing the work. Considered in that light, the type of work accomplished in a step is irrelevant and actually distracts attention from more important information, the flow. While you are working on the initial flow diagram, you want to maintain momentum and not have to stop to ask, "what kind of step is this?"

The second and more important factor is that if you use all these different symbols, some people won't approach the diagram at all, and, to many of the others who do, it won't be obvious what the symbols mean without referring to a legend. They add noise, not information, which is why we claim that the greater the number of symbols you use on a diagram, the worse the signal-to-noise ratio (SNR) will be. And the worse the SNR, the more effort it takes to discern the message. We keep it simple—a step is a step, and a step is a box. Simple boxes and arrows don't seem to discourage anyone from taking a closer look, which is important, given the range of

3.   See http://www.worksimp.com.

people who should be participating (painlessly) in process analysis and redesign. We have found that even in high tech companies, some people refuse to look at one of these charts if it contains something as simple as a decision diamond—"Ewww, that's one of those icky IT flowcharts" is a reaction we've heard.

To summarize, the whole point of business-oriented workflow modeling is to make the key aspects of the process—who, what, and when—as obvious and accessible as possible, without requiring training or interpretation. We always opt for visual simplicity, so the models are understandable to the *most* people with the *least* effort, because participation and buy-in are critical success factors.

This isn't to say ignore different types of steps, just that you don't need to distinguish among them on a swimlane diagram.[4] However, certain types of steps will always be named with the same verb, for instance, "decide."

In the same vein, we make liberal use of annotation on diagrams—a textual comment is often better than a complex diagram or the use of arcane symbols.[5] Once in a while, we'll add an iconic symbol if it will help to convey a concept. Rather than adding a separate swimlane and step for a holding area, we might place a wire basket over a flow line representing an inbox or an outbox. A telephone, fax machine, or e-mail symbol placed on a flow line can serve a similar purpose. It is very easy to go overboard, so we rarely add symbols like these.

Which Steps to Include?

One of the difficulties you'll encounter is deciding which steps to include in your workflow model. For instance, an actor might tell you about many activities they carry out, but that doesn't mean they all belong in the process being studied. Remember, you're modeling a specific process, from trigger to result, not all of the activity a person or department is responsible for! The opposite case came up at an insurance company, where not enough of the activities were shown on a swimlane diagram. Five percent of incoming claims were routed to Internal Audit and then returned a few days later to the normal claims flow. Whatever was done by Internal Audit never made any difference to the subsequent handling of the claims, so some analysts argued that Internal Audit and the step(s) they carried out weren't part of the process and shouldn't be on the diagram. In cases like these, two simple guidelines always help.

First, remember that the process will usually trace a single work item or "package" of work items from triggering event through to result. That work item might be a service problem, an order, an engineering upgrade, a building permit request, an item being manufactured, a material requisition, a replacement part, or whatever it is the process deals with. In this case, it was a claim. The work item might appear to be transformed along the way (e.g., when the replacement part request is "transformed" into the actual replacement part). It might even split and follow different paths, as when the replacement part heads for the courier company and the invoice or warranty details head off in another direction.

4.   However, when we later assess the as-is or design the to-be process, we'll ask the questions implied by these categories—for each step, we'll ask, "does this step make a contribution to the process, and, if so, what type?"
5.   Rummler and Brache add two symbols for specific types of annotations—goals or observed problems for a process step.

Second, any activity that "holds" one of these work items, in any way, shape, or form, should almost certainly be part of the process, whether or not it adds value to the process. To be more specific, we offer the chant we use when making these decisions:

"Show every actor that holds the work, whether they:

1. Add value,
2. Move the work along, or
3. Introduce delay."

A friend reduced this to "transforms, transports, or ties up." Simply put, if the work is held, whatever is being done, show it.

The first guideline, "adds value," could be stated as "causes a state change in the direction of completion." Strictly speaking, it could also subtract value, or cause a state change in the opposite direction of completion. In either case, work is being performed on the work item, which includes inspection or validation activities. "Moves the work along" indicates that some steps may not change the work item in any way, except to transport it between other steps in the workflow. As we'll see, many people mistakenly exclude these transport activities from their workflow models (e.g., by not showing internal or external delivery services that handle the work item). In those cases, factors that are important to process behavior are missed. Finally, "introduces delay" covers the third case—a step may not change the state of the work item or move it along, but some subsequent step can't proceed until the "delay-introducing" step completes. Our claim-handling example is a good illustration—subsequent steps in resolving the claim could not proceed until a claim returned from the audit step, even though the audit step didn't actually do anything *to* the claim. Internal Audit should be shown as an actor, with a decision step indicating that only 5 percent of the claims took that path.

In the Issue Building Permit example, the zoning compliance officer added value by completing an assessment, Administrative Services and the Mailroom moved the work along, and the zoning manager's contribution was to introduce delay.

Process Steps: Naming Guidelines

Anyone who reads the diagram should be able to follow it, so we want to avoid cryptic step names like "MS-17" in Figure 8.11. To ensure this, follow the same guidelines for naming a process step as for naming a process (see Chapter 5). The step name is in "verb-noun" format, or "verb-object," if you prefer, and often includes additional detail. In those cases, the text box for a step isn't just a name that tells us what is being done, it's a description that tells us how, if that is relevant. The components of the step name are as follows:

- Action verb (assign, validate, sort, …);
- Optional qualifier (initial, replacement, …);
- Noun(s) (service request, payment, …);
- Optionally, information on how (on Form MS-17, by fax, …).

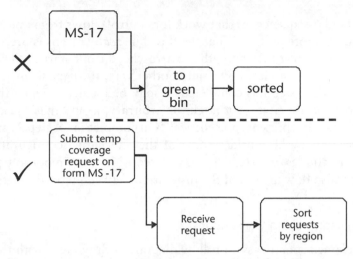

Figure 8.11 Step naming guidelines.

The step name should convey the result achieved by the step. Just as we did when naming processes, flip the verb-noun step name into "noun-is-verbed" form, as in the following examples:

- Name—Receive PNO application;
  Result—PNO application is received.

- Name—Apply parking citation;
  Result—parking citation is applied.

- Name—Issue replacement license plate;
  Result—replacement license plate is issued.

As final reminder, the name is:

- Not an area or function such as "titling," "accounting," or "inventory";
- Not an event or result such as "claim arrives" or "claim is registered";
- Not a state such as "sorted";
- Not based on "mushy" verbs (see Chapter 5) or jargon.

Flow

Flow is the passing of work from one step to the next, shown as lines with arrowheads. In other methods, flow is known as routes, events, communications, or transitions. Sometimes, accomplishing the flow may actually be a step in itself, such as "Retrieve tray from mailroom." A handoff is a special kind of flow, one in which the work passes, or is handed off, from one actor to another. It's a flow from one swimlane to another. They are a focus for process analysis, because they are often a source of the "three deadly sins"—delay, errors, and expense.

Like swimlane diagrams as a whole, the concept of flow is usually self evident. Everyone immediately understands that the flow line indicates that tasks happen in a particular sequence, or that work (or control) flows from one task to the next. But we can be more precise. What the flow line *really* means is precedence and dependence—the step at the end with the arrowhead can't start until the step at the other end has been completed. Or, put another way, the dependent step can't begin until the preceding step has completed. It may be a rule, as when the second step uses results from the first, or it might be arbitrary, as in "that's just how we do it." In either case, it represents precedence: "On completion of step A, step B can begin." In this section, we'll consider some of the alternative configurations for flow lines entering and leaving steps. First, we'll consider two important points: how to best draw those flow lines, and the distinction between workflow and data flow.

Flow Diagramming Conventions

One element of an easy-to-follow diagram is drawing it with the output flow lines leaving the step from the right edge and the input (or triggering) flow lines entering from the left edge. If the flow line means "B follows A," then the graphic should depict this—the left edge of step B should be somewhere to the right of the right edge of step A. All too many diagrams visually convey the impression that steps are occurring in parallel when in fact they are sequential. We never draw diagrams with flow lines entering the top or bottom edges.

Avoid the forms in Figure 8.12—the flows may be accurate, but they don't convey timing and precedence. The objective is to graphically show sequence, dependency, time, and so on—the objective is *not* to save paper.

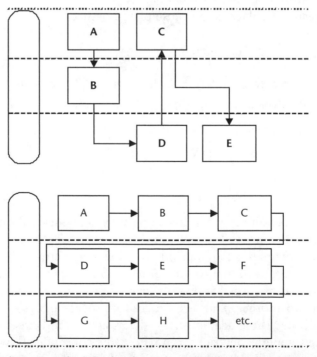

Figure 8.12 Flow lines enter the left edge, leave the right edge, and go left to right.

Workflow Versus Data Flow

If you have experience with an older form of process modeling, data flow diagramming, you might inadvertently confuse the concepts of workflow and data flow.[6] The distinction is subtle, because whenever you have a workflow, it's virtually certain that data either *is* the item that flows or *accompanies* it. However, a data flow does not necessarily imply a workflow. Before we thoroughly confuse you, a definition is in order. On a data flow diagram (DFD), a data flow line between steps (they're called *processes* on a DFD) indicates that data produced by the originating step is used by the receiving step. For instance, a step Provide Quote early in a process will produce data (the discount percentage) that is used by a later step Issue Invoice. On a DFD, these two steps might have a data flow between them, perhaps interrupted by a "data store" where the data "waits" until it is needed. A workflow model, on the other hand, might show a long sequence of steps before the process gets as far as Issue Invoice because that is the flow of the *work*. The two cases are illustrated in Figure 8.13. When data flow is superimposed on a workflow model, the result is usually such a maze of lines that the workflow isn't evident any more.

Different Types of Flow

In most of our examples so far, the flow has been simple—one step followed by the next and so on. This is a sequential flow, the simplest case, in which work flows from one step to the next in order. Of course, real processes also exhibit more complex flows, which can be generalized as either parallel or conditional. In a parallel flow, one step is followed by flows to two or more steps (or sequences of steps) that *all* proceed independently. In a conditional flow, a decision step is involved, so one step is followed by flows to two or more steps (or sequences of steps), but *only one* of those flows is followed. This is what is represented by the traditional decision diamond in flowcharting, which indicates that exactly one flow out of two or more alternatives will be taken, depending on the particular condition. The condition typically involves checking certain data values against rules (e.g., "if the estimated claim value is greater than $5,000...").

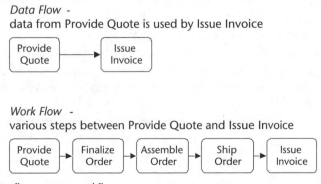

Figure 8.13 Data flow versus workflow.

---

6. For some reason, workflow is usually written as one word, and data flow is often written as two—we have no idea why.

This is a bit of a simplification. A conditional flow could involve more sophisticated rules, and it could be that one or more flows will be followed, but for most business-oriented workflow modeling, all you'll need is the ability to represent sequential, parallel, and conditional (decision) flows. Sequential flows have already been illustrated, so now we'll take a look at the other two cases.

Decisions

Mutually exclusive (conditional) flows are common when a decision is made that directs the workflow to *one* of two or more alternative flows. Many diagramming approaches use the diamond symbol to indicate a decision, but in the spirit of simplicity, just use a box as you would for any other step. Figure 8.14 illustrates a simple conditional flow with two alternatives. The key points to note are as follows:

1. Be consistent in naming this type of step—we most often use "decide."
2. When showing a decision, there is exactly one flow line leaving the step, which then splits into two or more branches.
3. Each branch is labeled to indicate which decision outcome will follow that path, along with statistics if appropriate.
4. The branches are mutually exclusive—*exactly one* is followed. If parallel flows are involved, a different representation is used.

As noted, "decide" is a verb that should be reserved for specific situations. Use "decide" or "determine" when the process looks at data values (typically) to decide on which action to take next (e.g., decide if purchase price >= manager limit). "Sort" and "route" are similar reserved verbs, but are used when deciding where ("to whom") a work item should go next.

This structure can also be used to depict a single optional step. However, as shown in Figure 8.15, we'd take the easy way out—simply annotate the optional step.

Parallel Flows

The last two illustrations showed mutually exclusive branches—there were two or more branches, but only one would be taken. In the case of parallel or concurrent flows, there are multiple simultaneous flows, and therefore multiple flow lines, leaving a step. For instance, after booking an order, there might be a flow that begins fulfillment activities such as allocating inventory, and another, parallel flow that deals with setting up the receivable. Even more flows could begin that deal with other

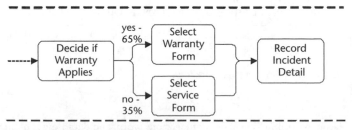

Figure 8.14 Showing decisions (conditional flows).

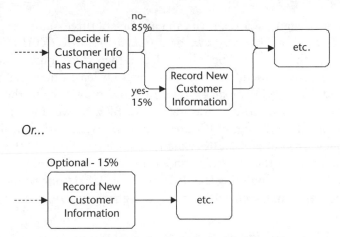

Or...

Figure 8.15   Using an annotation instead of a decision to show an optional step.

aspects of the order. Parallel flows are illustrated as shown in Figure 8.16 with multiple flow lines leaving a step, and the flows are drawn one above another to visually convey that they happen in parallel, even if we can't precisely indicate the timing of particular steps.

We've had objections from people that it's essential to add more symbols, such as the BPMN "gateways," to indicate the different alternatives, but our experience is that it's only necessary when laying out logic very precisely for an entire process (all cases) for implementation purposes. We find that when using our simple "boxes and lines" convention, depicting one scenario, for one case, of one process at a time, business people instantly grasp the distinction between parallel ("and") and conditional ("or") flows because of a simple visual cue—the number of flow lines leaving the *right* edge of the step tells us how many flows will take place. For a sequential flow, it's obviously one. For a conditional flow, it's also one but will take one of two or more alternatives. The use of the verb "decide" coupled with the labels on the alternate flows makes it clear what is being represented. For parallel flows, there is a separate line for each flow that will occur. Later, when implementation is at hand and you need to include all these different scenarios and cases on a single diagram, the additional logic provided by BPMN will be useful.

Alternate Representations

You might encounter another diagram style similar in intent to BPMN that adds specific symbols to indicate different types of flows. In this style, illustrated on the

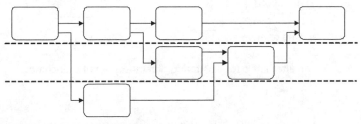

Figure 8.16   Parallel flows.

right side of Figure 8.17, a fork can have one of three qualifiers, sometimes called an *AND branch*, an *OR branch*, or an *exclusive OR (XOR) branch*. In the AND branch, all the forks will be followed, and their steps must be accomplished eventually. In an OR branch,[7] one or more forks (at least one and possibly more) will be followed. In an XOR, exactly one (one and only one) of the forks will be taken, which corresponds to our "decide." Like BPMN, we don't use this style for business-oriented modeling, but it does have the strength that it differentiates between OR (one or more) and XOR (exactly one—a decision). In the rare cases where we have to illustrate the OR situation, we draw it as we would draw parallel flows, but with a dotted arc spanning the flows with the label "one or more" at one end. This, plus the step name, seems to provide enough information that people can see what is going on.

Parallel and Conditional Input Flows

One of the most important aspects of a workflow diagram, sometimes the *most* important, is accurately showing what input flows are necessary for a step to begin. When you construct your initial workflow model, most of the lines will represent a

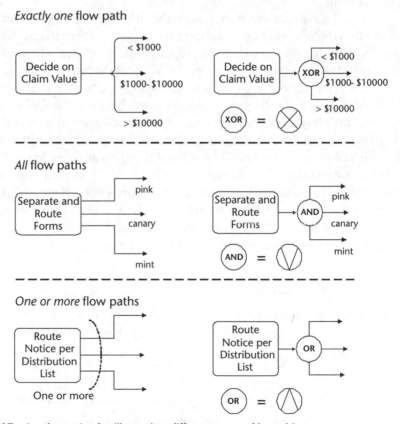

Figure 8.17 An alternative for illustrating different types of branching.

---

7.   This OR branch is sometimes called a *logical* OR to distinguish it from the exclusive OR.

simple sequential flow between two steps. Later, when refining the diagram, a critical question to ask is "does the second step *actually* begin then, or is another step or event necessary, or possible, *before* the second step begins?" Often, there should be multiple triggering flow lines entering a step, but modelers have missed some of them due to not explicitly asking this question. Your job as a workflow modeler is to find them all! Let's look at the different situations that can arise and conventions for representing them.

We've seen four alternatives for *output flows* leaving the *right edge* of a step:

1. A single flow;
2. Two or more parallel flows (AND);
3. A conditional flow that takes exactly one of two or more alternatives (XOR);
4. A conditional flow that takes one or more of two or more alternatives (OR).

Exactly the same situations can arise for *input flows* (*triggering flows*) entering the *left edge* of a step, and the conventions for depicting triggering flows are exactly symmetric with those for depicting output flows. First is the convention that the number of flow lines entering the left edge of the step tells us how many flows have to arrive from previous steps or events before the step will begin. With this in mind, we'll take a quick look at the triggering flows that correspond to each of the output flows described in alternatives 1–4.

1. A single flow enters a step, connected to a single preceding step, which indicates the simple sequential flow so common in the examples we've looked at. It says that when the preceding step completes, the following (or dependent) step begins.
2. A single conditional flow enters a step, which is exactly one of two or more alternatives. Think of this as a reverse decision. On the output side, we showed decisions (mutually exclusive output flows) as a single line that split into two or more branches. The input side is the mirror image, with two or more lines joining and then a single line going into the step. This is the XOR situation, indicating that *exactly one* of the triggering flows can arrive and initiate the step. To be more precise, it means that the triggering flow could come from only one source. This happens most often because a decision step earlier in the process sent the flow down exactly one path, and now the alternate paths are rejoining. Please note the consistency here—*exactly one* line is entering the left edge of the step, indicating that *exactly one* flow will trigger it. Contrast that with the situation in point 3, where there are *two or more* lines entering the step, *all* of which must arrive to trigger the step.
3. Two or more parallel flows enter a step, each connected to a preceding step. In some cases, one of them won't be connected to a preceding step, it will be connected to a temporal event, indicated by a clock symbol, or some other event. (Temporal events are described shortly.) This is the AND situation, indicating that *all* of the triggering flows must arrive before the step begins. The flows do not have to arrive at the same time and in fact almost never will.

4. For symmetry, we'll describe the fourth case, although it's of limited practical value. Two or more parallel flows enter a step, as described in point 3, but they aren't all necessary to trigger the step; one or more of the flows will trigger it. As we did for output flows, we indicate this with a dotted arc spanning the input flows with the label "one or more" at one end. Practically, this means that as soon as any one of the flows arrives, the step begins. It is possible that the step then carries through to completion, or perhaps it then decides that because of some particulars, something else is needed so it waits for another flow to arrive. We differentiate this from the case in point 2, in which as long as one flow arrived, the step could proceed, no questions asked. In a more precise symbology like BPMN, there are ways to indicate this situation, such as a gateway with a rule, but because we're drawing one diagram for each significant case of the process, it almost never comes up.

Situations 2, 3, and 4 are depicted in Figure 8.18.

Flows with No Fixed Sequence

A common situation is steps that don't happen in any fixed sequence or may happen iteratively. For instance, in an insurance claim scenario, customers who have an automobile accident call in to register a claim. The claims representative attempts to identify the customer in order to determine what coverage their policy provides.

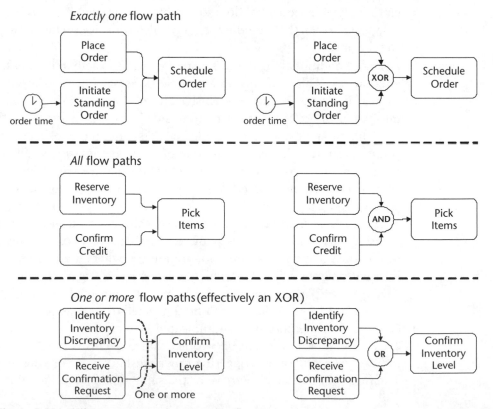

Figure 8.18   Different situations for triggering flows.

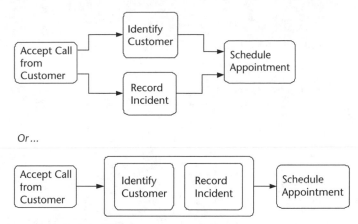

Or...

Figure 8.19   Steps that don't happen in a set sequence.

However, some customers would immediately launch into a description of the accident, which the rep would dutifully record. Eventually, usually when the customer paused for breath, the rep would determine who the customer was and then possibly return to capturing more incident details. To illustrate all the permutations ("decide if customer will let rep get a word in edgewise") would soon get ridiculously complex, so of course we opt for simpler representations that still gets the point across, as shown in Figure 8.19. Both options show that Identify Customer and Record Incident can happen in any sequence, or even interleave, but *both* have to complete before Schedule Interview can happen. We prefer the option on the right, where the concurrent (or "nonsequenced") steps are placed within a larger box. In the option on top, the fact that two flows enter Schedule Interview indicates that both must occur before that step will begin.

What's Next?

Armed with this review of the basic symbols and conventions for drawing swimlane diagrams, you could start to model a real business process. That's what we did when we first saw this diagramming style, and we quickly ran into the problem of managing detail—everyone does. It's not uncommon for progress on a workflow model to stall completely. The examples at the beginning of this chapter provided some specific techniques, notably "the three questions," for making sure you don't get hopelessly bogged down in details that prevent you from ever getting to the end of the process. The next chapter will formalize those guidelines and define the progressive levels of detail to which you can take a diagram.

CHAPTER 9

Process Workflow Models—Managing Progressive Detail

The Curse of Detail

When you set out to model the as-is process, your purpose is to understand it, not build the Winchester Mystery Model. Sarah Winchester's famous home, the Winchester Mystery House, is located in San Jose, California. Sarah, the heir to the Winchester Arms fortune, became convinced she would live only as long as it would take to finish building her house. So she set out to build on to her house forever. Some analysts seem to have a similar goal in modeling the current process—never finish! Unlike Sarah, who was sure she'd meet her fate if she *stopped* building, you will surely meet a terrible fate if you *don't stop* modeling—your project will be canceled and you'll never get to work on the to-be process! Once you *understand* the as-is process, you have completed enough modeling, and it's time to move on. In this chapter, we'll look at techniques to help you achieve that understanding with a minimum of pain, so you can stop when it's time to stop and move on to assessing the current process and designing a new one.

What's the Problem?

Two reasons account for most of the problems encountered in managing detail. First, analysts jump immediately into modeling minute details instead of building layers of progressively more detailed models. Remember that before you even start swimlane diagrams, you should have two levels of detail modeled—the overall process map will decompose a process area into business processes, and process framing will decompose each business process into subprocesses. By diving into detail too quickly, process modelers almost guarantee they will immediately be thrust into unmanageable complexity. Imagine trying to develop blueprints for a house by starting with the details of the trim around the front door—you might eventually finish, but it won't be easy. That's why we stressed "flow first, detail later" in the previous chapter.

The second source of difficulty arises when the modeler keeps adding more and more detail, seemingly unable to stop. In fact, they probably can't stop, because they're sliding down a slippery slope—each additional level of detail invariably raises more exceptions, each less significant than the exceptions dealt with in the previous level. Many analysts are compelled to deal with every one of these, but there's no end to it. For an analogy, consider that polishing metal is the introduction of progressively finer and finer scratches—you never eliminate the scratches, they just get smaller and more numerous until the polish is "good enough." So it is with modeling a business process—eventually, it's good enough, even if there are countless tiny flaws. As we said before, "the purpose of a workflow model is to show the flow of work" and we'll add to that the phrase "and the main contributions of each actor." The "main contributions" will emphasize another familiar refrain, "what, not how." Following this guideline, you will probably be surprised to see how little detail is needed to conduct a good as-is assessment. Save your energy for detailed modeling of the to-be process.

Achieving a Controlled Descent

Three Levels of Workflow Diagrams

Our main contribution to the problem of managing detail is that we have defined three progressive levels of detail for swimlane diagrams. The first seems almost absurdly simplistic, but it allows you to get all the way through the process. The second adds specific kinds of detail, and the third even more. These three levels are referred to as:

- Level 1 or *handoff-level* diagram;
- Level 2 or *service-level* diagram;
- Level 3 or *task-level* diagram.

Two key points before we go further:

1. In the first edition, we called the service level the *milestone level*. That's still an accurate name, but we now use *service level* because the steps on one of these diagrams correspond strongly to the business services we'll describe in Chapter 15. This relationship is of special interest to anyone integrating Service-Oriented Architecture (SOA) and Business Process Management (BPM). The new name emphasizes the relationship.
2. We haven't developed a task-level diagram of a complete business process for several years, although in a few cases we took a small part of an as-is process down to this level. As we'll see, the step-by-step work that is described at this level is better documented in procedure descriptions, use cases, or other separate documents.

This approach was developed the hard way, through trial and error. The fact that we don't do task-level diagrams anymore reflects this. However, the basic principles have been successful time and again on our own consulting engagements, and readers around the world have reported enthusiastically how well the handoff-level (in particular) and service-level diagrams have worked for them. Their natural inclination was to start at a level closer to our task level, so learning about the higher-level models "saved them from themselves."

The most important concepts are that by beginning with a very simple model, you can establish a framework within which it's easy to add progressive levels of detail and also see when it's time to stop. Most of the examples we'll discuss are concerned with modeling the as-is process, but you will use these same levels of detail when designing and assessing the to-be process. Let's look at the details of these three levels of workflow model.

Level 1: The Handoff Diagram

Level 1 is the handoff-level diagram, or simply handoff diagram. This is the one we'll spend the most time discussing, because it's arguably the most important. It makes the overall structure of the process visible, and, if you get this level right, adding a subsequent level (or levels) of detail is fairly straightforward. The concepts will be familiar, because the first two examples we considered in Chapter 8 illustrated handoff diagrams. Figure 8.3 showed the simplest possible handoff diagram for a forensic sciences process, and Figures 8.4 through 8.6 showed the evolution of a handoff diagram by asking "the three questions." Since its purpose is to highlight handoffs, every handoff is shown, but detail about the steps is absolutely minimized. This is the diagram that concentrates on the "flow" part of workflow, not the "work." Each time an actor is involved in a process, no matter how large or how small their contribution, it is shown as a single box. Thus, it has only one step (box) each time there is contiguous or uninterrupted work by an actor, from receiving a handoff (starting a task or series of tasks on a work item) to initiating the final handoff for that work item (completing a task or series of tasks). An actor may have many steps in the handoff-level diagram if each takes place at a different time in the process.

Figure 9.1 illustrates a handoff-level workflow diagram. Each step summarizes the actor's involvement at a specific time in a process. The guideline for handoff diagrams that we introduced in the previous chapter is worth repeating here. Whenever an actor holds the work, whether they do a *lot* or a *little*, draw *one* box and *move on*. We regularly hear from people that this is one of the two most useful guidelines they have learned about workflow modeling. (The other is that you must show every actor that holds the work, whether they add value, move the work along, or introduce delay.) Note that the sales rep's step Determine Required Credit will decompose into multiple steps on a service-level diagram, while the credit admin clerk's step Order Credit Report will still be shown as one step at the service level. This illustrates the idea that the handoff diagram provides no visual clue to the relative amount of work any actor is performing; that distinction becomes apparent with the service diagram.

This might be easier to follow if we look at it in reverse, or, more accurately, in a bottom-up fashion. Assume that an actor receives a work item, via a handoff, and begins to work on it. This work might involve many individual actions, including decisions and handoffs, but proceeds without interruption until either the final handoff for that work item to some other actor or until work ceases awaiting a future event or handoff. On a service diagram, we would see a series of steps in one actor's swimlane, generally beginning with the receipt of a handoff and ending with

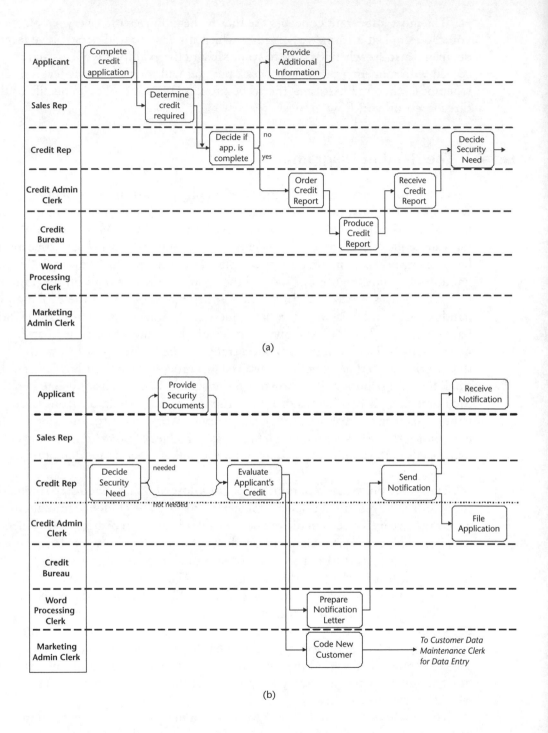

Figure 9.1   (a, b) Handoff level diagram for as-is processes.

a handoff to another actor. All of the intervening steps, even if there were eight of them, would be reduced to a single step on the handoff diagram. The exception would be if part way through these eight tasks, the actor stopped working on that work item to wait for the arrival of another handoff or a predetermined time. In that case, the work would appear as two steps, each representing contiguous or uninterrupted effort. (Cases like this are explored shortly.)

These diagrams are usually simple to produce, although there could be minor difficulty when there are multiple handoffs along the way or decisions that might cause a handoff. These will all have to be combined, in which case there would be multiple flows leaving the step or one large decision fork that summarizes various intermediate decisions. If the diagram becomes unwieldy, consider drawing two or three versions, each reflecting a particular scenario.

Issues and Observations with the Handoff Diagram

Simplify Steps, Not Actors

One of our clients chose to call a handoff diagram an "involvement diagram," because it highlights each point in the process where an actor is involved. This leads to an important rule for these diagrams that at first appears counterintuitive. Even though we simplify the steps greatly, we don't simplify the actors at all—every single actor in the process is shown. The corollary is that as you progress through subsequent levels of detail, you'll add many more steps, but no more actors. The diagram will grow from left to right, but not from top to bottom. A common objection to this rule is that if we're simplifying steps, we should also "simplify" the actors, perhaps by combining the different roles within a department and just showing the department as an actor. In extreme cases, you might choose to do this, but it eliminates one of the main benefits of the handoff diagram. Because each handoff is "a potential source of delay, error, and expense," there can be tremendous benefit from a diagram that so clearly illustrates all of the handoffs. In fact, one of the fascinating things about handoff diagrams is that they can make process timing and dynamics visible when they were hidden in more detailed diagrams. In one case, the handoff diagram made "yo-yoing" immediately evident—the workflow kept returning to the same actor, for review and approval, over and over again. In the detailed diagrams, which the project team had developed first, this wasn't obvious even though it proved to be a significant factor. Over the course of the process, this approval step introduced significant delay, because completing the review was not a high priority for that actor.

"I'm Too Important to Be Just One Box!"

Each individual step may be simplified or abstracted so much from the actual steps being completed that a step effectively says only "this actor is involved at this point in the process." This can be a little distressing for the participants. One of the consequences of reducing an actor's involvement in a process to a single box is that trivial contributions and major contributions look exactly the same—just a single step is shown. Consider a real example. The manager of a retail store had many responsibilities at the end of the day, including balancing the day's receipts against the records in the system and then preparing the bank deposit. This was a considerable amount of work, comprising many individual steps, and was often stressful as well. However, it showed up as just a single box on the handoff level swimlane diagram.

Adjacent to it was a box of the same size that represented just a few moments of work for the sales assistant who signed a form witnessing that the deposit bag had been placed in the safe. Understandably, the store manager was a little miffed by this apparent trivializing of their contribution, so we had to explain (again) carefully that this part of the workflow model would soon be expanded, while the adjacent step would stay the same. As we'll discuss in Chapter 11, we now deal with this situation in advance, during the introduction of a modeling session, by showing a service-level diagram to introduce swimlane diagramming and then showing a handoff-level diagram and explaining that we'll build one of these first, to establish the overall flow.

Adjacent Steps by One Actor?

A common situation is illustrated in Figure 9.2, which is borrowed from the front end of the issue building permit process we looked at in the previous chapter. In this example, the builder working alone completes a step, then has a meeting with the permit control clerk, after which the permit control clerk completes another step working alone. (It could just as well be the builder completing the third step, or both of them doing independent steps subsequent to the meeting.) To people new to the idea of a handoff diagram, this appears to violate the rule about reducing all contiguous work by an actor to a single box, but it is the right way to diagram this situation. The key to understanding this is to see that it isn't *contiguous* work done by *one* actor, it is *noncontiguous* work being done by *separate* actors. For the first step, the actor is the builder, for the second step, the actor is the builder and the permit control clerk working together, and for the third step, the actor is the permit control clerk alone. As well, the work isn't necessarily contiguous—there could be considerable time, interrupted by other work, between when the builder prepares the permit application and when they go to City Hall to submit it.

A similar situation, also troubling while getting the hang of handoff diagrams, is shown in Figure 9.3. Here we have three adjacent steps by the same actor in a

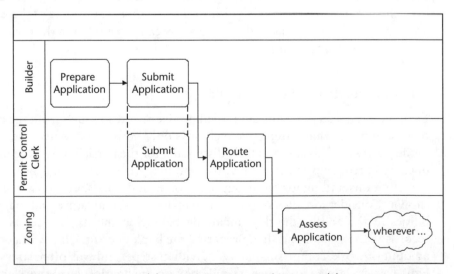

Figure 9.2   Not contiguous work by one actor—noncontiguous work by separate actors.

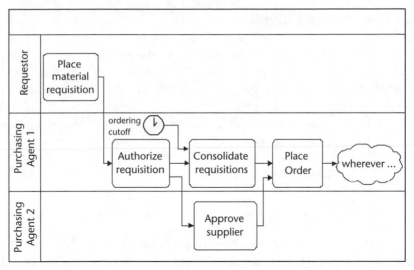

Figure 9.3   Noncontiguous work by one actor.

handoff diagram, and we can't argue that there is another actor involved in one of them. Again, though, it's the correct representation, this time because the work isn't contiguous. The second step represents separate activity that isn't started until some predetermined time, a temporal event, indicated by the clock symbol. Between the first second steps there could be hours or days of waiting or working on other tasks. Between the second and third steps is a similar situation, except that in this case the third step is waiting for some other step to complete.

Can We Stop Now?

Our first guideline for when to stop modeling the as-is process is simple—as soon as you've done enough modeling to understand why the process behaves the way it does, you can stop. This can happen at the handoff level, when something like a timing issue, convoluted workflow, or bottleneck is identified as the root cause of performance problems. Now that we've become more comfortable with the idea of stopping as-is modeling at the handoff level, we find that we do it increasingly often. Much of the time, we're not so lucky and have to proceed to a second-level diagram.

Recap

Handoff diagrams emphasize *who* is involved throughout the process and *when* that involvement occurs in the process, but they only provide an overview of *what* the actor does and essentially nothing about *how* they do it. These diagrams support understandable presentations by providing an overview, and they give us a view of the overall pattern of involvement, which can be very illuminating. While running a session, you will find that the main benefit is that the initial pass of modeling the as-is process is completed much faster. This is because of the clear guidelines that override our natural tendency to "dive for detail" too soon and lose the forest in the trees.

Level 2: The Service Diagram

The service diagram is used to understand the primary contributions made by each actor, including key steps that determine flow. Steps at the service level will be "smaller" than steps in a handoff diagram, but will still represent significant activity, so this type of diagram is also suitable for presentations. Building this one is easy if you have a good handoff diagram. Break each step in the handoff diagram into separate steps on the service diagram, as necessary, to illustrate:

- Completion of a significant achievement or milestone, which is a service to the process;
- A decision that affects the flow in a significant way.

Examples of decisions that affect flow include "Decide if claim requires extended handling," if that caused a handoff to actors (e.g., the Fraud Investigations group) that wouldn't otherwise be involved. A minor decision within one actor's involvement wouldn't be depicted, unless that led the actor achieving different milestones. A decision to repeat a step or set of steps is also an example of a decision that affects the flow.

Milestones are often significant events in the life of the work item. They usually entail a change in state or status that moves the work item toward completion. For example, a handoff diagram at an insurance company includes the step File Claim. On the service diagram, this step is broken down into the individual services the actor provides, such as Record Incident Detail ("incident detail is recorded,") Register Claim, Describe Loss, Confirm Coverage, and Schedule Appointment. It might take a number of small tasks to achieve each milestone, but don't slip into listing these. An important guideline to prevent that is that steps on the service diagram will tell us *what* is being done, but should say little if anything about *how*. If you did start detailing the individual tasks or steps leading up to a milestone, you would find that they often reflect how the step is completed (e.g., the use of particular systems or mechanisms). We used to suggest that these diagrams include any handoffs (both the "pass" and the "receive") in which the method used introduced delay, errors, or expense (e.g., "Photocopy forms" and "Submit forms to internal mail"). However, we've found that not only is that a definite move onto the slippery slop of detail, but the inclusion of *how* diminishes the value of a diagram that would otherwise only reflect *what*.

Another critical guideline is that steps on a service diagram tend to have the same level of granularity as the business services we'll cover in Chapter 15. One of the guidelines we'll look at there is that a half-done service doesn't accomplish anything of value, so you wouldn't want to define services of that size. In the recent example, either coverage is confirmed or it isn't, and an appointment is either made or it isn't—you wouldn't want to break either of these steps into smaller ones. We use this guideline in the method we use to develop a service diagram. Under each step on the handoff diagram, using Post-its so we don't permanently alter it, we list what we believe to be the main accomplishments that go into that step. In practice, you will usually gather more detail than you need, so individual items on the list will then be clustered into steps that meet the "don't want it half-done" guideline. This pattern of gathering more detail than you want, and then reducing it, is repeated daily in the life of a business analyst.

As Figure 9.4 illustrates, a level 2 (service) diagram is usually three to five times as large as the level 1 (handoff) diagram. This provides a clue as to why you don't

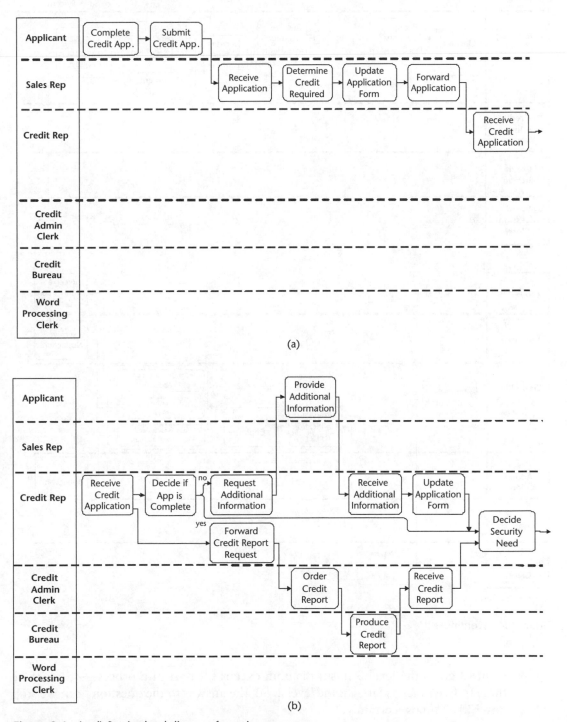

Figure 9.4   (a–d) Service level diagram for as-is processes.

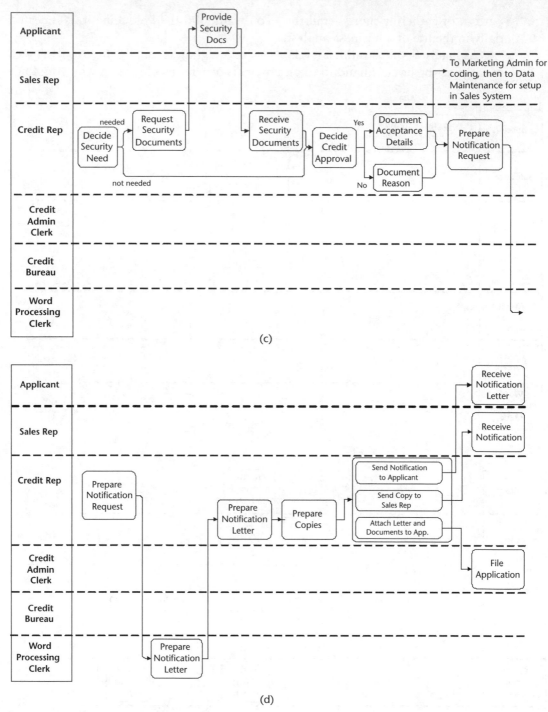

(c)

(d)

Figure 9.4   (continued)

want to go to the level 3 (task) diagram except for part of a process—it might be three to five times as large as the level 2. So, the answer to the question "can we stop now?" is "almost certainly."

Level 3: The Task Diagram

As we noted before, we don't develop this level of diagram for entire processes, but we'll include the description for symmetry with the first edition and to illustrate why we don't build these. This will lead into valuable guidelines on when to stop workflow modeling.

The previous levels show *who* is involved *when*, and *what* is accomplished, but not much detail on *how*. A task diagram makes the transition into describing the details of *how* the process is implemented—it contains individual tasks carried out by an actor leading up to a milestone, as well as details that characterize how the workflow is implemented, such as "Retrieve estimate from file," "Photocopy estimate," "Mail estimate to shop," or "Set up appointment using Adjuster Workbench System." This sounds like plausible information to show on a workflow diagram until you realize that the work isn't really flowing—it's being completed at someone's desk, or workstation, or wherever they perform their duties. And if you took an entire business process to this level, on a single diagram, it could get very large and certainly would be of no use to anyone. Unless, that is, they were trying to make the process appear as overwhelming as possible.

Our workshop participants have come up with various ways to tell when you're going too far on a workflow model. Two of our favorites:

- "It's a flow model, not a user manual."
- "If you're drawing step-by-step instructions on a workflow model, you've gone too far."

That doesn't mean this level of information shouldn't be captured, just that it shouldn't be captured on a swimlane diagram, which is intended to show the flow of work among multiple actors. Figure 9.5 illustrates that this sort of detail belongs in standalone documents such as:

- Procedure descriptions;
- Use cases;

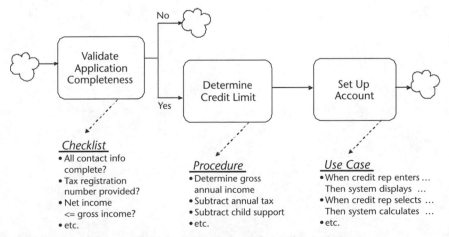

Figure 9.5 When to stop workflow modeling and switch to other techniques.

- Checklists;
- Decision trees or table;
- Traditional flowcharts;
- User manuals;
- Online help facilities;
- Any other format that describes how a step should be completed.

Closing Thoughts

Remember—diagrams convey concepts and structure, while narratives, tables, and other forms convey detail. If the diagram would be a complex maze of crisscrossed lines and decisions, *don't bother drawing it*. In general, if it's too complicated to draw, it's too complicated to generate an "aha!" Instead, record your findings (but only if they're important!) in some other format. There's a big difference between process analysis and task analysis; if you're supposed to be doing the former and drift into the latter, someone will eventually be disappointed, even if it looks as though you're being productive. Remember too that one of the frustrations in most forms of analysis is that you usually have to go too far to be sure you've gone far enough. That means leaving some detail "on the table" (well, maybe in an appendix) and resisting the normal urge to diagram it.

Restraint also has to be applied while developing the swimlane diagrams. Exceptions and errors will crop up regularly, which are tempting to follow up on, but stick with "sunny day" case first. That means flagging branches that you aren't going to worry about just now so you can come back to them later. We'll have lots more to say on this topic in Chapter 11, when we discuss techniques for developing swimlane diagrams, but in the meantime the essential guideline is to follow the mainstream case all the way through the process first and then come back to the other variations later.

Managing detail is a big issue, but it's just one of the tricky problems you'll encounter. In the next chapter, we'll examine other questions and difficulties.

CHAPTER 10

Process Workflow Models—The Finer Points

Introduction

The last two chapters have covered the basics—the essential components and conventions in workflow modeling, and how to stay out of the morass of endless detail. Now, we'll look at the weird stuff that typically arises when as you get into building a swimlane diagram for a real project. We'll address the questions and difficulties that we struggled with while we were learning the techniques so you'll be better prepared than we were when they come up on your project. Many of these situations were raised in the Really Big Telephone Company example in Chapter 8, and now we'll see how to handle any that haven't been dealt with yet.

To prepare for writing this chapter, we wrote each of the questions we most commonly hear on a Post-it, and then sorted them according to the three components of a workflow model to see what would emerge. That's another example of our bottom-up, Post-it-driven development (PDD) approach in action. Stepping back, we saw a great cloud of questions about the first component, actors, so if you have questions about whom or what can be an actor, you're not alone. Only one question about steps was in the mix, and that revisited the point we made in Chapter 8 about every step being shown as a simple box. There were only a few questions about flow, and then a couple of outliers that generally dealt with complexity. Even though the numbers weren't balanced, those categories seemed like the best way to organize the chapter, so it is organized into sections corresponding to the three main components of a workflow model—actors, steps, and flow—plus a fourth section on dealing with complexity.

Actors and Other Characters

Some of the concerns that are typically raised include "what actors do I include in a swimlane diagram?" and "how do you handle cases where the same actor participates in different ways in a process?" and "can there be actors that aren't people, such as systems or devices?" The respective answers are "all of them," "it depends," and "yes." You would probably like a little more meat on the bones of those answers, so we'll expand on them in a question and answer format.

Every Actor? Really?

Do I Really Have to Show Every Actor?

This is the most basic of the common questions, and the answer is "Absolutely!!!" If someone handles the work item in any way, shape, or form, they're an actor, and you must show them. Our inclusion mantra, "Show every actor that *holds* the work, whether they add value, move the work along, or introduce delay" was created for a reason. If you don't show every actor, there are good odds that you are committing deception by sanitization. Without showing each actor and their steps on the diagram, you can't assess whether their participation—the steps, and handoffs to and from—is value-added, neutral, or a source of delay, error, or expense.

People tell us that "actor holds the work" a simple, useful guideline for deciding what steps to include. That's because in practice, it's easy to get caught up in trying to decide if a particular actor is, for instance, "adding value" or simply "moving the work along." Don't worry about it! As long as they "hold the work," they're part of the process.

An important corollary of showing every actor is that even in very high-level diagrams, all of the actors must be depicted. You can summarize and simplify *steps*, but not *actors*, because it's so important to see *all* of the handoffs, even those that take place within an organization unit (see the next question). In fact, as our Chapter 8 examples (forensics and building permits) demonstrated, it's at the highest (handoff) level that showing every actor is most beneficial, because it makes the overall pattern of the flow visible. When you add additional detail to a diagram, it will grow to the right (get longer) but it will not grow vertically because the roster of actors should remain the same.

Do I Really Have to Show Every Actor Within a Department?

Seeking to avoid having all those swimlanes on their diagram, the next question, usually in a pleading voice, is, "Even different actors in the same department? Couldn't we just show the department?" The thinking is that maybe we wouldn't be "sanitizing" the diagram if we simply showed the department as an actor (e.g., Customer Service) rather than showing each participating actor within the department (e.g., customer service rep and new service specialist). Again, show all the distinct actors, as per Figure 10.1, because they perform different steps, and the handoffs will surely affect the process. In the Customer Service example, the customer on the line will certainly be aware of the handoff because of the time it will take, as well as the need to reexplain their situation.

As always there are exceptions. That's why we sometimes raise the quote "rules are for the guidance of the wise and the obedience of fools." For instance, we have modeled situations where there are different job titles, perhaps based on seniority, but they all perform the same steps. In that case, there would just be a single swimlane.

A common situation where we don't show actors within an organization is when they're within an internal department, or an external company or agency, and we have no control over "who, does what, when" within that organization. Certainly if one of the actors (swimlanes) on a diagram was the Postal Service, or a courier company, we wouldn't try to break it out into all their internal actors. A similar

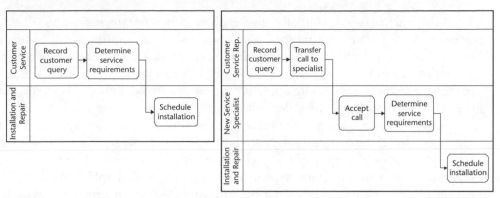

Figure 10.1   Showing multiple actors within a department.

case is when your job is strictly to look at flow across organizations and not within them. In models depicting patient flow through a hospital, we showed the major departments involved (admissions, transportation, medical imaging, cath lab, finance, and so on) but not the individual actors within them, because that wasn't part of the scope of the study. Please don't be tempted, though, to use that as an excuse not to look at the reality of workflow within a department. In one memorable case, when a simple interagency handoff was handled using the internal courier service, we found over fifteen actors were involved and the delivery took several business days.

Jobs, Roles, and Committees

Should I Show the Actor's Job Title or the Role They Play?

In Chapter 8, we said there was usually no practical reason to differentiate between an actor (e.g., a job title) and a role (a part played in a process), so our default is to label swimlanes with the job title. As often as not, the job title gives a pretty good indication of the role anyway, such as customer service rep or investigating officer. This perhaps makes the diagram less generalized, but it definitely makes it more concrete and relevant, which is a good tradeoff.

How Do I Show Two Actors with the Same Job Title but Different Roles?

The example here shows up regularly in cash-handling situations. There are two clerks, each with the same job title, handling a cash deposit. One's role is to prepare the deposit, while the other confirms the accuracy of the deposit slip. Clearly, there are two different actors, and they both should be shown in their own swimlane. There is no need to get fancy in naming the actors according to their role—they would simply be retail clerk #1 and retail clerk #2. The step names will make it abundantly clear what the role is that each is playing.

What About the Case Where One Person Performs Two Distinct Roles?

Do I show just the one actor, or is there a swimlane for each role?

As a starting point, initially give each role a separate swimlane. Place the swimlanes adjacent to one another, and provide some indication that the same person performs them all. You might treat the person as if they were a department in your diagram to illustrate the situation—one wide swimlane (a *pool*) for the actor containing two narrower swimlanes, one for each two role. This will help you gather the facts to support your final decision.

Now you can move on to the real question, which is why they appear to be two separate roles. If the work done by each is of a different nature, and is being handled by only one person because of resource constraints, then it should be remain as two separate swimlanes. Or, if an auditor would say, "Split this up!" you should show two separate roles. As a final test, if you hired another person, and each would take on one of those roles, then you should definitely show each role as a separate swimlane. On the other hand, if you'd now have two people, each performing the same work, they aren't really separate roles.

Another factor to consider is how the handoffs flow from one role to another. If there aren't really handoffs, or the work flows seamlessly from one role to another (they don't do role A work in the morning and role B work in the afternoon), then you really don't have separate roles any more than separate steps denote separate roles. However, if the handoffs prove to be a source of delay, error, or expense, then leave the swimlanes separate to ensure that the situation is highlighted.

Should a Committee Be Shown as an Actor?

We frequently encounter situations where an actor performs as an individual as well as a member of a committee. For instance, an actor (a capacity engineer) also served on two committees, the Joint Integration Team (the JIT) and the Joint Operations Team (the JOT). The capacity engineer, the JIT, and the JOT should each have a separate swimlane. Another example was when a faculty member is also sitting on an appeals committee. In virtually every case, we model the committee as an actor, even if all of its members are already represented on the swimlane diagram because of their separate and distinct responsibilities in the process.

One decision you'll have to make is whether you want to explicitly show the member's participation in committee work as a collaborative activity or you want to show steps only within the committee's swimlane. That's what we would normally do, unless there was a need to visually highlight the participation of other actors in the committee, because it was an intrusive burden.

Systems as Actors

Should Systems Be Shown as Actors at All?

This is a question that raises some extreme positions. We once encountered a reengineering firm that insisted only people, not systems, should be shown on a swimlane diagram. This led to some very misleading models, which led to some very wrong analysis, because the models hid the reality of the situation. A multiday stream of batch programs introduced *many days* of delay into a process they were trying to speed up, while the total "human" part of the process they illustrated amounted to less than an *hour!* Considerable effort was expended on data entry and reformatting, which was also not shown because it was "system work."

Without intending to, they had committed deception by sanitization. They weren't showing every step that added value, moved the work along, or introduced delay, and therefore weren't showing every handoff that was introducing delay, error, and expense.

Consider another example—would a diagram of the Execute Trade Order process for your online broker be accurate is the systems were omitted? Undoubtedly not, since so much of the process is done by the system, not by people. In certain cases, the entire process is completed without any human involvement at all, from the system triggering a trade when a preset price limit is reached, through to the final settlement and issuing of confirmation. How could you depict that without showing systems?

Part of the reasoning behind the resistance to including systems is the idea that what happens inside the machine is just "techie stuff" and isn't part of the "real" process. We've already dealt with that argument, and the bottom line is, if it holds the work, it is part of the process. The system definitely needs to be shown, although it might be simplified and abstracted. The other reason for resistance is the fear that if the discussion gets into IT issues, and systems people are involved, it will rapidly spiral downward into excruciating detail. Unfortunately, that fear is often well founded! This must be managed using the "flow first" and "levels of detail" approaches.

Now, let's consider how we actually show the systems.

How Should Online Systems That Support a Human Actor Be Shown?

A common situation is that an information system assists a human actor in completing a step, such as a Web-based online shopping system, or an Oracle Human Resources system. Certainly the person doing the shopping or completing the HR transaction is an actor with steps in the process, but how should the supporting system be shown? We use one of two alternatives, the first being simply to mention the system in the step name: Create Order via Web or Assign Employee using Oracle HR. In the second alternative, illustrated in Figure 10.2, the human actor has a step in their swimlane, connected to a step in a "systems" swimlane by a vertical, dashed, "supports" line with an arrowhead at each end, intended to indicate interaction. This example also illustrates batch systems and other internal or external processes.

Note that rather than a separate swimlane for each system, we generally use a single swimlane labeled "systems" and then preface the step description with the name of the system, and, if appropriate, the system function being used.

How Should Batch Systems Be Shown?

A batch system, such as overnight production of invoices, is a good example of a system that should be shown, because it takes control of the work item, adds value, and it introduces delay because subsequent steps can't proceed without until it's done. It is shown as an appropriately labeled step in the systems swimlane, as

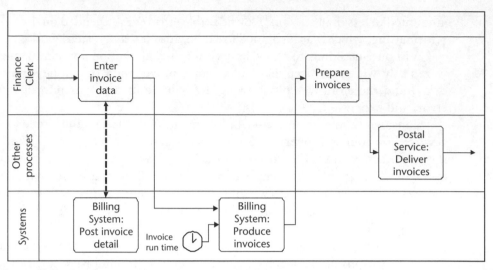

Figure 10.2 Systems as actors.

illustrated in Figure 10.2. We can see clearly that it is a batch system, or at least a system that involves no human interaction, because there is no "supports" line up to a step carried out by another actor.

Many examples aren't so straightforward. In an example from our experience, which we described earlier, a government licensing agency had a complex batch job stream that was part of many of their business processes. This part of the process was not understood at all by business people and was poorly understood by IT—individuals understood their piece of the job stream, but no one understood the whole thing. It had a major impact on client satisfaction because between the batch jobs and the post office, clients had to wait more than two weeks for a license to arrive. After the initial modeling failed to get at the real sources of delay, we were able to convince the team to illustrate the batch jobs. The real challenge lay in depicting what actually happened in the batch job stream without getting into the complexity of every sort, merge, copy, and processing step. To gain understanding of a process like this, you must abstract the detail into understandable business terms, using the swimlane format that the rest of the process will be described in, but it's going to be hard.

The main difficulty will be to find IT resources who have the technical skills to trace through the batch processes, but who can also explain in everyday language what's being accomplished. In some cases—and this is frightening—no one knows anymore what some of the programs are doing. Fortunately, during Y2K remediation, many organizations "opened up" these old programs, figured out what they were doing, and documented them. Better yet, sometimes they actually restructured them or threw them out!

We've tried various approaches, not all of which worked. For instance, we have tried creating swimlane diagrams on which each subsystem was represented as a separate step or even had its own swimlane. That works well when the subsystems are clearly delineated, but, as often as not, it's hard to agree what constitutes a subsystem and its boundaries. Also, splitting work across subsystems often drives you to too low a level of detail, so no business person could follow the diagram anyway.

One option that worked well was to add one swimlane to the workflow model for *each* day in the cycle that a typical license request would work its way through and create a step for each significant milestone on that day (e.g., day 4: "Transmit contract record to national clearinghouse"; days 5 and 6: "no activity"; day 7: "Receive activity report from national," "Merge with secretary of state activity reports," "Print summary reports"; and so on). Showing each day as a separate actor was unusual, but it did a good job of highlighting the delays and serial nature of the process. Remember a point we made in Chapter 8—arrange the swimlanes to tell a story. As usual, it was hard to "synthesize out" the main milestones because the actual job steps were so arcane that only skilled, experienced professionals could tell us what was actually happening.[1]

In a similar example, we followed our normal practice of only one swimlane for systems, but we added vertical markers to the diagram to indicate "day boundaries"—each time the process went through an overnight batch job cycle.

And of course, there has been the odd case where we couldn't interest the business people in seeing a model of the batch processes, so we just had to tell them the conclusion—"It takes eight days to accomplish what should happen almost instantly. It you're interested in improving this, we can prepare estimates."

Should People Doing "System Support" Work Be Shown?

The answer is "yes." In one organization, we were stunned to find out how much "babysitting" of production systems was being done by the IT staff that developed the system, not by the operations department. They were monitoring batch jobs for successful completion, recovering from failures, checking report outputs, correcting bad data "by hand," and so on. This absolutely had to be shown—the IT person definitely had a role in the process that was neither widely known nor funded.

In other cases, there are process steps that are substantially less automated than many people are aware. A classic case was the e-commerce site where orders were captured on the Web, printed, and manually entered into the order entry system! No discussion here—these "human glue" steps must be shown.

Should Devices or Machines Be Shown?

Devices such as ATMs and IVR systems can certainly be shown as actors—they take control and add value. An ATM also holds work for subsequent processing, so it can be said to introduce delay. Figure 10.3 illustrates the addition of an IVR system as an actor. In other models, we have included actors that were machines, like a sorting machine in a mailroom, and pieces of equipment, like a machine doing DNA amplification that operated unattended in a laboratory for extended periods of time.

---

1. This is similar to a business process in which each actor's tasks are so small and specialized that it's almost impossible to discern the overall process. In batch jobs streams, technically similar tasks (e.g., edits) might be combined into one program, so complete business steps or activities are spread across many programs. Only the developer or a good systems analyst can help you figure out this situation.

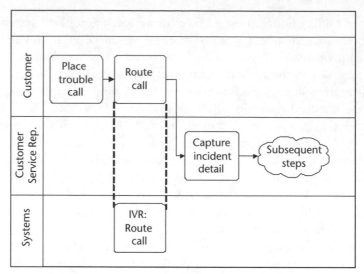

Figure 10.3   A device (an IVR unit) as an actor.

Passive Actors

Should Holding Areas Be Shown?

Does an actor really have to be, you know, "doing something?" Is it fair to include something like an inbox or a loading dock on a swimlane diagram? For a long time, we said, "no," the reasoning being that, per the opening questions, an actor had to "do something." Alec remembers very clearly (and with some discomfort) making this point several years ago while conducting a workshop. Two participants looked dubious, and said, "All right, Alec, let's try your own guidelines on the situation." Immediately, Alec had that sinking feeling you get when your children turn your own rules around on you. Sure enough, an inbox "held the work," and while it didn't "add value," the case could be made that it helped to "move the work along," and it certainly "introduced delay." Point made. Since then, showing this situation on a diagram has frequently been important.

So, a passive storage or holding area like an inbox can be shown as an actor, generally completing the step "hold work." Without explicitly showing them, we might hide an important aspect of the process, the points when the process's work item is sitting, waiting. It also gives us the opportunity to ask how and when the work item gets to the inbox (or whatever), and how and when it is removed. There have been cases where doing this uncovered important sources of delay, for example, when an inconveniently located "pigeonhole wall" was only checked once a day for arriving mail.

Examples of passive objects that could be added to a diagram include:

- An inbox or outbox where items await attention or transport;
- The little metal carousel your order goes onto at a restaurant (handoff from waiters to cooks);
- A cabinet or freezer where samples await testing;
- A loading dock, receiving platform, or staging area at a warehouse.

In Figure 10.4, a "pending orders" board is added as an actor. However, we usually add a single actor called "Holding areas," and into this swimlane we place steps labeled with the name of the holding area, and a step name that essentially says "hold work," but in a more informative fashion. For instance, a step might be "New order board: Hold Orders for Routing." This is completely analogous to how we show systems. An important benefit of having all holding steps shown in a single swimlane is that it's easy to see all the points in the process where work is waiting.

This isn't to suggest that you have to include every single holding area and "wait" step, because they may not be of consequence and can distract attention away from more important issues. We usually don't show them on our models and only do so when observation has proven that they're an issue. If showing all of the "hold work" steps will make the diagram grow too long, there's an alternative that looks the same as an online system supporting an actor completing a step. The difference is that the "hold work" step has a "supports" vertical, dashed line to the flow line that is supported by that holding area. Refer to Figure 10.5.

Should Transmission Mechanisms Be Shown?

We don't show mechanisms like the telephone network because it's more or less instantaneous—it doesn't really hold the work for any time and doesn't introduce delay. In the case of asynchronous communication, we're more likely to show some element of the transmission mechanism. An e-mail communication would be asynchronous, because the sender and the receiver don't have to interact synchronously, the way they would in a telephone conversation. We would often show an e-mail inbox as an actor, because actors don't check it instantly and it holds the work in the meantime. It can also be interesting to determine what triggers the step that retrieves

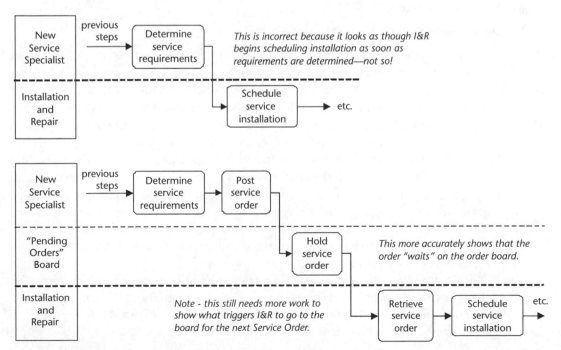

Figure 10.4   A passive holding area as an actor.

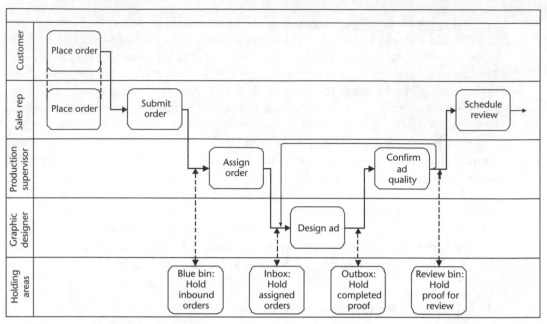

Figure 10.5   A holding area supporting a flow.

something from an inbox—is it done on arrival (there's a "You've got mail" alarm), according to some set schedule (a temporal event), or is it more or less random? Also, don't show something that physically holds the work but is in turn held by or is under the control of another actor, such as a truck, a delivery cart, or a mailbag.

Processes as Actors

Can a Separate Process Appear As an Actor?

Yes, if it is a process your process depends on in the sense that there is a handoff of work *to* that separate process, and then a wait for something to come *back* from that process. The most common case is that many concurrent instances of one process hand off to a single instance of another process that provides some sort of shared service. After the shared service is provided, all of the instances of the original process "wake up" and proceed through to their result. An example came up at a bulk marine shipping terminal, where on any given day there were multiple pending orders to load freighters with the commodities stored at the terminal. Once a day, all of the order details flowed from the various instances of Fill Order into the single process Allocate Resources, which would assign labor and equipment to each Fill Order instance. After allocate resources completed, the Fill Order processes would start up again. This situation was described in Chapter 5 and illustrated in Figure 5.10, as part of process discovery.

Illustrating this situation is exactly analogous to illustrating batch systems. An "other processes" swimlane is placed on the diagram, and a step is placed in that swimlane labeled with the name of the other process. See Figure 10.6. Figure 10.2 also illustrated the involvement of another process.

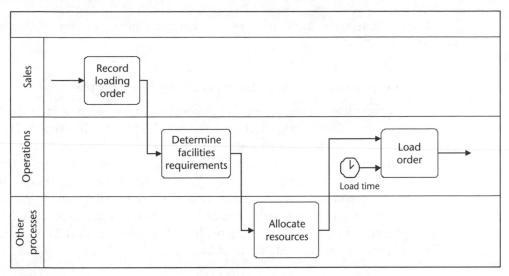

Figure 10.6   Other processes as actors.

If you do not expect a response from the other process (i.e., it is a one-way handoff), you can illustrate the other process with a step in the "Other processes" swimlane that only has a flow going in, or you can indicate the other process by putting its name on a flow into a "stop" symbol.

Steps and Types of Steps

Can We Really Get By with Just Boxes?

This question revisits, briefly, a point we made in Chapter 8. In a business process, the steps perform different kinds of work. Some steps move a work item, some store or retrieve it, some enter or display data, some make decisions, and some add value by transforming the work item in some way. Ultimately, though, a step is a step, and we show them all with the same, rounded-corner rectangle. Depicting the flow is enough to ask of the diagram without burdening it with additional detail.

We're repeating this cautionary note because there are various workflow modeling tools, including the Work Flow Diagram Shapes stencil in Microsoft Visio, that use many iconic symbols such as a telephone, a desk, an envelope, a meeting, a truck, a sack of cash, and so on. These have their place, but are not the kind of workflow model we're discussing here. Incidentally, we use Visio extensively, and the starting point is the Cross-Functional Flowchart Shapes Horizontal stencil.

What Makes It Go? Flow!

You can describe an awful lot with no more than boxes and lines, but a few special symbols will be helpful without adding significant complexity. The questions that come up about flow illustrate the need for these additional symbols. Note first that we use a lot of narrative annotation on our diagrams, often in a layer that can either be displayed or hidden.

How Do You Show Steps That Are Done According to a Schedule?

These steps are started in response to a temporal event, shown as a little clock icon. When the process itself is triggered by a temporal event, as the Report Quarterly Results process would be, the first symbol on the workflow diagram will be a temporal event triggering the first step. It will be labeled with the value of the temporal event, such as "quarter end minus 3 days." When a step within a process is triggered by a temporal event, it is usually one of two or more parallel flows triggering the step. For instance, if there is a step at the end of the business day that consolidates all completed transactions, it will be triggered by a flow from the Post Transaction step AND a temporal event labeled "close of business."

How Do You Show Batching, Counters, or Limits?

Most batching is triggered by a temporal event, the way overnight batch jobs in your system processing cycle are initiated. When a counter or some limit has been reached, the usual way to express that is with a decision, essentially "decide if limit has been reached." The slightly trickier part can be determining which actor actually makes the decision, so you can put that step in the appropriate swimlane. On rare occasions, we have added a little symbol similar in concept to the temporal event, except that it looks like the odometer on your car, and the mileage reading shows the counter value that would trigger the step. In BPMN you might show this as a "rule event." Like the temporal event, the flow from the "odometer" would be one of two or more parallel triggering flows.

How Do You Show "Just Because"?

It sounded strange at first, but you can have steps that are triggered randomly. In one case, at a government taxation agency, an auditor could decide randomly to reach into a "tub file" to select a case that had been set aside for audit. The tub file, so named because it was a big plastic tub, was just like the proverbial "job jar." That situation seemed odd to us, until we drew it as an untriggered (no flow lines entering the left edge) step, Select Case File, and placed it at the very beginning of the audit tax filing process. That's when we realized it wasn't actually so strange after all—most processes begin because of a decision event, and these are essentially random. After all, you never really know when a customer will call to place an order or register a complaint. Most processes are triggered this way, and begin with a step in the upper left corner that has no flow line entering it—the step *is* the triggering event.

Can I Highlight Where a Process Starts and Stops?

For many years, we were content to show the start of a process as an untriggered event and an ending point of a process as a step with no output flows, or a flow into either a stop sign graphic or flowcharting terminator symbol. Now, we've adopted the convention that most of our clients use, which is to add the "start" and "stop" symbols, which have their origin in UML Activity Diagrams and in state transition diagramming before that. We introduced these symbols in Chapter 3. The event that starts the process is shown as a solid black circle, labeled with the triggering event, such as "auditor selects case file" or "customer detects service problem." As described earlier, if the trigger is a temporal event, the clock will be shown.

The stop symbol is used to indicate an ending point in a process and is a hollow circle with a black circle at its center, somewhat like a bull's-eye. We use these to indicate the point in a process at which a result has been delivered to one of the stakeholders and place a label next to the stop symbol indicating the stakeholder and result received. We also use these when there has been a one-way handoff to another process, in which case we label it with the name of the other process and what is being handed off. If it's not one way—that is, we expect the flow to return to the process under consideration—then we depict the other process as an actor.

BPMN offers symbols that mean much the same thing, but the start is a hollow circle and the stop is a hollow circle with a thick border.

Can a Step Have No Output Flow?

Sometimes, you will have a step that just dangles—it has no output—and sometimes that's okay, and other times it's not. The question to ask is: "Has this actor fulfilled their responsibility at this stage of the process?" If so, and there is no follow-on activity or handoff to another actor, then this "dangling activity" is fine. For example, the File Clerk actor completes the step File Original, and that's it—they have no further work at this time, and the process's work item, the original they filed, is not going anywhere either.

How Do I Show Repeated Activities (Looping)?

This can be a tricky situation, proving the contention that a swimlane diagram can't simultaneously tell a good story and be totally precise and generalized. To illustrate, consider a process in which a designer builds a new Web site for a client. They meet, the designer does some work, they meet again, the designer does some more work, and this continues until the client accepts the work. How many "meet—design" cycles should be shown? We could just draw one, ending with a "client accepts?" decision, and a mutually exclusive flow that either carries on into implementing the design, or "loops back" and joins the flow entering Meet Client. (At that point, it's a mutually exclusive trigger—Meet Client is either triggered by the initial contact or by the returning flow.) The problem with that is that it doesn't really tell the story visually, especially if the typical number of meetings is something like seven. What should you do?

This is another example of learning from our students. For years, we would have drawn one cycle of activity with the loop as we just described. However, one group of students rebelled and pointed out that the looping flow was going back in time! They felt it would be more appropriate to repeat the cycle of activities a typical number of times, even if that was 10, because that more accurately and visually told the story of what was happening. Of course, they were right, and this is our usual approach now. We usually draw a dotted outline around the entire set of activities (i.e., one box around all 10 repeated sets of steps) with an annotation explaining that we have shown a typical case and perhaps also noting best and worst cases.

A cautionary note—always draw the first cycle separately, because it will almost always contain setup activities that aren't repeated in subsequent cycles. The same may be true for the last cycle. In Figure 10.7, a set of activities that is typically repeated twice is shown, with the diagram also supporting "looping back" to handle the cases when the activities are repeated three, four, or more times.

How Can I Show Time on a Diagram?

In one of our examples relating to showing a batch job processing cycle, we described how we handle this, which is simply to add vertical lines to the diagram, each indicating some time boundary or milestone. Each was labeled just as you would on any timeline—day 1, day 2, and so on. Figure 10.8 provides an example. Of course, the timing could be in hours or weeks, or you could be labeling the lines according to the subprocess or phase—intake, assessment, and so on. If you're using Visio, the stencil for these diagrams includes a symbol called the "separator," which is intended for this use.

How Can I Show a Part of the Process I Don't Know About (Yet) or Care About?

We get a lot of use out of a cloud symbol. When we put a blank cloud before or after part of a diagram, it means "there's something there, but it isn't relevant right now." We've used this in many of the examples in the book. A cloud with a question mark means "we know something's going on here, but we don't know yet what it is—we'll get back to it." Finally, the cloud can contain narrative explaining what is happening when it is too complicated to depict with a swimlane diagram but needs to be captured. We also use this to indicate collaborative, creative work in a process that just cannot be reduced to a sequence of steps and decisions.

Dealing with Complexity

At some point, you will have to deal with somebody else's convoluted, overly detailed diagram. We're often in that situation, and are a little embarrassed to admit that over the years, cleaning up these diagrams has been a good source of income. We don't feel bad about it, though, because clients always report high value from the product, because they can then see things about the process that were hidden before. We'll provide a quick overview of the steps we go through in these situations, which will also provide guidance to help ensure that you're not producing a diagram that we'll have to come in and clean up.

The heart of the approach is summed up in a quote from Thomas Mann's "The Magic Mountain": "Order and simplification are the first steps to mastery of a subject." That's where we'll start.

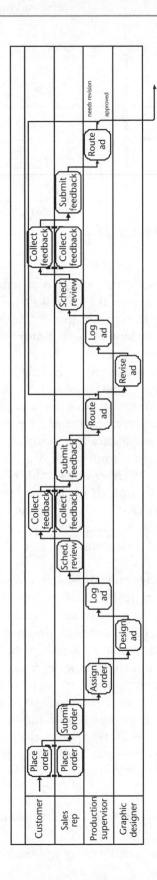

Figure 10.7 Diagramming repeated activities (looping).

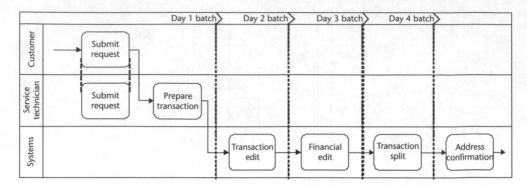

Figure 10.8   Adding a time scale to a diagram.

First, "order" the diagram so the flow goes strictly from left to right. We typically use Post-its and plotter paper, the same way we'll describe in Chapter 11 on running a workflow session. Don't start on the "simplification" part just yet. The odds are that there will be some looping back, but try to get the main flow following a left to right timeline. If it's impossible to draw the diagram this way, you have likely encountered the situation covered in the following point.

Next, ensure that it's diagramming a *single* process. You might have to separate one diagram into several. Many of the most complex "process models" we've encountered turned out to be anything *but* a process model. Sometimes, you'll actually be looking at a data flow diagram of a complex processing cycle that doesn't have a beginning or an end. There's not much you can do about this, because there isn't a process model to simplify. Other times, multiple processes and activities have been rendered in a single diagram that depicts the entire life cycle of some entity, even an entire division, rather than a single, specific business process. This was the case recently when we were asked to decipher a "process model" of standard operating practices (SOP) by a baffled plant engineer who had been told to validate it and, even worse, use it.

It was laid out in swimlane format, but within this one diagram was the hiring, training, and assessment of employees, their clocking-in for a shift, the start-up and shut-down of plant systems, the monitoring and inspection of the plant, and other activities too numerous to mention. In addition to being impossible to reorder from left to right, another clue that it didn't trace the flow from a single event was that activities were clearly on a different time scale, triggered by different events. Some inspection activities happened only a few times per year, while clocking in for work happened hundreds of times per day. You could show all these different activities in a decomposition diagram, but not on a flow diagram that traces a single triggering event through to its results. When this happens, the power of the Post-it comes into play, because you'll move parts of the flow onto separate diagrams. We look for chains of activities that flow from a single event to the final result. Three examples on the SOP diagram were:

1. From hiring an employee through to certification that they could start working in the plant;
2. From clocking-in of an employee for a shift through to clocking-out;

3. From a scheduled inspection being triggered through to corrective action being completed.

Once you've separated out different processes, you will sometimes be able to simplify even further by separating out variations for one part of a process where alternative flows have been depicted. For instance, the front end of a process has several alternatives, but the rest is the same. A simple example would be a request for replacement parts arriving from a retailer, from a repair agency, or direct from the consumer. If each variant is just a few steps, they can probably all go on the same diagram. However, if they are more complex, with multiple steps and multiple actors, and those actors participate in the other variations as well, you have a recipe for a spaghetti diagram that won't tell anyone anything. Each variant should then be diagrammed separately. Include the most common case on the main diagram, with a dotted box around it to identify it as one of some number of alternatives. Other "empty" dotted boxes on the diagram can each serve as a reference to a variant drawn on a separate "subdiagrams." All of these dotted boxes can flow into an "OR" leading into the rest of the process. In the same fashion, there can multiple variants within the process or multiple endings.

If the whole process is significantly different in each situation, you need to put each on its own diagram. That's exactly why we identify the cases of a business process during framing, so we only have to worry about diagramming one at a time.

Now, it will be safe to start "squashing" steps together using principles of handoff and service diagrams. Before you do, take photographs of the details, as you might need them later. If the diagram is much too detailed, you'll want to combine steps until you have an approximation of a service diagram. This can be a good point to rearrange the order of the swimlanes (customer, core, supporting, and so on) to better tell the story. Finally, you can combine steps in the service diagram to produce a handoff diagram.

If this works out for you the way it usually does for us, some useful analysis of the process workflow can now take place, and you'll have earned your keep for a while longer.

Flowing On

We could carry on into the modeling of more and more obscure or theoretical cases, but we've covered the vast majority of what will come up in practice. Now it's time to put what we've learned to work and develop a real workflow process model. Chapter 11 tells you how to go about building and validating a workflow model in a facilitated session with the participation of subject matter experts.

Develop As-Is Process Workflow Model

Introduction

You're Ready to Go!

Now, at last, it's time to conduct your initial workflow modeling session. The good news, assuming you've taken Mr. Fosdick's advice from Chapter 1 about not skipping any steps, is that you are pretty well prepared for it. Consider what you have:

1. Sponsorship and a team you've already facilitated through process discovery and framing, many of whom will participate in the upcoming modeling sessions;

2. A properly framed process, including triggering event, final results, subprocesses, main cases, and a roster of the actors and their main responsibilities in the process, all of which will help "swimlaning" proceed, dare we say it, swimmingly;

3. A good foundation in the techniques (rules and conventions) of workflow modeling, including the finer points we covered in the last chapter, and guidelines that will be invaluable in practice, such as "flow first, detail later" ("FFDL!") and "show *every actor* that holds the work" ("EA!");

4. Exposure to the approach we illustrated in Chapter 8 for building a handoff diagram by asking "the three questions," beginning with "who gets it next?"

After some practice, you will really appreciate that last point, because it will get you all the way through the process, from trigger to result, building a framework on which you can *iteratively* and *quickly* build a more accurate and complete swimlane diagram. After that, you can much more easily develop progressively more detailed models, as necessary.

The Overall Flow for Flow—What We'll Cover

With all that background, we now move into methods for building an as-is workflow model. It's not quite as simple as just grabbing a pen and starting a diagram, but with the background you now have and the techniques we'll cover, it's not all that difficult either. We'll progress through:

1. Preparing for the workflow modeling session;
2. Initiating the session;
3. Building the initial handoff (level 1) model by applying the three questions;

4. Validating and extending the model by applying five more questions;
5. Adding detail, as necessary, with a service (level 2) model;
6. Transitioning into task-level documentation.

Is a Session Really Necessary?

You might wonder "Do I really need to conduct a modeling session?" Perhaps you feel that you could build a workflow model by observing people on the job or that you know the process pretty well already. Regarding the first point, starting the modeling process with a facilitated session is almost always the most workable approach, because it's hard to abstract behavior into a model while observing it. Remember that while watching people at work, they will likely be participating in multiple processes, and you won't know which. On top of that, the complete business process probably takes place at multiple locations, and stitching these disparate observations into a cohesive model will be much harder and more time consuming than the session would be. However, you should always finish by confirming your conclusions through direct observation, what is known as *walking the flow*.

Regarding the second point, you might know the whole process well enough to develop a swimlane diagram, but that isn't what really matters. What does is whether the process actors, the people who would attend your modeling session, know the overall process and everyone's contribution. Probably not, so there is almost always benefit in terms of learning and buy in from having participants jointly develop a workflow model. However, not all of the work will be carried out in sessions. The usual cycle is:

1. Prepare for the modeling session.
2. Conduct one or more team sessions to build the handoff-level model.
3. Interview individual areas or participants to collect additional detail about their parts.
4. Consolidate your findings into one or more cleaned-up handoff diagrams, and service-level diagrams if you gathered that level of detail.
5. Reconvene the group for review and verification of the models.
6. Walk the flow—confirm the workflow models by direct observation in the workplace. You might do this earlier, but we prefer to get the model as close as possible first.

Will This Work for Me?

While every situation is a little different, and each analyst has different strengths, we've found that the techniques we'll describe work well in a wide variety of situations. Of course, the right technique is the one that works—the one that produces the necessary model without having to quell a rebellion—but these approaches have a great track record. Even if you're a little dubious, we recommend you try them as is and then adjust them as necessary to adapt to your situation. Here is a relevant lesson. One of our friends recently did a study at his company, a global enterprise, on the lessons learned through the adoption of a new application provisioning and requirements definition methodology. The number one lesson? "When in doubt, trust the method." We've learned a similar lesson over the past several years, which is that we can make progress even faster than we used to think possible by sticking to our own methods as strictly as possible. That's what we call "eating your own dog food" in the consulting business.

Not everyone trusts your method, though, or wants to eat your dog food. You might encounter resistance to as-is workflow modeling from people who believe "we all know how things work" or " we all know what the problem is—let's get on with solving it." In reality, the situation is often "we all know how *our* part of things works—sort of" and "we all know what *one* problem or symptom is—but not the root cause." Let's spend a few minutes considering how to deal with this resistance.

Dealing with Resistance to As-Is Modeling

To avoid stirring up unnecessary angst, we'll point out that when you get this far, there is seldom resistance to spending a reasonable amount of time on as-is modeling. You've already demonstrated how much can be accomplished in a short period of time by following well-defined methods and so have usually earned the faith of the sponsor and participants.

In a small percentage of cases, however, there will be pressure to skip as-is modeling altogether. This used to be much more common, perhaps because the advice in the early days of BPR was that you shouldn't waste time mapping a process you planned to replace anyway. That turned out to be profoundly bad advice, and many people who followed it were burned and now recognize that as-is modeling is essential. That doesn't mean they're thrilled about it, but experienced project leaders and analysts recognize that skipping it is a false economy.

Still, reluctance will arise. As noted, one explanation is that the problem is already known, and presumably understood, and it's time to get on with implementing a solution. The trouble with this explanation is that it is virtually always wrong. Because a true business process is larger than people think it is, their understanding of the problem is also limited. More precisely, their understanding of the impacts of any proposed solution will be limited, taking us right back into the world of "local optimization, global suboptimization" and conflicting functional objectives that we've thoroughly discussed already. You can't just tell someone "you're wrong," so as a first line of defense, try explaining that experience shows you'll pay later if you skip the as-is because:

- The as-is must be fully understand order to identify specifically why it behaves the way it does—the good aspects to preserve and the bad aspects to eliminate, improve, or replace. A cross-functional process is such an interconnected set of actors, activities, departments, locations, systems, metrics, objectives, and so on that if you make changes to one part without the knowledge *and participation* of the whole, there will inevitably be unanticipated consequences. Whether or not it was part of a business process initiative, everyone has experienced this.

- The only way to truly understand the current situation is to identify who (job titles or actors, and organization) works in the process now to get their input on how things actually work and how things should work in the future;
- The as-is ensures focus on fact, not opinion, and demonstrates to the involved parties that improvement is needed and possible, speeding up redesign and implementation.
- It will establish an accurate performance baseline so you can demonstrate improvement later and justify the project.
- You need to know who will be affected in order to prepare for job change and training. A critical and sometimes overlooked point—you must know who does what in the current process if for no other reason that to be able to tell them "don't do that anymore."
- You will also need to identify all interfaces to other systems and commitments to other processes that must be maintained. This is also critical—there are *always* important interconnections and dependencies that will be disrupted if they aren't identified. Similarly, some are "useless" and might be reimplemented unnecessarily if they aren't understood.
- Most of all, experience shows time and again that even though workflow design is usually not the real issue, the workflow model provides the best framework for uncovering what the real issue is. It shows every point of involvement, by every actor, and so lets us evaluate all of the enablers.

If you've reviewed this list and "the resister" really does think all seven points are covered, it might be worth going through an example. Here's one that a friend recently recounted from his days at one of the top global consultancies. He was part of a process improvement team working at a large energy company, and senior management refused to support as-is modeling. The reason given was "the usual suspect"—"we all know what the problem is, so just get on with it." Dutifully, the team tried to implement the suggested fix, and then countless revisions to it. Every time they got into the details of implementation, some factor or other emerged revealing that the proposed solution wouldn't work, and so it was revised. Again and again and again, for six months. Eventually, management agreed that the effort was going nowhere because the process was more complex than they had realized. The entire six months of effort was scrapped, which was a significant expense due to staff time, consulting bills, and the cost of lost opportunities. The irony, which you probably saw coming, was that a useful job of as-is modeling was then completed quickly, and redesign then proceeded relatively smoothly, all in far less than six months. In some ways, this is a "good news" story because we've seen cases where the lost time was closer to a year than six months.

The other underlying reason for opposition to modeling the current state is personal experience with a never-ending process modeling death march, where months and months of effort are expended gathering information of less and less significance. If this is the case, you'll have to point out that we're seeking to *understand* the as-is, not *document it in excruciating detail*, and if the as-is *really is* well understood, this step will go quickly. Make your point by showing examples of handoff- and service-level diagrams, and your guidelines for stopping workflow modeling as soon as you get into describing step-by-step procedures. That should persuade the dubious that you won't let the as-is modeling effort get out of control.

This might not fully convince people, but it could be enough to set you up to try the "please, humor me" approach, which we have fallen back on more than once. Say, "Let's just spend enough time to confirm that we all share the same understanding of how the process works." Stress that the goal will simply be to identify or confirm the main actors in the process, determine the sequence of their involvements, and their main responsibilities. Get permission to run a three-hour session to produce an initial handoff-level model, using the "three questions" approach we saw earlier. You will likely have time to make some progress on other cases, or even on the service-level model as well. If the modeling goes smoothly, fine—you'll have a useful product without having invested much of anyone's time. If it doesn't go smoothly, you will have demonstrated that there isn't a shared understanding of how the process works, and that usually amounts to agreement to proceed.

Assembling the Team

If you've made it this far on your project, you have a pretty good idea who needs to participate in the workflow modeling session. Anyone who participated in the process identification sessions that has a role in the process to be mapped is a candidate, along with any additional folks you identified during framing. In the simple case, you'll have representatives from each organization unit that participates in the process, and won't have to worry about having multiple participants to represent variations across geography, product line, or market segment. Good luck!

What we will cover in this brief section are a few additional pieces of advice that relate to common questions, such as:

- Should management attend, or only the hands-on workers?
- Do we need the actual workers, or would others who know the process do?
- Should IT or other staff that support the systems used by the process attend?
- Should external parties like customers or suppliers participate?

Management and Front-Line Participants?

Participants should include management or supervisory personnel and front line workers or "individual contributors." Here's a reaction we've heard to this—"Oh no! Not all at once. They can't work together!" Well, they do in successful organizations, and, besides, they have to, or process improvement will fail. Both perspectives are essential, and in our experience, each group always learns from the other. Individual workers learn what other areas do and what the interdependencies are, and they learn from management about the organization's issues and direction. Management learns what *really* happens at the front lines (now as opposed to 5, 10, or 15 years ago), and what issues or obstacles their people face. It may initially be uncomfortable, but the facilitator (that's you!) and the structure imposed by building a model help everyone to participate. Working on an as-is model has proven so successful at improving communication, developing a broader understanding, and team-building that clients bring us in just to do this even when the process doesn't apparently need improvement.

Front-Line Workers or Representatives?

There is occasionally the desire not to include front line workers because (a) they're really busy, and (b) "we know what they do." The suggestion is that the session instead be attended by delegates "who know the process" such as the training department, the people who designed the current process, or policy and standards groups who know how it's supposed to work. We're always a little amused that these people can apparently be freed up to attend the session, but the actual workers can't. Perhaps there is some concern that front line workers won't know how to participate in a session, but that has never been an issue. Whatever the reasoning, this is among the worst ideas that come up during process improvement projects. The problem in all cases is that knowing how things are *supposed* to work is no substitute for knowing the day-to-day reality of how things *actually* work. You will always get a better understanding of process behavior when the people in the process participate. Looking ahead, participation leads to buy-in that will be invaluable when you get into process redesign and implementation. Even if it's expedient, don't be tempted to map the as-is process without the people who make it work.

IT and Other Supporting Players?

In general, every organization and preferably each individual role that "touches the work" should be involved. That doesn't mean you should invite all the administrative support people or drag representatives from the mailroom to every session, but some support staff should attend, with IT at the top of the list. One reason IT staff should be there is that they're often the ones who have to make all the systems "play nice together," and so they might have a more end-to-end view than people working in the different business functions the process crosses. We have encountered numerous cases where IT staff performed significant, daily "babysitting" of systems, such as watching for exceptions, revising or correcting data, or routing work. They were definitely "holding the work," not just supporting systems that held the work. In any case, those systems might play a critical role (add value, move the work along, or introduce delay) so IS or IT representatives need to represent those systems, although with the caveat to stay out of eye-glazing detail.

That note about "eye-glazing detail" is much less of an issue than it used to be. Thankfully, the stereotype of the nerd who speaks in code is disappearing, and we consistently work with IT architects, project leaders, and analysts who are every bit as business-oriented as anyone else, and sometimes more so. In fact, we have seen many business process initiatives originally formulated by IT staff. These didn't necessarily involve technology—they just came about because IT had to stitch all the pieces together, saw the inherent conflicts, and therefore saw how the complete process could be improved.

Of course, this doesn't mean that IT staff should forget about IT. Participating in process mapping can help them spot opportunities that will be considered during process redesign. Many times, knowledge gleaned during process mapping sessions has helped to identify places where significant process improvement can be accomplished using modern BPMS or enterprise application integration (EAI) tools to support straight through processing (STP) by linking batch (and other) steps in real time.

External Participants

Participants should include customers, suppliers, or whatever other external party is part of the process, although we seldom get agreement from our clients. The typical reaction is a variation on "Oh no! We can't let them see how messed up we are!" We point out that "they certainly already know how messed up you are—they've told us—and that's why we're doing this work in the first place." Besides, they almost surely know some things about the process that you don't. Sometimes the customer does substantial work that the internal process performers weren't aware of. The customer might ride herd on the process or monitor it to ensure that things keep happening. Other times, the customer carries out handoff and transport activities—they're the so-called human glue that joins the different parts.

A personal example—I contacted the dealership when a major home appliance failed, and they provided me with paperwork for the authorized service organization, which in turn provided me with paperwork for the local repair agency. I can attest this was an opportunity for delay, error, expense, and frustration. Customers and suppliers may be internal to the organization or external to it. There is the most reluctance to including external customers, suppliers, or other trading partners, but in the age of e-business, e-commerce, and the extended enterprise, where business processes "cross the firewall" (i.e., organizational boundaries), it is becoming a fact of life.

Preparing for the Modeling Session

Scheduling

How Long Will It Take?

Everyone wants to know "how long will it take?" and hopes we can provide some formulas or heuristics for estimating. Unfortunately, we just can't tell you, just as we couldn't say in Chapter 5 how long process discovery would take. We've tried to discern a metric that uses the information from framing such as the number of participating organizations, the number of individual actors, the number of main responsibilities each has, the number of subprocesses, the number of cases, the time from trigger to result, and estimates of complexity. No luck. This shouldn't really be surprising, because if you already knew enough about a process to estimate how long it would take to map it, you probably wouldn't need to hold a mapping session. Simply put, you don't know what you don't know. The other factor is that the time taken depends on the people involved, and, of course, people are people, so variation is expected and substantial. Some facilitators are masters at keeping a group moving forward; others aren't. At some companies, the culture supports rapid development of a "good enough" model, at others, the culture demands more discussion and involvement even when following our guidelines for getting through a handoff diagram quickly.

There is, however, some good news. We said in the first edition that it will take "longer than you think" but experience has shown that it will usually be "faster than you think," *as long as you are diligent about following the guidelines.* With solid preparation, hard-nosed facilitation ("FFDL") and adherence to the "one process, one case, one scenario, and one flow at a time" guideline, we are usually able to build at least a substantial handoff diagram within a single three-hour session. This includes processes that involved 20 or more actors and scores of steps. Within that same three-hour session, we've often been able to cover two or three cases of the process and even gather some of the details for the service-level diagram. There are no miracles—this level of accomplishment depends absolutely on having done a good job of framing.

We've avoided answering the "how long?" question, but, in practice, we're expected to estimate how long it will take, and so will you. Our approach is to employ the time-honored and generally effective approach of "time-boxing" the problem. We arbitrarily state how long it will take to produce the initial iteration of the model(s) and then work to that. Most often, the objective of the first mapping session (approximately three hours) will be to produce a handoff diagram for the main case of the process. Then, when you conduct the session, there are three typical outcomes:

1. The target is met, in which case everyone is happy with progress, and you congratulate the group.
2. The target is exceeded, in which case everyone is *very* happy with progress. As a facilitator, you are sure to congratulate the group on their accomplishments.
3. The target is not met, and the amazing thing is that participants are *still* typically satisfied with progress. Why? Because the process has been shown to be more involved than was originally thought, which reinforces the need to invest time in modeling it. And of course, as a facilitator, you congratulate the group on sticking with it and getting as much done as they did.

It doesn't always work out this well, but it usually does.

Once the initial handoff diagram is completed, that might be good enough to understand the as-is, or you might invest one or two further sessions in refining it and ensuring that all the main cases have been covered. You should also have a sense of whether taking the model down to a service-level diagram is necessary. If it is, we recommend producing that through one-on-one interviews or small meetings with each of the functional areas involved in the process. These are typically no more than 90 minutes or two hours in length. After you consolidate what you've learned into a single model (or multiple models—one per case), it's a good idea to conduct a walkthrough with the entire group. That way, everyone gets a better sense of what everyone else is doing in the process without having had to sit through the development of the entire model.

How Often and How Long Are the Sessions?

Realistically, two or perhaps three sessions per week, each lasting half a day (the morning is preferable) is the most that is practical. Three is often too much to ask people to participate in. Twenty years ago, we had no trouble scheduling people into *several weeks* of three, half-day sessions per week, but those days are gone. Everyone is extraordinarily busy these days, and getting the right people to attend just one or two sessions is an achievement. Our default schedule is half-day sessions on Tuesday and Thursday mornings, which avoids problems with Mondays and Fridays such as travel, four-day work weeks, and the "Monday morning blahs." Serve refreshments as an incentive to get there early, work hard from 8:30 am until noon or so, and then let people get back to their job. Session time in the afternoon is never as effective as session time in the morning. You can probably remember struggling to stay awake during a 1:00 pm meeting.

If it seems that more sessions would be better, remember that if your session is productive, it will take you several hours of work to clean up and document the results. As we noted earlier, our guideline is that for every hour in a facilitated session, your team will invest three additional hours—two in documenting the session, and another in preparing for the next. A half-day session therefore represents a total of two days of work—a half day in the session, a full day documenting it, and another half day preparing for the next session. This breakdown is approximate, but has been borne out over the years. The key point is that you can put *more* session time into a week, but it won't necessarily be the *most effective* use of everyone's time. Participants are energized when they return to the next session and see the results of the previous session properly cleaned up and documented, possibly even in a form they can take back and review with coworkers. They are further energized when they see that the session has been thoroughly prepared for—the necessary flipcharts, Post-its, and other resources are ready to go, answers have been developed for questions that arose in the last session, key questions and topics for the session have been identified, and so on. We hear again and again from participants how much they appreciate this "behind the scenes" work.

But We're Using a Global Team!

A complicating factor in determining the schedule is that many of the participants might be traveling long distances to attend, and it simply isn't feasible to only have two, half-day sessions on Tuesday and Thursday, with Wednesday off. As organizations and their people become more geographically distributed, distance and travel are more common issues. In these situations, we've reluctantly run five days of back-to-back, all-day sessions, because this was assumed to be the best use of everyone's time. It wasn't. Keeping sessions to a maximum of two-thirds of a day has been at least as effective, and often more effective, than all-day sessions. Why? Because a properly run session can be fairly intense, and people just don't have the mental energy to participate fully for eight hours and then go back to their desk or hotel room to deal with all the phone calls and e-mails that are stacking up. Plus, the core team won't have the time to invest in preparing for a fully productive session the next day. What we do now is run a session from roughly 8:30 am to noon, have food brought into the session room (don't let people leave!) for a stand-up lunch from noon to 12:30 pm, and then carry on with the session until 2:00 pm, give or take half an hour. Conversations during the lunch break are often an important source of ideas and information, especially if people remain in the session room. For instance, a core team member might notice a few people discussing a particular flipchart or part of the swimlane diagram, and join the group to find out what it is that is interesting them. Now, even when travel isn't involved, when a client requests a single, all-day session we suggest this 2/3 of a day format instead.

Of course, when you need to bring people together who are geographically distributed, possibly globally, there will be resistance. You'll need to stress that the group only has to be brought together for development of a handoff-level model. If you just can't secure this involvement, maybe a virtual (electronic) meeting is possible. We have used NetMeeting with a simple drawing tool like Visio or electronic Post-its in some cases and videoconferencing tools in others. New Web-based collaboration tools are appearing all the time. Your organization's training or corporate services department may be able to help.

Facilities and Supplies

The main facilities requirements were already covered back in Chapter 5, on process discovery. The only significant change is that for process discovery sessions, we wanted to accommodate a wide "U" shape, but for swimlane diagramming the most important factor is to have a long, plain wall to use as a work area. You will curse every pillar, every piece of permanently affixed artwork or equipment, and anything else that interferes with your ability to put a 30- or 40-foot-long roll of paper up on the wall. We used to do a lot of this work on whiteboards, but there are almost never enough of them all together to model a complete process, so we use rolls of paper. You will also want plenty of room for the group to stand around the paper, because they will be doing a lot of the moving and placing of Post-its. Once, when we were unable to secure a proper meeting space, we were able to use a long, wide hallway on the executive floor, and arrange for artwork to be temporarily removed. We taped up 40 linear feet of brown butcher paper, handed out pens and Post-its, and got to work. A happy benefit was how impressed the executives were with the process maps that illustrated how work flowed through the company's divisions and functional support areas!

The supplies needed are also much the same as what we suggested in Chapter 5—multicolored flipchart and whiteboard markers, bright white flipchart pads, Super Sticky neon Post-its in both 3 × 3-inch squares and 4 × 6-inch rectangular sizes, and a roll of white plotter paper or similar product. Our friend Mathew in Seattle shared a great trick for working with plotter paper when he saw me start to draw long, crooked, dotted lines for the swimlanes. Take a length of paper about 15 or 20 feet long, fold it in half lengthwise, and crease it. Fold and crease again, and then once more, and your length of plotter paper will have eight swimlanes clearly marked via the creases, and they'll be just about the right size for the Post-its. Typically we place two or three of these, one above the other, on the wall, giving us 16 or 24 swimlanes to work with. If we think the length will be necessary, it's usually easier to put up two 20-foot lengths than work with a single 40-foot length.

Before we go any further, a cautionary note—*don't write anything on the paper (actors, flow lines, notes, and so on) until the last possible moment!* If you do, you *will* regret it, because new actors and steps will always arise, and you need to be able to move things around on your work surface without being constrained by markings in indelible ink. For instance, don't write the names of the actors you identified during framing on the plotter paper. Instead, write each on a Post-it, and place it at the left edge of their swimlane, so they will be easier to resequence later on.

The Kickoff

Approach

First and foremost, remember that getting a first-cut, as-is workflow model completed within your (and the project's) natural lifetime is the immediate goal. Horror stories abound, like the "as-is" model that grew to more than 100 feet long, completely consuming time and resources, and leading to the cancellation of a promising project. Many initiatives get into similar difficulties because the team gets bogged down in detail, the participants (subject matter experts) get bored and/or frustrated and stop participating effectively, and the project dies on the vine. The problem—detail begets detail, which begets even more detail. It's critical that you and the participants internalize a key concept—the purpose of the modeling sessions is to *understand* the as-is, not document it in excruciating detail! The introduction (the "kickoff") for the modeling session addresses this by giving everyone a quick introduction to the purpose and philosophy of the methods that will be employed and immediately getting underway with as-is workflow modeling. We will make use of the different levels of detail we covered in Chapter 9 and the techniques we introduced in Chapter 8 for quickly getting *through* a process before diving *down* into details. We will quickly build a handoff-level (level 1) workflow model, refine and extend it, and then add a controlled amount of detail, but only after confirming the need.

To accomplish this, you must immediately give the group a sense of urgency and forward momentum, and a long introduction to the first workflow modeling session won't help. That's one reason the kickoff for the workflow modeling session will be different than your process discovery session was. Most of the participants have already been in sessions together, so you won't need to have a "pep talk" from an executive, a tutorial on what a business process really is, or a time for venting. Essentially, you'll spend as little time as possible answering two questions:

1. What are we doing? You'll answer this by explaining the basic principles and methods of swimlane diagrams.
2. What process are we modeling? Now, you'll recap scope and context using the overall process map and the information gleaned during framing.

This shouldn't take any more than about 10 minutes. Then, you'll reinforce the scope by placing the triggering event and the final results on the swimlane diagram and get started on mapping the flow.

If you have attendees who didn't participate in the earlier session, you'll take a little more time for introductions, but you should brief the new participants about background and overall objectives before the session.

Let's return to how we handle these two questions.

Question 1: What Are We Doing?

The facilitator or lead workflow modeler (that's probably *you!*) will introduce workflow models, the principles, and the method the session will follow. If the group hasn't seen one before, show a sample swimlane diagram, but not one depicting the process they're about to study. If you do, they'll immediately start critiquing it or wondering why a session is necessary when you already have the model done. A service-level (level 2) model can be used to explain the four components—actors, steps, flow, and handoff. Explain that this can easily get bogged down in detail, perhaps with another real-life example of a complex diagram, and explain that this is why we start with a handoff-level (level 1) diagram. Then, show the handoff model corresponding to the service model you just showed them and explain the concept—whenever an actor holds the work, no matter how much or how little they do, draw one step and move on. Tell them that it might be frustrating at times when important details are omitted, or the magnitude of someone's contribution is apparently minimized, but this will ensure we get all the way through the process and provide a framework for gathering detail about everyone's contribution that was missed along the way.

You should also summarize a few of the guiding principles, especially:

- "GEFN"—good enough for now;
- "Flow first, detail later"—get through the process first;
- "Flow first, assessment later"—don't slip into judgment about what's value-added or not;
- "Flow first, improvements later"—don't slip into developing ideas for the to-be;
- "Main flow first, others later"—the initial emphasis will be on tracing the flow that leads to a result for the customer, with other flows added later;
- "Reality, not policy"—the purpose of the session is to model what really happens, not what should happen according to policy, the training program, or the current process design;
- "One process, one case, one scenario, and one flow at a time"—we want to minimize how many variations we're modeling at one time, right down to the point that if there are two or more flows out of a single step (e.g., if the step is a decision), we'll only follow one of them during the first pass.

Summarizing these on a flipchart is a good idea, and you can explain that you're doing so because you'll try to adhere to these guidelines, but you really need their help.

You might have to remind people that we separate a process into different "cases" in order to make the workflow models manageable and understandable when each case has a substantially different workflow. You might want to recap one of the examples we used in Chapter 6, such as the idea that the Receive Shipment process at a manufacturer might have three cases:

- Receive *consumable* Shipment (for fuel, gases, cleaning supplies, and so on);

- Receive *indirect inventory* Shipment (for factory equipment repair or service items);

- Receive *direct inventory* Shipment (for raw materials or product components).

The point is to avoid putting too much on a single swimlane diagram—multiple understandable diagrams can be produced much more quickly than one complex one and are also much more useful.

Question 2: Which Process Are We Modeling?

The overall process map (or process landscape) should be on a flipchart, posted in a location where it will always be visible, because you'll probably have to refer to it during the session when participants drift out of scope. During the kickoff, simply remind people what the overall set of processes is and then place a big, bright "we are here" Post-it on the process you'll be modeling. Flipcharts summarizing that process' framing, initial assessment, and goal-setting can also be posted, but all you need to review at this time is the triggering event(s), the final results, the subprocesses, and the cases, highlighting the case that will be covered initially. The trigger and results will be repeated in just a moment, when you start mapping.

You can quickly review guidelines for "session behaviors" if you feel the group could use a reminder, and then get started on mapping.

Building the Handoff-Level Diagram

The Mechanics and the Methods

Readers of the first edition will notice significant differences in the mechanics of how we now build the workflow models:

- The default approach is to work on a "wall of paper" rather than whiteboards. As organizations get better at identifying true, end-to-end business processes, the standard 4 × 8-foot whiteboard just isn't big enough, even for a handoff diagram, and few meeting rooms are equipped with multiple adjacent whiteboards (and competition for these is stiff).

- We use blank Post-its to indicate a point of involvement (one or more steps) rather than drawing a cloud on a whiteboard.

- We use Post-its for everything else, too—the roster of actors, triggering events, results, flows to be followed later, and annotations.

- We avoid drawing flow lines, and even naming steps, until as late as possible, at least until we're pretty sure we have the main flow and all of the actors depicted.

- We typically add three general-purpose lanes at the bottom of the diagram—systems and tools, other processes, and holding areas.

Collectively, the intent is to concentrate on getting the "depth" of the diagram (all or most of the actors) and the "length" of the diagram (the main path) fairly complete as soon as possible. That way, when other flows are traced, there will be minimal disruption from having to move everything around. That's also why we avoid drawing flow lines until we're quite confident that the overall layout is correct. Even then, we'll work with pencil as long as possible.

What remains the same from the first edition is the philosophy, which is to get all the way through the process, tracing everyone's involvement between the triggering event and the result for the customer, before coming back and addressing details, errors, exceptions, and all those other tempting diversions. Also unchanged is that we offer two main methods:

1. Building the handoff diagram by tracing the flow, asking "who gets it next?" and then again "who gets it next?" and so on. This is by far the most common method.
2. Building the handoff diagram bottom up by first identifying activities by actor and then sequencing them into flows. This is an unusual method, and it is only employed when the current process is so fragmented the actors don't know the flow.

A final piece of advice—remember that the problem might not be in the workflow, but having a workflow model will ensure that you understand the contribution made by each actor and therefore have a much greater chance of uncovering where problems really originate. Along those lines, don't let your as-is modeling session drift into assessment, but do be sure to keep your ears open for comments and complaints made by participants that relate to the other enablers—IT, motivation, human resources, and so on. This information will be very useful when it comes time for assessing the as-is, so perhaps a team member can be assigned to discreetly make notes.

Option 1—Trace the Flow (The Three Questions Approach)

Getting Set Up

You have already seen this approach described thoroughly in Chapter 8 as "Example 2: Getting to the Essence Without Diving into Detail." There, we built an initial workflow model for the issue building permit process by asking three questions. If you skipped over it, or can't remember the specifics, please go back and read through it now.

The essence of the approach is that starting with the triggering event you ask these three questions, each time completing one pass through the entire process, from trigger to result:

1. "Who gets the work next?"
2. "How does it get there?"
3. "Who *really* gets the work next?"

Do not stop along the way to ask, "What do you do?" and do not attempt to follow multiple flows simultaneously. Do focus initially on the flow that leads to the result for the customer before going back and picking up other flows. The goal is to trace the involvement of the actors without worrying (yet!) about what they actually do at the points they're involved.

Prior to the session, prepare the "wall of paper" and place a Post-it labeled with the actor's name on the swimlane for each process actor you identified during framing. Also place labels on the three swimlanes at the bottom for systems, other processes, and holding areas. Leave some empty swimlanes between the known actors and those three lanes at the bottom because you'll probably find additional actors. Also prepare a Post-it for each triggering event, which will either be the start symbol (a solid circle) labeled with a short description of the event or a clock labeled with the temporal event or time. As well, prepare a Post-it for each final result, which will be the stop symbol (a bullseye) labeled with the name of the stakeholder and the result they expect. You and your team should also have decided which case you'll start with and developed a representative scenario for that case. If there is one case that is clearly the most frequent, start with that one. The first scenario you model should be the most common example of how process unfolds. Be careful about describing this as the "sunny day" example, because it might not illustrate how the organization *wishes* the process happened but rather shows how the process *most often* happens. The key elements of the scenario should be summarized on a flipchart.

Before you start diagramming, remind everyone what case of the process is being modeled and recap the key elements of the first scenario. If you didn't create a scenario in advance, have the group create one by describing the most common situations. Sometimes, we'll split the group into smaller teams and ask each to come up with three scenarios—the most common, the ideal, and a problematic example. Reconvene the group and either select one of each type or create three composite scenarios using the best ideas from each. Surprisingly, this can be fun, because people like inventing stories, and it encourages participation. Just be sure to emphasize that the scenario just needs to be good enough, not perfect.

At last, you can get started with the group in building your initial handoff-level diagram.

The Method—"Seven Steps to Success"

1. Add the bookends. Place a prepared Post-it labeled with the initiating event at the beginning of the diagram, either in the swimlane of the actor that raises the event, or in the upper left. At the other end of the diagram, place a prepared Post-it for each stakeholder result that must be delivered by the process, pointing out to the group that initially we'll trace the flow to the customer's result.
2. Go back to the initiating event and ask the all-important question: "Who gets the work next?" Ignore all the details of the work performed by that actor and just place a Post-it in their swimlane. While you're doing this, don't cram the Post-its close together—leave at least enough horizontal space between them to add another Post-it in another actor's swimlane.

3. Again, ask, "who gets it next?" If it always goes to the same actor next, place a Post-it in that actor's swimlane and repeat the question. If it varies because there is a decision being made, or because there are parallel flows, place a "bookmark" (a smaller Post-it) on the right edge of the Post-it, then choose the mainstream path that eventually leads to the customer result and place a Post-it for the next actor's involvement. The bookmark can be labeled to indicate the situation—with a forking flow line to indicate that there's another path from a decision, with a couple of parallel flow lines to indicate there are parallel flows, with a cloud to indicate "something else happens here, too," or simply with an annotation. Don't agonize about it—keep moving forward. Keep repeating this question until you hit the actor's step that delivers the customer result you were aiming for, and then place the Post-it for the customer result next to the appropriate step. Don't stop just yet—often the flow will continue after the customer has received their result (e.g., if there is follow-up activity). Keep asking "who gets it next?" until you can't go any further.

4. Go back to the beginning, and, retracing the flow you just modeled, ask, "how does it get there?" at each handoff, which will often uncover additional actors such as couriers or systems that are moving the work along. Note that we don't worry yet about the other flows that we "bookmarked" the first time through, because we want to identify as many additional actors as early as possible. Keep repeating this question, adding actors and steps as necessary, until you get all the way through the process.

5. Go back to the beginning, and, retracing the flow you've been developing, ask, "who really gets it next?" after each step to determine if you've accurately identified the next actor. Often, you will discover intermediate players, such as an administrative resource that first gets the work or a manager who first assigns it. Keep repeating this question, adding actors and steps as necessary, until you get all the way through the process.

6. At this point you have traced a single path—a series of involvements—from trigger to customer result. If this also passed through involvements that delivered a result to another stakeholder, the prepared result Post-it should be moved so it is next to the appropriate step. Now, go back to the earliest bookmark that indicated a flow that wasn't followed, and pick it up from there, following the same method. You'll probably notice that by now the group is less likely to miss points of involvement the first time through, so this will not require such heavy iteration. Remember to stay within the scenario you started with and check that ultimately every stakeholder receives their expected result.

7. Make the model more readable by adding step names (remember—action verb + noun) and rearranging actors' swimlanes in order to better tell a story. Whether or not you also draw the flow lines now depends on how different the other scenarios will be and whether you think you'll be able to add other cases to this diagram. If you do choose to draw the lines, a dark pencil like a carpenter's pencil is a safer bet than an indelible flipchart marker. This is less of a concern if you've been working on a whiteboard. We often take digital photographs after each of the three questions, so we can illustrate the

evolution of a workflow model. Even if you haven't taken a picture so far, you'll want to now so you have a record of a single scenario.

A few other points:

- If you think your swimlane diagram will be short, without too many actors, a whiteboard will be easier to work on than paper, because you can be more relaxed about drawing flow lines, notes, and so on.

- If your process is fairly simple, then putting up blank Post-its will keep things moving; if the process is more complex, you'll want to name steps as you go, but don't agonize over the name. A mushy name like "routing" is adequate for the time being.

- If your process is quite a bit more complex (e.g., having lots of parallel flows and collaboration), then you'll also need to start adding flow lines fairly early on. That's why you want to identify all the actors, and the full length of the process, as early as possible.

What Next?

Congratulations—you did it! You have built the initial handoff-level diagram. Now you're on your own.

Just kidding, but at this point we can't be as definite about how you'll proceed because it depends (the consultant's favorite phrase) on whether you'll add the other scenarios to the workflow model you just built or create a new diagram for each scenario, and on whether you'll add the other cases to this model or create a new diagram for each case. Most often, we will add multiple scenarios to the diagram illustrating a single case, but create a separate diagram for each case. But how will you decide what to do on your model? Generally, we talk the group through the diagram for each of the other scenarios of the case being studied, one at a time, without actually adding anything to the diagram. If we find that the other scenarios will simply add a few alternate flows and a manageable number of additional steps, or that they result in bypassing steps that are already on the diagram, then we'll add the other scenarios to the diagram. With luck, this won't involve much juggling, especially if you resisted the urge to draw flow lines. We then continue working on the same case by going through a thorough validation and refinement that is described in the next section, "Refining the Initial Model—the Five Key Questions." Having added the other scenarios will uncover many of the refinements that the five questions are intended to uncover.

If the scenarios are substantially different, the situation is more complicated. You either bite the bullet and start a new diagram for the next scenario, or you continue working on the same scenario and start on the five questions for refinement. We almost always keep people in the same mental space by sticking with the initial scenario and going into refinement and validation with it. You'll then have to come back, build the diagram for the new scenario (salvaging as much as you can from the first) and then validate it. Either way, you definitely want to photograph what you have now!

Option 2—Bottom Up (Gather Activities, Then Assemble)

The Approach and When You Would Choose It

The second approach is to brainstorm individual activities (who does what?) on Post-its, without regard for sequence, flow, or even relative granularity, and then sequence and cluster the activities to produce a handoff-level diagram. This bottom-up approach is similar to the method so often used by project planners. Once an overall, first-cut flow for the process has been determined this way, you can flesh it out by using the three questions and then refine and extend it with the five additional questions.

Why would you ever choose an approach like this? Well, we don't very often, but once in a while we encounter a situation where the participants don't have a good grasp of sequence and flow, and this is the only workable method. In old-line organizations, where there is a very hierarchic, top-down style of management coupled with tightly defined jobs, this approach might be the only one that will work. For instance, we worked in a government agency where most of the participants picked up inbound work from their inbox and placed completed work in their outbox, without a clear sense of what was happening on either side. Strange, but true. This was one of those cases when seeing the entire process was quite an emotional experience for the participants.

The Method

As you would have done in the other method, prepare the "wall of paper." Even though you won't initially worry about placing activities in swimlanes, you might as well crease the paper now, because you'll want swimlanes eventually. If you have some framing information, post it on flipcharts, but in this approach we don't begin with labeled swimlanes or with Post-its showing the trigger and the results. You're operating on the assumption that you have an incomplete view of the process, so you don't want to constrain things too much at the outset. For preparation, that's about it, except for ensuring that you have lots of pads of 4 × 6-inch Post-its and enough markers for everyone. As before, you'll review with the group whatever has been decided about the process, the case, and the scenario that you will start with. That can be quite sketchy when we find ourselves using this approach. The steps you'll go through are as follows:

1. Brainstorm for significant activities (steps or tasks) completed by each actor, using the form "actor: step description." Place the actor's name at the top of a Post-it, and the step description below. As the facilitator, you can canvass the group, recording each suggestion on a Post-it as it is made and then placing it on a flipchart to the side of the wall of paper. This single-threaded approach can get tedious and lead to herd mentality, so our preference is to have individuals or breakout groups separately identify activities. Then have all the individual Post-its placed on flipcharts or on your "working wall," and see if synergy results in additional ideas. If people can't put each step in verb-noun format, don't worry—anything that captures the idea is good enough for now. Don't let perfection be the enemy of the "good enough"; just get something down you can refine later.

2. Have the group organize the steps in approximate sequence on the work surface you have prepared on the wall. This is when the "power of the Post-it" becomes apparent—they're easy to sequence, cluster, and move around. Don't worry about precision at this point—you won't know the exact sequence and flow of steps and only want to show roughly where steps are happening in sequence or in parallel.

3. Now, have the group look things over and ask, "Did we miss any important steps?" This is where one of the strengths of this approach becomes apparent—by laying out the approximate structure of the process, missing steps become much more obvious. Steps can be added while it is still relatively easy to do so, because swimlanes and flow lines aren't yet specific, so it's easier to slide the Post-its around.

4. Next, label the swimlanes by actor (using Post-its, of course) and place the steps in the right swimlane.

5. Wherever an actor has a contiguous set of steps (from receiving a handoff to initiating a handoff), reduce them to a single step as per the central principle of the handoff diagram. Don't throw out the details you've captured—you'll want to save that for subsequent diagrams. A good technique is to stack the steps being reduced and add a new Post-it on top with a summarized step name. Naming this summarized step will often be awkward, so if you have to use "and" and "or," or otherwise get wordy, don't worry about it.

6. Add flow lines between the steps, being careful to depict any mutually exclusive or parallel flows, inbound and outbound, that have emerged. The handoff-level step might summarize several steps, with flow lines coming in or out along the way, and these will all "stack up" at the left and right edges of the step.

7. Try to improve step names to reflect the totality of what happens while that actor has the work. It's likely that a few step names will still require "and" and "or" (e.g., "accept and route application").

At this point, as described under the heading "What Next?" in the previous section, you now have an initial handoff-level diagram that can be extended by considering other scenarios and cases, and then the five questions described next.

Refining the Initial Model—The Five Key Questions

Any time substantial progress has been made on your swimlane, such as completing a case, you should stop and validate the model. A proven method is to review each step in the swimlane diagram, one by one, and ask each of five specific questions about it. This is especially useful when applied to a handoff diagram, because it will verify and extend it before you proceed to adding more detail at the service level.

The questions first consider how work arrives at a step though a handoff and then what the step actually does, before proceeding through the step from left to right, beginning with the inputs (the flow lines coming in from the left), the actors involved in the step, and the outputs (the flow lines going out from the right). Asking these questions almost always leads to the discovery of additional actors, steps, triggers, and flows. This rigorous procedure prevents glossing over ambiguities and missed details. After we review the questions, we'll provide a real example of a swimlane diagram that was significantly altered (and improved!) by asking these questions. The five questions, in sequence, are:

1. If there's a handoff, "how does it get there?" You will recognize that we've asked this before—it was the second of the three questions we asked while developing the initial diagram. However, when we ask it again, we look specifically for external "courier processes" and systems. When we ask, "how is the work transported from the previous step to this step?" we sometimes discover that additional actors who perform a delivery service are involved. An upcoming example is full of such cases. In some cases the handoff is accomplished by an information system. In either case, the additional actors might introduce delay, error, or expense. See Figure 11.1.

2. "Does the name of the step convey the result of the step?" The purpose of this question is to ensure that there really is a legitimate step, the participants agree on what the outcome of that step is, and that the name conveys the result. Practically, this most often means ensuring that a "mushy" verb hasn't been used unless there is absolutely no other choice. Remember the list of "mushy verbs" from Chapter 5? Use it! Common ones we encounter are "process" or "handle," which say nothing, and "monitor" or "review," which are usually hiding decisions. Sometimes, before getting started on the five questions, we'll go through any obvious mushy verbs to accomplish an initial cleanup before starting the more thorough, step-by-step evaluation. See Figure 11.2.

3. "What makes it go?" Now we're looking at the left edge of the step. This is a critical question, because it uncovers missing trigger conditions for a step, which is a fundamental aspect of workflow. Often the initial diagram will show a single flow line entering a step, but the question is "is the flow line shown *really* all that it takes to trigger the step?" Often, it turns out that a flow from a step performed by some other actor is also required. Also common is the case when a temporal event (e.g., "close of business") and/or a condition (e.g., "total receipts >= cash drawer limit") is also required before a step can begin. The example we'll review includes many steps that are triggered by a schedule. See Figure 11.3.

4. "Is anyone or anything else involved?" Now we're looking at the upper and lower edges of the step. What we're looking for with this question are as follows:

   a. Activities shown as being serial that are actually collaborative. See Figure 11.4(a), where clearly the complainant (the customer) and complaint taker (the customer service rep) are both involved at the same time.

   b. Activities shown as being performed by one actor that are actually collaborative. See Figure 11.4(b).

   c. Activities that an actor carries out but with support from a system that hasn't been shown. Sometimes, this question also uncovers the use of systems operating in a batch mode that have so far been missed. See Figure 11.4(c).

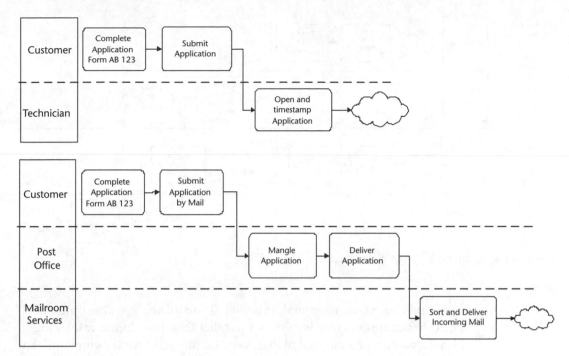

Figure 11.1   Question 1, "How does it get there?"

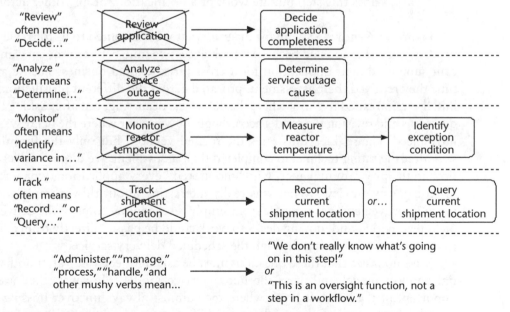

Figure 11.2   Question 2, "Does the name of the step convey the result of the step?"

5. "Are all outcomes shown?" Now we're looking at the right edge of the step. Sometimes a diagram will show a single flow line leaving a step. One common error, often appearing along with a mushy verb, is to show only one outbound flow when in fact a decision is being made and there are two or more possible outcomes. If there's any doubt, we'll specifically ask, "is a

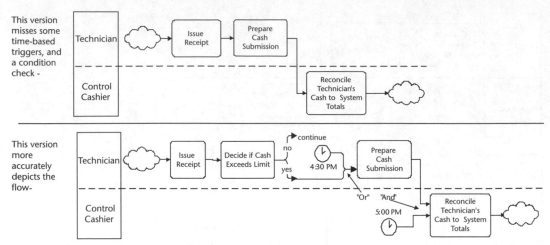

Figure 11.3   Question 3, "What makes it go?"

decision being made here, and, if so, what are all the possible outcomes?" The other common error is to miss a parallel flow line. In the case of Figure 11.5, it wouldn't be unusual to discover that the step "route complaint" had a flow to the appropriate specialized service rep, but missed a notification (flow) to the customer's assigned sales rep. To drive out cases like this, we ask, "does this step initiate work or a notification for any other actors?"

Figure 11.6 shows a swimlane diagram that was presented to us for review. The process had been modeled because it took excessive time between the time an applicant submitted their application for a cross-jurisdictional business license and the time they received their assessment, prorated across the different jurisdictions. This initial version failed to show where the delay was occurring, but after asking the five questions and revising the model accordingly, it was clear where the delay was being introduced. Figure 11.7 illustrates the revised version, but only the first third or so—after the rating technician completed their assessment, we discovered a parallel flow to the program manager, who "monitored" every application, which resulted in an extensive review! What was really interesting about this example was how much improvement was possible from simply rescheduling some of the delivery and pickup activities, and moving desks so work could be passed directly from one actor to the next without going through the scheduled delivery service.

We emphasize that these questions must be asked for each step after both the initial handoff model and after the initial service model. However, they are most important at the handoff level, where they almost always uncover missing actors and steps—the rest of the work proceeds far more smoothly, without continual redrawing, if all of the actors and their "contribution points" have been identified.

"Can We Stop Now?"

Workflow models can stretch to absurd lengths, depicting the smallest procedural details of work tasks or individual human-computer interactions. That much detail

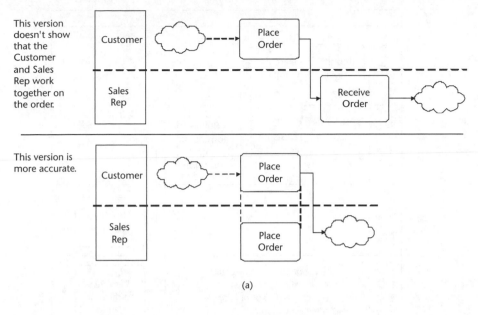

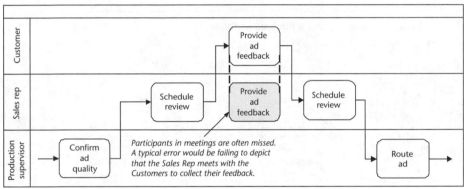

(a)

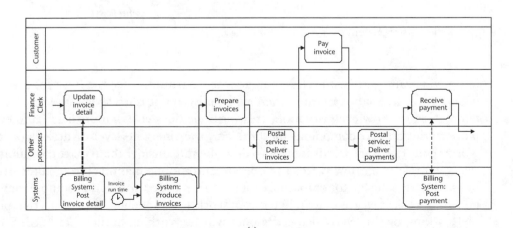

(b)

(c)

Figure 11.4 Question 4: "Is anyone or anything else involved?" (a) confusing serial and collaborative work; (b) confusing solo and collaborative work; and (c) missing system-supported work.

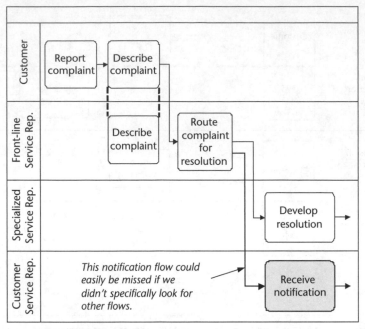

Figure 11.5   Question 5, "Are all outcomes shown?"

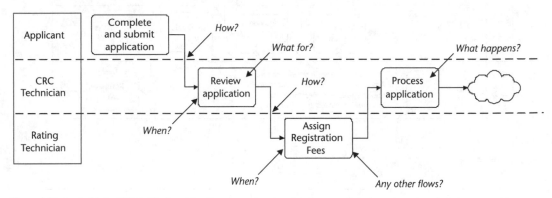

Figure 11.6   Initial version, before the five questions review.

in one diagram is at best useless, and at worst harmful, since the finer the level of detail, the more slight variations there will be. Even if it is irrelevant, there will be a temptation to show each variation, creating a vicious cycle of more detail and even more variation. To compound the problem, the finer the level of detail you are working at, the more words it takes to describe it. Consider that you could summarize a company in a few words as "operate automobile manufacturing enterprise" but to describe the lockout procedure for a single piece of production equipment will take hundreds of words of text. In terms of workflow modeling, this means that people working on an overly detailed model will be working harder and harder, but contributing less and less to understanding overall process behavior.

Thus, it is important to stop before you slip into modeling useless detail, and the point to stop might be sooner than you think! Remember the modeler's motto:

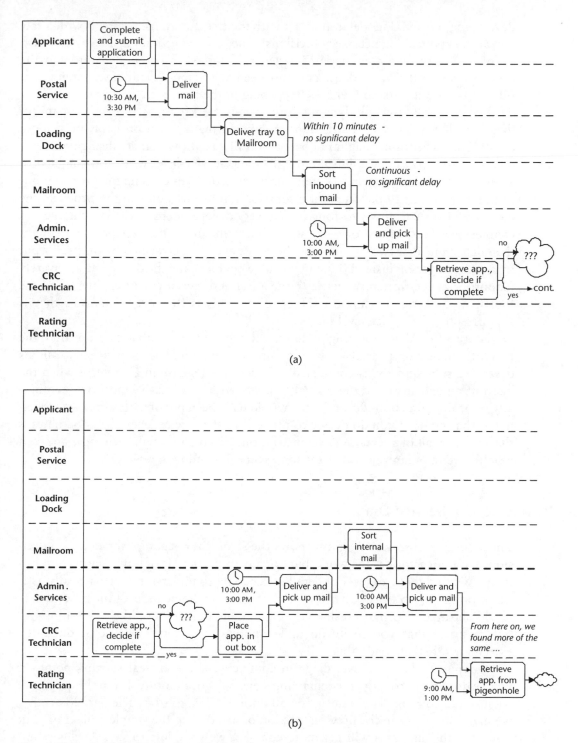

Figure 11.7 (a, b) Revised version, after the five questions review.

"Good enough for now!" If you are unsure about whether to go further, ask, "what is the underlying purpose of this model, and will more detail further the goal?" If not, it's "good enough." So, after completing the handoff diagram (for instance, developing the initial model, refining it with the five questions, testing it with a few scenarios, and making necessary revisions), one more question must be asked: "Do we really need to add more detail?" In general, stop when you understand why the process behaves the way it does. You only need to add more detail if you aren't confident that you understand what is happening in the process.

If the overall flow and dynamics of the as-is workflow, as shown in a handoff diagram, doesn't clarify what is impacting performance, you probably need more detail. That is because it might not be the overall workflow that is causing unacceptable process performance, but a more detailed, service-level workflow might provide the framework for you to determine what actually *is* causing the problem. For instance, you might take an actor's contribution at one point in the process (one handoff-level step) down to four or five service-level steps and then conduct an enabler-based assessment of each, as we'll describe in the next chapter. You might then determine that two of the steps shouldn't even be performed by that actor but by a support person instead (human resource enabler), the third step has an entirely inappropriate performance metric (motivation and measurement enabler), and the fourth needs better IT support (IT enabler). This is the sort of analysis that is supported by the service-level model.

More often than you might think, though, you'll be able to stop after the handoff model, or possibly a handoff model annotated with further details as described subsequently, is completed. We described a case in Chapter 8 when the handoff model illustrated the central problem with a process's workflow (continually returning to a control point), so it would have been possible to stop as-is modeling at that point. If you do decide to proceed to the service level, the good news is that most or all of it can be developed in one-on-one or small meetings, and you won't have to organize another session except to conduct a review.

Producing the Service Diagram

The second-level service diagram shows the significant accomplishments and decisions while an actor has the work, but not any of the details of how they accomplish them. We find that this level of detail is adequate to understand virtually any as-is situation that wasn't clear after the handoff diagram. Some parts of the process may need to be taken down to a task-level diagram, but that will not likely be for insight, but to prove that you really do understand what a particular actor does. It's extremely rare that we do this.

Getting the handoff-level diagram completed is the critical starting point—if you've done that properly, the remaining steps will go smoothly. From this point on, we just add controlled amounts of detail until it's time to stop. The paradox is that we had a lot to say in the previous section on producing the simplest diagram, but now that the diagrams will get more complex we have less to say. At this point, we're just applying the guidelines on progressive detail that we explored in Chapter 9. Here are a few key principles...

- When collecting additional detail, it's generally easier to capture it in list or point form rather than trying to swimlane it immediately. When building a list, it's easy for people to spot missing or incorrect steps and rectify. With diagramming, there can be tendency to resist changes, even essential ones, because it seems like a lot of work. So, begin the service level by looking at each handoff-level step, asking "what are the significant accomplishments here?" and then listing them under the step. Often, the list will be adequate, and you'll choose not to turn it into a service-level diagram but instead produce an annotated handoff diagram.

- Encourage participants to think in terms of milestones (e.g., the point when an actor could say, "there—that's done!" as opposed to each work task).

- Follow the principle of expanding by "five plus or minus two." Each step in a handoff diagram should typically ("typically"—there are always exceptions) expand to no more than five or so steps at the next level. Some will not expand at all, some just to two, and only rarely will you find a step performed by a core actor that expands to more than five. If it does, check that you aren't actually documenting steps in a procedure rather than milestones in a process.

- In most cases, and this is important, you usually have to go too far before you know you've gone far enough, which we noted in Chapter 9. You'll gather some information, but essentially abandon it without turning it into a diagram. That is, you'll list some points about the next level, and then say, "hey, these aren't milestones" or "hey, there's no 'aha' in here." When that happens, save your notes but don't take the time to develop a swimlane diagram! Some analysts find this very difficult—"I've gathered the information, I must format it!"

Some specific guidelines for the level 2 service diagram:

- First, remember what Chapter 9 said—this level adds steps that show achievement of a significant, intermediate milestone while the actor holds the work, or it adds decisions that affect the flow in a significant way, including branching to a different flow or returning (looping) to a previous point.

- Therefore, for each step in the handoff model, start by listing the significant milestones and decisions, trying to keep it under five. Remind participants that a milestone is just that—the point where an important state or result has been reached, which is different than a simple task. Some steps in a handoff diagram won't break down any further—they represent a single milestone.

- If there's a mandatory sequence in an actor's steps, put them in that order and ask: "What have we missed?" If there isn't a mandatory sequence, the steps can be placed in a larger box when you draw the diagram.

- Continue listing service-level steps until you get all the way through the process before drawing the service-level diagram. Don't automatically assume you have to draw the service-level diagram. You should only do this if a graphic depiction of the information will be useful. Otherwise, as is often the case, it will be adequate to produce a handoff diagram annotated with the service-level steps.

- Walk through a few scenarios to ensure that all steps, decisions, loops, and handoffs are shown.

• Verify and extend the model by going through the five key questions.

As noted earlier, if we go to a task-level diagram, it is only ever for a part of the process, and the intent is usually to prove that part is understood. Generally, though, that level of detail is virtually always best left for separate documents like procedures or use cases, which are not typically part of as-is modeling and assessment. They will be developed for the to-be process to support training and implementation.

Issues During As-Is Modeling

Unfortunately, modeling the as-is process doesn't always sail along smoothly. During the session, certain problems commonly arise, and this section will arm you with strategies for dealing with them. It's a bit of a grab bag of issues and approaches arranged under five broad topics:

1. Misapplying workflow modeling;
2. Modeling different versions of the same process;
3. Inability to model a particular situation;
4. Facilitation issues;
5. Dealing with disagreement.

Before we look at specific problems, there are two things to remember about staying out of trouble in the first place.

Many of the difficulties people report could have been avoided by framing the process well, so don't skip that phase or you'll waste time and frustrate the participants. A particular example is that many people get tied up in modeling a complex process that would have been much easier if they'd identified the different cases of the process, which is part of framing, and modeled each one separately.

Second, some issues, especially those of the "how do I model XYZ situation" variety were covered in previous chapters. In the heat of the moment, you might forget certain guidelines we've covered already, such as those that address handling (or, more precisely, not handling) detail and complexity. Chapter 10 in particular, which covered the finer points of swimlane diagramming, should be reviewed before your modeling session. Chapter 9, on managing progressive detail, also contains guidelines about staying out of the weeds.

Misapplying Workflow Modeling

There are cases when the approach in this book and the problem area you're working in don't match. Swimlane diagrams are a fabulous tool, but they aren't the solution for every problem. Use them for what they're good for, and switch gears when they're not. Don't let the tool get in the way.

Imagine you are running a session and are getting the uncomfortable feeling that "workflow" as you understand it wasn't the right perspective to take. Framing went well, but now you're chanting "flow first, detail later" to yourself in the hopes the flow will come, because there doesn't seem to be any defined flow of steps among actors. Instead, you constantly hear "well, it depends…" And rather than a repeatable sequence of steps and decisions, you find there are:

* Many ad hoc activities;
* Lots of creative and collaborative work;
* Much sharing of information;
* Occasional milestones or gating points.

You've stumbled into the "other workflow." Many tools, notably Lotus Notes, are referred to as "workflow" tools, but they're a different kind of beast that perhaps should be called "information flow" or "information exchange" tools. They are suitable for unstructured or less structured work, like developing a strategy or a marketing campaign, which we refer to as *creative/collaborative* processes. They are characterized by information exchange and milestones, but without a fixed "roles, responsibilities, routes" structure. Workflow modeling is best used for *transactional* processes, and those highly nonlinear creative/collaborative processes do not translate well into workflow diagrams. If we encounter one of these situations, we run. Well, not really. We actually focus on clarifying the structure, content, and meaning of the information, and defining the milestone or gating parts of the process. We might even draw a rough swimlane diagram for these defined parts of the process and leave the areas in between as clouds labeled "MHH"—"magic happens here." Then we run and find someone with experience in this area to take over.

Here is another case. Someone (maybe you, maybe the client) has decided to follow a process workflow–based approach on a project, but it turns out that "process" isn't really the problem. In a particular example, a client retained us to look at a business process that was experiencing difficulty, so we developed a process-based agenda. The session went just fine, but it was clear that the process workflow was not the issue—the right people did the right things at the right time. The real problem was information access—in this, and other processes the participants worked in, access to complete, accurate information was the limiting factor. Note that a situation like this usually bears more than a passing resemblance to the previous case—the "other" workflow. We still managed to use our process-based agenda, but careful as-is modeling and to-be redesign weren't part of it.

Instead, we moved into a general discussion of what types of information were needed without getting too specific. We focused on the topics, not the details. This helped us understand the basic terms and definitions that applied to their information. Then we brainstormed the events that drove a need for information (e.g., "complaint is received," "license renewal is due," and so on). We strung the events together into a semblance of a process, which also made missing events stand out, so they were added. This was done for completeness; otherwise, people tend to zero in on one area. Finally, we walked through the events (essentially, the steps) that made up the process and for each asked, "what information is needed here?" In the end, we were able to build an *information map* that showed the different information topics they needed to access, how they related to one another, and also a progressive drill-down through more and more specific information. So, while workflow wasn't the issue, our process-based agenda ensured that we covered the field rather than zeroing in on one area. Also, we did end up initiating minor process changes, especially where support staff was involved in retrieving information.

In another situation, you're stuck in a silo, dealing with much less than a complete process. The scope of your project is a particular function or department, but you've been asked to develop workflow models. Actually, you've probably been asked to "improve our department's processes," even though, by definition, you're not dealing with a complete process. Try to identify the "pieces" of the various processes the department deals with. Otherwise, you'll go crazy trying to fit it all on a single swimlane diagram. Identify "arrival" events, "departure" events, and the paths that connect them. Clean up the really goofy steps, and then really concentrate on the "boundaries"—getting work in and getting it out—so you don't inadvertently commit local optimization and global suboptimization.

Modeling Different Versions of the Same Process

Sometimes you will have to build different models of the same process. There are many reasons to do this in both as-is and to-be models, and it's often a judgment call whether or not you will. For instance, as-is modeling might reveal variances in how different locations carry out a process, but that doesn't mean they all need to be illustrated. Don't bother documenting variations that don't matter—ones that don't contribute to a significant difference in process behavior.

The main situations in which we model different versions of the same process are when they must be understood, so you can discover if differences are important and must be preserved, do gap analysis (i.e., compare them to a new "master" process), perform implementation planning, or discover best practices. Typical cases are when processes vary:

- *By location.* For instance, "pay employee" is different in the United States and Korea because of legal and cultural differences; it will be different in the to-be as well. In Korea, the expectation is that payment will be in cash, whereas this would be almost unheard of in the States. We frequently encounter situations where legal constraints vary across an organization's operating locations, and this must absolutely be understood in order to meet legal requirements.

- *By organization.* For instance, the packaged goods division receives shipments differently than the health and beauty division. This could be important for discovering best practices, or because of conventions among an industry's trading partners that will require some differences to be maintained in the to-be.

- Note that there can be different versions in both the as-is and to-be processes. For example, the as-is may have different versions by location, which are eliminated in the to-be, while the to-be may now have different versions by case or by differentiator. For to-be, we generally build one "master" version, and then adjust it for local conditions—legal or regulatory requirements, pragmatic/operational differences (e.g., different skills or resources), or cultural norms that must be addressed.

The main point is that while organizations strive for consistency in the way their processes are implemented, there will always be geographic or business concerns that demand variation.

Inability to Model a Particular Situation

"I can't model this! I don't know how to show this!" If you're struggling mightily with how to swimlane a situation, maybe you shouldn't bother. It could be that swimlane diagrams are not the appropriate tool for the task. At some level of detail, words work better than pictures, and maybe a paragraph of explanation will be more enlightening than a swimlane. Especially for details, exceptions and variations, an explanatory note can be easier to produce, and communicate better, than a complicated diagram. That's why we keep stressing that procedural level details belong in, well, a procedure.

Don't let the swimlane diagram technique get in the way—never let your inability to model something prevent you from capturing it. Some techniques:

- Describe it in quasi–use case format or narrative format. That is, "actor does action" form or just a point-form description. Use traditional tools such as "structured English" or pseudocode (e.g., if, then, else), decision trees, or truth tables. If this works, you were almost surely below the level of detail that belongs on a swimlane diagram.

- Simply add an annotation to the diagram (we do this all the time).

- Add a big dotted box or a cloud with some narrative in it and move on to another part of the process. (A difficult situation sometimes resolves itself while you work on an easier area.)

And, if you discover something important, and don't know how to depict it, feel free to invent a symbol or apply a different diagramming technique.

- For instance, if tasks by a certain actor are continually interrupted, show lots of jagged arrows labeled "interruptions" coming in to the area. Draw flow lines with zigzag lines as well. Also show the same process step drawn multiple times with zigzag connections between them to illustrate interruption.

- Another example—you might sometimes add an icon such as an inbox. This is an example of "inventing" a symbol to get a point across. Various modeling tools or graphics tools (e.g., Visio) have icons for all sorts of things. You should use them when they help, *but sparingly!* Remember that we use a simple "everything is a box" diagramming style because it provides maximum clarity and accessibility to the maximum number of people. Diagrams with literally dozens of different icons are cute, but they confuse more than they inform.

- Don't be afraid to use some other kind of diagram, especially of something physical that people can relate to like an office floor plan or a shop floor layout. If you investigate Lean (visit www.lean.org) you'll see that tools from that arena such as value stream diagrams or physical flow diagrams can provide an excellent alternative to workflow models

Over the course of a project, you might need to highlight different aspects, such as:

- Wait time;
- The role of systems;
- Total cost;
- Duplicated effort;
- Unnecessary constraints;
- And so on.

But don't try to show them all at once—if you highlight everything, you highlight nothing. That's one reason you shouldn't use a lot of special symbols. You might draw one diagram that highlights the time a work item spends in actual or virtual in-baskets (e.g., by time-scaling the diagram and "flat-lining" the periods when an item is waiting), and you might draw another diagram that emphasizes something entirely different, like duplicated effort. When the special diagram has served its purpose, go back to the plain vanilla model before highlighting another aspect.

Facilitation Issues

The real message here is "read books and take courses on facilitation skills, and presentation skills, too." All the modeling skills in the world won't help if you can't focus a group on the task at hand, obtain balanced participation, and keep the session moving. Here are some miscellaneous issues that relate to facilitation in general, and workflow modeling sessions in particular.

- There are a few ways to deal with off topic, out of scope, late, or ahead of time points; with ideas that come out of the blue; and with total nonsequiturs:
    - First principles—you need the overall process map, the process framing material, and your session plan posted so you can use it when asking how the point fits. Without them, you're lost. Having displayed and reviewed them during the session kickoff gives you a form of "moral authority" to question points that you aren't sure are in scope. They also give you something to compare the point to, other than your opinion, which depersonalizes the situation.
    - Second, just because you don't understand how a comment or point fits, don't assume the participant is off topic. Do the Lt. Columbo routine—"I'm not clear on how this fits in..." When we apply *constructive ignorance* (asking "dumb" questions), we often uncover important facts or ideas and discover the "off the wall" comment was right on the money.
    - If, however, it can't be related to the topic at hand, use the parking lot, bin list, or whatever you call it to record the point. This acknowledges the contribution and gets the point out of mind so everyone can concentrate on the topic at hand. Often, items on the bin list resolve themselves.

- Jargon is fun to use, because it makes you feel like you're one of them, but be careful. Things always seem to make sense at the time, so be sure you record what's actually happening so you'll remember later. Someone from another area should be able to follow the model. *Always* use the terms that you agreed to in the glossary or data model, and stick with "verb-noun" format for step names.
  - Bad: "Complete form CS-39";
  - Good: "Request transcript using CS-39."
- Another pitfall is confusing the "as is" with what "should be"—per a guideline we gave you earlier, model reality, not policy, and discourage criticism from the "rule happy" folks. You know, internal audit, training, or some other group that "knows" how it ought to be done, and insists on attacking participants with "That's not how it's supposed to be done!" This stifles participation, to put it mildly. Remind everyone that whether or not this is how "it's supposed to be done" is immaterial, because the purpose of workflow modeling is to uncover the reality (no matter how painful or ugly) of how things are really done. You may have to take the critic aside and explain that if they don't stop jumping on participants, the facts won't emerge at all, which won't help anyone.
- Similarly, stay focused on "as is" not "could be." Note any improvement or redesign ideas or "low hanging fruit" on an "ideas" flipchart and move on *with no discussion*. Above all, control the urge to leap into the design of a solution like an Access application—we've seen it happen, and it's a sure-fire way to get into trouble by designing the to-be before you understand the real problems in the as-is.
- After the modeling session, you may find that the client really likes "version 1." They might say, "That's great—now we know how it works!" But don't stop unless you've confirmed the model by reviewing it with others (who weren't in the session) and by direct observation.
  - Before you conduct "direct observation by walkaround," be sure the project is discussed with staff and they know who you are and why you're there. Major problems develop when people assume the worst, which is that you're the "downsizing police" and are engaged in a "reduction in force" (RIF) initiative.
  - Accept that sometimes the situation is too sensitive for you to have a walkaround—leave it to one of the managers or supervisors people are used to seeing.
- If, during the session, people are a little reserved, it may be perfectly natural. People define themselves in terms of the job they do, and if you're messing with that, you're messing with their identity. Be sensitive. Not like the one analyst who still makes us cringe. In a process-modeling session, he traced one group's swimlane with his index finger and happily exclaimed, "Wow, this is so cool—these people add absolutely no value whatsoever." "These people" represented half of the participants in the session, and they quickly became nonparticipants.

Dealing with Disagreement

This is another facilitation issue, but it's the one that seems to terrify people new to running sessions, so we give it its own topic. The fear is "What if I'm up there running a session to build a swimlane diagram, and everyone's arguing about how the process actually works?" Sounds bad, but if you take a deep breath and step back, you can handle it. Some general principles:

- Usually there is some difference in perspective for the "disagreeing parties." The key is to discover what it is:
  - Geographic location is the most common ("Akron handles receiving differently than Sydney"). European Union versus North American versus Asian differences have been striking.
  - Organizational location ("sales awards bonuses differently than tech support").
  - As-is versus should-be ("what is actually happening is different than what the operating procedures state").
  - In minor cases, the difference is that individuals perform the same step differently ("Juan and Alice conduct follow-up inspections differently"). It might be procedure, not process, and you shouldn't be diagramming it anyway.
- Before diving into detail, try to list or describe (in narrative form) the key differences. Then try to ask, "Are these significant differences?" and "How important is it to resolve them?" Do people agree on "what" must happen and therefore the differences are "how"? The question is whether there is value in drawing out all the different versions. Maybe not. Perhaps you can build one good-enough model of the typical situation and then document as narrative annotations the variations—at most, one diagram per geographic area, with annotation.
- If the differences are substantial (more than just one piece of the process) and they matter, then the best approach is to do a separate model for each variant. You'll eventually have to understand each location's as-is process anyway, to plan implementation, and you can sometimes identify best practices from various sites. Always agree to model *one case at a time*—this avoids the endless circling that will happen if you try to model them all at once.
- A second alternative, almost as good, is to have representatives from the most typical site (if there is such a thing) participate in drawing their form of the process. Then review with other groups, and they can usually highlight the differences easily.

Generally, we find that people are less concerned with differences when we put them into context by showing how much of the process is agreed, and the differences arise only in a limited part of it. One of our core facilitation principles is to "seek out areas of agreement," because it so often makes the area of disagreement seem small by comparison.

Conclusion

This chapter will have taken you to the point where you are ready to make a thorough assessment of the current process. The next chapter will cover that in detail and marks the beginning of Phase 3: Design the To-Be Process.

PART IV

Phase 3: Design the To-Be Process

CHAPTER 12

Conduct Final As-Is Process Assessment

What's going on here??!!!
—Everyone, or so it seemed when you were a kid.

Introduction

So, what have we accomplished so far? First, we completed phase 1, *establish process context, scope, and goals,* during which we established the target process and its boundaries and performed initial assessment (stakeholder-based) and goal setting. We've just finished phase 2, *understand the as-is process,* during which we completed as-is workflow process modeling to whatever detail was useful and learned a lot more about the process along the way. Now, in phase 3, *design the to-be process* it's time to transition into rethinking and redesign. Our immediate concern in this chapter will be to consolidate our understanding of the factors impacting current process performance and at the same time identify ideas that *might* address those factors. We'll resist the urge to leap straight into modeling the to-be process workflow, a common urge, and instead take a short time to conduct a holistic assessment, enabler by enabler, of the as-is process.

Actually, as illustrated in Figure 12.1, with final assessment we *are* taking a step into the design of the to-be process. Assessment is part understanding the as-is and part designing the to-be—they're inseparable. When assessment identifies a specific fault in the as-is process, it's only human to think of a fix to implement in the to-be. Up until now, we've discouraged people from thinking about solutions, but at last we're going to start recording improvement suggestions as they arise. Recording them, though, doesn't necessarily mean we'll act on them. In the next chapter, we'll look at techniques for identifying other potential improvements and then assessing all ideas in a holistic manner (also enabler by enabler) before deciding which improvement ideas to proceed with. Only then will we start to lay out the new workflow. By the way, during the assessment, we won't just dwell on "what's wrong"—we will also identify the good aspects of the process that should be preserved.

Perhaps this all sounds time consuming, as if we're falling into analysis paralysis. What if you have completed as-is workflow modeling and are sure you know the root causes of the problems and even what the likely solutions are? Not so fast! If you perform an assessment as described in this chapter, you might find the root cause of an issue is completely different than your initial impression. For instance, your initial assessment for a permit application determined that the cycle time was far too long. After as-is modeling, your team feels that an IT solution based on a

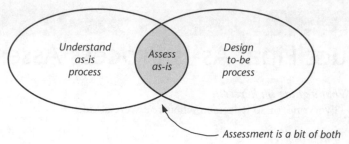

Figure 12.1   Final assessment is part as-is, part to-be.

BPMS will address the problem by expediting the movement of the permit through the process. However, an enabler-based assessment might determine that the real problems are inappropriate staff performance metrics (rewarded for finding fault, no matter how inconsequential) and narrow job definition (too many people each looking at too small a piece of the puzzle). The IT solution will have virtually no impact if these other factors aren't addressed. We've seen it more times than we care to count. Reward for finding fault is common, and it leads to...well, a lot of fault found. Take a moment to think about cases you've seen where new procedures or IT really didn't make the desired improvement. Why didn't they effect change? Probably because they didn't look at the whole process, didn't address the most important issues, and didn't address all of the enablers.

You will avoid this by performing an assessment that ensures your project addresses the issues that really matter. Let's see how, starting with a recap of the goals of this step. One goal of *conduct final as-is process assessment* is to determine the root cause of unsatisfactory performance in the process, specifically addressing stakeholder issues established in phase 1 during *conduct initial as-is process assessment*. The other goal is to suggest ideas for consideration during the next step, *determine to-be process characteristics and workflow*. These ideas (and that's all they are right now—ideas) will include process changes and aspects of the current process to retain. We'll also confirm whether or not we need to proceed with process change at all.

Characteristics of the new process, whether current features to retain or new features to introduce, won't be finalized until the next step, in Chapter 13. So, in a way, this is like brainstorming—capture ideas and then let them gel a bit before assessing them and making decisions. The approach follows a step-by-step method that has evolved over many consulting assignments. The intent is to ensure you don't jump into solutions until you properly understand the problem and the environment in which it arises.

The approach is step by step, but it isn't Industrial Engineering 101. It's less formal, and perhaps more subjective, but it seems to strike a good balance that works in practice. It won't always be easy—like redesign, it's part technique, part flashes of insight. As Edison said, "Genius is 1 percent inspiration, and 99 percent perspiration." But this chapter will provide a framework to help inspiration come. It utilizes a framework, an assessment based on the six enablers introduced in Chapter 4 (workflow design, application of IT, motivation and measurement, and so on) to ensure that a broad view is taken. Otherwise, it's too easy to drill down in one area while ignoring others. It often yields surprising discoveries—people focus on workflow design and IT (naturally), but the solution might lie in motivation and measurement or in job definition, as in the building permit example. To prevent diving into the wrong details, we identify the process' leverage points. In the best Stephen Covey tradition, this forces attention on the "big rocks first." The key steps within *conduct final as-is process assessment* are:

1. Confirm stakeholder assessment and process goals from initial assessment;
2. Capture first impressions of process strengths and weaknesses;
3. Identify leverage points;
4. Assess by each enabler in turn, generating process improvement ideas;
5. Assess individual steps (optional);
6. Make the initial decision on what to do with the process—leave it as is, abandon it, improve it, and so on;
7. Consolidate process improvement ideas.

Getting Ready

In addition to the core team, this step will involve the content experts who participated in the as-is mapping. Along the way, everyone has built up a lot of knowledge and impressions, probably much of it undocumented, and you want to capture it in the form of an assessment ASAP. This should never be a back-room activity involving only the consultants, analysts, or process improvement experts. That's been tried, and often when a supposed fault was found in the process there was a good reason for it to be that way. More important, process team and the folks back at the ranch will never buy into an external assessment—they must participate.

As usual, this is best done in a facilitated session. You may have individuals or small teams do detail work, but the norm is that it all happens in session. You have probably covered this already, but if your group isn't familiar with the business of process improvement, and the kinds of things that other organizations are doing, prepare a brief presentation. It should be less than 30 minutes, and cover the principles and practices of process improvement. The examples in the *assess by enabler* section of this chapter can provide raw material for the presentation. Be careful about covering examples from your own line of business—sometimes a group will simply want to duplicate other "best practices," whether they're appropriate or not.

Confirm Initial Assessment and Goals

Look at your initial assessment, especially the summary poster, and ask:

- Would the process case for action (especially the stakeholder assessment) be any different now based on what you learned while doing the mapping? Be sure to ask the question for *each* stakeholder.
- Would the process vision be any different now based on what you learned while doing the mapping?

Make whatever changes are necessary, bearing in mind that you might have to reconvene some of the earlier participants if they aren't currently involved, to confirm the changes with them.

Capture First Impressions

We don't want our formal steps to get in the way of recording the obvious. At this point, participants will probably have some strong ideas about the process. Open up the floor, or a blank sheet of flipchart paper, and brainstorm for first impressions, including significant problems, features to keep, and possible improvements. These ideas will eventually come out anyway, but you're better off to do it now—let participants get the ideas off their chest so they can focus on the enabler-based assessment. Otherwise, they'll be distracted while they look for an opportunity to make their point. That's why we introduced the idea of "venting" back in Chapter 5.

You must strictly control this, or it will spiral into minor details. You really do only want first impressions, and there might not even be any significant ones, so don't let the group go off on a quest for material. Try time boxing this step by allowing only 20 to 30 minutes of session time. Or, you can limit content—give each participant three slips of paper, one for each of their top three concerns. Toss the slips in a box, then record each anonymously on flipcharts. Wait until all have been recorded before capturing any comments and additional points.

Identify Leverage Points

This is a continuation of capturing first impressions in which we ask, "What's really important in the process?" Looking for "leverage points" can help you find out. A leverage point is a part of the process that has a disproportionate impact on overall performance. It's likely to be the root cause of the most significant problems. In other words, if you could fix the problems at the leverage points, you would significantly improve process performance, possibly with surprisingly little overall redesign. Leverage points often occur at the front end of a process, where improvements can have disproportionately large benefits throughout the rest of the process. For instance, "If we could avoid taking on those cases that end up generating a lot of work and frustration for little benefit, all the other cases would benefit." Note that you might discover leverage within a specific aspect of the process (e.g., at a particular step or in the absence of a needed enabler), but you might find it only within a specific case of the process. As an example, it could be that "issue building permit" works well except for a single type of new construction within a particular zoning area. Let's look at two examples of leverage points:

1. An order fulfillment process based on a "build to order" model had unacceptable fulfillment time and defect rates. Finished goods were currently shipped to a separate quality control facility (a holdover from an acquisition) for inspection and calibration, and then shipped back to the production site for consolidation and shipping to the customer. As well as the obvious delay, the shipping introduced more defects than if the goods had stayed at

production site. So, the leverage point was to "eliminate shipping of finished goods to a separate quality control facility." Presumably, this would be accomplished by moving quality control to the production area, but remember, we're not going to decide to do that until after the assessment of ideas, which we cover in the next chapter.

2. Another advertising order fulfillment process, very similar to a radio advertising example mentioned in Chapter 7, generated unacceptable error rates and stress levels in the production department of a monthly magazine, which led to customer complaints and lost revenue. A mobile sales force took orders for advertising that required custom production work back at the magazine's offices. The assumption was that something was wrong with the internal order booking and production activities, but when pressed for the leverage points ("what single change would make the most difference?") a different story emerged. Because they were expected to "sell, sell, sell," the sales reps stayed in the field selling and didn't submit orders until the last minute. This led to a "pig in a python" effect, with a glut of orders arriving all at once and overwhelming production. If the reps could somehow "get the order back to the production department in 'real-enough' time" (the leverage point), then the major problems would disappear with no other process changes. Possible remedies appeared in workflow design, the use of IT, the motivation and measurement scheme, and so on, but finding solutions isn't the immediate concern. If ideas can be captured now, fine, but there's still time to do this at the next step.

If time isn't taken to consider leverage points, there is a tendency to start looking at comparatively minor aspects of the process, typically local irritants. Perhaps it's just easier for people to focus on the 80 percent cited in the famous 80/20 Rule. This is also known as the Pareto Principle, after V. Pareto, an Italian economist. He noted that in distributions, in particular income distributions, 80 percent of the distribution usually goes to 20 percent of the observations. For example, 80 percent of the wealth is held by the richest 20 percent of households, 80 percent of the workers are employed by the largest 20 percent of companies, and so on. By this reckoning, we would expect that 80 percent of your problem could be caused by 20 percent of your process steps or cases. In some circumstances, and your process might be one of them, the 80/20 rule becomes the 90/10 rule: 90 percent of the problems are caused by 10 percent of the process. We have seen entire processes reduced to a shambles because of problems in the first couple of steps. As noted earlier, improvements at the front end of a process often have an outsize impact through the rest of the process. You must concentrate on the vital few defects that cause the majority of loss, not the trivial many.

In practice, leverage points are fairly obvious, provided you take the time to step back and look for them. If they aren't obvious, take a quick walk through the process map and at each step or area ask if there are problems that affect the entire process. Don't fall into the trap of looking for "the big issue" when it's not there. If you do find a real leverage point, record any improvement suggestions on an "ideas" flipchart for use during the *determine to-be process characteristics and workflow* (Chapter 13).

Assessment by Enablers

The concept of "process enablers" introduced in Chapter 4 is familiar by now, but here's a quick recap. An "enabler" is one of the aspects of a process that "enables" it to perform properly. More to the point, if an enabler is absent or inappropriate, it is a "*dis*abler." Finding both cases is important. The six enablers are:

1. Process workflow design;
2. Information systems (use of information and communications technology);
3. Motivation and measurement;
4. Human resources;
5. Policies and rules;
6. Facilities design (or some other categories appropriate to your situation).

Figure 12.2 expands on Figure 4.1 and puts this in context. It shows the process, supported by the six enablers. Above it, effectively constraining the process, are the organization's mission, strategy, goals, and objectives; the process' goals, objectives, and differentiator; and the organizational environment. This is how we look at it:

- A process supports the organization's mission, strategy, goals, and objectives.

- A process has its own goals and objectives according to the chosen differentiator.

- A process must operate within the reality of the organizational environment ("culture").

Look at each enabler in turn, and canvass the group for suggestions on how that enabler manifests itself in the process, whether positively or negatively. Record these

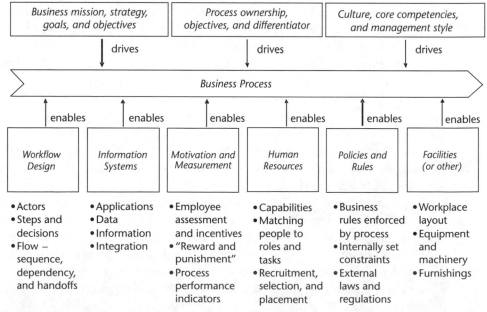

Figure 12.2   A process in context with constraints and enablers.

assessments, and, when improvement ideas emerge (they will!), also record them on an "ideas" sheet. Keep all of these suggestions, even if they appear dubious at first. If you want to be a little more structured, capture assessments and ideas in a matrix with four columns: enabler (e.g., IS), issue (the problem), alternative (a potential improvement), and notes. You might want to do this now, because you'll do it eventually—for each significant process change under consideration, you'll document the issue and its impact, along with each improvement idea and its expected benefit.

Participants often struggle with this, because they can't always say a problem is specifically one enabler or the other—"I don't know whether this problem belongs in human resources or in workflow design." For example, if a process has too many handoffs, is that workflow design, or is it a human resources environment that has defined excessively small jobs? It's probably both, *but it doesn't really matter*. The idea of following this framework isn't to force an issue into one category or another; it's to force us to identify factors that might otherwise have been missed. Now let's look at some of the things we'll be looking for when we consider each enabler.

Workflow Design

Workflow design isn't necessarily the most important enabler, but it is the topic of this book, so we'll provide a little more information here. Besides, a workflow model provides a step-by-step framework that allows us to uncover issues that would otherwise be missed. We've never yet had an assignment where this wasn't the case. There's no end to the possibilities, but here are the usual suspects when looking for workflow design flaws:

- Are there too many actors, for instance, three people doing minor tasks that could easily be handled by one of them?
- Are there too many handoffs (see previous)?
- Are there non-value-added steps, for instance, rekeying information or reconciling different sources? A good test: would a reasonable customer pay to have this step completed?
- Are there noncritical steps holding up the main flow? Does the work item wait while recording, filing, or whatever are completed?
- Is there excess serialization? Are steps happening in a sequential fashion when they could occur in parallel? This often happens with processes that were originally paper-based, and the source document (like a claim, credit application, or manuscript) could only be on one desk at a time.
- Is there an obvious bottleneck? That is, is there an under-resourced step that all work items must pass through, whether it's value-added or not? Note that a "bottleneck" isn't automatically bad—sometimes it can serve to regulate the flow of work through the process, or through parallel paths in the process, and actually prevent worse problems (collisions and backups) later on.[1]
- Does the process yo-yo, continually returning to the same control point?

---

1. We'll expand on this point. See the restaurant example coming up shortly.

- Do exceptions or "tough stuff" get in the way of the other 80 or 90 percent? Do problem customers get the attention, while the easy ones wait? Process redesign often involves "triage" at the front end to direct an instance of the process into a flow that is designed for that particular case.

- Does the process require something—a work item, a worker, or a customer—to continually shuttle among different locations? This could also surface when looking at the facilities enabler.

- Conversely, is there a tracking mechanism to ensure that tough stuff eventually gets dealt with instead of languishing in a "dead file"?

- Is the process "one size fits all" with one complex process that has lots of decisions, exceptions, or complexity to cover all situations? For instance, a purchasing process we saw cost hundreds of dollars in administrative costs, whether it was for a significant purchase like a laptop or $5 worth of office supplies.

- Are escalating approval or information loops built in? For instance, does each layer in the corporate hierarchy decide if the dollar amount of a requisition requires a higher authority? The alternative is to send the request directly to the appropriate level, with some parallel mechanism to keep intermediate levels happy and "in the loop."

- Is there a role that coordinates other roles or tasks? This is often a symptom of a bad process in which actors are working in isolation, lack information or authority, and so on.

- Is the process undocumented, leading to each individual or area doing it their own way?

- Are individual tasks or desk procedures undocumented, again leading to inconsistency?

- Are roles undefined, leading to confusion about who is responsible for what?

- Are cause and effect separated in some way, or, more commonly, are work and inspection separated? This introduces delay, it requires rework of intermediate steps, and the doers don't learn what they are doing wrong.

As a separate category, we'll look at what we've come to call a "Goldratt assessment"—looking for workflow designs, or policies and rules, that impose constraints on inputs or outputs to the overall process or to steps within the process. The prime examples are unnecessary delays or batching driven by technical concerns or by policy. We find it useful to think in terms of straight-through processing (STP). STP occurs when a process that formerly had many delays built into it for batch processing now takes place virtually instantaneously, without human intervention. This is accomplished by having the automated facilities of some EAI technology or BPMS shepherding the transaction through various systems. The BPMS tool automates human interventions and performs the necessary translations along the way, and invokes each system in real time rather than waiting for batches or limits. Imagine that every transaction or work item could sail through the process with no delay or human intervention. Then look at every obstacle to that. This includes the following:

- Batching by time (hourly, daily, and so on);

- Batching by numerical limits (wait for 50 orders);
- Batching by dollar limits (wait for $1,000 worth of orders);
- Batching for transport or delivery;
- Batching for approval;
- Batching for data rekeying or reformatting.

We're not saying that all batching is bad, because it isn't, but it has to be considered, not taken for granted. At one company (probably many) handwritten forms were batched and then sent overseas every night for data entry, with the results transmitted back electronically. No other option was nearly as accurate and cost effective.

The batching examples were all variations on not doing something as soon as possible, because an artificial M:1 connection has been introduced into the process. That's why, back in Chapter 5, when we were analyzing linkages (1:1, M:1, …) for process boundaries, we cautioned that you need to consider if the M:1 connection is intrinsic to the process (many passengers board one flight) or has been introduced for policy or technical reasons (many orders are billed on one invoice).

Please note that these symptoms are not always problems. For instance, having separate inspectors and coordinators may use the abilities of experienced individuals to leverage the effectiveness of entry-level workers. An example:

When one of my sons was a teenager, he got a part-time job in the kitchen at a well-known "casual, high-energy, high-quality" restaurant. In no time, he was cooking appetizers and then supervising. I expressed amazement: "Son, I know you can grill a mean sandwich, but how in the world do you cook all those appetizers, and start them at the right time, and get them to the right spot all at the same time? It's amazing!" He said: "Dad, it's the process!" I couldn't believe my ears. "The process?" "Yep, the process. The procedure for making each appetizer is precisely defined, so anyone can do it. Also, they know how long it will take, within seconds. So a "line coach" tells each worker when to start what, so that a table's order of appies will be ready all at the same time." He also explained the role of an inspector at the other end of the line, expediters, servers (as opposed to waiters), and so on. By designing a repeatable process and putting skilled people in the right coordination roles, the restaurant could achieve excellent results with junior kitchen staff. Note, however, that coordination and inspection didn't take place invisibly—it was instant and "right there."

Information Systems

This is a big topic, too, but we'll restrict our discussion to a few key questions. Are any of the following characteristics evident?

- Unavailable information, or a lack of shared data;
- Rekeying (duplicate entry) of data;
- Data structures that have inconsistent formats, structures, or semantics;[2]

2.   See Chapter 14 on data models for further explanation.

- Reconciling different information sources;
- Missing functionality, or manual activities that could be automated;
- Awkward interfaces;
- Lack of support for workflow;
- Existing automation that blindly replicates an earlier paper-based process, known as "paving the cowpaths."

Wherever possible, is IT being used to:

- Automate activities and free up human labor for higher value-added work?
- Support self-service, or elimination of intermediaries?
- Resequence or parallelize steps that otherwise would happen in some strict sequence?
- Duplicate scarce expertise?
- Eliminate barriers of space (geography) or time the way the Internet has in many processes?

Are modern alternatives being used wherever beneficial?

- Mobile computing (pen based, wireless, PDA, GPS, ...);
- Things that know what they are: self-identifying tags, SmartCards, RFIDs, ...;
- Biometric interfaces devices: voice recognition, face recognition, hand geometry readers, retinal scan, and so on;
- The device that hasn't been invented yet!

Do IT architectures include the following?

- Use of middleware or EAI technology to integrate applications across disparate platforms into a single composite transaction, or to integrate different data sources into a single "canonical" view;
- Use of BPMS or other technology to integrate applications into business processes, and business activity monitoring (BAM) to monitor the progress of individual transactions;
- Inventory of shared data services and business services;
- Evolutionary or disposable applications.

Motivation and Measurement

Motivation and measurement is the enabler that surprises less experienced analysts with its importance, but experienced people almost invariably know that it's the most important of the enablers. The bottom line is captured in the C. R. Luigs quote mentioned earlier: "People don't pay much attention to what management says;

they pay attention to what management measures." And experience has confirmed this time and time again—no matter what management says about what they want a process to achieve, it's what management measures (and rewards or punishes) that dictates how people and processes behave.

Here are a couple of case studies. Motivation and measurement as an enabler first crystallized for me in the mid-1980s. I'd been studying the slow rate of behavioral change in an IS department where I was consulting. Management strongly wanted certain changes to take place, but it just didn't happen. Presentations, pep talks, and bulletins from management didn't change anyone's behavior, no matter how passionate the delivery was. It dawned on me that this organization revered adherence to project budgets and schedules. Project leaders were "dinged" if they came in more than 10 percent over estimates or (unbelievably) if they were more than 10 percent under estimates, and they were showered with praise and promotion if they consistently came in on target. Management wanted to improve client satisfaction, and encourage good analysis that would lead to application stability, flexibility, and extensibility, but there were no measures for these variables and consequently no change.

That's when I saw Luigs's quote, and shortly thereafter had a chance to put the idea that "measures drive behavior" into action. This case was introduced in Chapter 7. The VP of IS had stated his extreme dissatisfaction with a computer services department that was in charge of a high-volume, production, transaction-processing environment with thousands of users expecting subsecond response time. Along with maintaining and tuning this environment, the computer services (CS) group was responsible for migrating new applications into production. The VP's complaint was: "Our application developers have to jump through flaming hoops to get a new system into production. It seems as though the CS people feel that their entire function is to keep anything new out of "their" production environment. I've told them I want to see some responsiveness and flexibility, but nothing has changed, and I'm ready to outsource the entire function!"

I suggested we take a minute and look at how this group was measured, and, sure enough, that explained everything. First, there were absolutely no measures in place relating to getting new apps in quickly. All that was measured was up time and response time, and statistics on these were summarized hourly, daily, weekly, and monthly. They were analyzed, trended, charted, and distributed to every operational manager in the organization. They were also conspicuously posted in public areas. So, it was no mystery to CS what they were measured on. And what's the surest way to negatively impact up time and response time? You guessed it—migrate a new system into production. Case closed, or at least explained.

Another classic example: After the fall of the iron curtain, a team of Western manufacturing experts visited a tractor factory in the former Soviet Union. One of them spotted a lab-coated individual walking among the newly built tractors. Every so often, he'd scratch a fender, break a headlight, or pull out a wire. More amazing, this individual worked in a quality control function. Can you guess the motivation? QC was measured on the defects they found. When quality improved, there weren't enough defects anymore, so QC had to artificially introduce them in order to justify their existence. This may be an apocryphal story, but we've seen exactly the same phenomenon in office environment, and so have you:

- If the project control office is rewarded for finding faults in a project plan, then, no matter what, they'll find faults.
- If a software quality assurance group is rewarded, one way or another, for finding defects in software, they'll find defects.

We have seen this phenomenon repeatedly in the fields of health care and justice. A recent article in the *New York Times* by Dr. Sandeep Jauhar made the point beautifully. Dr. Jauhar writes [1]:

> I recently took care of a 50-year-old man who had been admitted to the hospital short of breath. During his month long stay he was seen by a hematologist, an endocrinologist, a kidney specialist, a podiatrist, two cardiologists, a cardiac electrophysiologist, an infectious-diseases specialist, a pulmonologist, an ear-nose-throat specialist, a urologist, a gastroenterologist, a neurologist, a nutritionist, a general surgeon, a thoracic surgeon and a pain specialist. He underwent 12 procedures, including cardiac catherization, a pacemaker implant and a bone-marrow biopsy (to work-up chronic anemia).
>
> This man's case, in which expert consultations sprouted with little rhyme, reason or coordination, reinforced a lesson I have learned many times since entering practice: In our health care system, where doctors are paid piecework for their services, if you have a slew of physicians and a willing patient, almost any sort of terrible excess can occur. Though accurate data is lacking, the overuse of services in health care probably cost hundreds of billions of dollars last year, out of the more than $2 trillion that Americans spent on health.

We have seen precisely the same phenomenon in the justice system—if the court-appointed defense lawyers are paid by the motion or by the filing, then you'll get a lot more motions and filings.

The key point: "distortions" in behavior are often caused by local measures or piecework measures, rather than more sophisticated metrics that include all relevant customer outcomes or process results. Take a moment to identify some of the examples from your own experience—they're surely there. A second key point: as we pointed out in Chapter 7,[3] implicit measures are every bit as important as explicit, statistical measures. Implicit measures include "Way to go!" from management or the approval that comes from adhering to cultural norms. We remember the systems manager who was always thrilled to see a prototype, so she always got one whether it was appropriate or not.

Now, after that preamble, it turns out that there aren't really very many questions to ask. It's just important that they be asked in a structured way. Start at the "outside" of the process, with the process's customer, and working inwards.

From the customer's perspective:

- What are the desired outcomes? (This is reflected in the process result, and in the process differentiator.)
- What measures would emphasize the desired customer outcome?

---

3.   Speaking of Chapter 7 ("Conduct Initial As-Is Process Assessment"), many of the ideas in this section hearken back to that topic. If you skipped it, or can't remember it, this would be a good time for a review.

- Is that how the customer currently measures the process? (You might have to negotiate some "attitude adjustments" with the customer. In one case, there were process problems that led to constant hand holding, adjustments, and "favors" for the customer. They had come to expect this, but it was now interfering with what they really wanted—predictable, lower-cost service.)
- Are there other external stakeholders to consider?

From the organization's, or the process owner's, perspective:

- How is the process currently measured?
- Is that appropriate? Is there appropriate focus on customer outcomes or inappropriate attention to internal convenience or efficiencies? (In one software development environment, all that mattered was getting the initial release developed, no matter how flawed it was or how long it took to get a stable, second release developed. Those targets were driven by IT ego, not what the customer valued.)

From the perspective of the departments or functions involved in the process:

- How is their contribution to the process measured?
- Is that appropriate? Is the process considered at all, or do the measures stress task completion, convenience, or efficiency within the function? (This is the most common problem of all, and we've seen many examples so far of measures that emphasize tasks or efficiencies within a functional area as opposed to process-oriented or customer-focused measures that focus on outcomes.)

From the perspective of the process's individual actors:

- How is their contribution to the process measured?
- Is that appropriate? Are the measures based on task completion, or on quality or contribution to process (or process phase) outcomes? (An example was the kitchen designer measured on rapid turnaround of the first draft. This inevitably led to more cycles of revision than would be necessary if they had time to do a better job the first time. A better metric would take into account the number of iterations, the time to approval, the value of the overall job, and so on.)
- Are there measures that reward new abilities?

What you're looking for in all cases is a misalignment between how the customer would measure the process and how the organization measures the process and its participants. And it's not that internal efficiencies shouldn't be measured at all, just that there should be balance with measures important to the customer. And we certainly want to eliminate measures based on tasks that simply shouldn't happen. For example, "transcriptions per hour of field inspection report to head office format"—don't measure it, eliminate the transcription. A "reasonable" customer wouldn't pay for reformatting and transcribing, which is classic non-value-added activity. Another example is "settlement corrections handled per clerk per hour"—it's better to eliminate the errors than to measure the correction activity.

A relevant example arose just this week, at a provider of automobile insurance. Changes in the renewal process for a core product offering were coming, and customer service knew they would be facing an avalanche of calls, which they were trying to figure out how to handle. Meanwhile, what were the people designing and implementing the process changes doing to minimize the number of calls? Nothing, because customer support calls weren't a concern to their department. Contrast this with what we've seen in enlightened companies—customer service actually *reports to* product development,[4] and when a new product or feature is launched, the responsible development team is assigned to handle customer support calls for the first few weeks. Needless to say, their incentive is to introduce a product or feature on time and within budget, but also to ensure that it is as hassle-free for the customer as possible.

Human Resources

"Human resources," encompassing organization structure, job definition, recruiting, skills, and training, is a complex and sensitive topic. Entire books and Master's degree programs are based on single aspects of human resources so we can't do it justice in a page or two. But that doesn't mean we'll ignore it—we'll just keep it simple by listing a few simple questions to consider.

We haven't included any questions that address organizational structure. That's because the design of the organization (divisions, departments, sections, teams, and so on) in the absence of other factors doesn't make much difference. What really seems to matter is how people, organizations, and processes are measured, and how individuals, jobs, and tasks are aligned.

Let's see if you agree—collectively, the authors have more than 60 years of experience in private and public organizations, and neither of us can recall a case where the dreaded "re-org," in the absence of other significant changes, had a positive impact. Mostly, the impact was negative. How about you? On the other hand, there are lots of examples of organizations remaining intact, but new job definitions and measurement schemes having a huge impact. This is highly relevant to process improvement, because so much has been made about the problems of functionally based organizations and the superiority of team-based organizations (especially the self-directed, empowered, cross-functional, process-based, customer-focused variety). But whatever their faults, functionally based organizations are generally easier to manage than the alternatives—you have similar people, with similar backgrounds, performing similar work. They're also easier to staff, a pool of expertise develops, and all the other advantages appear that made specialization attractive in the first place.

As an alternative to vertical, functionally based organization structures, some companies experimented with organizations based on horizontal, cross-functional processes. This was an outgrowth of the mid-1990s belief that teams were a panacea for all an organization's ills, just as reengineering was a few years before. Certainly, a cross-functional team is the best structure when they are brought together for a particular project, like the process redesign projects that are the subject of this book.

---

4. Think about how much sense that makes. Who is in more constant contact with the customers, and knows more about what they like, don't like, and want, than customer service?

However, when you create permanent organizations based on cross-functional teams, all manner of problems start to arise. Companies that tried this report three main problems:

1. They can be very difficult to manage, because you have different sorts of people, with different backgrounds, language, and interests, all making different contributions to some overall goal. This requires a degree of management skill, and attention to motivation and measurement, training, and other factors, that isn't easy to come by. A case in point: how do you motivate, reward, and retain a "star" performer in an environment where measures and rewards are team-based, and competition for stars is intense?
2. While staff in the process-based organizations developed a breadth of skills, the absolute level of expertise in any one function began to decline.
3. Efficiencies were lost because there was no longer a pool of functional experts in a field such as international logistics, which could support multiple processes. Instead, you ended up with each process having to staff that need separately, and, as mentioned, the level of expertise wouldn't get as high.

Currently, we see the best results from a combination of:

- Functionally based ("traditional") organizations;
- Appropriately "rich" job definitions;
- Well-designed processes, IT systems, and metrics that encourage the flow of work toward the desired process outcome.

The functional organizations and the roles within them should be appropriately broad. You want to avoid the situation a U.S. federal government official cited when explaining problems with the Hurricane Katrina response: "Too many players and too many layers." If you really think that organizational structure is a problem, it's time to bring in the professionals from your human resources or organizational development department. These people may also be able to help you develop the best metrics for the people and organizations that support a process.

In some organizations, especially in small startups, the notion of job definition is foreign—a nonissue, in fact. Everyone is expected to be highly skilled and motivated, and to do whatever needs doing. Generally, it's only with size and complexity that job definition becomes an issue. Size and complexity come at you fast, though. We've seen organizations as small as 20 people failing because of unclear job responsibilities, and by the time an organization has 40 people it appears that formal structures are essential. And, as noted earlier, it's often hard to separate process design issues from job definition issues—if the workflow has too many handoffs, then it's possible that on the HR side the jobs are too narrowly defined. What you're investigating is alignment among the following:

- Skills, knowledge and experience of the people in the jobs;
- The boundaries of their responsibilities, as constrained by job or role definitions;
- The requirements of the process activities and steps they'll be responsible for.

Let's look at some of the questions. This will not be an exhaustive list, so just remember the key point: "Are the right people, with the right skills, in the right jobs, performing the right tasks?"

Are the skills, knowledge, and experience of the actors well matched with the tasks they perform? This can go both ways. Highly skilled or scarce resources might spend too much of their time doing clerical or administrative tasks that are not a good use of their time. This has emerged as the most common HR issue we've seen over the past decade. Poorly considered layoffs of support staff have left expensive knowledge workers spending a lot (often 50 percent or more) of their time doing work that could be better done, more economically, by clerical and administrative professionals. It's strange that we see this in environments like justice, medicine, engineering, and R&D, but on a large construction site no one would consider firing the laborers and having carpenters, steelworkers, and electricians doing their work instead.

In one (failed) reengineering project, doctors had been provided with word processing software so they could update their own records rather than having medical data entry staff do it from dictation or handwritten notes. It was a disaster—the doctors resented it, most being inept typists at best, and it took far too much of a scarce, expensive resource's time. On top of that, the data entry staff was trained in arcane coding schemes that were essential to proper record keeping, while the doctors struggled with them. Naturally, the bargaining unit wasn't happy with the loss of jobs, which caused problems elsewhere. Eventually, the experiment was abandoned, but not without hard feelings and lost credibility. In another case, an outside sales force was burdened with a lot of administrative activities that could have been handled much more effectively by sales assistants.

The reverse can happen. In one case, all customer service reps, from the newest hire to the most experienced individuals, had to handle any type of issue from any type of customer, even though there was a call screening and routing function. Experienced staff didn't spend their time dealing with cases that required their skills and experience, and junior staff made many errors in handling calls that were beyond their ability. The reasoning, by the way, was that a sink-or-swim environment ensured that only the best candidates stayed around; we were unconvinced. Ironically, reengineering projects have led to many mismatches, such as the case where technical specialists were suddenly expected to participate in customer service and sales activities without any training, or, frankly, without even the temperament (or appearance!) for client contact. Assembly line workers have been burned out by "enriched" job responsibilities that were beyond their natural abilities, even with training. Sometimes long-term workers are perfectly happy with their routine jobs because they can talk or daydream while doing them.

Look for skill dilution from excessive specialization and fragmentation. This is a common problem after 200 years of specialization. In addition to getting less from human resources than is possible, boredom and lack of ownership lead to more errors, not fewer. Some clues: what is logically a single task requires multiple participants; individual contributions are almost mechanical; people frequently say, "That's not my job!"; jobs aren't *vertically loaded* (workers don't use the information they create, or detect and correct errors that they have introduced). Has a job been created to coordinate fragmented work—a tracking clerk, traffic manger, expediter, lot coordinator, and so on? This isn't automatically a problem, but it can indicate that other jobs are excessively limited or operating without the information they need.

Has recruiting become an issue because either the jobs are so complex that no entry-level candidate is suitable or the jobs are so simplistic that no one wants them? Many companies have realized they have been recruiting the wrong people because they have focused on particular experience. A retailer experienced significant benefit when it began to hire people who were affable and liked helping other people, rather than hiring for cash register experience. The phrase "hire for attitude, train for skills" is a good summary.

Policies and Rules

This is fairly straightforward, and will probably have been caught when you inspected the workflow and saw some decision points and checks that left you asking "why?" Those were probably "policies and rules" that have gone unchallenged but are ripe for rethinking.

- Why *do* we hold special book orders until the total value for a publisher exceeds $1,000?
- Why *do* we require the applicant to provide three years of income tax returns when a valid credit card would handle any conceivable risk?
- Why *do* we require at least three bids on any service requisition with an estimated value of less than $5,000, especially when we know that it will cost more than that to solicit, review, and select from the bids?
- Why *do* we refuse to allow credit card payment for international orders, including Canada–United States transactions?
- Why *do* we insist that vendors emboss a contract with their corporate seal?[5]

You get the idea. What you're looking for is any constraint or requirement that the business imposes that impacts the conduct of a business process. Many of these are easy to spot, because they show up as a decision point in the workflow, but others may be more subtle. Just ask if every validation or decision is truly necessary. While you're at it, ask if an assumed policy or rule really is just that—*assumed*. We often encounter situations where, somehow, a rule was thought to be in place that really wasn't, or it had been years ago but most people "didn't get the memo" letting them know it had been rescinded. If you don't catch these now, the *challenge process* that we introduce in the next chapter will almost surely highlight them. Note that these "assumed rule" situations are quite different than cultural norms, which are also unwritten but are powerful shapers of behavior.

Facilities

With "facilities," you're looking for cases where the workplace and equipment interfere with the process. The local library was a good example until a redesign.

---

5. We told the legal department at that client that we couldn't bring in the corporate seal, because he'd been sold to the circus. They didn't laugh.

There used to be separate counter areas; one for checkout and the other for paying fines or fees, picking up holds, and so on. Each area required a person to staff it, because they were enclosed and there was no easy way to move from one to another. This meant that even in slow periods, two people had to be on counter duty. Customer satisfaction suffered as well—if a customer was checking out books and found that a fine was due or that a reserved book was available, they'd have to leave the checkout line, stand in line at the other counter, complete their business there, and then return to ("butt into") the checkout line to complete their transactions. Also, there were two separate checkout lines, and one always seemed to move more slowly (the one I was in) than the other.

The solution was obvious. A single, large counter area now serves both functions, with a single checkout line up being handled by one or two staff members who can also accept payment, retrieve reserves, and so on. In busy times, a third person handles a line just for fines, registrations, and so on, and in slow periods only one person needs to be at the counter.

In recent times workflow modeling has been used in the design of new facilities, as it always has been in industrial environments. We have seen this in a hospital environment, where the physical layout of various nursing stations and labs now matches patient flow, and in a testing laboratory, where sample storage, preparation, and testing workstations are now arranged to match sample flow.

A few questions to ask:

- Does distance between people whose tasks are linked introduce transport or communication delays?
- If work is collaborative in nature, are there suitable facilities (i.e., meeting spaces)?
- Does the physical environment make the job more difficult or unpleasant than it would be otherwise (ventilation, glare, noise, interruption, lack of privacy, and so on)?

Other Factors

Please don't feel constrained to consider only our list of enablers. Something not explicitly covered by the six enablers could be more important in your organization, and so you should feel free to add it as a category. For instance, a reader in the Netherlands [personal communication, Olga Melnik, January 14, 2007] suggested that on two of her assignments, documents that supported the processes had to be considered as a specific enabler, or, more to the point, a disabler. In her words, some of the issues to consider included:

- No clearly defined set of documents to be provided for the activity to start;
- No templates/forms for documents that could be developed to replace ad-hoc informal Word files;
- Irrelevant data in the documents that consumes much time to collect;
- No clearly defined sources to extract certain data/access supporting documents, templates;

- No consistency in document output for a certain activity;
- Mistakes/excesses/gaps in distribution lists for the output documents of an activity, and so on.

Besides showing *what* documents, it's also helpful to show *how* they are transmitted (e-mail, paper, or internal workflow after transition to a Document Management System), and check whether the receipt of the document is a sufficient or appropriate trigger for the following activity.

Our correspondent also suggested, as we might have done, that documents could be a special case of another enabler such as information technology, or part of the data management layer. That's true, but highlighting it as a separate enabler makes the most sense to us, because it would make the most sense to the subject matter experts in the field. In fields such as justice and construction, documents are everything, and so should be recognized.

Assess Individual Steps

Assessing the individual steps in detail is optional—it can be overwhelming—so you should do this only for critical or complicated processes. The other assessments will probably catch any problems that this very detailed assessment would, and we have a step in the next phase (the "challenge process") that will probably catch anything that's been missed.

There's a book on writing called *Bird by Bird* [2]. The origin of the title is advice the author's father gave to her brother when the lad had to write a term project about ornithology and felt overwhelmed by the work ahead. The advice: "Just take it bird by bird." So, if you need to do a detailed assessment, but feel overwhelmed, our advice is to "just take it step by step." For each step, questions you could ask include:

- Is this step necessary?
- Does it yield a useful result?
- Would a "reasonable" customer pay?
- Does the most appropriate performer handle it?
- Do handoffs to or from the step introduce error, expense, or delay?
- Is the step triggered in the most appropriate way?
- Is this the step occurring at the best point in the sequence?
- Is this the step implemented or supported in the best way?
- Is all the necessary information available to the performer?

Another way to look at assessment of individual steps is this: "A process can be seen as a value chain. By its contribution to the creation or delivery of a product or service, each step in a process should add value to the preceding steps" [3]. Ultimately, what is most important about each step is whether it is adding value, or is non-value-added.

Consolidate Improvement Ideas

In addition to documenting the assessment, you'll want to organize the list of process improvement ideas that were generated along with the assessment. They'll be needed soon when we'll assess the main improvement ideas and select those that will become features of the new process—what we refer to as "characterizing the to-be process" Actually, two things will be listed: ideas for improving the process and process characteristics to preserve.

This may also be a good time for the team to highlight "quick wins," also known as "low-hanging fruit." What is critical is that a quick win really is just that:

- Is it quick and "cheap" (cost effective)?
- Is it a win: a significant improvement that doesn't have an opportunity cost (i.e., one that will distract the team from more important long-term stuff) and doesn't impair things in the long run?

Be very careful here! All too often, so-called quick wins become projects with a life of their own, detracting from important project goals and leaving a dead-end solution as their legacy. We're not picking on Microsoft Access, because it's a great tool, but it isn't always *applied* in the best way. In large corporations we're seeing substantial investments in redeveloping Access applications that were originally seen as quick wins but didn't have the architecture to scale up past a few desktops. You've been warned.

Decide on Approach

Before going any further, take some time to decide if you need to. Go further that is. The future of the process is not necessarily that it will be redesigned. There are five possible courses of action:

- *Drop/abandon*: This process is not necessary, or the benefit will never justify the cost. Rare, but we had a case where a software license validation process cost several hundred thousand dollars per year and consumed skilled resources, but delivered no benefit (never uncovered problems). The company decided to abandon the process rather than reengineer it. (Technically, this is the "ultimate" in reengineering.)
- *Outsource*: It would be a more effective use of resources to have a supplier carry out the process. Traditionally, this has been the choice for generic infrastructure activities such as cleaning and catering. Companies are increasingly doing this in areas such as billing, receivables, help desk, network operations, PC support, and so on.
- *Leave as is*: The process is fine; the issues were elsewhere, for instance, no one follows the process, or training is needed.
- *Improve*: The basic structure of the process is okay, but specific improvements are possible.
- *Redesign*: The process should be fully redesigned.

Looking at what's right and wrong, would you be comfortable deciding to embark on significant improvement? Could the quick wins conceivably be "good enough," especially with respect to other opportunities? Remember, just walking away is sometimes a highly cost-effective approach.

By the way, except when we're making this decision, we don't distinguish between "improve" and "redesign," and use the terms more or less interchangeably. In the early days of reengineering, they were characterized as very different efforts, but in practice, it's a continuum, and within a process, some aspects may be improved, while other phases are redesigned from the ground up. Either way, the intent of this step is to provide a moment of reflection before carrying on.

We've done a lot of work without actually getting into redesign yet, but we'll see that all of our effort so far will make redesign much easier and more effective than it would have been.

References

[1]   Jauhar, S., "Many Doctors, Many Tests, No Rhyme or Reason," *New York Times*, March 11, 2008.

[2]   Lamott, A., *Bird by Bird: Some Instructions on Writing and Life*, New York: Doubleday, 1994.

[3]   Rummler, G. A., and A. Brache, *Improving Performance: How to Manage the White Space on the Organization Chart*, San Francisco, CA: Jossey-Bass, 1995.

CHAPTER 13

Determine To-Be Process Characteristics and Workflow

...there is always an easy solution to every human problem—neat, plausible and wrong.
—H. L. Mencken

If at first the idea is not absurd, then there is no hope for it.
—Albert Einstein

Look Before You Leap!

In most process reengineering books, the section on actually designing the new process is short, containing guidance like "Be creative" (why didn't *we* think of that?) or the always helpful "Think outside the box!" Sometimes, to aid in rethinking the process, you'll be treated to an exercise in "creative thinking," like the infamous "try to connect all the dots in the following picture without..." People find this exercise entertaining or irritating, but utterly useless in rethinking the process. In BPR courses, the section on mapping the current process is typically followed by a segment on mapping the new, improved process, with a coffee break in between. How to get from the as-is to the to-be isn't explained, so we conclude that during the break, the famous ATAMO procedure is invoked—"And then, a miracle occurs."

This reflects the central problem of process redesign. In some cases, it seems like a miracle really is required, because it's hard to pry people loose from their accumulated paradigms about the process. What will be done, by whom, when they will do it, and how, have been ingrained by years of experience. In other cases, the issue isn't prying people loose but restraining them a bit before they rush headlong into implementing what seems like a great idea or the best practice from another industry.

In this chapter, we'll substitute method for miracles with proven techniques that enable project teams to creatively invent ideas for the to-be process, assess them in a holistic fashion, and then select the ones that will actually work. When we select ideas, we'll ensure that they are consistent, address the process goals, and are feasible with respect to culture and resources. As usual, the methods we'll describe are based on our experience with what works and what doesn't. In fact, the most important techniques we want to share with you are based on the three most common problems we see in process redesign efforts:

1. *Tunnel vision*—focusing exclusively on workflow and IT. We saw how to avoid this in the last chapter, when the assessment by enabler forced a holistic view of the as-is process, and generated relevant improvement ideas.

2. *Paving the cow paths*—simply automating or reautomating the as-is instead of rethinking it. In this chapter, we will employ the challenge process to uncover and challenge underlying assumptions, generating improvement ideas and ensuring we don't just speed up the old process.

3. *Unanticipated consequences*—implementing "improvements" without understanding what it will take to make them work and what the consequences will be. We will assess each potential improvement enabler by enabler to ensure that process requirements (and consequences) are understood. This will demonstrate a new framework that has proven to be extremely useful on process redesign projects in recent years.

Goals

The primary goals of *determine to-be process characteristics and workflow* are as follows:

1. Describe each important characteristic of the to-be process in terms of each of the six process enablers. Collectively, these are the "specifications" for the new process.

2. Develop swimlane diagrams at two levels of detail (handoff and service) depicting the process workflow that supports the desired characteristics of the process.

One way to look at this is that we're starting with "conceptual process design"—we'll identify the main concepts and characteristics of the new process, and only then do we perform "detailed process design" by specifying the workflow.

Philosophy/Approach

Two ideas characterize this approach. First, there are ways to generate creative ideas and to "think out of the box." This is not a random, hit-or-miss activity—we can specify techniques. It won't replace sheer brilliance and flashes of inspiration, but it might help you be more creative and look at a process in new ways. By the way, if you're interested in techniques for creative thinking, or *lateral thinking*, check out the works of the man who invented the term—Edward de Bono.

Second, a process improvement idea that looks great may not be so appealing when you look at it in context. That is, when you look at the ramifications of the idea on all six enablers, you might be surprised—sometimes, an idea works synergistically with changes across the enablers, but other times, it turns out to be destructive or much more involved than originally thought. This approach hinges on generating ideas and assessing them with respect to all enablers (in context) before diving into workflow design or "leaping into solution space" by applying technology to the wrong problem. Since we wrote the first edition, we've had consistent reports from readers and clients that this method really works.

The three core activities are done in sequence:

1. Generate ideas for the new process (some of which was already done during assessment).
2. Assess those ideas (in context!) and select the ones that will work and meet the goals.
3. Develop the to-be workflow, one level of detail at a time.

Three techniques are central to this approach:

1. Generate enabler-specific ideas while performing the final assessment.
2. Generate process improvement suggestions by challenging the assumptions embedded in the as-is process.
3. Assess each suggestion in context by defining its impact on each of the six enablers.

The key steps within *determine to-be process characteristics and workflow* are:

- Post and review the key findings from the initial as-is process assessment and final as-is process assessment.
- Collect additional ideas, using some or all of these techniques:
    - Bring forward and expand on the improvement suggestions from final assessment.
    - Generate ideas that specifically address the leverage points identified during final assessment.
    - "Steal" successful ideas by reviewing best practices.
    - Brainstorm—wide open and by enabler.
    - Conduct a challenge session to discover implicit assumptions and generate ideas.
- Assess each idea by defining its impact on each of the six enablers in an "idea versus enabler table.
- Select ideas that will become the "characteristics" (specifications) for the to-be process.
- Develop ideal to-be process flow (optional).
- For each level of the to-be workflow (handoff and service):
    - Develop new workflow.
    - Assess and revise as necessary before proceeding to the next level.
- Road show—get feedback from a wider audience.

You don't have to go through all of the "collect ideas" steps, and you don't have to do them in the order listed. In fact, we struggled with the order because there is not a fixed sequence—it's up to you and the unique needs of your project. For instance:

- If you're concerned that your group is stuck in the status quo, start with the challenge process to shake them up.
- If you have an excitable group with no shortage of ideas, and your concern is focusing them, start by generating ideas that address the leverage points.
- If the process "ain't broke" in any particular way (i.e., there aren't distinct leverage points), then brainstorming by enabler will help the team take a balanced approach.

This book covers process identification, scoping, initial assessment, modeling, final assessment, and redesign, with the emphasis on identification, modeling, and assessment. We won't spend a lot of time on redesign, but you'll find practical techniques that you can easily put to use on your projects. We've organized these techniques into a "process for process redesign," but there is no fixed process for Design Process any more than there is a fixed process for Paint Masterpiece. Many of the famous process redesigns came about because of a critical insight or flash of inspiration, not finding and fixing flaws. The techniques in this chapter have helped generate their share of inspirations, too, but don't be a slave to methodology. If you feel that the structured method described here is stifling some flash of brilliance, by all means experiment with alternate techniques. With that caveat behind us, let's get into the techniques we have on offer.

Post and Review Key Materials from Previous Phases

If you've done much facilitation, you know that people have an amazing ability to go off on tangents or to forget the points they agreed to the day (or the hour!) before. That's why facilitation has been compared to herding cats—*other people's cats*. As a facilitator, you need all the help you can get, which is why you must have the key findings from previous work posted during your session. By "posted," we mean summarized on flip charts that are visible to the group and easy for the facilitator to refer to. When it appears that the discussion is going off topic, the facilitator can ask (in a nonjudgmental way, of course) how the current points relate. The participants make the decision without the facilitator seeming heavy handed.

The key materials to summarize and review are:

- Overall process map that shows related, but out of scope, processes;
- Scope (or "frame") of the process being addressed—the event, results, subprocesses, and the cases;
- Process case for action (stakeholder-based initial assessment) and goals, to ensure we focus on the right things. In particular, have the group refocus on the "improvement dimension"—the facet of the process that *must* excel to satisfy the key stakeholders;
- The as-is workflow models, which might still be in Post-it and plotter paper form. If you want to use a version produced by a process modeling tool (e.g., Visio), then try to have it printed in large format on a plotter. It's an entirely different experience when people are standing around a wall-sized diagram

compared to having participants look at copies on the table or, even worse, on their laptops.

- You'll also be posting the key findings from the final, enabler-based assessment of the as-is process, as well as the ideas generated during that step, but there are alternative ways to handle this, as we will describe shortly.

Collect Ideas—Getting Started

A few points to remind the participants in your process redesign session:

- Just as a landscape architect begins with the major structural elements—the "bones" of the landscape—we're after the central features of the new process. The details can be worked out later on when we develop the to-be workflow and the mechanics of individual tasks.
- We're not just gathering new ideas—we'll also identify aspects of the current process to consider retaining.
- Finally, it's extremely important to remind participants not to judge the ideas while collecting them—they'll be assessed in a separate step. Just as in brainstorming, we discourage criticism of the suggestions, because of the following:
  - Ideas that seem unreasonable at first often "improve with age."
  - An idea that truly is impractical can nonetheless inspire other, useful suggestions.

Build on Ideas Generated During Assessment

We'll start with the work that's already been done—the ideas for the to-be process that were suggested while assessing the as-is (Chapter 12). They're probably already on flipcharts, and you'll have hung them on the wall while preparing for the session. Another approach is to organize the suggestions by subprocess or workflow. Prior to the session, summarize each idea on a large (4 × 6-inch) Post-it, and then arrange them under a wall-sized, left-to-right list of the subprocesses or under a wall-sized swimlane diagram. Don't agonize about correctly placing every suggestion, because every idea won't necessarily fit under a specific part of the process. Some will relate instead to more general factors, such as resourcing decisions or policies. Then, invite the team to spend a few minutes looking them over with the intent of suggesting revisions or extensions, or capturing new ideas that they inspire. We do this because suggestions evolve, often unconsciously, during the downtime between sessions. What once seemed outlandish can seem practical after some settling-in time, and new ideas emerge. You'll have to remind the group that suggestions will be assessed later, and so they must try not to be judgmental. You'll also have to be strict about controlling the time spent because the upcoming steps are more important in terms of generating proposals.

Generate Ideas That Specifically Address the "Leverage Points"

Unless you deliberately focus the group on them, the leverage points can be forgotten and people, as they so often do, will go off into the less important 80 percent instead of the crucial 20.

One good way to accomplish this focus is to build a "leverage points versus enablers" matrix. This would be similar to the matrix we'll construct while "assessing in context" a little later on. It isn't so important that you do this in matrix form—what's important is that for each leverage point, the team specifically asks, "How could this leverage point be supported by a change within this enabler?" This is a good time to focus on the enablers that often get ignored:

- Motivation and measurement;
- Human resources;
- Policies and rules.

The review of common improvement practices in the next step might trigger additional ideas, so you might need to revisit this step.

Steal Ideas by Reviewing "Best Practices"

"Best Practices" in General

A "best practice" is a tactic or process characteristic that has been employed at one or more other organizations with excellent results. "Benchmarking," the companion term, takes a variety of forms but typically involves comparing one of your processes with the same or a similar process at other organizations, usually with metrics to quantify the relative performance. There has been much heated writing and discussion of best practices, with industry pundits either strongly pro or con. In general, the "pro" is that studying best practices can expand your horizons by exposing your team to ideas they wouldn't have thought of otherwise. The con is that they can contract your horizons when they are slavishly copied and misapplied. Michael Hammer described Ford's breakthrough "invoiceless accounts payable process" in his classic 1990 article on reengineering, and, in the following years, you would not believe how many companies we encountered that were suddenly busy instituting the same, whether it addressed their problems or not. Critics are right when they point out by the time they're documented, "average practices" or "common practices" might be better terms. And benchmarking can degenerate into "industrial tourism" without concrete results. However, these criticisms miss the central points:

- Even the average practices may be better than what your organization does.
- The people you're working with may not be aware of what's possible because they are not all professional analysts or process consultants who live and breathe this stuff.

Depending on your assessment of the group you're working with, you could decide (as we often do) that a short presentation on common process redesign practices would be worthwhile. On the other hand, they may be well aware of current practices or have been exposed to the ideas while you conducted the "assess by enabler" step. If you decide a presentation will help, you'll have to stress that the examples are "food for thought," not dogma to be blindly implemented. In developing a presentation suitable for your team, there are many sources to draw on:

- A Web search on "best practices" (or "benchmarking") and "business process" will direct you to many sources, including, of course, "best practices" consulting firms and "benchmarking" organizations. As of this writing, a Google search of "business process best practices" yielded 35.6 million hits—that ought to be enough to keep you busy for a while.

- Books—a search of online booksellers for "best practices" and "benchmarking" will uncover many titles.

- Management and IT consulting firms often publish white papers (many industry-specific) on best practices.

- Most large consulting firms have offerings in this area, although many are subscription-based, so have your credit card handy.

- Industry organizations or software vendors dealing with a topic of interest such as supply chain optimization or customer relationship management document best practices and success stories.

The previous chapter can provide material for a review presentation—the *assess by enabler* sections highlighted many *worst* practices, and either implied or stated an alternative. Following are a few examples of common practices according to the primary enabler involved. These practices don't fit squarely under a single enabler. For instance, eliminating a management approval step is a change in *policies and rules,* but it also implies a change in *workflow* (the process proceeds without the handoff for review) and new *information systems* (to provide management information in lieu of the approval step).

During the review, or after each enabler has been covered, ask the group if any of the reviewed practices are relevant to the process or if any ideas have been triggered. Capture all suggestions on your ideas list.

Workflow Design

- Instead of having one, complex process with many decisions based on the type of transaction, establish a reasonable number of distinct processes (say, three to five), each tailored for a particular type. Using available information to direct each case into the appropriate process is referred to as "triage," after the medical term for directing the initial treatment of injured persons. Once the type of case is determined, it flows through the appropriate process without unnecessary steps or decisions. An example is to have different problem-resolution processes depending on the customer's history or different purchasing processes depending on the value of the product or service.

- Regarding approval or information steps, many organizations have eliminated them from the workflow or have them take place "after the fact." One organization found that purchase requisitions sat in heaps at an "approver's" desk waiting for approval, so they instituted a simple fix. All requisitions were considered by default to be "approved" and went straight into purchasing for action. The onus was then on the "approver" to quickly locate the ones that really shouldn't proceed and catch them before they went too far. This was backed up by clear guidelines and consequences, spot audits, and management information. You wouldn't want to do this in life or death situations, but in this case it certainly changed the dynamics, and the throughput, of the process! You could just as well consider this to be an example of changing *policy and rules.*

• In the case of escalating approval or inform steps, they can be done in parallel or directed immediately to the highest necessary level.

• Where serialization is a holdover from a paper-based process, IT can support shared access and therefore a parallel workflow. For instance, at an airline, the fleet maintenance, crew scheduling, and airport operations groups had to approve, in sequence, a new flight schedule. Any change "late" in the process meant the proposed schedule had to start all over again. Instead, each group simultaneously checked the first cut flight schedule for significant problems and got it "close" before the final approval, which still happened in sequence.

Information Systems

Even in the popular media, we're so inundated with stories about leading-edge technologies that some of the basic, workhorse technologies are forgotten:

• The use of bar coding or self-identifying tags to eliminate error-prone, redundant data entry;

• In general, the use of shared databases (or data transformation middleware) to eliminate gaps, inconsistencies, and the errors introduced by rekeying data from system to system;

• In particular, shared databases that include full contact history to make all customer and case information available to any sales or service representative;

• The use of discussion forums and social networking sites to enable interested (and unpaid!) volunteers to provide information and support for a company's products and services;

• Workflow automation technology has been around, it seems, forever. Now, there are business process management systems to implement end-to-end processes, and business activity monitoring tools to monitor individual transactions as they move through the process.

You can no doubt find examples of the clever use of IT within your industry or process.

Motivation and Measurement ("Reward and Punishment" Schemes)

Perhaps we shouldn't be surprised that this most-important enabler receives so little attention in the literature on best practices and benchmarking. This reflects a general obsession with technology, and with task, job, and process design, to the exclusion of the measurement schemes that motivate particular behaviors. We've made this point in Chapter 12, but to help fill the void, we'd like to describe a reference that might assist you in making the point at your organization.

It predates the "reengineering revolution," but Wickham Skinner's "The Productivity Paradox" [1] makes the point convincingly that what you measure matters, and it remains one the most-requested *Harvard Business Review* reprints ever. The article begins by outlining a massive productivity program at a large manufacturing organization that is representative of many organizations he studied. It sounds like a case study in reengineering, complete with "operation-by-operation analyses to improve efficiency," "retraining employees to work smarter not harder," and "streamlined work flow." However, after three years it netted an almost negligible 7 percent productivity gain, far short of the goal and not at all commensurate with the effort. Skinner then makes the point that by focusing on productivity and providing "daily performance reports on every operation, worker, and department" the company has inadvertently set up a cycle that ultimately does little for productivity because many other variables (especially the ones that matter to customers—product quality, meeting committed delivery times, order accuracy, and so on) are negatively impacted. Our experience has been similar, but substitute the word "productivity" with "efficiency"—we've seen so many ill-advised initiatives aimed at improving "efficiency" that we cringe when we see the word. (By the way, so do the people in your organization.)

Some quotes will convey the feeling of the article, but do yourself a favor and obtain a copy:

> When low cost is the goal, quality often gets lost. But when quality is the goal, lower costs do usually follow…A productivity focus inevitably forces management into a short-term, operational mind-set. The emphasis on direct costs, which attends the productivity focus, leads a company to use management controls that focus on the wrong target…The reward system based on such controls drives behavior toward simplistic goals that represent only a small fraction of total costs…When managers grow up in this atmosphere, their skills and vision never fully develop… As long as cost and efficiency are the primary measurements of factory success, the manufacturing plant will continue to repel many able, creative people."

We couldn't have said it better! The good news is:

> … a number of companies have broken out of the bind with extraordinary success. Their experience suggests, however, that breaking loose from so long-established a mind-set is not easy. It requires a change in culture, habits, instincts, and ways of thinking and reasoning. And it means modifying a set of values that current reward systems and day-to-day operational demands reinforce. *This is a tall order.* [Italics ours.]

Perhaps this is why we don't see enough attention placed on measurement and motivation as a lever to effect process change.

Although the article deals with manufacturing, the same phenomenon is demonstrated in all types of enterprises. Here is a favorite example—a telephone company (two, actually) measured customer service reps on short phone calls and backed it up with negative consequences for longer phone calls (a flashing red light above the "offending" CSR—you can't make this stuff up). Naturally, they got what you would expect—short phone calls. Of course, they came at the cost of the CSR moving on without dealing with the customer's problem, and sometimes even disconnecting the call as the time limit approaches, but the calls were indeed short. This is a perfect example of "perverse incentives"—task-based measures with either incentives (reward) or disincentives (punishment) attached that encourage behavior that could only be described as perverse. At both of these telephone companies, expensive programs aimed at having CSRs also perform sales functions failed completely, because they brought yesterday's measures into tomorrow's process.

On the other hand, measures that focus instead on improving the quality of products or customer service, such as "recurring problems detected" or "problems solved on the first call" or "defect-free product introduction" yield quite different results. We recently read about a company that reversed defections to its largest competitor by putting entirely different objectives in place for their CSRs. Rather than encouraging them to end the call as quickly as possible, the company essentially said, "stay on the line as long as it takes, just *keep the customer*." An objection we've heard is that "we don't have the resources to provide each customer with that much time." Probably true, but in many fields (including customer service) it's been observed that it's more cost-effective to get it right the first time (i.e., on the first call) than to invest in scrap and rework.[1]

If you can't find examples of innovative measurement schemes that are suitable for your project, this could be a good time to reopen the discussion that began during assessment. Have the group identify current measures that are counterproductive and new measures that would encourage the desired outcomes. This is where the workflow model is invaluable, because it has identified every participant in the process. You need to consider the measurement targets that every actor in the process is striving to meet, because problems introduced in one part of the process might not show up until much later.

Human Resources

- The most obvious and widely cited change is to recombine tasks into fewer job functions. (In general, as processes become simpler, jobs become more complex.) In some industries, more than 300 job titles have been reduced to 30. This is especially important where the customer is aware of the handoff. At an insurance company, a clerk recorded claim details, and then "routed" the claimant to an adjuster. The customer often had to go through the story twice, and good customers got the same treatment as everyone else. Now, the clerk

---

1. We could also get into a discussion of using IT to identify high-value customers and give them higher service levels, but you get the idea.

takes on some adjusting responsibilities. Within certain parameters, such as claim type (e.g., vandalism), estimated value (e.g., under $1,000), and customer characteristics (e.g., five years or more with limited claims), the clerk can settle the claim on the spot. However, this also required new IT, workflow, and performance measures.

- Another common practice is an expanded role for front-line customer contact personnel, (e.g., the integration of sales activities into customer service). For instance, a customer service representatives fielding billing inquiries for a telecommunications company now sell calling plans that will reduce the customer's bill. Again, like most "enriched" jobs, staff must be supported with tools (e.g., expert systems or operational data stores to present integrated customer history) and the whole thing can backfire if *motivation and measurement* isn't handled properly. The telephone company example from a few paragraphs back is a prime example of backfiring.

- Similarly, back office specialists can receive additional training and be moved out to customer contact positions providing faster, more personal service. A useful guideline is that no one in a customer-facing process should be more than one actor removed from the customer. In other words, everyone either has direct contact with customers or deals with others who do.

- Sometimes, a job needs to be split when scarce resources are spending a significant percentage of their time performing work that could be done by support staff or more junior staff. In a laboratory environment, sample preparation and analysis was assigned to support staff and junior scientists, while the senior scientists did the interpretation that required their years of experience.

- Where work is too complex for a single person, and functional expertise is required, a cross-functional team organization can be adopted. As we noted in Chapter 12, this isn't a panacea and has to be approached with caution.

Policies and Rules

- Eliminate approval steps by providing regular information or audit reports to management. On the same topic, eliminate the delay inherent in review by allowing the process to proceed while review happens, as we described in the section on the *workflow design* enabler. This puts the onus on the reviewer to complete the review before the transaction gets too far into the process. This isn't always appropriate, but if a high percentage of cases routinely pass the review anyway, it's worth considering.

- Eliminate delays due to credit history checks and proof of financial responsibility where a valid credit card or bond could cover any possible financial loss.

- Some organizations have gone so far as to eliminate volumes of policies, rules, and guidelines and replace them with a simple statement of principles. These can be the ultimate examples of the oft-cited "empowered workforce." In general, the empowered workforce requires the following:
    - Defined (and presumably greater) authority;

- Defined accountability for decisions, with consequences;
- Clear policies to guide front-line decision making;
- Tools and training;
- A backup mechanism (a "safety net") so individuals can "delegate upward" in difficult cases.

Facilities Design (or Other Factors)

This may not apply in your case, and can be substituted with some other more relevant category appropriate to your situation. The library example described during assessment is a good, simple example. Also, in organizations where there is a constant mix of collaborative and individual work, traditional fixed workstations (cubicles) are replaced by movable "pods" that can quickly be assembled in a way that each opens into a common area. Sort of a twenty-first century circling of the wagons.

As noted in the previous chapter with the example of a document enabler, please feel free to add an enabler that is critical to your industry or field and provide examples of best practices.

Brainstorming Additional Suggestions

This step is entirely optional, because you have probably covered the same ground already during "final assessment" when you collected first impressions and then leverage points.

If you think your group needs it, begin with a quick statement of the guidelines:

- Each participant makes one suggestion during their turn or says "pass."
- Record the idea without editing, except perhaps to have the participant restate it more briefly.
- No criticism or negative comments—this is about collection, not assessment.

As described in Chapter 5, we usually begin with an open brainstorm to encourage unrestricted ideas and then follow a framework to ensure complete coverage of the subject area. In brainstorming for process improvements, one approach to do this is as follows:

- First, brainstorm for *any* improvement, tactic, or process characteristic that comes to mind. This is the step that may have been accomplished with "first impressions."
- Then, brainstorm on improvements for each of the enablers, one at a time. Many of the enabler-specific ideas will already have been identified during assessment by enabler.

As suggestions arise, record them on the "ideas" flipcharts for later assessment.

Apply the Challenge Process

The "challenge process" is simple and can be described quickly, but that doesn't reflect its importance—it's often the critical step in breaking people free from assumptions about how a process has to work and generating those brilliant insights. The challenge process is all about not "paving the cowpaths," a popular phrase in the reengineering community that refers to blindly applying new technology to an old process. Examples abound; many of the early imaging-based workflow applications "duplicated paper flow in silicon," and we've seen online, database applications handling financial transactions in batches of 25 for no other reason than that was how the paper-based process worked.

Here's how the challenge process works. Begin with the level 1 (handoff) or level 2 (service) swimlane diagram for the as-is process that you probably already have posted on the wall. We usually prefer working with the hand-drawn Post-it version of the diagram—it sets the right informal tone. Before getting into the challenge process, you might eliminate some of the steps from further consideration, if the group has already decided that they are obvious flaws; we usually don't, because leaving the obviously "wrong" steps in can make the process even more fun (and it is usually fun, believe it or not). The central idea is to take each step (or linked series of steps) and its implicit assumptions, and restate it as hard and fast rules. Not just restate, but *overstate*. For instance, in a claim-handling process, the workflow might depict the following:

- The customer initiates a claim by telephone.
- The claim is recorded by a telephone claims representative (TCR).
- The TCR schedules an interview with the customer at a company office.
- An adjuster interviews the customer.

Overstating this as hard and fast rules, we might come up with the following challenge statements:

- *Only* a customer (beneficiary or policyholder) can initiate a claim.
- Claims *must* be initiated by telephone.
- We will *never* consider compensation until a claim is filed.
- The customer *must* be interviewed in person before a claim can be settled.
- The interview can *only* take place on company premises.

Note that we have overstated by using words like "only," "must," and "never." This makes it much easier for participants to challenge each of the statements by asking, "is that *really* true?" I like to think of this as "overstating the disobvious,"[2] but my friend Theo tells me this is a variation on the Latin quote "reduction ad absurdum"—"reduction to the absurd." If you take an assumption and overstate it enough, the underlying absurdity becomes evident, which helps people identify

---

2.   This is a reference to a favorite *Peanuts* cartoon that ends with Lucy yelling, "Obvious? It may be obvious to you but it's sure disobvious to me!" And then, to herself, "Unobvious? Exobvious? Antiobvious? Inobvious? Subobvious? Nonobvious?" Charles Schulz, United Features Syndicate Inc, 1974.

alternatives that wouldn't have occurred to them otherwise. That's why we think of this as a structured approach to thinking out of the box.

In some cases, though, even when overstated to absurd lengths, the statement is still true. We would say it has survived challenge, and so it is recorded on the list of ideas (characteristics) for the new process. For instance, the group might decide that a claim really can only be initiated by the beneficiary or policyholder ("no third parties, please"), in which case the point will be recorded on the ideas list as a potential characteristic of the to-be process. (Remember, we haven't decided for sure yet—that comes later.)

In most cases, the statement can be challenged. For instance, the team might decide that initiating a claim via e-mail or the Web is an option to consider or that interviews can take place at a location more convenient for the customer (home, place of work, and so on). These too would be recorded on the idea sheet.

You can even take one of the statements, and break it down word by word (or is that "bird by bird?"):

1. The *customer* must be interviewed in person before a claim can be settled.
2. The customer must be *interviewed* in person before a claim can be settled.
3. The customer must be interviewed *in person* before a claim can be settled.
4. The customer must be interviewed in person *before* a claim can be settled.
5. The customer must be interviewed in person before a *claim* can be settled.
6. The customer must be interviewed in person before a claim can be *settled*.

Some alternatives to each of the numbered points:

1. If we have a police report, do we need to talk to the customer?
2. Couldn't the customer complete an incident report form by post or e-mail?
3. Even if the customer wasn't there? Could the interview be conducted by phone?
4. Couldn't we settle a small loss without actually going through the formality of a claim?
5. Does a claim have to be filed if the insured and victim are both are customers and the insured admits fault?
6. Could we pay the customer the undisputed portion before settling? (It could reduce lawsuits.)

You may have noticed that this is an alternative to step-by-step assessment, which can be very tedious, as we suggested in Chapter 12. The challenge process is a more effective way of addressing the kinds of questions we'd answer if we were assessing each individual step:

- Does this step yield a useful result?
- Does it have to be done at all?
- Does it have to be done by the actor currently doing it?
- Does it have to be done in the sequence it is being done in?
- Does it have to be done where it is being done?

  • Does it have to be done in the manner it is being done?

By this point, enough improvement ideas have surely been generated, so it's time to move on to assessment and selection.

Assess Ideas in Context and Select

Like the challenge process, this step is so simple as to be almost obvious, but it has proven invaluable in practice. It involves taking each suggestion and considering its impact on all enablers before deciding to proceed with it. Here's the process:

- Post (tape up) the "idea lists" that have been generated so far.
- Perform an initial review of the list to eliminate any ideas that are clearly not going to make it. They might be illegal, a poor fit with skills and culture, too resource-intensive (to implement or to operate), or not a contributor the process' goals. (Set them aside, rather than tossing them out, because they may warrant reconsideration after the other ideas are assessed.) If there is disagreement on whether an item should stay or go, leave it in—the next steps should settle the discussion.
- Build an "assessment matrix" with eight columns—one for each idea, one for each enabler, and a seventh for "notes/conclusions." As with the "leverage points versus enablers" matrix, it isn't necessary that this be done in matrix form—we just find it convenient if there's enough whiteboard space. The key point is to ensure that you explicitly consider each of the enablers.
- Select an idea for assessment and record it in the "idea" column. For instance, a significant change to a support process could be "customer service reps (CSRs) take on sales responsibilities." We used to try to assign the idea to a particular enabler, but that often caused too much argument over which column to put it in.
- Now, the key step—fill in the rest of the enabler columns in the new row of the matrix by asking what the consequences of the idea are for each of the other enablers. We find it useful to ask, "what will have to be changed in this enabler to make the idea work?" See Figure 13.1, which illustrates the CSR example:
  - The workflow will clearly change. If the customer agrees to purchase a new service, will the CSR set it up, or will a "closer" be brought in? If the CSR makes a sale, how will it be routed for fulfillment? What about clients who are interested, but don't have time right now—where will these leads be routed to? And many more...
  - Sophisticated IT solutions will be required to present a composite view of the client's business with the company, in real time, and suggest alternate service packages.
  - The motivation and measurement package for the CSR will have to change radically. Will they be paid more, now that they have increased responsibility and skill requirements? Will they be paid a commission?

Suggestion	Workflow Design	Info. Tech.	Motivation & Measurement	Human Resources	Policies & Rules	Facilities (or other)	Feasibility & Notes
Customer Service Reps (CSRs) take on sales responsibilities.	Will the CSR or a "closer" set up the new service? Who follows up with interested Customers not ready to commit?	System to present real-time view of Customer's total business, and recommend alternatives.	CSRs paid more for additional responsibilities? Current measure is "call time" – must change. Commission? What impact on commissions for current sales force?	Sales training? Displacement of current sales reps?	What will CSR's authority be for discounts, etc.?	CSRs may need more desk space for product catalogs that aren't online.	What will Customer reaction be?

Figure 13.1   Assessing potential process characteristics by enabler.

The primary current measure is "call time," which will have to be changed.

- There will be HR consequences. First, the CSRs will have to receive training in sales techniques and more training on the company's service options. Also, the impact on the existing sales force, and on any CSRs who aren't comfortable with or able to perform sales duties, must be considered.

- Regarding policies and rules, will the CSRs have authority to offer special deals?

- Are the current facilities suitable for any paper-based product literature the CSRs will have to refer to?

- Assess the suggestion now that the consequences are visible—does the whole "row" make sense, whether or not you used a matrix format? Record impressions in the "feasibility and notes" column. You might decide at this point that the idea still has merit—the potential improvement isn't negated by other consequences. This may require research, though, to assess costs and other impacts versus benefits. Or, you might decide to revise the suggestion (and, of course, redo the assessment) or eliminate it.

- Continue with the next improvement idea. You can go through the list in sequence, or try to consider the "big ticket" items first, or consider similar ideas together.

- Once all of the plausible ideas have been assessed, go through the matrix and select ideas ("rows") that will become the "characteristics" or specifications for the new process. This will involve judgment that can't be reduced to a step-by-step procedure, but the key elements are as follows:
  - Impact on process goals;
  - Feasibility;
  - Consistency with other characteristics.

If an idea has successfully made it through this assessment, and is now one of the characteristics of the to-be process, we document it more carefully using the format illustrated in Figure 13.2. This will be distributed to a wider audience, so you need to

Characteristic or improvement name
Forensic strategy ("applying science at the front end")

Description
A Senior Scientist, typically the Case Manager, will meet with the Submitting Officer and develop a case strategy specifying which avenues of investigation, which items, and which tests are most likely to yield the needed results in the least time, with the least effort. The goal is to do this for as high a percentage of cases as possible. This is the first decision point in another characteristic, *multiple decision points*. Visually, this is the first stage in a funnel, in which the work being performed on a case is continually reduced as new facts arise.

Issues addressed
There is a tendency for the Customer (the police) to submit all possible items, and request all possible tests, or at least submit more items for more tests than are necessary or justified. This is known as "forensicating" a case, and is ironically a primary cause of the delay and expense that the customer is unhappy with. Currently, Forensics accepts all items and performs all requested tests through to completion. In some cases, the suspect has become the accused and then the defendant, and has been convicted and incarcerated, yet testing continues.

Anticipated outcomes/benefits
For the Customer—deliver a positive result in less time, at less cost. For Forensics—free up resources by reducing submissions, and performing fewer tests on fewer items, thereby providing better throughput for all cases. In the future, Forensics will only perform those tests that will help, which will stand up in court because we can say "we chose these tests for these reasons." On an ongoing basis the customer will become more aware of the avenues that are most effective.

(a)

Enablers	
Workflow Design	Performers ("actors"), tasks, sequence, dependency · Senior scientist Senior scientist "meets with" appropriate scientist, not necessarily in person · Assessment and agreement and recording of *requirement* which is not contracted yet. · The requirement must be made available to the Process Manager, who will assess it with respect to current capacity. · The Case Manager and Process Manager will then negotiate and refine the requirement. They will then agree on "what and when"and commit capacity, which might involve another provider.
Information Technology	Systems, automated support, data and information, communications · Capture requirement · Real-time view into work-in-progress and committed capacity (Forensics and subcontractors)
Motivation and Measurement	Measurement, assessment, consequences · The Process Manager will be measured on accurately estimating capacity and throughput. · The Process Manager makes a commitment for Forensics, and will be measured on having done the least to get the necessary result ("lean consumption").
Human Resources	Recruitment, placement, education, roles, matching task to role · New front-end role for scientists · Process Manager role · Provide service 24x7 will impact some staff. · Recruitment, recognition, and reward are fundamental to making this work.
Policies and Rules	Internal: policies and guidelines. External: laws and regulations · The overall submissions policy must be revised to reflect forensic strategy vs. "take it all." · Investigate legal consequences of forensic strategy. · Mechanism to protect the individual scientist from pressure. ("Forensics, not the individual scientist"–this is a corporate decision, not a personal decision.) · Scientists can't make commitment without the Process Manager. · A 10 minute phone call and a 4 hour conference both constitute delivery of a service. A request to confer with a Case Manager constitutes contract initiation.
Facilities and Equipment	Physical accommodations, layout, equipment, furnishings · Some place to meet—in person, teleconference, ...

(b)

Figure 13.2   Documentation format for selected process characteristics.

ensure that the process change will not be misinterpreted. We give each characteristic a short name, for convenience, and then describe the change precisely in order to avoid misunderstanding. We also document the issues the change is expected to address and the anticipated benefits. This format has been extremely popular in practice, because it forms a high-level, easy-to-read "process requirements document."

As a final check, here are some general principles to follow:

- Ensure that every step is value-added. For every step, ask "would a reasonable customer pay for this if they knew it was being done?" Ideally, each step should accomplish a state change in the direction of completion, which usually excludes moving and checking.
- Measure outcomes, not tasks or handoffs.
- Information must be available when and where needed, unfiltered by layers of management.
- Eliminate or minimize approval or information steps that require a handoff to the approver and then another handoff back into the flow. Instead, automate the production of information for management, especially exception/variance/excursion reports.
- Similarly, don't handoff to make a decision—push the decision to the front lines, where the work is being performed.
- Ensure that the process produces the necessary information for automated monitoring.
- Avoid cumbersome translations and interfaces such as rekeying data from one system to another (see next point).
- Seek STP—automate clerical activities, especially those that move a "transaction" from one system to another.
- As few people as possible should be involved in the process.
- Make individual jobs "rich" enough that people are working up to their potential.
- Parallelize wherever possible.
- Control the work that enters the process—the sooner a problem with an inbound work item can be detected, the less expense will be incurred.
- Ensure that a work item can always be located in the process.
- Ensure that a work item can be maintained—revised, cancelled, held, and so on—by the customer through the same mechanism they created it with.

When you're done, the new process is "characterized"—you have a description of the important characteristics of the to-be process, enabler by enabler. Many of the points will describe elements of the workflow—who does what and when. So, armed with this information, it's time to express the new process as a workflow.

Develop Ideal To-Be Workflow

Before starting on a swimlane diagram showing who, what, when, and how, it's useful to step back and express the essence of the process—the what and when. This is the "ideal" workflow, unconstrained by technology, human abilities, space, time, or other very real concerns. It's not an exercise in fantasy, though—such a model can provide a target our "real world" swimlane diagram should strive for.

At the heart of this is the concept of an "essential" or "fundamental" step. We introduced this idea in Chapter 3, while defining business processes. The essential steps are what remain after all references to "who" and "how" are removed, leaving only the essence of "what" has to occur. Imagine perfect database and communication technology, as if there were no barriers of space or time.

We like the way the concept was described by Daniel Whitney in an article [2] from our favorite publication, the *Harvard Business Review*. When designing robots (i.e., to automate manufacturing activities) too much focus is placed on *how* a person (the *who*) currently does the task, rather than the essence of *what* the task is. The goal is to understand "what, not who or how."

He explains: "I often ask beginning robotics students to design a robot to wash a stack of dishes. Usually the students conceive an expensive machine with two hands that lifts up each dish in turn, inspects it visually for dirt, picks up a brush, dips it in soap, scrubs the dish, and so on. After the discussion has gone on for a while, I remind the class that local department stores sell automatic dishwashers for about $250."

Whitney highlights the key point: "The mistake here—plausible as it might seem—lies in confusing *what* people do with *how* they do it. The goal in robotics should be to reproduce *what's* done (getting results), not *how* it's done (using certain methods)." When we use this article in our class on service specification, this is the point at which we introduce the recurring chant "what, not who or how!" The identical goal arises in systems development when we define the "services" that make up the business services layer, and in process redesign, when we define the "ideal" process flow.

That was a generalized example of the principle—here's a case from a process improvement assignment at a large government agency. The subject matter was the process Issue Business License, which included an inspection of the business premises. Here are the relevant steps from that phase of the process:

- The inspector gets to the next inspection location.
- Inspector conducts inspection (these first two are repeated throughout the day).
- Inspector returns to field office.
- Inspector telephones head office (HO) technician.
- Inspector reads each inspection report while HO technician transcribes information onto HO transcription report.
- HO transcription reports are batched, and three times per week they go to data entry.
- Data entry enters each HO transcription report into a locally hosted inspection system.
- The inspection system prints a three-part report on an impact printer detailing each inspection.

- An operator separates the three copies ("bursting and decollating," for you former machine room operators).

- Pink copies are attached to the corresponding original HO transcription report.

- All of the reports for an inspector are collected and mailed back to the correct field office.

- The inspector matches their original inspection report with the printout from the inspection system.

- If there's an error, they check the HO transcription report to determine if the error occurred during transcription or data entry.

- And so on. (We won't get into the error-correction process, but trust us, it's a beauty.)

At a session to identify improvements to the process, suggestions included:

- The inspectors could be equipped with mobile phones so they could phone in each inspection report immediately.

- Inspectors could fax their reports so HO technicians could transcribe them without tying up the phone or dealing with miscommunications.

- The batch update job could be run daily instead of three times a week.

- The reports could be printed on laser printers (three times) to eliminate the separation step.

You see the problem—participants were so locked into the current "who and how" that their improvement ideas were extremely limited. They really thought, for instance, that transcription was a fundamental part of the process. To be fair, this was a last-minute, "late in the game" engagement, so the participants hadn't been "opened up" by going through steps like identifying leverage points, assessing by enabler, or using the challenge process. Nonetheless, we encounter the same basic phenomenon all the time, and the idea of "essential processes" can help people break free of their current assumptions about what's really essential.

In the business licensing example, after being introduced to essential processes, participants were surprised to conclude that virtually all of the steps were "who and how." The essential step was simply Record Inspection Results, or even better, Conduct Inspection, based on the principle that an essential process step should record its own results.[3] The focus then shifted to how inspection findings could be captured electronically in real time (or "real-enough time") with minimal intermediaries. Tablet computers or scannable forms were two options.

So, the essential process steps are the "essence" of what the business does. They are the steps remaining after removing any reference to who (performer, such as job function or organization) or how (technology, whether high tech, low tech, or no tech). They often correspond very strongly to "services" (units of work from the business services layer) that are introduced in Chapter 15.

---

3.   You could claim that completing each inspection item—checking for signage, office space, fire extinguisher, and so on—is a an essential step, but let's not split hairs—the main point is the same.

Getting comfortable with the concept is the hard part; once you've got that, applying it is relatively straightforward:

- Identify the main essential steps using the as-is models and the process characteristics as a guide. Most essential steps will clearly be milestones or significant state changes.
- Recheck—if a change in performers or technology would change your essential steps, you're not done yet.
- Identify the dependencies among the essential steps—which ones *must* happen in sequence, and which can happen in parallel.
- Depict the dependencies graphically, as shown in Figure 13.3, just as you would if you were laying out a project plan.

What you now have is a template for the ideal workflow. It's worth noting that many processes use EAI or BPMS tools to implement straight-through processing and have achieved workflows that contain almost nothing but essential process steps. All human intervention, delays, batching, transport, and so on have been wrung out of the process, with a process integration engine shepherding the transaction through various systems in real-enough time. This is especially prevalent in the financial services sector, where financial transactions (e.g., a stock exchange trade) that used to require multiday batch processing cycles are now completely processed instantly.

Next, we'll consider the constraints of technology and the actors in our workflow and develop a swimlane diagram.

Develop To-Be Workflow

We're tempted to say, "And now, the easy part!" Admittedly, it still isn't easy to design a new workflow that meets your objectives. However, with all of the information you've assembled to this point, it will be much easier than it would have been if you had just dived right in.

Using the characteristics matrix (to provide the "who" and "how") and your ideal workflow (to provide the "what") as guides, propose a handoff level first, then

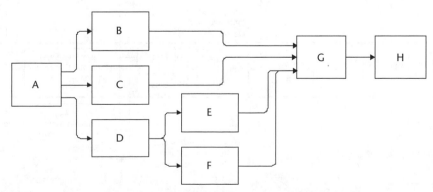

Figure 13.3   The dependency among essential steps is a template for the ideal.

add detail in layers. You'll use exactly the same guidelines when developing each level of the to-be model that you used when you were developing the as-is model:

- Handoff (level 1) shows contiguous activities by the same performer.
- Service (level 2) adds significant accomplishments or milestones.
- Task-level details will be documented later on separate documents (procedures, use cases, flowcharts, decision trees, or checklists) after the new process design is agreed to.

After your first effort at each new level of detail, assess whether the workflow still meets process goals and is feasible. By "feasible," we primarily mean, "does each actor have the skills, resources, and information to carry out the designated process steps?" If not, revise or refine it. It is often the case that new jobs have to be defined, so you should consider having human resources professionals participating. We also suggest treating each new level as an as-is model and assessing it. Applying the challenge process to a to-be model can be an interesting exercise.

Figures 13.4 and 13.5 illustrate samples of handoff and service to-be models. You should heavily annotate the diagrams to indicate what's noteworthy about the new process. Unless you highlight these points, many people won't notice!

Road Trip

At this point, you may want to take the new process on a road trip to review it with a wider audience. In addition to getting suggestions that might further improve the process, there are two reasons to do this.

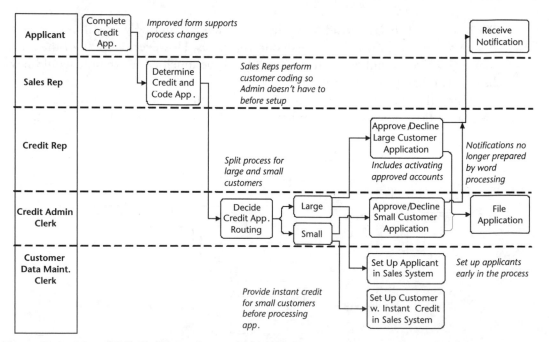

Figure 13.4 A handoff-level diagram for a to-be process.

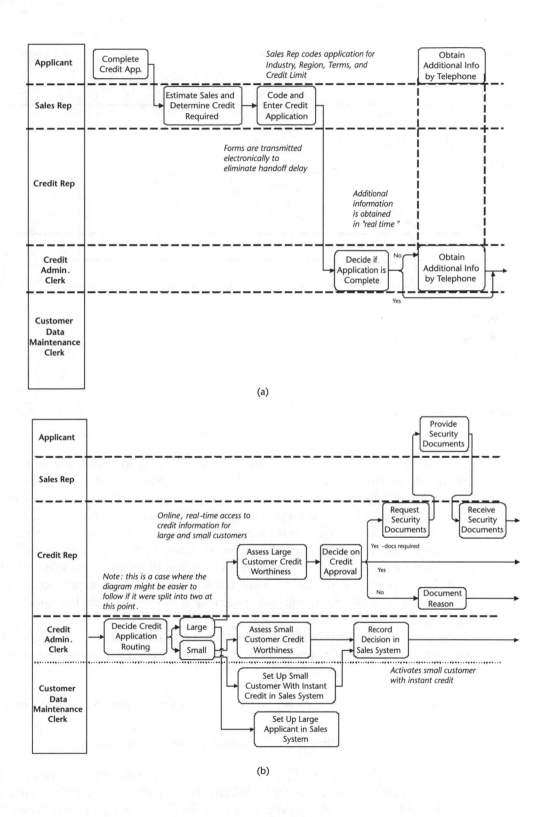

Figure 13.5 (a–c) A service-level diagram for a to-be process.

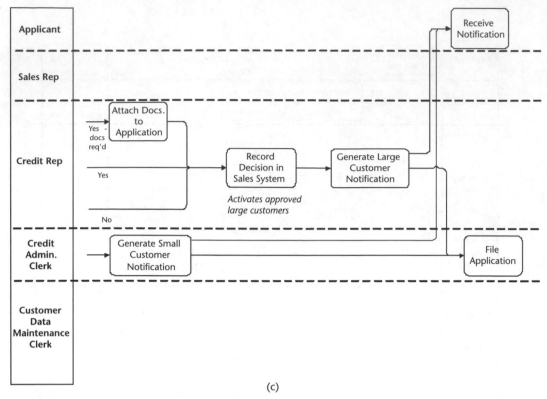

(c)

Figure 13.5   (continued)

First, especially if your organization is geographically distributed, you'll need to find out about any constraints due to local conditions or regulations. These may require changes to the version of the process operating at that location. However, before stepping out onto the slippery slope of local process versions, we suggest that if you have the necessary executive support it's best to vary the process *only* if there are legal issues. This eliminates all manner of issues related to training, staff rotation, certification, and so on. However, in practice, there are often variations that must be accommodated due to local resources and business practices. "Copy exactly!" is a good goal, but for practical reasons it often becomes "Copy intelligently!"

Second, you can gather information for "force field analysis," which will help your preparations for training and implementation. Two topics need to be addressed:

- What aspects of the new process/systems are people positive about? These are your *drivers*.
- What aspects are they negative about? These are your *barriers*.

Armed with this knowledge, you can develop implementation strategies that promote/maximize the drivers and minimize the impact of the barriers. Here is a short list of factors that we find regularly contribute to making a new process easier to implement and easier to sustain.

- Make the process *visible*:
  - *Consistency and repetition*, especially the process versus function chart.
  - Wall-sized swimlane diagrams in the workplace—some of our clients print huge versions on plotters.
  - Smaller job aids detailing procedures, use cases, and checklists.
  - *Physical* versions will often have more impact than *electronic*, although those should be there as well.
- Proper training in the new process, for current and *all new* staff. If you leave it to experienced staff to teach new staff on the job, the old process will creep back in.
- Allow *time* for the new process to take hold before introducing change. *Continuous* change ought to mean *regular*, but not *constant* change.
- The most important factors, though, are determined during process design—*alignment of all enablers*.
  - The single most important factor is that *every* department's and *every* contributor's performance metrics (motivation and measurement) be aligned with the desired outcome of the process, and the differentiator.
  - *All* of the enablers matter.

Now that you have a new process and its supporting workflow designed, it's time to make a major transition into determining how information systems can support the actors in the new process. That's the purpose of requirements modeling with use cases and services, which is the topic of Chapter 15. First, though, Chapter 14's introduction to data modeling is in order, because it's an important aspect of requirements definition and is very helpful while working with use cases and services.

References

[1]   Skinner, W., "The Productivity Paradox," *Harvard Business Review*, July–August 1986, pp. 55–59.

[2]   Whitney, D. E., "Real Robots Do Need Jigs," *Harvard Business Review*, May–June 1986, pp. 110–116.

PART V

Related Requirements Definition Techniques

CHAPTER 14

Business-Oriented Data Modeling

Data Modeling—What It Is, What It Isn't

Data modeling is certainly one of the most widely used techniques in modern business analysis, but it isn't always used well. Too often, technically oriented "modelers" jump straight into excruciating detail, dense jargon, and complex graphics—incomprehensible to process-oriented participants and other mere mortals.

The root problem is a misconception—data modeling has been equated with database design. That's like equating architecture with the drafting of construction blueprints. Of course, the architect's work will eventually lead to precise, detailed blueprints, just as the data modeler's work will eventually lead to precise, detailed database designs, but it shouldn't start there. In fact, it can't start there, or the subject matter experts will mentally "check out." Without their participation, the data model won't be a useful and accurate description of their business, which is exactly what it *should* be. A data model should be seen above all else as a description of a business, not the commonly held misconception that it's the same as a database design. Consider some ways to describe a business:

- An *organization chart* describes an enterprise in terms of managerial structures and reporting relationships.

- A *financial statement* describes an enterprise in terms of its fiscal health.

- A *process workflow model* describes an enterprise in terms of the work it must carry out in order to deliver value.

Each of these is a model that helps people communicate about the subject matter it represents. A *data model* is no different—it describes a business in terms of the *things* it must record information[1] about and the *facts about those things* that must be recorded. And just as we've seen with process modeling, data models must be simple and accessible during the early going. We'll now cover the basic concepts, structures, and terminology of data modeling and also help you get the most from this technique by reviewing practical techniques for developing a data model and managing detail. Let's dive in.

---

1. Strictly speaking, organizations maintain data—"the facts"—and from that data they can produce information—"data presented in answer to a specific request or query," or as Drucker put it, "data imbued with meaning and purpose."

Basic Terms and Concepts

Essentially, a data model depicts:
- The *things* of significance to an enterprise that it needs to maintain records about;
- The *facts about those things* that the enterprise needs to know.

"Things"—Entities

"Thing modeling" wouldn't cut it as a discipline, so a *thing* of significance is referred to as an *entity*. Hence the other common terms for data modeling—entity modeling and entity-relationship modeling. Some of the main entities at a mail order retailer would be Product, Customer, Order, Warehouse, and Supplier. When a business process or any part of it (subprocess, activity, step, and so on) is named in verb-noun format, the noun is most often an entity (e.g., Schedule Order). If not, it will likely be either a fact about an entity (e.g., Calculate Customer Status Level) or a report made up of entities and facts (e.g., Produce Customer History Report).

This should be sounding familiar, because you've already had significant exposure to data modeling in Chapter 5, when we employed an approach for analyzing the terms used by a business. We didn't call it data modeling, but what we were doing was the earliest step in the development of a data model—entity identification. We sorted the terms we'd discovered (through interviews, reviewing documents, and so on) into categories, the first and most important of which was the "things"—the entities.

Facts About Things—Relationships and Attributes

There are two kinds of *facts* about entities in a data model—*relationships* and *attributes*. *Relationships* are associations or connections between one entity and another that must be recorded, such as Order *placed by* Customer. Relationships are always bidirectional, so the same relationship named in the other direction is Customer *places* Order. Other relationships could include Order *requests* Product, Product *stocked at* Warehouse, and Product *available from* Supplier.

Attributes are individual data items that describe an entity. For Product, they include Product Number, Description, and Unit Price. For Customer, the attributes could include Customer Number, Name, Status Level, Since Date, E-mail Address, Telephone Number, and so on.

Think of an *entity* as a standardized description for a set of essentially similar instances the business needs to keep track of. "Joe Smith," "Sumi Ganesh," and "Able Enterprises, Inc." are each a unique individual or organization, but if they all meet certain qualifications (as per the entity definition) then we consider them to be *instances* or *occurrences* of the Customer entity, and we record the same kind of facts (*attributes* and *relationships*) about each.

Strictly speaking, we should use the term *entity type* rather than *entity*. An *entity type*, such as Customer, is a standardized description of a whole set (or *type* or class) of instances, and an *entity* is a single instance—Joe Smith and Emily Dixon. Most modelers, for clarity, would simply refer to Customer as an entity, and Joe and Emily as *instances* or *occurrences* of Customer.[2]

A Simple Example

Later, we'll provide guidelines and tips for entities, relationships, and attributes, but first we'll put this in context by illustrating the development of the two parts of the data model—the graphic and the narrative. The graphic illustrates the interrelationships among the entities using an *entity-relationship diagram*. The heart of the narrative is the entity definitions, which ensure that all parties share the same understanding of what is represented by the entity. In the early stages of a process-oriented project, the narrative—a glossary of terms and definitions—is the most important part of the data model, so we'll start there.

The Narrative Component—the Entity Definitions

A glossary might seem like a strange thing to produce, but one of the most common sources of difficulty on projects is a failure to define common terms, especially the entities, on the assumption that everyone "knows" what they mean. After all, won't everyone working on an order fulfillment process agree what "order," "product," and "customer" mean?" Surprisingly, no—even the most common terms will have different interpretations that will cause grief when they become evident (it's inevitable!) late in the game. The more important and fundamental the term, the more likely you are to be astounded by the differences of opinion that will arise. Consider this moment of discovery—"Oh no! You mean we're supposed to be able to handle internal customers too? I assumed we were only talking about external customers, so that's how we designed the system. Maybe we can add dummy customer records for internal customers, with some sort of a pointer to our legacy system—that's where internal customer records are now. Of course, that involves a lot of reprogramming, we'll have to redesign the user interface, and our report generator will be blown out of the water..." This real-life example illustrates why a project should develop a glossary as soon as possible, whether it's treated as part of data modeling or a separate undertaking. (That's why our preferred method for process discovery involves identifying the central things or entities of the business.)

During the development of the definitions, discussions *invariably* get interesting. It's without question our favorite part of data modeling. Participants are surprised, even shocked, to learn the different interpretations that others have for terms they've been "communicating" with on a daily basis. Alec vividly recalls a marketing VP being dumbfounded by accounting's definition of customer (an account held by a corporation with more than $2,000 of business within the past six months), and then saying, with some exasperation, "That's why those customer reports you've been sending us for all these years are so useless." Another indelible memory

2.   If you're working within an *object-oriented* (O-O) methodology, the concepts are identical, but the terms are different. An entity is referred to as a *class*, and a single instance is an *object*. In the O-O world, everything is a class (or an object), including transactions, screen widgets, devices, and so on, so many distinguish the *data-oriented* classes that we call entities by prefixing them—"entity class" or "business class," and their corresponding instances, "entity objects" and "business objects." Terminology in the world of information systems can get confusing, but at least it's getting better—it's more standardized than it was 20 years ago.

involved running a session in a criminal justice environment and asking, "What is a case?" The first reaction was "that's an awfully silly question" but Alec persisted ("please, just humor me") and when a police representative offered a definition, it was immediately disputed by a prosecution representative. He offered an alternative, which was then, predictably, countered by someone from forensics. Surfacing these previously unknown differences of opinion was, of course, the original intent of the question, and the group quickly agreed that it wasn't such a silly question after all.

Think of the possible interpretations of "customer" at your organization. Is a customer an individual contact person, an operating location, a division, or the customer organization (legal entity) itself? Is a "client" the same thing as a "customer"? Perhaps marketing will want to consider prospects or mailing list subscribers as customers, while accounts receivable will be convinced that "customer" means "someone who has purchased products from us and has a customer account" (even if many organizations have more than one customer account). If one part of the enterprise requests a product from another, does that mean the enterprise is its own customer? And we haven't even touched on the other entities. Is that internal request considered to be an "order" or something else? Does "product" imply goods only, or are services included? The distinction between "supplier" and "vendor" at a manufacturing company raised a lot of eyebrows.

A good definition comprises a few sentences, at most, and possibly some clarifying bullet points. It will answer the question "What is *one* of these things?" Generally, we begin defining an entity by asking three questions:

1. "Can anyone in the group think of any anomalies or potential sources of confusion around this entity?[3] For instance, can you think of an example of what you consider to be a customer that might surprise someone else?" At one company, that uncovered the fact that recipients of a charitable donation had to be recorded as customers for tax purposes because they had received a beneficial good or service from the company. At another, in the highly interdependent electronics industry, it uncovered that the company's largest competitors were also its largest customers.

2. "Could we list 5 to 10 examples (instances) of this entity?" While defining "customer" at an insurance company, this revealed that customers were individuals, corporations, or other types of enterprises including government agencies and not-for-profit societies.

3. "Does this entity represent specific individual instances, or does it represent types or categories?" At the insurance company we just mentioned, we found that to some participants, "vehicle" meant a *specific* vehicle owned by a policyholder, while to others it meant a *kind* of vehicle—a particular make and model—that had to be tracked because each make and model had specific information that had to be recorded, including rating category, safety ratings, repair costs, and so on.

Here is a definition of their Customer entity used by one of our clients:

---

3. At this point, you might have introduced the term *entity* to the group you're working with, or you might still be calling it a "thing."

A customer is a person or organization that is a past, present, or potential user of our products or services.

This excludes cases where the company uses its own products or services.

The customer does not necessarily have to pay (e.g., a charity).

"Client" is a synonym, but "account" is not, because one customer could hold multiple accounts.

By the way, the definition of Product clarified that both goods and services were considered to be Products.

These distinctions aren't academic—consider the impact they have on the scope of a new Fulfill Order process, and the huge impact on the functionality of the supporting information system. If these ambiguities aren't dealt early in the project, they will eventually surface (count on it!), causing rework, delay, and expense. Data modeling, especially glossary development, should begin early in the project while discovering business processes, and the data model should be refined throughout (e.g., while framing the process and developing workflow models).

The Graphic Component—the Entity-Relationship Diagram

The graphic is called an entity-relationship diagram, because in its simplest form it shows only the entities and the relationships between them. Other common terms are E-R diagram or simply an ERD. Figure 14.1 is a simple example—the entities are shown as labeled boxes, and the relationships as labeled lines between them. It shows the significant things—the entities—and how they relate to one another.

Adding Cardinality to the Relationships

In Figure 14.2, the model has been revised to show an important property or "business rule" of relationships—*cardinality* or *multiplicity*. Cardinality is an arcane

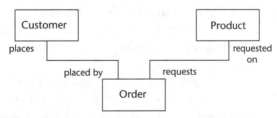

Figure 14.1 Simple entity-relationship diagram.

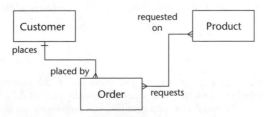

Figure 14.2 Adding cardinality to the relationships.

term for a simple concept—for a *single instance* of an entity, it shows the *maximum* number of instances of the entity at the other end of the relationship. If you "looked across" a relationship to the entity at the other end, how many would there be, *at most?* The answer is either "one" or "many."[4] *Each* Customer could place a maximum of *many* Orders. They may have only placed one, or even none if our definition of Customer includes people who are on our mailing list but haven't ordered anything yet (see why definitions are important?), but our concern is with the potential *maximum*. The "many" is shown on the diagram by the "crow's foot" adjacent to the order entity, indicating that there could be multiple orders for a single Customer.

Now, we go to the other end of the relationship, from Order to Customer, and ask the same question to determine cardinality. The possibilities are again one or many, but, in this case, the answer is one. *Each* Order is placed by a maximum of *one* Customer. Note the emphasis on the word *each*. Even though we first agreed that a Customer places *many* Orders, we start again from one ("each") Order when asking how many Customers it could be related to. We stress beginning the statement with the word "each," because a common error with new data modelers goes like this—"Hmmm, a Customer could place many Orders, and if we have many Orders, I guess we must have many Customers." Wrong! The "one" is shown on the diagram by the "hashmark" (a small dash perpendicular to the relationship line) adjacent to the Customer entity, indicating that there could be at most one Customer for each Order.

The Customer places Order relationship is described as a one-to-many (1:M) relationship. Order requests product is a many-to-many (M:M) relationship—each Order requests a maximum of *many* Products (a shirt, a pair of socks, and a pair of slacks), and each Product is requested on a maximum of *many* Orders. The third type of relationship is one to one (1:1), but they are quite rare in practice. In fact, they are almost always the result of an error in analysis. Either the relationship will ultimately prove to be 1:M or M:M, or it will turn out that the two entities related on a 1:1 basis are actually different views of just one entity, and so they will collapse into a single entity and the relationship will disappear.

You might have noticed that we drew the M:M relationship from side to side, rather than from the bottom of one entity to the top of another. We'll explain why shortly when we introduce the idea of laying out your diagram to show dependency in a top-down fashion.

These rules will often have a significant impact on business processes, which is why we recommend the development of a simple data model (even if you don't call it that!) early in the project. If you find that each Order can have many Delivery Locations, that will lead to a different process than if each Order could have only one Delivery Location. Making these rules visible separately from the process model will increase accuracy, because the two models will tend to correct each other.

---

4. The other phrase used in place of "many" is "one or more," which gets around a potential source of confusion. "Many" implies "lots of them," but we don't actually care as data modelers whether it's a couple, a few, several, dozens, scores, hundreds, or a gazillion—in our simple counting scheme, the choices are "one" and "anything greater than one," which we reduce to "many."

Adding Attributes to the Entities

With the basic structure laid out, we can add some attributes to the entities, as shown in Figure 14.3. During the early stages of data modeling, we don't try to identify every single attribute. Only the main ones are depicted, to help clarify the meaning of the entity. An important principle that we'll explore later is that each attribute belongs in only one entity. For instance, we wouldn't show the attribute Customer Name in the Order entity because it's really a fact about Customer. It's true that someone looking at an order would want to know the name of the customer the order was for, but behind the scenes the system can put that information together by following the relationship from the Order to the Customer and retrieving the Customer Name.

Each of the attributes fits neatly into an entity except one—the Requested Quantity for each Product specified on the Order. At first glance, this seems like an attribute of Order, which is how we've drawn it, but there's a problem. A particular attribute should appear only once in an entity, but there is a Requested Quantity for each Product requested—if the Order specifies three different Products, there are three separate values for Requested Quantity. For instance, the order might request one of Product Number 1719, a French blue dress shirt; but six of Product Number 4223, a pair of black dress socks; and two of Product Number 3764, a pair of black dress slacks. In data modeling terms, we say that Requested Quantity is a "multivalued" attribute, and it will require some additional work because an attribute should have at most one value in an entity. We could get around the problem by including multiple Requested Quantity attributes, but that introduces various difficulties. Which value of Requested Quantity goes with which Product? How many different values will we allow for? Five? Ten? Whatever we choose, someone will exceed it. There are other issues, but let's move on.

The key to the solution is that Requested Quantity is actually an attribute of a relationship, not an entity. It is a fact about the "Order requests Product" relationship, because it is the Requested Quantity of a particular Product requested on a particular Order. In this style of modeling, only an entity can carry attributes, so the

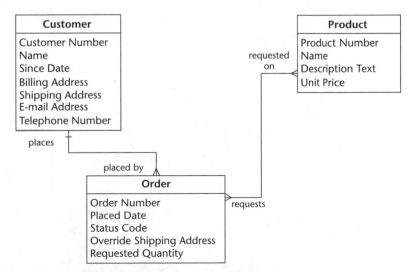

Figure 14.3 Adding attributes to the entity-relationship diagram.

solution is to introduce an entity in the "middle" of the relationship to hold this attribute and any others that might arise. As shown in Figure 14.4, this new entity is Order Line Item. This isn't unreasonable—if you visualize a paper order form, it is made of some "header" information at the top, and then a separate line for each ordered product. Each Order is made up of many Order Line Items and each Order Line Item requests one product. Starting in the other direction, each product is requested on many Order Line Items, and each Order Line Item is part of one Order.

Note that this diagram is drawn following the "top-down dependency" convention, which vastly increases the readability when models get more complex. Some entities in a data model are *dependent*, because they can't exist unless they are related to one or more other entities that are referred to as their *parent(s)*. Order is dependent, because it can't exist unless there is a Customer that placed the Order, so it is drawn below customer—that's top-down dependency. An Order Line Item cannot exist unless it is related to both the Order that it is part of and the Product that it requests, so it is drawn between and below these parent entities. Customer and Product are drawn at the top, because they aren't dependent on any other entity. They are referred to as *independent* or *fundamental* entities. Before we resolved the M:M relationship between Order and Product, it was drawn in side-to-side fashion because neither Order nor Product depends on the other.

This example demonstrates a couple of key points about data modeling. The first is really *the* central point in data modeling—the data model *must* represent the "essence" or "natural structure" of the entities, not a particular physical implementation. We say it depicts "business reality," not a particular technology or record-keeping system. That's why we made the point at the beginning of this chapter that data modeling shouldn't be confused with database design—a database design is only one possible implementation. Our Order – Order Line Item model

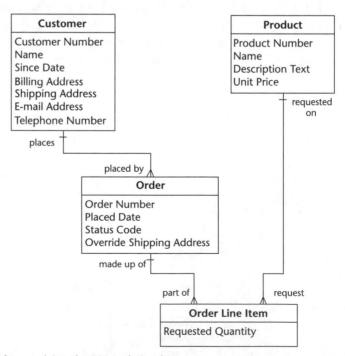

Figure 14.4   After resolving the M:M relationship.

works whether the Order is a "shopping cart" on a Web site, a paper order form with a header and multiple line items, a list of items conveyed to a sales rep via the telephone, or an XML message moving between two systems. The importance of this is that from the data model, we'll eventually derive the structure of the record-keeping system, usually a database of some sort. If the design of this database is based on the "natural structure" of things, it will be much more flexible in meeting new requirements and accommodating new technologies. Experience with "long-lived" databases has proved this absolutely. From the business process perspective, the importance is that the most successful business processes have a base of consistent, shared data from which all participants get the information they need. Clearly, an order fulfillment process will work more smoothly if sales, manufacturing, logistics, and accounts receivable all work from the same "picture" of order.

The other point is a well-known pattern in data modeling—a M:M relationship is always "hiding" another entity, and it will be "resolved" by adding a new entity and a pair of 1:M (usually) relationships. This doesn't have to be done right away—M:M relationships are just fine while the model is at an overview stage, although the detail-oriented modelers we mentioned earlier tend to obsess about resolving the M:M relationships immediately. Don't worry about resolving the M:M relationship until the discussion turns to attributes that can only be captured in the new entity. By the same token, the multivalued attributes we cautioned you about earlier are actually just fine during the early stages of data modeling. Even very complex data models can be developed by applying a few basic patterns, like this one for handling M:M relationships.

One final point on the E-R diagram is that the symbols will vary slightly among the different data modeling "dialects." For instance, we've used the "crowsfoot" to indicate "many," while other notations will use a small circle or arrowheads. These are minor differences, easily learned, because the underlying meaning is constant. Over time, these differences will continue to disappear—currently, the symbols are much more standardized than they used to be.

Levels of Detail

Earlier, we stressed that data modeling shouldn't start at the detail level. This is true of all types of models—they go through progressive levels of detail, each highlighting different aspects, each serving a different purpose and perhaps a different audience.

A house will progress through the following:

1. Use, style, general features, location on the site;
2. Floor plan/front elevation (sketch);
3. Detailed blueprints.

As we've seen, a business process progresses through the following:

1. Identification (overall process map) and framing;
2. Business-oriented workflow diagrams;
3. Specification-oriented workflow diagrams, for instance, using BPMN.

Similarly, data models have the following defined levels of detail:

1. Contextual data model (the scope and glossary of core terms);
2. Conceptual data model (an overview);
3. Logical data model (the details).

A contextual model is similar in appearance and use to the overall process map. It can also take the form of a block diagram, except that it shows *subjects* or *topics* within an area rather than business processes within a process area. A subject or topic is a collection of related entities that deal with the same matter, such as Inventory, Product, Customer, or Orders. Each topic will eventually break down into multiple entities (e.g., the customer subject will contain entities such as customer Operating Location, Customer Contact Person, Customer Organization, and, of course, Customer). Like an overall process map, it could be depicted with a simple list. It also has the same purpose, which is to establish context by clarifying what is in or out of scope. The intent is to show what data subjects will be required to support some initiative, which in our case is a process improvement undertaking. To support processes in the Order Fulfillment process area, the corresponding contextual model would probably show the subject's Customer, Order, Product, Inventory, and perhaps Carrier.

The contextual data model can also include a *glossary* or *vocabulary*, which is our main interest. It lists the main entities (and other important things, such as metrics) and the agreed upon definitions. Many practitioners would see this as an extract of the conceptual data model, which is fair, but we treat it as a separate level of model to stress the importance of developing a common set of terms and definitions.

The Order data model in Figure 14.3 is a simple or initial *conceptual data model*, which serves to get the main ideas across (the main entities, attributes, relationships, and rules). On a real project, even the conceptual model would be more complex and would include additional entities such as Customer Location, Carrier, Shipping Route, and so on.

In a conceptual data model, many of the M:M relationships are left unresolved. The main purpose of a conceptual model is to improve communication and clarify scope—the details needed for physical design are added while our conceptual model evolves into a logical model.

A *logical data model* contains all of the excruciating detail that is needed to actually build a database. This includes keys (primary, foreign, and alternate); every single attribute broken down to its most atomic level; the definition, data type, length, and validation rules for each of these attributes; and a host of other details. It will include many more entities (usually about five times as many) than the conceptual model—a conceptual entity may prove to be a whole collection of entities related to a subject that we hadn't yet discerned the details of. Customer, for example, may in the logical data model become many entities to record a Customer along with multiple operating locations, divisions, contact persons, products, industry groups, ownership records, and so on. Eventually the logical model will become "physical" when the database administrator (DBA) uses it to produce a database design for the particular DBMS (e.g., DB2, Oracle, SQL Server, or Access) used by your computer system.

Much of the difference between conceptual and logical is in the handling of attributes. In a logical model, attributes are *atomic*. For instance, name is a legitimate conceptual attribute, but in the logical model it is broken down into its atomic components—the smallest parts of the attribute that would ever be handled independently. Name would become prefix (Mr., Ms., and so on), first given name, second given name, last name, goes by name, and so on. Address could become suite/unit number, street number, street name, city, state/province/county, country, and postal code, and so on *if* there was a need to deal with these parts independently. Otherwise, it might become address line 1, address line 2, city, and so on. If international addresses were to be handled, the simple attribute address in the conceptual model could become a very complex data structure in the logical.

Another difference is that in the logical model, attributes are not multivalued or repeating, as per our Requested Quantity example earlier. Returning to the name example, if it turned out (as it often does) that the model must record a history of name changes, we would say that Name is a repeating attribute, because one Customer could have many Names. (The same thing would likely happen to address as well.) In the logical model, this would be handled by creating a separate Customer Name entity connected to the Customer entity with a 1:M relationship (each Customer has a maximum of many Names, but each name is attached to a maximum of one Customer). Each Customer Name would record an effective date range during which the name was valid, as well as all of the atomic attributes described previously. Another wrinkle—a different format will be required for Customers that are organizations, not persons.

During logical modeling, we also strive to eliminate redundancy, so if we encounter an attribute whose value would be recorded multiple times, we will place it in the entity it fundamentally describes so that its value is only recorded once. This obsession with redundancy stems from the simple fact that if you maintain multiple copies of the same fact, they can easily get out of sync—wrong, in other words. A special case is when we discover a descriptive attribute such as Industry Type or Customer Status and want to maintain a list of the allowed values. In this case, we create a new entity called a *reference entity* that is used to record the allowable values of one of these descriptive attributes. Usually they also maintain a code or short abbreviation for each value. For instance, for the attribute Customer Ranking, the values of the abbreviation and the full value could be PL for Platinum, GO for Gold, and SI for Silver.

Applying guidelines like nonredundancy and elimination of multivalued attributes is referred to as *normalization*, and the result is a *normalized* data model. Figure 14.5 illustrates some of the things that occur when we apply normalization to the model and move from conceptual to logical. We don't want to get bogged down too early, but when we move into design and implementation, these details will have a major impact, not just on database internals but on the design of the user interface that actors in the business process will deal with. We'll consider that further in the following chapter on services and use cases.

There are other important differences between conceptual and logical models, but we may have already covered more than you wanted to know. However, it is important to illustrate why both overview and detail models are necessary, what the main differences are, and why it's important not to get too detailed too soon. By the

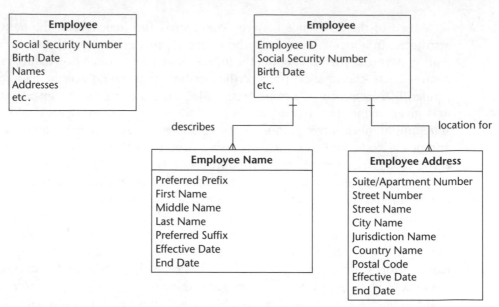

Figure 14.5 Normalization—dealing with attributes in a logical data model.

way, like many IS terms, *conceptual* and *logical* are a little strange— we'd prefer to call these the *overview data model* and the *detailed data model*, but we don't set the standards. Speaking of that, not everyone uses these terms consistently, and the detail-oriented folks we discussed earlier often don't even recognize the existence or need for conceptual models, much less contextual models or vocabularies.

A key point! As you add detail, your conceptual model will evolve into a logical data model, but don't lose the conceptual view!!! It will be an absolutely vital tool for presentations, orientation, training, and discussions about new requirements.

To summarize, here are the characteristics of each type of model.

Contextual Data Model

- Illustrates the topics or subject areas within the scope of some initiative;
- Provides a *context diagram* to help clarify high-level scope;
- Generally includes a glossary comprising terms and definitions for the main entities (the ones that would be in the conceptual data model);
- May be the starting point (top-down) or may be a summary from your conceptual data model (bottom-up).

Conceptual Data Model

- Shows the main entities, relationships, and attributes within the scope of a project or subject area;
- Provides an "overview" to ensure everyone is on the same wavelength before diving into detail;
- Most entities will be important things that people refer to on a daily basis;

- Lots of M:M relationships;
- Relationships will show cardinality but not optionality;
- Main attributes only;
- Attributes will often be nonatomic and multivalued;
- No keys shown;
- No reference entities shown except those that are necessary to link parts of the model;
- Generally fits on one page;
- Represents about 20 percent of the data modeling effort;
- *Save a copy before it evolves into the logical model!!!*

Logical Data Model

- Shows every single entity, relationship, and attribute within scope;
- Provides the "excruciating detail" needed for first-cut physical database design (the DBA will likely refine this to meet other factors—performance, security, geographic distribution, and so on);
- Typically about five times as many entities as the conceptual model;
- No M:M relationships (all are resolved);
- Relationship optionality is shown;
- Fully "normalized"—no redundant, multivalued, or nonatomic attributes;
- Multivalued attributes all moved into separate entities with a 1:M relationship;
- Nonatomic attributes all decomposed into their smallest (atomic) component parts;
- All attributes completely documented (defined, data type and length specified, validation rules including allowable values documented, and so on);
- Primary keys, alternate keys (unique but nonkey attributes), and foreign keys all shown;
- Lots of reference entities shown;
- For readability, may be partitioned into multiple one-page diagrams;
- Represents about 80 percent of the data modeling effort;
- *Save a copy before it evolves into the physical database design!!!*

The Components—Further Guidelines and Pitfalls

You can skip over this section for now, or forever if you've learned as much about data modeling as you need. If you'd like to try it, we include some more specifics on the components of a data model—entities, attributes, and relationships.

Entities

An entity is a distinct thing the business needs to know about. It can be a person (Employee), place (Region), thing (Part), event (Police Incident), concept (Regulation), or organization (Corporation). Most entities fall into one of those categories, although many analysts add additional categories such as request (Order), transfer or transaction (Sale), work item (Project Task), specification (Vehicle Make/Model), and so on. An entity is always named using a singular noun meaningful to the content experts. Potential entities at a university include the following:

- Student;
- Instructor;
- Subject;
- Course;
- Class (or section);
- Tutorial;
- Room;
- Scholarship award;
- Residence;
- Residence room.

From another perspective, an entity is a standard description for a set of similar instances. The main criteria for something to be an entity is that it is a distinct thing we need to maintain records about, it has multiple occurrences, there are facts that must be recorded about it, there is a need (and the ability) to keep track of each individual occurrence, and therefore we can meaningfully discuss one of them. "Student" qualifies because there are multiple occurrences of it, all are essentially similar (i.e., have same facts recorded), the institution needs to keep track of each occurrence, they can differentiate one from another, and they can reasonably discuss a particular student.

You'll recall that a process must have a "countable" result, and you must be able to identify specific occurrences of that result. Entities are the same—you must be able to count the number of occurrences (not that you'd necessarily want to), and you must be able to refer to individual instances when necessary. Look over the list of entities at the university and you'll see that all of them meet the "multiple occurrences" criterion. In contrast, the university may have departments called Admissions, Accounting, and Facilities, but they wouldn't appear in a data model as separate entities, because there is only a single occurrence of each. Rather, there would be a Department entity, and these would be three of its instances. For that matter, if the university was Whattsamatta U,[5] we wouldn't expect to see the entity Whattsamatta U on one of its data models, because there is certainly only one Whatsamatta U!

Along with multiple, distinct instances, the criterion that it "has facts we need to record" is a simple and useful test for entities. Some of these facts are "attrib-

---

5.   Bullwinkle's alma mater.

utes"—individual pieces of data, like the fields on a screen or report. Others are "relationships"—an association between two entities. For example, some Student attributes are ID Number, Name, Birth Date, GPA, and so on, and some of its relationships are Student majors in Subject, Student enrolls in Class, and Student *currently occupies* Residence Room.

Many potential entities will arise during your analysis, but you must select only those relevant to your scope and objectives. In a data model somewhere, Product and Order are surely entities, but they aren't relevant to this university example.

Perhaps the most common error is to confuse reports, forms, screens, messages, and other ways of presenting or capturing information with the fundamental entities. For instance, "transcript" isn't an entity because it's really a report that presents data from other entities—a Student, the Courses they've taken, and so on.

Each entity must be named and defined. The entity name should be a short phrase (1 to 3 words) based on a noun, in the singular form. The convention is to capitalize the entity name and its attributes. It should be a phrase that everyone can relate to, not a technically convenient shorthand.

The entity definition tells which instances in the real world are included within our understanding of that entity. Another term is "entity qualification." For instance: The world has hundreds of millions of people who are "Students." Which ones would we expect to find in the Whattsamatta U Student database? Which ones would be excluded? Another way to look at it—are there any cases or anomalies that are likely to cause confusion? For example, is a Person a Student as soon as they've applied for admission? Are they still a Student after graduation? And what about a Faculty Member (another entity) that takes Classes? An example:

A Student is any person who has been admitted to Whattsamatta U, has accepted, and has enrolled in at least one Class within a designated time. Faculty and staff members may also be Students, but on graduation a student becomes an Alumnus.

Note that the definition is always in terms of a single instance. If you can't name the entity in the singular, and define what a single occurrence is, you probably don't have an entity. We recall working at an insurance company where Weather was suggested as an entity, but it didn't seem to fit the bill. It wasn't named in the singular—the question "what is a Weather" just didn't sound right. And it was hard to conceive of a singular instance of Weather. By having the participants list sample instances, we were able to see that the entity was Weather Event—they were interested in recording particular events like Hurricane Charles or Hurricane Katrina so they could tally the total damage due to each.

As that example illustrates, it's generally very helpful to get some examples—specific instances—as part of your definition of each entity. If you have only a vague notion of what the entity is, you'll be unable to come up with examples of specific instances. For instance, when you start listing examples of a Product, it may become evident that some participants are thinking about a product family, others are thinking about a base product, others assume that Product means a particular configuration of options and packaging, and still others are thinking about a specific unit (i.e., with a serial number) that must be tracked for warranty purposes. You might have four distinct but related entities—Product Family, Product, Product

Configuration, and Product Unit. That's how models that start out small and simple become larger and more complex!

Attributes

Correctly identifying the entities is the more challenging (and important!) part of data modeling. Once that's been accomplished, attributes are fairly straightforward. An attribute, also called a data element or data item, is a fact about (property of) of an entity that can be expressed as a piece of data. The individual fields we see on screens, forms, and reports correspond to attributes in a data model. Traditionally, attributes in a data model are text strings, numbers, or alphanumeric strings that contain both characters and digits, as per the following examples for the university:

- Student Name;
- Course Description Text;
- Course Code;
- Admission Date;
- Special Admissions Flag;
- Fees Due Amount;
- Maximum Attendance Quantity.

New types of attributes are appearing in data models because of technical advances in what can be recorded in a database, such as Student Portrait (a picture), Student Résumé (a word processing document), or Student Presentation (a video clip). Note that these were always "naturally occurring" attributes of the Student entity, but they wouldn't have appeared in the data model because there was no way to capture them in files or databases. This is one of the dilemmas of data modeling—we seek to produce a technology-neutral representation of the required data, but what gets included in the data model is always constrained by the available technology.

The basic criterion for an attribute is that it is a necessary fact, something the enterprise needs to know. Student shoe size is a fact, but is unlikely to be a necessary fact, unless the athletic department has a need to know.

The attribute should contain one and only one fact—otherwise, we say it's "semantically overloaded." The attribute male special admissions flag contains two facts—gender and admission status—and so should be split into two attributes. This is similar to guidelines we reviewed earlier—as the model progresses from conceptual to logical, attributes become atomic and single-valued.

The attribute should be a fundamental fact about the entity, not easily calculated from other attributes or relationships. Otherwise, it is referred to as a "derived" attribute. Student Age is derived, because it can be calculated using student Birth Date and today's date. Similarly, Section Current Enrollment could be derived (calculated) by adding up the number of students currently enrolled in a Section. Even Student Grade Point Average is derivable. Eventually, you'll get to the point where the calculation seems so onerous that it's more reasonable to include a derived attribute in the model. The classic example—your bank account balance, which could be derived if you wanted to go right back to the opening balance and apply every deposit, withdrawal, fee, and adjustment that had ever happened. You might wonder why we don't just show all the derived attributes, reasoning that doing so would make the model more understandable. In practice, that quickly leads to a cluttered and hard to follow model, so we document derived attributes where they'll be used (e.g., in report specifications or descriptions of how to calculate a metric). Where to draw the line isn't clear, demonstrating once again that data modeling is part science, part art. If you really want to show a derived attribute, be sure to document the calculation algorithm with the attribute definition.

Yes, we said "attribute definition." Along with entities, attributes must be clearly defined to avoid misunderstanding. For instance, we could have an attribute Enrollment Date applying to the enrollment of a Student in a Class. But does the date represent the date they requested the class, the date they were tentatively enrolled, or the date their enrollment was confirmed (e.g., payment had been received). Attribute definition can easily lead to one attribute becoming two or more, another example of how models necessarily grow larger and more complex if they are to meet all requirements.

Finally, the attribute should be attached to the entity it's a fact about. This seems self-evident, but in practice it's a frequent point of confusion. For instance, Instructor Name seems like a reasonable attribute of Section, but it isn't—it's a fact about Instructor, which is a related entity via the Instructor *is assigned* to Section relationship. This illustrates a common error—adding an attribute to an entity instead of creating a relationship to the entity the attribute belongs in.

Relationships

A relationship is a named association between two entities. The relationship name will be verb-based (assigned to, located in, transported by, and so on), as opposed to an entity name, which is noun-based. Eventually, you'll name the relationship in both directions, ideally using the same root word. Shipment *transported by* carrier would be Carrier *transports* Shipment in the other direction, just as Organization *located in* Building would be Building *location of* Organization in the opposite direction. Depending on the conventions at your organization, you might add "is" to the relationship name for readability—Organization *is located in* Building and Building *is location of* Organization.

During conceptual modeling, you determine the *cardinality* of each relationship—the maximum number of one entity that another entity can be related to. The choices are one to one (1:1), one to many (1:M), or many to many (M:M). Eventually you need to resolve all M:M relationships into a new entity and a pair of 1:M relationships, because databases can only store 1:1 and 1:M, but during conceptual modeling M:M relationships are fine.

Later, during logical modeling, the *optionality* of each relationship is determined, which answers this question: for each entity involved in the relationship, is it mandatory for every instance to participate in the relationship, or is it optional? Consider the 1:M relationship Course *offered via* Section. The Course "English 100" may be offered by many Sections, each at different times and locations. In the other direction, the relationship is Section *offering of* Course. Each course *may be* (optional) offered by the scheduling of a Section. It's optional because a new Course may not have any Sections scheduled yet. Each Section *must be* (mandatory) an offering of a Course, because you can't have a Section unless there is first a Course to offer in that Section. Different data modeling dialects depict optionality in different ways, but the concept is always there in a detailed model. In the style we use, an open circle (a zero) is used to indicate *may be*, which is the equivalent of saying there could be as few as zero, hence the symbol. A hash mark (a one) is used to indicate *must be*, which is the equivalent of saying there can be no fewer than one, hence the symbol. Optionality is also called *minimum cardinality*, which is why these symbols are based on the minimum number of instances of a related entity. The symbols are added next to the hash mark or crow's foot you used to depict cardinality, just slightly further away from the entity. Optionality is illustrated in Figure 14.6.

Two common errors are redundant relationships and irrelevant relationships. A redundant relationship occurs when a "shortcut" relationship is added between two entities that are already connected via more fundamental relationships involving another entity. For instance, Student *enrolls in* Section and Section *is offering* of Course are both fundamental relationships that the model must record. If we added a relationship directly connecting Student and Course (e.g., to make producing a transcript a little easier), that would be redundant, because the information is already available by going from Student to Section and then from Section to Course. This may seem inefficient, but in the grand scheme of things, it's better to avoid redundancy. One reason is that it is very easy to build an incomprehensible "spaghetti" model where every entity is connected to every other entity, the first law of ecology being that everything is ultimately connected to everything else. Another reason is that somebody has to write and maintain program logic ("code") to keep all those redundant relationships in sync whenever a fundamental relationship changes. It's exactly the same reasoning we described earlier to justify avoiding redundant attributes—eventually, redundant versions of the same information will get out of sync.

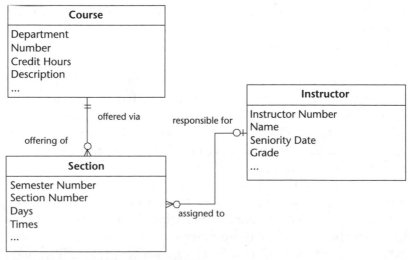

Figure 14.6 Adding optionality to a relationship.

Irrelevant relationships are those that, while true, don't contain information that must be maintained. For instance, it might be true that Student *had coffee with* Instructor, but if no one cares, why add it to the model?

There's a lot more to learn about data modeling—at the end of the chapter, there are references for some excellent books on the topic.

Starting Your Data Model

There are many possible approaches to starting a data model, but to simplify things, let's consider two choices you have for your overall approach:

1. Covert or overt?
2. Bottom-up or top-down?

In a *covert* approach, like the terminology-driven method we illustrated in Chapter 5, people aren't necessarily aware that you're initiating the development of a data model. This is the approach we usually take on a process-oriented initiative. In an *overt* approach, you let everyone know that the group is about to construct a data model, and you will typically begin with an overview of data modeling. This is the approach we often use on a requirements definition or business intelligence project, as long as no one has any problem with the idea of data modeling.

In a *bottom-up* method, like Chapter 5's, you gather a lot of detail and then synthesize a simpler model out of it by classifying the items and identifying the things or entities. In a *top-down* method, you educate the group on what an entity is, and then have them directly identify the entities. This sounds more effective, but the catch is that if you start top down, you will still have to do some sorting and synthesis anyway, and by having them focus on entities you will miss some other things that would have been good clues to entities, such as reports or metrics. That's why in practice we almost always use a bottom-up approach, and, as you'll see, whether we're being covert or overt about it, the steps are almost identical. By the way, top-down in this context refers to the approach, not the top-down style of drawing the ERD.

Starting Covertly

In this approach, you're like a covert operative, except that instead of getting someone to divulge state secrets, you're getting them to willingly but unknowingly help you identify entities. This is the subtle approach we usually take on a process-oriented initiative. The rationale is that many participants will rebel if you suggest building a data model because they have either suffered through some excruciatingly detailed data modeling or they just don't see how it's relevant to process improvement. Don't try to *convince* a group like this that data modeling really is a useful activity—instead, *demonstrate* it. (We always advise people that a good mindset is "demonstrate, not convince.") Get started without referring to "data modeling" and let valuable insights emerge naturally before explaining that a data model is being developed, if you do at all. This is "guerrilla" data modeling, which beats "gorilla" data modeling every time!

One starting point is to collect all of the terms you can through pre-session interviews and other research, as described in Chapter 5. This is done early in the project, during process discovery. The other starting point is to wait until later when you will locate all of the nouns that have been used in the verb-noun process, subprocess, or step names. Ideally, this is done during "framing the process," but certainly by the end of as-is modeling. If you leave it that late, though, you may discover you missed some important cases and have to redo some of your earlier work.

Whichever way you start, some of the nouns will refer to things that are clearly central to the process, and you can say to the group "let's define some of these terms to ensure we're all on the same page." After the definitions are sorted out, which almost always raises enough interesting points to justify the time taken, a reasonable next step is to ask, "how do these things relate to one another" while starting to draw an ERD. Then ask, "what facts do we need to know about each of these things?" Use as many ideas as you think you can from the "starting overtly" method—ultimately they're very similar. You may even complete a substantial amount of data modeling before the detractors realize what you're up to!

Starting Overtly

If your group doesn't have any problems with the idea of data modeling, you can set aside some time in your plan for it. You'll want at least a half-day session to sketch out a basic data model. In point form, here's a proven, seven-step (there's that magical number again) approach for developing the initial conceptual data model in a facilitated session:

1. *Don't begin with a treatise on data modeling*—people's eyes will glaze over and they'll tune out. Simply state that along with a process model, you're going to develop a data model to help understand the information needs of the process, or words to that effect. Let people know that you'll explain terms and concepts along the way, but it's best to just dive right in.

2. Brainstorm for *anything* "data-related" needed by the process and the supporting applications. Reassure the group that "anything goes," including things you need information about, facts, reports, metrics, queries, and so on. You can record suggestions on flipcharts or put each suggestion on a large Post-it as described in the note on that subject after this list.

3. *Option 1*: When you go through each item in sequence, ask, "Is this a thing, a fact about a thing, or something else?" We often use the phrase "other stuff" instead of "something else" to set a casual tone. Surprisingly, people usually don't need much explanation of "thing" versus "fact," and we explain "other stuff" as reports, metrics, forms, queries, and so on.

   - Circle "things" or record them on a new flipchart with lots of room around each entry.

   - When a fact is identified, ask what it is a fact about and record it next to the appropriate thing, creating new things if necessary.

   - Set aside "reports and other stuff" for later analysis.

3. *Option 2*: Using the same approach that we did in Chapter 5, review a flipchart that explains the different categories that an item can fall into (thing, fact about a thing, metric, and so on) and a second flipchart explaining the criteria for things (singular noun, need to know, has facts, multiple instances, and so on). Then go through each item in sequence and ask, "Is this a thing, a fact about a thing, or does it fall into one of these other categories?" As in option 1:

   • Circle things.

   • Cluster facts around the appropriate thing.

   • Mark anything else with a code to indicate which category it fell into.

4. Explain that the things are referred to as *entities* and check the validity of the entities:

   • Consolidate obvious synonyms.

   • Set aside those that are outside the scope of your project.

   • Ensure again that they meet the basic criteria: multiple occurrences, have facts, the business needs to know about them, and so on. If there is overlap—the same facts appear in two entities—that may indicate one of the entities is actually a report, query, form, or something else.

5. Starting with the fundamental entities, develop entity definitions. Remember that you're answering the question "What is *one* of these things?" Use the guidelines we provided earlier—look for anomalies, list examples, and determine whether it refers to instances of a thing or categories of a thing.

6. Draw an entity-relationship diagram:

   • Fundamental entities should be at the top.

   • Dependent entities should be below.

7. Brainstorm important additional attributes for each entity up to a maximum of seven or so.

As time permits, you can validate the model by "playing it back" to the participants as a presentation and asking if it sounds like a reasonable description of their business. The model will be further validated and refined if you carry on with requirements modeling as described in the next chapter.

As an alternative to step 2, do the brainstorm on Post-its, and for step 3 have participants arrange them into things, facts, metrics, reports, and so on. You could set aside a "thing" area and have participants post things at the top and facts under the appropriate thing. A separate flipchart can be used for each of the other categories. In recent years we find ourselves most often running sessions this way because of the important benefits—participants take whatever they're building *much* more seriously when they have been *physically involved* with creating and manipulating it. As noted before, 4 × 6-inch Post-it Super Sticky Notes in the neon colors are a good choice—they're bright, large enough to write on and see in a session, and they really do stick.

Starting by Reverse Engineering

The majority of our current data modeling work involves going through the process in reverse! This is done when there is already a database in place, either for an existing legacy or custom application or for a piece of commercial software that is in use or is being evaluated. This requires a degree of technical skill (e.g., a DBA) and data modeling experience that we can't get into here, but it's worth knowing that this is a valid approach. Essentially, we study the physical database design and some real data to figure out what's going on, and then work backward and represent the physical database as an entity-relationship diagram. Some tools help to automate this step, but human judgment is always necessary. It's needed to set aside entities (tables) that exist for the care and feeding of the system but have no business relevance, and also to spot cases where the database has been "denormalized" for some reason, typically performance tuning, security, or geographic partitioning. The result of this "working backward" will approximate a logical data model. We then apply simplification heuristics and turn it into a conceptual model. Finally, through a variety of techniques including interviewing developers and users, studying documentation (ha!), looking at screen shots and reports, checking with the vendor, and so on, we develop entity definitions. This leads up to a review presentation at which we "unveil" the model (without calling it a data model) and ask:

- "Is this what you expected?" (for current legacy or custom applications);
- "Will this work for you?" (for commercial applications being evaluated).

This provides important guidance on whether the database (and, therefore, the application) supports the scope and objectives of the new business process, or even the *existing* process. We've found repeatedly that participants are stunned—the phrase "shock and awe" comes to mind—to see the "world view" (as we call the data model) of the system they're currently using. It isn't unusual to hear comments like "Now we know why we hate this application!" When we're looking at a commercial application being evaluated, the result is often awareness that either the organization or the software package will have to change. To be fair, we've had many cases where the reaction was "Wow—that's so much better than how we do it!" In those cases, the organization adapts its processes and "world view" (data model) to the application, which is increasingly becoming the norm. Modifying or even extensively configuring a purchased application usually ends in unhappiness, so, if you need to do either, purchased software may not be the best option.[6] Purchased applications come with a set of assumptions about the business and its processes; if you can adopt them, fine, but if you can't, purchased software isn't the best option. Surprisingly, this determination can often be largely made just by inspecting the data model. This could be the subject of an entire book, but we'll remind ourselves that this is a book on business processes and avoid the temptation to dive further into related topics.

---

6. We're discussing purchased software that has application-specific functionality, like a manufacturing planning or benefits administration system, not software that provides a platform on which you can develop applications that meet your needs, such as that available from Salesforce.com.

From Conceptual to Logical

Techniques for developing the logical data model are well beyond the scope of this book, although we've provided some guidelines on what comprises a logical model. The basic principle of logical models is that they are primarily developed by discovering additional attributes and making entities more granular by normalizing the model.

These additional attributes are best discovered, surprisingly, by shifting our attention away from data and concentrating on other analysis techniques, such as use case modeling (next chapter), service specification (also in the next chapter), and report specification. While doing these, constantly check that all the necessary attributes are in the data model. If not, add new attributes according to the rules of normalization we covered earlier:

- If we need to record attributes of a relationship, create a new entity "in the middle of" the relationship.
- If one or more attributes repeats within an entity, push the attributes "down" into a new dependent entity to record them.
- If the values of an attribute would be recorded redundantly, push the attribute "up" to a parent (or grandparent or...) entity, or "out" to a reference entity.

This is a lot of work—developing the logical data model takes roughly four times as long as developing the conceptual data model—and is probably going to require the assistance of specialists. We won't get any further into data modeling, but there are several excellent books if you want to learn more. Two in particular stand out as excellent references. Graeme Simsion and Graham Witt's *Data Modeling Essentials, Third Edition* [1] is eminently readable and based on real-world experience—no idle theory here. David Hay's *Data Model Patterns* [2] isn't a book *about* data models, it's a book *of* data models—much can be learned by studying the "generic" (similar across enterprises and industries) data models the book presents. In the same vein are Len Silverston's excellent books on universal data models, *The Data Model Resource Book, Volumes 1 and 2* [3].

We'll continue our whirlwind tour of related analysis techniques in the final chapter, where we consider the important role of use cases and services in modeling application requirements.

References

[1] Simsion, G., and G. Witt, *Data Modeling Essentials*, 3rd ed., San Francisco: Elsevier, 2005.

[2] Hay, D. C., *Data Model Patterns: Conventions of Thought*, New York: Dorset House, 1996.

[3] Silverston, L., W. H. Inman, and K. Graziano, *The Data Model Resource Book, Volumes 1 and 2*, New York: John Wiley & Sons, 2001.

CHAPTER 15

Requirements Modeling with Use Cases and Services

From Workflow to Information System Requirements

A Time of Transition

While characterizing and designing the to-be process, we produced a service-level workflow model for the new process and identified where automation would be applied to support an actor completing a step in it. Now, we need to go down a level of detail to produce a *use case description* to describe *how* an actor (*who*) will interact with the system to complete that process step, and produce a *service description* to describe *what* the system will do in response. These descriptions must be accessible and understandable so managers, workers, functional specialists, and other stakeholders can tell if their needs, expectations, and rules are understood. The tricky part is that they must also be clear and complete enough that software developers can design or prototype the required functionality.

You could attempt to do this by adding detail to your to-be swimlane diagrams until you were describing every field entered on a screen, every time "enter" was pressed, and every system response. But what would be the point? You'd be drawing a *workflow* diagram, but you wouldn't be diagramming the *flow of work*, because the *work* would not be *flowing*—it would be at rest on an actor's desk. Instead, you would be describing a procedure—a step-by-step set of instructions that an actor completes at a single time and place to accomplish a step in a process. In this case, it would be a procedure for interacting with a system—a *use case*. The issue is no longer the flow of work among the various actors, it is determining how a system will help a specific actor complete a specific activity or process step. In other words, it's time to make some important transitions:

- From the flow of work to the details of how "work at rest" is carried out;
- From modeling process workflow to modeling system requirements.

Swimlane diagrams are, categorically, inappropriate for this purpose. We've seen it attempted, and it isn't pretty. They become large, complex (imagine trying to show every decision point and path in an event-driven interface) and fail to illustrate the central concern—system functionality and behavior. Instead, we make the transition to our particular variant of the use case technique.

Transition into Use Cases

We developed this approach through trial and error, mixing and matching from other approaches and just as often creating our own. The driver was the observation that even though use cases get a lot of attention, business analysts at most organizations have had limited or no success with applying the techniques. In fact, just last week at a conference for business analysts, we asked an audience of about 55 analysts, "How many of you have had experience with use cases?" About 25 or 30 hands went up. Next question: "How many of you would rate the experience as successful?" This time, something like 6 or 8 hands went up, which is typical of what we've seen in the field. The reason for this poor success rate is, frankly, that many of the published use case methods are so arcane or complex that they are suitable only for use by "rocket scientists" working in packaged (or military or aerospace or real-time) software development, or they are so vague as to offer no real method or benefit, or (like the original published works on the subject) they are really oriented toward internal software design, not discovering requirements for an application's external behavior.[1] That highlights another problem, which is that the approaches vary so widely it's hard for someone new to the field to even grasp what a use case is. As a friend pointed out, "a use case seems to be anything anyone wants it to be." Another significant issue is that use cases are often overloaded with too many different perspectives—the business process, user interaction, and internal system requirements. The approach we will introduce separates these into different models, as we will now see.

Separation into Business Services and Use Cases

The method we use is unique in various ways, one of which is that it treats the process workflow model and the data model as vital, but separate, products. The most important distinction, though, is that instead of loading everything into *one* product—the use case—it creates *two* separate but tightly related products—business services and use cases.

Product 1: Business Services

A *business service* is a fundamental unit of functionality offered by an information system, such as Place Order or View Open Orders. The business analyst writes a *service specification* that describes the invocation, validation, rules, logic, and updates for a single business service that the system will provide, completely independent of who is requesting the service or which platform they are using. The orientation is *what* the system will do.

---

1.   The book that propelled adoption of the technique was Jacobsen, Ivar, et al., *Object Oriented Software Engineering: A Use Case Driven Approach,* Reading, MA: Addison-Wesley, 1992. A key point that is often missed lies in the title—this is a book on software engineering, not requirements definition. Two popular books on use cases are Cockburn, Alistair, *Writing Effective Use Cases,* Reading, MA: Addison-Wesley Professional, 2001; and Kulak, Daryl, and Eamonn Guiney, *Use Cases: Requirements in Context, Second Edition,* Reading, MA: Addison-Wesley Professional, 2003. Note that these books describe fairly different approaches to the one we have described here.

From an IT perspective, a business service is a technical concept for packaging application logic (the "code" your programmers write) in a way that provides a complete, indivisible unit of functionality, assures the integrity of updates to the database, and achieves a measure of reusability. It's not purely a technical concept, though—they must be defined with respect to the business. A service is a discrete unit of business activity, with significance to the business, initiated in response to a business event, that can't be broken down into smaller units and still be meaningful—it's said to be atomic, indivisible, or elementary. Specifically, it is not a collection of related functions, like Order Management, but a discrete service such as Cancel Order.

Product 2: Use Cases

A *use case* is a single *case* in which a specific actor will *use* a system to obtain a particular business service from the system (e.g., Customer Places Order via Internet, Service Rep Places Order via Order Management System, or Service Rep Views Open Orders via CRM System). A use case is documented in a *use case description*, which traces a generalized sequence of interactions between the actor and the system. Eventually, those interactions will be described right down to a "back and forth" dialogue that the actor will go through to obtain the service. The orientation is *who* the particular actor is, and *how* that actor will interact with a system, in order to obtain the desired service. Most important, a use case describes system behavior *from the perspective of the actor* interacting with the system.

In terms of our three-tier systems model, the use case describes the behavior of the presentation services or user interface (UI) layer, while avoiding details of specific UI design elements or "behind the scenes" activity involving the business services and data management layers. Another way to put this is that use cases provide a "how used," not a "how built," view. This shielding is critical—the actors themselves provide the main input to the use case descriptions, and they mustn't be confused or misled by internal design considerations or prematurely making decisions on which UI widget is most appropriate. Refer back to Figure 4.5 for a reminder of how the different layers in our framework fit together.

There are two particularly strong reasons for an analyst to employ use cases. First, by focusing on a single actor obtaining a single service, you are working within a very strong context and so are much more likely to uncover requirements that would be missed in less specific approaches. Second, by taking the use case down to a series of steps, or a back-and-forth dialogue, we are more likely to develop an effective and workable interaction before beginning application design and development. Many times we have seen this approach deliver excellent results in fewer iterations of the development cycle, even in Agile[2] or rapid-application development (RAD) approaches.

Because they are specific to an actor, a service, and a platform, use cases in the form we use provide invaluable information for the user interface designers and

---

2.   Agile is the term attached to a style of software development that is highly effective, when appropriately applied, and deals more with sociology than with technology. See www.agilemanifesto.org for the original source. Like Extreme Programming (XP), more organizations *claim* to be doing Agile development than actually are.

human factors engineers who are responsible for the outward-facing (presentation services) part of an application. Even though they are specific to a particular technology, you will see they don't constrain the interface designer unreasonably because they don't try to design the user interface, just the sequence of interactions that will work in the actor's world. Some people object to the idea of use cases that are specific to a particular UI technology because it sounds like "getting into solution space" too quickly. We are sympathetic to this objection, but remember that the essence—the "what"—has already been described in the service. Once that has been accomplished, you can document some initial technology-neutral information about a use case, as we do. Beyond that, there is little or no percentage in trying to fully describe how someone will interact with a system without reference to a particular interface technology; the difference between interacting with a purpose-built kiosk, an IVR system, and Web browser are just too great. Figure 15.1 summarizes the idea that rather than develop use cases that try to accomplish too much, we separate our requirements gathering and modeling into internal (services) and external (use cases) perspectives. Figure 15.2 goes a little further, showing how use cases, services, and the data model interact.

Benefits

The separation of requirements into external (use case descriptions) and internal (business service specifications) works extremely well in practice. It makes requirements modeling easier, because it allows the analyst to focus on one aspect of the problem at a time—human-computer interaction (dialogue) in use cases and business rules in service specifications. This allows a better job of each, but also enhances synergy.

Looking at each technique separately, the advantages of a use case-driven approach—focus on one actor, one service—are fairly clear, even if the methods don't always live up to the promise. The advantages of a service-driven approach, however, aren't so immediately obvious, especially if you don't come from an IT background. We'll spend a little longer describing those benefits, which we summa-

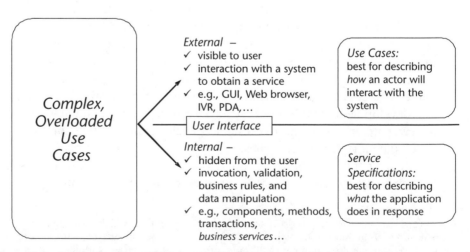

Figure 15.1 Separating the problem space into internal and external perspectives.

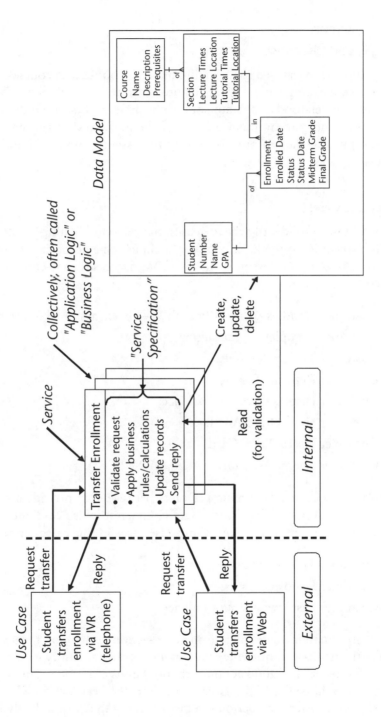

Figure 15.2 Use cases, services, and the data model.

rize as integrity, flexibility, and reuse. First, though, here is an example that will make the discussion about use cases and services more concrete.

A Quick Example

Apologies and Disclaimers

We're almost embarrassed to do so, but like most books and courses, we'll rely on a retail banking example employing an automated teller machine (ATM) because it's universally understood and demonstrates the main points. It won't precisely follow the methods and conventions we will describe in the rest of this chapter because it has been put together to quickly convey the essential points about use cases and business services.

Identify Use Cases

First, you'll want to identify the use cases that the retail banking system should provide. In a traditional method, you would choose one actor at a time and then list their use cases. For a customer at an ATM, use cases that come to mind are as follows:

- Customer Handles Banking (via ATM—this is assumed in the remainder);
- Customer Completes Transaction;
- Customer Transfers Funds;
- Customer Deposits Funds;
- Customer Displays Account Balance;
- Customer Signs On to ATM;
- Customer Inserts Bank Card;
- Customer Selects Account.

Some of these are legitimate use cases because they provide a service that has value to the customer. That is, they can complete the use case and leave, satisfied that they have accomplished something. Use cases in this category are as follows:

- Customer Transfers Funds;
- Customer Deposits Funds;
- Customer Displays Account Balance.

Our strict naming rules dictate an actor–action verb–noun format (or actor-service) for the use case name where the noun is usually an entity or fact from the data model. "Transfer" is a good action verb, but Funds is a little vague, so a more rigorous name would be Customer Completes Transfer Transaction where *completes* is the verb and *transfer transaction* is a distinct thing that would likely be an entity in the data model. For this example, we will stick with the simpler "transfers funds."

The suggestions that are not valid use cases, and why, are the following:

- Customer Handles Banking—too vague, not a discrete service;

- Customer Completes Transaction—still too vague or too large, because it doesn't meet a specific goal like deposit, transfer, or withdraw;
- Customer Signs On to ATM—doesn't deliver value to the actor in itself, although it is a necessary and commonly repeated set of interactions, so it would be described once as a "sub-use case" or "out of context use case";
- Customer Inserts Bank Card—this is only one-half of a clause (a when-then interaction) and a use case dialogue is made up of several clauses;
- Customer Selects Account—this is one clause or step within a use case.

Describe Use Cases: Questions

At this point, if we provided no further guidance and asked you to describe the use case Customer Transfers Funds via ATM, you would attempt it and most likely come back with these questions. For brevity, we've included our answers with the questions:

- Should I tell a story, list the steps, or show each interaction (back and forth) between the actor and the system? Answer: You might do all of these. In the initial use case description, a short vignette in the form of the "use case brief" is very useful, and we will suggest that you can optionally list the main steps in the use case. However, real value emerges in the final use case description when you describe each interaction in "when-then" format, which we will see shortly.
- Should I describe the entire preamble, such as accessing the system, signing on, selecting the desired service, and so on? Answer: Absolutely! You don't need to do it for every use case, but you need to do it for enough use cases to ensure that navigation to the desired service isn't an unwieldy dialogue.
- Should I show "behind the scenes" activity, such as validation or important system functions, or only what's visible to the actor? Answer: Contrary to what is often advised, we include the important background work in our use case dialogues because it adds important context.
- Should I show the various error and exception conditions? Answer: Yes, but not immediately. After you have documented the dialogue for the main successful case in pass 1 of the final use case description, pass 2 will add those other conditions;
- Should I refer to specific UI mechanisms such as pull-down menus, function keys, and so on? Answer: No, not unless you absolutely have to. For instance, when describing a dialogue at an ATM there probably isn't any alternative to referring to the receipt printer or the deposit slot. However, you want to describe a useful dialogue without constraining the UI designer, so "customer selects account" is fine but "customer pushes selection button next to desired account" is not.
- Can the main banking system or other automated facility be an actor? Answer: Yes. For instance, on a regular basis a central banking system might poll the ATM for recent activity, and initiate a dialogue to upload log files or surveillance video.

Describe Use Cases: Sample Dialogue

An initial use case description (concept level) would usually be created before you would develop a dialogue, which is part of the final use case description (detail level), but for the purpose of this example, we'll get right to a dialogue for customer Transfers Funds via ATM:

1. When Customer inserts bank card:
   Then ATM prompts "Language?"
2. When Customer selects "English":
   Then ATM prompts "Receipt?"
3. When Customer selects "yes":
   Then ATM prompts "Password?"
4. When Customer enters password:
   Then ATM validates customer and password and prompts "Transaction?"
5. When Customer selects "transfer":
   Then ATM displays list of customer accounts with balances and prompts for "from" account.
6. When Customer selects "from" account:
   Then ATM confirms "from" account status and displays list of remaining accounts and prompts for "to" account.
7. When Customer selects "to" account:
   Then ATM confirms "to" account status and prompts "Amount?"
8. When Customer enters amount:
   Then ATM summarizes transaction and prompts "Confirm?
9. When Customer selects "confirm":
   Then ATM initiates transfer funds and confirms success and prompts "More?"
10. When Customer selects "no":
    Then ATM ejects bank card and prompts Customer "Remove."
11. When Customer removes card:
    Then ATM prints receipt and terminates session and returns to waiting state.

The point of all of this is to determine if this is a functional and satisfying dialogue. Some of the points that could come up include:

- In general, should it take 11 interactions to accomplish the transfer?
- Do we need to prompt for language, or should this be a default for the customer?
- Can the initial clauses (language, receipt, and transaction) be combined somehow? And do we need to ask so soon if a receipt is desired, given that some use cases don't require a receipt?
- Bank security might point out that it is poor practice to display all of the available accounts and balances in case a thief is using the bank card fraudulently or the customer is under duress. A different dialogue for selecting accounts is indicated.

It seems like a lot of work to develop these detailed dialogues (we haven't even touched on errors and extensions yet!), but we find again and again that this drives out assumptions, misunderstandings, and requirements so effectively that it's always worth the time.

Describe Business Services: Sample

In this example, we illustrated use cases first, but in the approach we will cover in the rest of this chapter, the core services are identified and described before developing use case dialogues. This initial focus on the "what" clarifies what must be accomplished by the "who and how."

The initial service description for transfer funds would include the following actions:

- Confirm Customer existence, status, and password;
- Verify "from" Account existence, status, and available balance for transfer;
- Verify "to" Account existence and status;
- Debit and credit Accounts;
- Create transaction number and log transaction;
- Commit transaction and return message to UI.

Later, in the final service description, this will get much more precise. We will also specify other information, such as the input message required to invoke the service. In this case, that is customer number, password, from account number, to account number, and amount.

You might feel that the description is already too specific in some areas. For instance, why should the service validate the "from" Account details when this was already done at the UI during the use case? The answer is that the service has to be able to accept a request from any sort of UI, including very primitive ones where validation isn't feasible. In short, the service doesn't trust any input message—it always validates it as if it came from a raw text editor.

A given service might be accessible through multiple use cases, each supporting a different dialogue, with navigation and hand-holding appropriate to the needs of the specific actor and platform. For instance, the same Transfer Funds service is available via the following use cases:

- Customer Transfers Funds via ATM;
- Customer Transfers Funds via Web browser;
- Customer Transfers Funds via telephone interface;
- Teller Transfers Funds via Teller Workstation.

Each of these would have very different interaction. Withdraw Funds, for instance, is only available to the Customer via the ATM or indirectly via a Teller using the Teller Workstation. Each of the Transfer Funds use cases would have very different interaction, optimized for the UI technology, but accessing the same underlying service. The power of the concept lies in this reuse, and in focusing analysis on what the service must accomplish before delving into how it will be accessed. These ideas are explored further in the upcoming section.

Business Services—Why?

This Concept Sounds Familiar...

Before discussing why business services are such an important concept from both business and IT perspectives, a little history is in order. The point is that although the concept gets a huge amount of attention these days, as evidenced by the interest in service-oriented architecture (SOA), it has been around for a long time, with the name and supporting technologies changing more than the fundamentals. In the IT field, when a new idea comes around, the lessons from previous incarnations of the same idea are often lost, and services and SOA are no different. We've tried to ensure that some of the good techniques of the past aren't tossed aside in the rush to embrace the seemingly (but not really) new.

In the first edition of this book, we used the term *transactions* rather than *services*, and some of the definitive literature does as well. In Component-Based Development (CBD), all the rage a few years ago (and still perfectly valid), each component interface exposes a specific function that will often correspond to, not surprisingly, a business service as we define it.[3] Earlier, in object-oriented methods, public operations or methods associated with a "business class" (an entity) correspond to services. Before that, in the Information Engineering methodology, the same concept was called an "elementary process." Years ago, going back to the late 1970s and early 1980s, we documented the same concepts as (you guessed it) services. Adherents of a particular method will always claim, "Oh, no, you don't understand—it's different this time," but as we noted, it's the technology that changes more than the concept. The common denominator was always the desire to make the same service available to different actors, via different user interface facilities, without having to recreate it.

The Benefit Case for Services—In General

Three key benefits ensue from packaging system functionality into well-formed services.

1. *Integrity.* If business rules and updates are documented and implemented in one place, in a service that has precisely one function, the odds of getting it right are much higher than if the logic was scattered around in disparate pieces or jammed into huge, multipurpose programs. This becomes even more important when you consider maintenance of the services by future generations of programmers. Picture yourself lifting the hood of a modern automobile and seeing the baffling array of interconnected pieces—that's what it can be like looking at a large, multipurpose program. As it does in

---

3. "Component" means many things, but in this context we mean a functional "chunk" or "repackaging" of a system that offers a related set of services. An order-management component would provide services such as create order, revise order line detail, add order line, drop order line, cancel order, and so on

process redesign, focusing on "what" (business rules and expected actions) rather than "who or how" (actors and interaction) often leads to new insights about what the rules should be.

2. *Flexibility.* This requires that we first cover another important rule for services—they are completely independent of the user interface by which the actor is communicating their wishes (the business event) to the system. The service doesn't know or care whether the user interface was on a SmartPhone, a Web browser, or an IVR system, as long as the UI can send the right message. This is possible because the transaction processing (TP) monitor or application server isolates the service from the UI and manages the communication between them. The benefit of this isolation is huge, as it provides the flexibility to use new interface technology or modify existing user interfaces, without rewriting the services. Organizations with their application logic packaged into services (although they used different terms) had a much easier time migrating their mainframe systems to client/server platforms, and then later making those available via the Web.

3. *Reuse.* This is closely related to the previous point, flexibility. Services are like building blocks that can be reused as needed when applications require functionality that is already coded as services. Not only does this save development time, it ensures that there is one version of the business rules. Most important in the context of this book, it supports the design of new business processes with the rapid development of "assemble to order" applications. Increasingly, the functionality offered by visionary companies like Amazon.com and Salesforce.com is made available as services that are accessed from other applications.

The promise of reuse isn't achieved as often as we would all like, but even if you never reused a particular service, the first two benefits—integrity and flexibility—are enough to make this a superior approach.

The Benefit Case for Services—Project Participants

The service specification format described here has worked extremely well for the three main constituent groups:

1. Process actors, subject matter experts, and others who work in or with the process being supported find that the focus on *what* a single, well-defined service must do, exclusive of all the complications of the *who* and the *how*, provides clarity and focus, which makes it much easier for them to define rules and requirements. We have been pleasantly surprised on occasion to see that working on a "pure" or "essential" service specification can lead to new insights into *what* their business really does. In one memorable case, a government licensing process involved so much document handling, so much redundant data entry and copying, so many back and forth phone calls and faxes, and so much checking and cross-checking, that people in that division had literally lost sight of what they were really trying to accomplish. When we reduced the work to a small set of essential business services,

they were stunned to see what their fundamental business activities were and how much of their work was pure protocol, procedure, and overhead.

2. Business analysts, like the aforementioned group, find that studying one specific service at a time makes it far easier to complete their analysis. The alternatives, such as asking, "what do you want?" or "what are your rules?" are so open ended that there is almost no chance that rules and requirements will be enumerated completely.

3. Application architects and developers who design and create the backend, server-side logic commonly thank us for a format that tells them *what* must be done, without implying *how* they should write their code. (It wasn't always thus, but after being told a few times by developers that it looked like we were trying to write code and weren't very good at it, we devised better approaches.) Some aspects of the templates, such as explicitly referencing the data model, greatly increase the odds that the business analyst will uncover the important rules, which reduces the number of iterations, and therefore frustration, for the developer. A service also provides a clearly defined level of modularity for making functionality reusable in an SOA.

Important to all of these groups, especially the aforementioned architects and developers, this format allows the development of a service *once*, even though it might be accessed by *many* use cases. As an example, we might create a single service implementing the logic and rules to Place (an) Order. We could then develop two different use cases, one being Customer Places Order via the Internet and the other being Inside Sales Agent Places Order via Sales System. Each use case will depict very different dialogues. The Customer use case will likely involve plenty of "hand-holding" and navigation aids suitable for a novice, leading to a UI with lots of point and click or pull-down widgets, while the Sales Agent use case will be designed for efficient use by an expert user, probably leading to a UI relying primarily on keyboard input. Behind the scenes, though, the underlying rules and logic will be the same. As noted, this improves integrity (correctness), flexibility, and reusability, and is an example of SOA at work.

This "build once, deploy many" model also benefits each of the three stakeholder groups during analysis, specification, and development:

1. Process actors and others involved in the process will by and large only have to answer questions about a service's rules and requirements once.

2. Business analysts will only have to analyze and document that service once.

3. Developers will only have to create the service logic once, or at least only once for any particular platform and always from a common specification.

It certainly won't be this close to "systems Nirvana" every time, but it's a much better situation than the norm.

Services and BPMS

Another benefit area that is rapidly growing in importance is that a business service can be invoked by means other than a human actor interacting with a user interface, as documented in a use case. For instance, a BPMS might detect a condition in the demand chain that leads it to automatically invoke the Place Order service, and then orchestrate the execution of subsequent services such as Schedule Order, all without human involvement (use cases). This illustrates why SOA and BPMS are so interdependent and how services support the implementation of flexible business processes through a BPMS. Savvy architects and developers are ensuring that all process workflow logic is removed from application logic (the services) and instead implemented in the BPMS, where it can be easily reconfigured as process needs change.

Disclaimer and Direction

Before going any further, we acknowledge that services and use cases are major topics, the focus of entire courses and conferences. Each warrants its own book, not just a section within a chapter of a business process book. So, for those of you with knowledge in this area…yes, we know we've omitted important concepts and details. For the rest of you, our goal is to cover enough information to get you well on your way. People with a background in process redesign find that these techniques are a great transition into the world of requirements modeling; those having experience with requirements modeling find that workflow process models (and data models) provide an excellent framework for developing use cases and services. Our goal is to provide an approach that bridges or integrates these techniques synergistically.

The Approach and How It's Different

It would seem logical, especially in a book called workflow modeling, that we would start with the workflow model to identify and then develop use cases and services. A reasonable sequence would be as follows:

1. Identify a point in a workflow model (probably a step in a service-level diagram) at which an actor interacts with a system.
2. Document that interaction as a use case.
3. Document the underlying rules and logic as a service specification.

This would be an "outside-in" approach, progressing from the actor in toward the user interface and then system internals. Although we use it in some situations, we most often take an "inside-out" approach, starting with the most fundamental element—the noun or entity. This will be familiar from the approach for process discovery in Chapter 5. Whether or not you use this sequence, it turns out to be the best way to explain the concepts and methods, so we will follow it. The general sequence is as follows:

1. Identify business services for each significant entity.
2. Complete service specifications.
3. Identify use cases by determining which actors need which services.
4. Complete use case descriptions.

Fleshed out a bit more, the steps are as follows:

1. *Identify business services*. For each significant entity (or noun or thing, if you prefer) within scope, such as Order, identify the services (verb-noun) that must be provided for that entity, such as Place Order, Schedule Order, and Fill Order. Many people find it helpful to take the intermediate step of identifying the events (noun is verbed) that happen to the entity, such as Order is Placed, Order is Scheduled, and Order is Filled, and then "flipping" these around into verb-noun form to identify the services. We will employ this method.

2. *Describe business services*. For each service, document the expected outcome, confirm the size or granularity of the service, and later document the specific rules and logic in the form of a service specification.

3. *Identify use cases*. For each service, identify which actor needs to access that service via which platform (actor-service-platform or actor-verb-noun-platform) such as Customer Places order via the Web, Customer Places Order via In-store Kiosk, and Inside Sales Rep Places Order via Sales System. Specifying the platform isn't necessary if there is only one choice, but when there are multiple platforms, each with difference interaction, it's very useful.

4. *Describe use cases*. Document the user experience and stakeholder expectations, and later the dialogue (interaction), in the form of a use case description. Initially the dialogue will trace the normal flow and later will be extended to cover alternate or error conditions.

In practice, the steps are more granular than illustrated by that simple outline. In the approach we'll describe, you will complete initial service specifications and then complete initial use case descriptions, which in turn might uncover refinements for your service specifications. Then, you will complete the final service specifications, and then the final use case descriptions. With more iteration, of course!

We use this inside-out approach as the primary method on many smaller requirements modeling assignments. On a very large process-oriented project, it might not be our primary approach for discovering use cases and services, but we will always use it to ensure completeness. Later, in the section on identifying services, we will review the alternative approaches and when to use them.

Unique Aspects of This Approach

Before getting into the details, we offer a few cautionary notes for those who are already familiar with published use case methods. Many features of our approach are quite different from others, and reading this will be easier if we highlight five differences up front:

1. As described earlier, the explicit separation of use cases (external requirements) from the service specifications (internal requirements) is something we haven't seen in use case literature. For that matter, we have seen little in the service-oriented literature that provides explicit guidelines, as we will for identifying and documenting *business* services.

2. This approach uses and integrates with workflow models and data models. In contrast, it is sometimes suggested that a business process is just a big use case and can be documented the same way. Other methods make no reference to the business process or workflow models at all. Most published methods ignore data models entirely, or propose that a data model is unnecessary because one can be derived from the use cases, or even that data models are a *detriment*. These perspectives are baffling until you realize that many experienced analysts have not worked with business-oriented data and workflow models of the sort we've described. We will use data models extensively to provide a common language and help discover services and rules. Workflow models will provide context and be used to discover use cases and services. Actually, we will describe three approaches to service and use case discovery—workflow-based, actor-based (the usual approach), and service- (or event-) based. Readers might be surprised to see that we most often begin with a service-based approach, as it provides excellent completeness and cross-validation when combined with workflow- and actor-based methods.

3. Some use case methods revolve around narrative stories, providing high context but low rigor; at the other extreme are methods using complex diagramming, providing low context but high rigor. Our method uses a tabular format that strikes a middle ground and provides both good context and good rigor.

4. We clearly distinguish between *use cases*, which provide a generalized description including alternate and exception situations, and *use case scenarios*, which are "test cases" that explore a specific "worked example" and add context and uncover requirements. Many professionals have independently arrived at the same distinction, although terminology in the field is far from consistent.

5. We have templates to guide the progression of use cases and services through scope, concept, and detail levels, and these fit well with the same progression for workflow and data models.

Related to that last point, we've found that development teams using Agile methods such as XP (Extreme Programming) really like the defined phases because they can quickly develop concept level models, to "get everyone in the ballpark," and then switch to iterative development to drive out further requirements. Other teams like the well-defined detail-level templates, which support different needs such as outsourced or offshore development.

Is This All New?

Most of the techniques we're describing here we developed independently, but we're certainly not saying that everything you read here is our invention. We borrowed bits and pieces from other practitioners, and there are some ideas that we have taken directly from Alistair Cockburn's work. For instance, the development of a use case "brief" (an illustrative story) and specifically looking for stakeholder interests that must be protected are two techniques we learned from Cockburn's book, and they solved real problems we had encountered. Other techniques we have deduced from negative examples, with some of the use case templates that are freely available on the Internet being a good (or bad, depending on how you interpret it) example. They are so complex, with so many different items to be documented, that in company after company we see analysts struggling to figure out what goes where, or what the difference is between items like "triggering event" and "initiating step." Our templates stress simplicity.

A final cautionary note: Whenever a technique becomes widely known, someone will try to take it too far, and use cases are no exception. A notable example—they have been proposed as the core technique of a process reengineering methodology in which a process is viewed as a use case—a *very large* use case—that is progressively decomposed until individual use cases are arrived at. This approach simply hasn't taken off, so if you're considering it, don't bother. Process framing and swimlane diagramming are better for dealing with complete business processes, just as use cases are better for determining how actors and systems will interact to complete their steps in the process.

Where to Now?

Now, we will get into the specifics and the methodology. The remainder of this chapter will do the following:

- It will introduce the terminology, concepts, and guidelines for business services. Emphasis is given to the relationship between business events and services, and how to ensure your business services are at the right granularity—neither too large nor too small.
- It will introduce the terminology, concepts, and structure of use cases and use case scenarios.
- With this foundation, we will close out the chapter by working through a successful, seven-step method for applying use cases and service specifications, along with workflow models and data models, in determining system requirements at progressive levels of detail.

Business Services in General

Services and Events—A Point of Confusion

"Services" have become "the next big thing" in recent years, with plenty of press devoted to SOA and Web services. These discussions remind us in some ways of those about process. We made the point early in the book that "process" means very different things to different people, from very large business areas down to very specific procedures. So it is with services. These can be very large and all encompassing, down to the trivial—one of our friends jokes about the "add two numbers" service he encountered. Just as we did with *business* processes, we'll need to develop clear guidelines for the granularity of *business* services.

Business Services and Business Events

Business services go hand-in-hand with business events, to the point that it's hard to tell them apart. The service Place Order is a response to the event "order is placed." Or, you could say that the event "order is placed" hasn't happened until the service Place Order has completed. In fact, it could be either. A baby is born (the event) and the service Register Birth records the event in the hospital system. Event precedes service in that case. Elsewhere in the hospital, someone wants to reserve an interview room, but the event "room is reserved" hasn't actually happened until the service Reserve Room has completed. Service precedes event in that case. The point is that events and services are so tightly related that many requirements modelers treat them as interchangeable. Besides, we find that the business people whose business we're trying to support don't worry about which came first—the service or the event. Essentially, something happened and the service updates the system to record it, or we want something to happen, and the service makes it so. What is important is that it is easy for business people to quickly and easily produce a fairly complete list of business events because it is the events that define so much of their working life.

What Is an Event?

In the context of information systems, an event is an occurrence outside of the system's control for which a "planned response"—a system function—is necessary, such as "section is scheduled," "section enrollment is completed," or "section is canceled." These are not interface events or individual interactions like "mouse is clicked" or "pick list item is selected," but events that have business significance. They require a *logically complete response*, a concept we'll clarify shortly. The event "order is placed" requires a logically complete response (the service Place Order) that accepts the order details, validates it, and records all of the pertinent facts.

A few events, like "order is placed," are especially important because they are the triggering event that initiates an entire business process, but we're considering *any* event (mainstream or exception) that happens *during* the course of a business process. We're not talking about every conceivable event, though—just those that will occur often enough and/or are important enough that they fall within the scope of the system.

The complete "planned response" provided by the system comprises user interface mechanisms (described in use cases) to get the necessary information about the event from an actor and convey the event to the system, and business logic (described in service specifications) to validate and process the event as well as to control database updates that record the outcome of the event. There is a service for every event, and, as we've said, the ideas are more or less interchangeable. Most services have an associated use case, but not those that are invoked by a batch system, a BPMS, or some other automated facility. There are some subtleties, such as cases when the same service can be triggered by two or more different events (e.g., by time or by a condition), but those are beyond the scope of this introduction.

Types of Events

There are three main types of events—action, temporal, and conditional.

1. *Action events* occur when an actor takes an action or makes a decision that the information system must have a designed response for—"section is scheduled," "section enrollment is completed," "section enrollment is dropped," "final grade is posted," "transcript is requested," and so on. Note that the object of the event is usually an entity or fact from the data model, a pattern we've seen before during process discovery. Also note the "noun is verbed" naming format, which you will recall adds useful rigor—it must describe a discrete, countable result. Some analysts separately consider internal and external events, depending on whether or not the actor triggering the event works within the organization responsible for the process. This is a less useful distinction now that processes frequently span multiple organizations, but if you think it will help focus attention, use it.

2. *Temporal events* occur when a predetermined time arrives that the information system must have a designed response for. These are prescheduled events such as time to produce account statements, time to publish semester results, time to produce payroll, time to submit government financial statements, and so on.

3. *Conditional events* require a monitoring activity to constantly scan for some condition that must be responded to. A security system will monitor for events such as a door being opened or a smoke alarm being triggered.

One or more descriptive data items always accompany action events. The event "section enrollment is dropped" must have an associated Student Number and Section Identifier. Stripped to its essence, a user interface is a means of capturing these data items and signaling the event to the system by invoking the correct service and passing it a message containing the necessary data items.

A temporal event, on the other hand, does not introduce any new data items, and so it doesn't have an associated use case. It is essentially like an alarm going off, and any required parameters are already somewhere in the database, although there may have been an event and use case to initially set them. Temporal events are typically handled by the services that run in the background or are part of the batch-processing schedule. The business services they require are important for complete requirements definition but aren't of interest in use case identification.

Conditional events have associated data (e.g., the event "door alarm is triggered" must have an associated door identifier and probably a date and time). This might require a use case if a human operator reports the condition, but even when the monitoring process is fully automated, you could still choose to document the event reporting as a use case. Many use cases describe the dialogue between systems rather than between a human actor and a system. For instance, establishing a dial-up Internet connection involves a dialogue between your computer and the service provider's computer during which protocols, line speed, and authentication are established.

Again—What, Not Who or How

Variations of "who, how, and why" are avoided when identifying events. This stands to reason, given the correspondence between events and services, and the service being focused on "what" and ignoring "who and how." This keeps the number of events manageable and encourages focus on the essential functions that must be provided. For instance, for "section enrollment is completed" we don't indicate whether the request came from the student or on their behalf from the departmental advisor ("who"). Similarly, the request may have been transmitted via the Internet, through telephony (an IVR interface) or using the university's registration system ("how"). "Section is cancelled" may have happened because enrollment was too low, facilities were unavailable, or the budget was cut ("why"). One of the associated data items might be a cancellation reason, but we don't recognize a separate event for each reason. In all cases, what is important is the essence of "what" happened, not the particulars.

Services—Granularity

We defined an event as an occurrence outside the system's control for which a "logically complete response"—a service—is required. A service, in a somewhat circular definition, is a "logically complete unit of work" that a system provides in response to an event. Building on what we know about events, we'll clarify this business of being "logically complete."

In the student registration environment, three services (following the usual "verb-noun" naming format) are as follows:

- Complete Enrollment;
- Drop Enrollment;
- Transfer Enrollment.

Note that each is a response to a discrete event—enrollment is completed, enrollment is dropped, and enrollment is transferred. Think about how you would expect the system to properly and completely respond to each of these events. For Complete Enrollment, you'd expect the system to ensure the Student had the prerequisites, check for available space in the Section, create an Enrollment record attaching the Student to that specific Section, lower the number of Available Spaces in the Section, and update the Student's Account Due. This description of the "expected actions" is the essence of the service specification.

Now, consider what would happen if the service was "subatomic," only going as far as creating the Enrollment record, but not updating the number of Available Spaces or the Student's Account. The system's databases wouldn't be in a state of integrity—the number of Available Spaces in the Section would be out of sync with the number of Enrollment records attached to the Section, and the Account Due would be inaccurate. In other words, the system wouldn't reflect the business' expected handling of the event, because the *indivisible was divided*. We would be dealing with *less* than a logically complete unit of work. Our responsibility as analysts is to ensure that the complete, indivisible set of expected actions is documented. Architects and designers may later implement it differently, but that's not our concern.

Once these actions are programmed into a service, IT facilities such as transaction processing (TP) monitors or application servers provide a variety of implementation capabilities, one of which is ensuring that services (or transactions, if you prefer) are *all or nothing*. This means that if a service successfully completes, *all* of the database updates are *committed*, meaning they become permanent. On the other hand, if the service fails part way through, for any reason, all of the database updates to that point are *backed out* and *nothing* is changed, as if the service never even started. It's one or the other—all or nothing. Service or business service is the current term, but the same concept was formerly known as a transaction, hence the importance of transaction processing capabilities.

Other lessons are provided by Transfer Enrollment, which responds to the event "enrollment is transferred" by ending one Enrollment in a Section and creating a new Enrollment in a different Section. You might think you could handle this by simply having the appropriate actor invoke two services—first Drop Enrollment and then Complete Enrollment—but that would eventually cause problems. For instance, if the actor completed the Drop Enrollment service and then went for coffee, the "from" and "to" Sections might both get filled by other Students before the Complete Enrollment service happened. Now the Student is in neither Section, they're in limbo, which certainly wasn't the intended result of the transfer event. The rule is that for each discrete event, there must be a single, discrete service.

Another way of looking at this example is that services are complete *business* operations, not single *database* create, update, or delete operations, and they must implement the business' complete, expected response to an event. Separately, it's highly likely that your application and data architects will define and create data services that provide a single way of achieving those data operations.

A Few More Guidelines

- Each service does exactly one type of thing. It's tempting to create multipurpose services that can handle a number of related events (enroll, transfer, drop, and so on), but the imagined efficiency of combining multiple services into one doesn't materialize because of the extra effort decoding different message formats, deciding what to do, handling different security requirements, and so on. Besides, "small is beautiful."

- All editing that takes place at the user interface is redone—the service trusts no one. It has to be assumed that in some cases, the message will come from a primitive character-based user interface, with little or no editing at the front end, or even from software that is *spoofing*—trying to masquerade the true source of the message. Normally, we expect the UI to do some validation so it can "hand hold" the user to correction.

- The service could be newly coded, or it could be a legacy application function "wrapped" and made available through a message-based interface, or it might be a "composite service" constructed out of existing functions (legacy, custom, packaged) using some integration technology. Be sure to check with your IT staff on the availability of tools and techniques like these—you might be able to make more use of your existing applications than you thought.

Want More?

There's much more to learn about services—the ACID test (atomic, consistent, isolated, durable), two-phase commits, reusable data services, techniques for business rule specification, long-running transactions, and so on. If the topic really interests you, *Transaction Processing* [1] is the bible on this subject, but isn't for the casual reader. If you really need to understand the theory and the practice, though, this is the book for you.

Now we'll return to use cases, and put the services in context. You will find that understanding services, the "what" of the application, will make use cases, the "who and how," far easier to discover and describe.

Use Case Concepts

Use Cases in General

The notion of use cases is appealing in its simplicity—a unit of functionality offered by a system to an actor (a user)—but it requires clarification to avoid the common problems encountered. Referring back to the ATM example might help to put the following guidelines in context:

- It is a unit of system functionality that is logically complete, because it's based on a service, which is by definition a logically complete unit of work. That is, it has business significance on its own and delivers measurable value to the actor or to the process. In the context of taking an order, recording the customer's name is not a use case, it's only part of one. Take New Order, which includes identifying the customer, establishing delivery and payment terms, and recording the items being ordered, would be an example of a logically complete use case. The cornerstone of our method is to describe business services first, thereby establishing logically complete units of work, before the complications of actors and interactions arise.

- A use case will usually take place at a single place and time.

- Use cases most commonly describe the steps by which an actor interacts with a system via its interface. This is commonly a graphical user interface such as a Web browser, but they can illustrate any other type of interaction, such as the dialogues for an interactive voice response system or a keypad-based interface such as an ATM. They can also show communication between systems or devices.

- Use cases are usually defined actor by actor. Some of the use cases for the actor Student using a Student Registration System would include:
    - Student Views Semester Schedule;
    - Student Views Course Details;
    - Student Completes Enrollment;

- Student Transfers Enrollment;
- Student Drops Enrollment;
- Student Views Account;
- Student Submits Payment;
- Student Views Transcript.

- Generally speaking, a use case satisfies a specific query or information request, or it invokes a specific business service. Some methods separate these into two different classes of use cases.

- "Actor" has the same meaning that it does on a workflow process model—a person, job function, organization, system, or device playing a particular role. The vast majority of use cases involve human-to-device interaction, but it's certainly valid to describe use cases that have no human involvement, such as a central monitoring system being the actor that interrogates a device like a failing network printer.

- A use case will generally involve one actor, but could involve more (e.g., a Customer, Customer Service Rep, and Credit Specialist could all participate in the Order New Service use case). If you treat the system itself as an actor, a common practice, then two actors will typically be involved.

- There will often be different use cases for the same service delivered to different actors. For instance, student completes enrollment and departmental advisor completes enrollment would each behave differently and provide different capabilities. The latter might include student search capabilities and more direct data entry (versus pick-list selection) to accommodate the more experienced user. There can also be separate use cases for each technology platform, because the interaction can be so different.

- There is a strong correspondence between use cases and service level workflow models. A step at the service level indicates an actor providing a distinct service to the process, and a use case represents an actor using a system to obtain that service. This is the natural intersection point between process workflow modeling and requirements modeling, and it indicates why swimlane diagrams provide an ideal framework for discovering the important use cases.

- Multiple use cases will often be employed in a single session or *use case scenario*. After accessing the Student Registration System, a Student might use most of the use cases in the sample list. Similarly, use cases can be combined to extend basic capabilities. For instance, while carrying out Student Completes Enrollment, the use cases to View Semester Schedule or View Course Detail might be used.

Extensions and Scenarios

One inherent challenge is ensuring that each use case includes the functionality to handle not just the normal situation, but all of the errors, exceptions, and alternatives that will surely arise. That's why we develop use cases following, no surprise, a phased approach. First, the *initial use case description* establishes the basic concepts. Then, the first pass of the *final use case description* establishes the dialogue for the normal situation, and the second pass refines it by considering all the other things that can happen at each clause in the dialogue. These are the *extensions*. Even then, we might not be done, because we could choose to develop *use case scenarios*. Essentially, a use case scenario depicts the dialogue between an actor and a system for a *particular scenario* (like a test case) that:

- Has named actors;
- Uses actual data values;
- Illustrates a specific sequence of interactions, including normal steps, errors, exceptions, extensions, or whatever the scenario is intended to illuminate;
- Illustrates a single scenario. *This is a critical point!* There is no branching ("If actor does X, then...") because the scenario follows a single path. This manages complexity by ensuring focus on one case at time.

A use case scenario may cover multiple use cases, the classic example being a session at an ATM. This is a single use case scenario, but includes multiple use cases such as Customer Deposits Funds, ... Pays Bill, and ... Withdraws Cash as well as Customer Signs On, a use case fragment that can be reused in various contexts.

These are the critical aspects of use case *scenario* analysis that differentiate it from the more abstract or generalized use case analysis that is often employed. We say "abstract" because a use case is an abstraction of all of the ways an actor could use a particular unit of functionality. This isn't meant to be a criticism, because separately inspecting each significant function via its use case is a big improvement over the even *more* abstract or disconnected forms of requirements analysis that we used to rely on. However, developing a "perfect" use case description without context is difficult. The use of scenarios provides the context that helps potential users relate to the example and provide much better feedback on how the system ought to behave. Important use cases might require several use case scenarios to uncover all of the requirements.

Note that a system has a finite number of use cases, but an infinite number of use case scenarios. Another challenge, then, will lie in defining a set of scenarios that is large enough to elicit all (or at least the great majority) of the requirements but not so large as to be impractical. This is addressed in the upcoming "how to" section.

The Methodology

Seven Steps to Success

You could get started with use cases the same way we did—jump in and try it. However, the "just do it!" approach has its limitations, including moments of fear, uncertainty, and doubt, and the likelihood that you will dive too deep in some areas before establishing even the basics of others. To help you avoid these issues, we will describe our proven approach that organizes business service and use case development into a manageable seven steps. Note that in parentheses we have identified which of the three levels (scope, concept, detail) each step deals with:

1. Identify services (scope) and complete initial service specifications (concept);

2. Identify use cases (scope) and complete initial use case descriptions (concept);

3. Complete final service specifications (detail);

4. Begin final use case descriptions (first pass at detail);

5. Refine final use case descriptions (final pass at detail);

6. Identify and describe use case scenarios (conditions and outcomes);

7. Complete use case scenario descriptions (dialogues); refine use cases as necessary.

You might choose not to develop use case scenarios. Or, you might go even further by describing archetypical actors or "personas" that embody characteristics of various types of system users, to ensure each of these will be satisfied with the system's behavior. Excellent books that explore these methods are on the market.[4]

Using Facilitated Sessions

Like the other work we have described in this book, modeling services and use cases begins with facilitated sessions. Participants should include some of those involved in the design of the to-be process and *must* include experienced people who will use the resulting information systems. They have to be there, because nobody else knows as well as they do what will actually work in practice. We clearly recall this being proven during our first-ever session to develop use cases. A dialogue had been proposed that began with a telephone claims adjuster asking the claimant for their automobile insurance policy number and entering it to retrieve policy information. ("When adjuster enters policy number, then system displays policy coverage details and claim history.") The experienced adjusters in the room immediately pointed out that half of claimants didn't know their policy number, and the other half were probably too upset about the incident they were reporting to want to start there. The rest of the session proceeded the same way, with use case interactions continually being revised and refined by the people who would use the new system. That, after all, is the whole point of doing use cases—to discover what will *actually work* before a lot of work goes into writing requirements or (gasp!) developing the first version of the system.

Preparation, facilities, and supplies for these sessions will be pretty much as they were for the earlier process discovery and process modeling sessions. You will of course want to have workflow models available for the relevant processes, which also provides an initial roster of actors who will use the system. Along with this, you should have a conceptual data model, even if you don't tell people that is what it is. You can get by without one, and just use a list of the nouns or things you have worked with already, which are the major entities that would appear in the data model. However, drawing them as an entity-relationship diagram arranged according to dependency will be very helpful because:

---

4.   Cooper, Alan, *The Inmates Are Running the Asylum: Why High-Tech Products Drive Us Crazy and How to Restore the Sanity,* Indianapolis, IN: SAMS/Macmillan Computer Publishing, 1999; and Constantine, Larry L., and Lucy A. D. Lockwood, Software for Use: A Practical Guide to the Models and Methods of Usage-Centered Design, Reading, MA: ACM Press/Addison Wesley, 1999.

- People always understand the meaning of an entity more clearly when they can see how it relates to other entities.

- You will begin looking for services at the "bottom" of the model, with the most dependent entities.

- Any time a service creates or changes an entity, you will look at closely related entities (the nearby ones on the diagram) to determine if they are affected as well.

Now we can get into the first of the seven steps, identifying and describing business services, beginning with deciding what your initial approach will be. This step establishes the foundation for all the others, and so is more complex and requires more decisions on your part. Take heart—it gets easier after this first step.

Step 1: Identify Services (Scope) and Complete Initial Service Specifications (Concept)

Choose Your Primary Approach

Initial service discovery is a highly iterative activity that uses a variety of perspectives:

- *Workflow-based:* inspecting the to-be, service-level workflow model for steps requiring an automated service.

- *Actor-based:* considering each actor and asking what services they will require. This is essentially a use case–based approach, because the results will be in actor-service form, which are use cases but without reference to technology.

- *Event- or service-based:* identifying the events that will target each entity in the data model and identifying a service for each. If this seems too indirect, you could simply ask, "what system functions—what services—are needed?"

Given the range of possibilities, it is difficult to describe a single generalized approach, but that is all we have the space for in this chapter. We have chosen to describe an event-based approach, because that is our default in practice, and because it has proven to be the best way to introduce and get practice with the concepts and techniques. Once you have some experience with this approach, applying actor-based and workflow-based approaches will be much easier. Here are a few thoughts to help you decide what your primary approach will be. Remember, one will always be the primary or initial method, but the others should always be used for completeness and validation:

- A workflow-based approach is a good choice for large, cross-functional projects, especially if new processes and activities are involved. It ensures focus on the main services but is less likely on its own to pick up unusual, less frequent, or administrative services.

- An actor-based approach is indicated for small, departmental projects, especially if there are no major process changes contemplated. Essentially, for each actor, you are asking, "what do you want?" which is the traditional use case approach.

- The event- or service-based approach is our usual approach because it focuses on the essence of *what* is required, rather than *who* and *how,* which are the natural focus of actor- and workflow-based methods. This makes it a valuable cross-check with the other approaches. Because it doesn't start out constrained by known actors or workflow models, it is much more likely to be complete—subject matter experts will identify events (and, therefore, services), whether or not they appear on the workflow models or they think a particular actor needs that service. Better yet, the focus on one entity at a time ensures your subject matter experts will have no trouble identifying events, which are such a large part of their working life.

Brainstorm for Events or Services

At this point, we assume that you've settled on an event-based approach, initiated the session, and introduced the concepts of services and use cases to the participants. This doesn't have to be a long explanation, and shouldn't be. A simple example like the ATM will illustrate that the objective is to discover *what* the system must do (the services) and *how* various actors will interact with the system (the use cases) in order to obtain the services.

Focusing on one significant entity from the data model at a time, brainstorm for events targeting that entity. The initial brainstorm can begin with the question "what events happen to this entity?" You could just ask, "what verbs go with this noun?" and simply list them, but we encourage participants to use the "noun is verbed" form. Some groups just prefer the "verb-noun" form, effectively going straight to services, and will offer their suggestions in that form no matter what you suggest. If that is the case, don't worry about it. What is important is that you check after the brainstorm that each suggestion passes the "noun is verbed" test for discrete, identifiable, countable results. That way, when you inspect the suggestion Monitor Enrollment (which sounds plausible on the surface) you'll find that "enrollment is monitored" doesn't really tell us anything, and you have to push by asking, "what are you monitoring for?" In one case, this led to several new temporal and conditional events such as Time to Finalize Enrollment as well as rules that had to be enforced in other services.

Because some groups will be most comfortable working with events ("section is canceled") and others will use the service form (Cancel Section), we will treat them as interchangeable for the rest of this section on discovery and use both terms.

Surprisingly, identifying events and services works best if you begin with dependent entities *lower* in the entity-relationship diagram and work your way *up* to the independent entities at the top. For instance, consider Enrollment, then Section, then course. If you start with an entity at the top, there's a tendency to try to cover all of the events for its dependent entities at the same time.

Once you have completed the initial brainstorm, you can open it up by asking the group to think about their experience and identify any events or required services missed in the first pass. Suggesting that they consider temporal and conditional events will uncover more, as will considering "query" or "display" events.

An alternative approach is start with an open brainstorm on events and then move into the more structured brainstorm by entity. The advantage of this is that it will indicate which events are most common or most important and might also uncover outliers that would be missed otherwise. If a group strikes us as being inclined to drift quickly into the unusual instead of focusing on the core, we start with the structured entity-by-entity brainstorm. Brainstorming by entity, or at least within a topical area on the data model, provides valuable focus. If a group seems to need a push to think in a more free-form manner, we start with an open brainstorm.

Refine the List of Events or Services

The brainstormed list will always require some cleanup. Some of the suggested events might be eliminated (with caution!) because they are beyond the expected scope of the system or are just too unusual to warrant effort. Others will have to be made more "essential" by removing references to who, how, and why.

Many suggested events will be synonymous or target the wrong entity, and these require a level of care in spotting them and resolving them. Synonymous events, such as "enrollment is completed" and "enrollment is made," must be dealt with because you don't want to start describing services for each only to discover there is really only one. They will be resolved by selecting the one with the best name or creating a new one with a clearer name. Just be sure to have a short discussion to ensure they really are the same event. Events targeting the wrong entity are more subtle, but the data model can help you spot these. For example, it's likely that participants will know that Students want to register in Sections and Drop Sections they have registered in, so the events "section is registered (or registered in)" and "section is dropped" will be suggested. However, the data model shows that students "get at" the Section via the Enrollment, so more appropriate events would be "enrollment is completed" and "enrollment is dropped." This might seem like hair-splitting, but when you specify validation, rules, and updates performed by the service, it is critical you are focused on the correct entities. Note that some events establish a relationship among entities, which will be reflected in names that include two or even more nouns in the form "noun is verbed (connector) noun." An example is "instructor is assigned to section."

Temporal events that don't require any action on the part of an actor, such as "time to open section for enrollment" won't require a use case, but do need to have a service defined and are part of your overall requirements specification. Conditional events are the same but require a special note of caution, illustrated by the example "waitlisted enrollment exceeds target." Conditional events often prove *not* to be a separate event but instead are an action within the service for some other event. In this case, whenever an enrollment is completed in "waitlisted" status, the Complete Enrollment service should check to see if the new total number of waitlisted enrollments now exceeds some target and then place a notification message or alert somewhere. (The "alert" might turn out to be another entity in the data model, related to the appropriate faculty member, depending on how the business intends to handle situations like that.) Dealing with that alert will probably be a separate event (and service) but detecting the condition isn't—it is part of another service.

A useful validation technique is to put the events into a normal or typical sequence—the *entity life cycle*—which makes missing events more obvious. You will be checking that the complete "birth to death" cycle of events or a phase within the overall cycle for some important thing has been described. Not all of these will end up within your scope, but it is better to identify them now and determine they are out than to miss them now and have them pop up later. For instance, once you have the events "enrollment is completed" and "enrollment final grade is posted," you might see that between these two are the events "enrollment midterm grade is posted," and "enrollment assignment grade is posted." (These might all get generalized into one event, "enrollment grade is posted," but at least you've discovered the possible flavors of the event.) Next, look for the exception events, such as "wait-listed enrollment is confirmed," "enrollment is dropped," or "enrollment is transferred."

Having refined the list of events or services, you can search for others by using the other two approaches as a cross-check. In this case, that means looking for events by taking a quick pass through the workflow-based and actor-based approaches.

Finalize the Scope-Level List of Services

For each event, you can now name the corresponding service. For the three events "enrollment is completed," "enrollment is dropped," and "enrollment is transferred," you will name the three services Complete Enrollment, Drop Enrollment, and Transfer Enrollment. If you chose to bypass events and go directly to service identification, you already have a list in this form. We always organize this list into three parts, services triggered by action events, temporal events, and conditional events, and, within each, by the object (the entity) of the service. Each will require somewhat different handling:

- Action event services will need to have use cases defined for the actor who raises or handles the action.

- Temporal event services will require that the time-based trigger is clearly defined so your application architects can decide how best to handle these. You will also need an administrative use case to "set the alarm" for the temporal event, unless it is absolutely fixed;

- Conditional event services also require that the condition be clearly defined. Again, we stress that these often prove not to be *separate* services, but rules that must be enforced as part of some *other* service.

It's worth noting that simply listing all of the events (or services) has tremendous value because it defines the scope of a system and clarifies expectations before further work is undertaken. In one memorable case, we were called on to "unstick" a stuck project, and a large facilitated session was organized to discover and resolve the problem. We had four breakout groups each build a list of the services they expected the new system to provide. They were time-boxed to 20 minutes, and then had to report out when the session reconvened. The result was "shock and awe" at how wildly different the expectations were. Even more value emerged when we identified the use cases by adding actors to the services, thereby highlighting major differences of opinion about "who will use this to do what?" This gave the team something concrete with which to clarify scope and organize the work into phases. It was also a bit of a shock for management from the business to see—clearly, unambiguously, and inarguably—the required amount of work for a project they had thought "couldn't be that difficult."

Describe Business Services

Good news! After all the decisions and work that went into discovering your initial list of services, things get much easier. This is a theme that has been repeated throughout the book—upfront effort in scoping and building frameworks always saves time later on.

The initial service specification includes simply the service name and result, just like a business proccss, and the main expected actions. The result should be in "business-speak" so your subject matter experts can confirm it, but it must also exclusively use terms from the data model, or your list of agreed nouns. You and the client initially might write "creates a registration in a class" in order to get something done quickly but this must soon be changed to "Creates an Enrollment in a Section." Similarly, each of the actions must make sense to the business, but use terms from the data model. Figure 15.3 provides an example.

A critical point: the purpose of this initial specification is to ensure that you and the client are "in the ballpark" or "on the same page," not to exhaustively enumerate all the actions and rules. We aim for (once again) 5 ± 2 actions, covering the "happy path" and the very most common exceptions. If you include more than that, your subject matter experts will focus on the details, questioning what you have and adding more, bypassing the question "is this a legitimate service?" The objective at this point is to verify the scope or granularity of the service, and you do not want to invest a lot of time in more thorough documentation only to discover that the service is too small or too large.

	Component	Description
1	Name	Complete Enrollment
2	Result	Enrolls a qualified Student in a single Section by creating an Enrollment record
3	Action	• Validate Student status and prerequisites • Confirm space in Section • Create Enrollment, link to Student and Section • Generate confirmation number • Revise remaining space in Section

Figure 15.3   Format for the initial service specification.

Confirm Business Services

Walk through each service specification with the experts, and first ask, "Would you ever do *less* than this and still consider that a useful service had been provided?" If so, the service is too large and needs to be split into smaller services, each providing a discrete, essential result that is of value to the business.

Next, ask, "Would you ever do *as little* as this and consider that a useful service had been provided?" If not, the service is too small, and needs to be combined with other potential services in order to provide a valuable, indivisible result.

At this point, you might choose to follow a different sequence than the one we have outlined here. You and the participants are focused on business services, so you might decide to stay on this topic and capture some of the final service specifications. There's no harm in this, and we often do it this way, but bear in mind that service specifications can't be considered finalized until you've done substantial use case work to validate them.

Here, we will proceed into identifying and describing use cases, because that often uncovers additional services.

Step 2: Identify Use Cases (Scope) and Complete Initial Use Case Descriptions (Concept)

Discover Use Cases

You will be pleasantly surprised at how simple this is, now that you have identified the required services and have workflow models and a roster of actors to aid in the process. The essence of what we are going to do now is as follows:

1. Consider one service at a time, assigning actors to services, yielding use cases.
2. Consider each actor, one at a time, asking, "what else does this actor need to do?"
3. Walk through the to-be workflow model, looking for additional use cases.

You also might have already completed step 3 as part of characterizing the to-be process. In that case, this is an exercise in validation and uncovering the outliers that didn't show up on the workflow models.

Of course, you might choose a different sequence based on the nature of your project. Or, as was the case with discovering services, you could begin with an open brainstorm and then shift to the three structured approaches. The open brainstorm can uncover the unusual situations (departmental advisor calls in sick), while the structured approaches ensure completeness by overlaying a framework on the subject area and then considering one perspective at a time. We used to advise, "start wide open, then use structured," but now find that starting with the structured approach is faster and less frustrating because it avoids trips into the wild blue yonder. One thing that remains the same is that the best results are obtained when multiple approaches are used to identify the required use cases.

Service-Based Discovery

We begin by posting the list of services that are triggered by action events—the services that require a use case. We will also post a list of actors, and a list of UI platforms if there are more than one. Sometimes the UI platform is specific to particular actors—the Internet and touch-screen kiosks might be primarily for use by students, and the registration management system (RMS) might be specifically for department advisors and other staff or faculty.

One service at a time, identify which actors require that service, optionally specifying which platform. For a single service such as Complete Enrollment, this could yield three use cases:

- Student Completes Enrollment via the Internet.
- Student Completes Enrollment via Kiosk.
- Advisor Completes Enrollment via RMS.

There will always be use cases that can be employed by multiple actors, so we usually identify whom the use case is primarily for, and, if it isn't too onerous, list the other actors who would access the same service via the same platform. (Use the same use case, in other words.) If there isn't a clear, primary actor for a given use case, you might have to create a "role" such as "enroller" and then list the individual actors who can take on this role. We avoid this approach unless it is absolutely necessary, because it quickly gets unwieldy and the use cases begin to lose context. Books on use cases can provide further guidance on this and the many other situations we haven't got room to cover here.

Actor-Based Discovery

The next approach is to look at the needs of each actor in turn. Focusing on the actors is the essence of the use case approach, and it will seem ironic that we didn't begin with an actor-focused approach. However, we will be helped tremendously in ensuring that we meet the needs of each actor by the work that has already been done—most of the core use cases have already been identified by matching actors to services and your earlier work characterizing the to-be process and modeling the to-be workflow. In preparation for considering each actor's needs, it is helpful to develop a "use cases by actor" list comprising the use cases that have already been identified. Then, you will extend it by asking four questions for each actor:

1. What other "normal" system functions will they require? Do the have regular job responsibilities that have so far been missed?
2. What error and exception situations will arise that require other capabilities?
3. What maintenance functions, such as updating scheduled events, code tables, or user accounts, will be needed?
4. What other supporting or recurring functions, such as help or search capabilities, will be needed?

As usual, some ideas may have to be consolidated or eliminated.

Workflow-Based Discovery

If you haven't done this earlier, now is the time to walk through the workflow model, possibly one actor at a time, looking for additional use cases. You might also annotate a version of the to-be workflow model to relate use cases to workflow steps, as this can be helpful later on during training and rollout.

Finally, check that all of the action-triggered services are covered by a use case. If not, decide which actor(s) will own the service and add it to that actor's list of use cases. Similarly, ensure that someone has use cases for setting the time for temporal events and for dealing with any conditional events that require human intervention.

The list of use cases you have produced is a valuable tool for unambiguously explaining the scope of the undertaking.

Describe the Use Cases

As with the initial service description, the goal of the initial use case description is to ensure that everyone is in agreement on the basics before undertaking detailed use case dialogues. We learned this the hard way on a project during which a couple of technically oriented analysts went off and completed several very detailed, and very inappropriate, use cases. They had completely missed the point about the user's expectations and capabilities, leaving us in the uncomfortable position of having to say "Sorry, but we have to scrap these and start over." We promptly adopted Alistair Cockburn's suggestion that a use case brief (or abstract) and stakeholder interests be documented and confirmed before further work is undertaken.

Figure 15.4 illustrates a possible format for the initial use case description. We keep it simple and focus on three essential elements—the name, a brief description, and the stakeholder interests. Some practitioners include much more, even in a basic description, and some of those additional components are illustrated in items 6 through 9 of Figure 15.4.

Keep in mind that detailed or not, your initial use case descriptions will be an approximation and will need refinement after you have developed use cases and use case scenarios. You might wonder why you should go back and refine the *initial* description after you have completed the *final* description. Hasn't it already served its purpose? It may have, but many organizations find that it's useful to maintain these brief descriptions as part of a catalogue of available functionality and even as part of an online help system. Now, we will provide some guidelines on the components of the initial description.

Use Case Name

The name is documented in actor-service-technology form, with the technology component optional. Sometimes the format will break the name down into these three discrete components to make it easier to sort or search the use cases.

Abstract or Brief

The idea of the use case *abstract* or *brief* is to create a mental image of the actor working through a use case to ensure everyone has a similar understanding. A

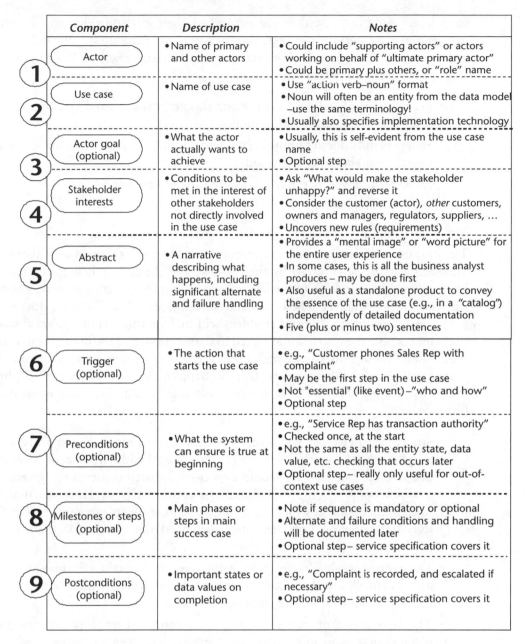

	Component	Description	Notes
1	Actor	• Name of primary and other actors	• Could include "supporting actors" or actors working on behalf of "ultimate primary actor" • Could be primary plus others, or "role" name
2	Use case	• Name of use case	• Use "action verb–noun" format • Noun will often be an entity from the data model – use the same terminology! • Usually also specifies implementation technology
3	Actor goal (optional)	• What the actor actually wants to achieve	• Usually, this is self-evident from the use case name • Optional step
4	Stakeholder interests	• Conditions to be met in the interest of other stakeholders not directly involved in the use case	• Ask "What would make the stakeholder unhappy?" and reverse it • Consider the customer (actor), *other* customers, owners and managers, regulators, suppliers, … • Uncovers new rules (requirements)
5	Abstract	• A narrative describing what happens, including significant alternate and failure handling	• Provides a "mental image" or "word picture" for the entire user experience • In some cases, this is all the business analyst produces – may be done first • Also useful as a standalone product to convey the essence of the use case (e.g., in a "catalog") independently of detailed documentation • Five (plus or minus two) sentences
6	Trigger (optional)	• The action that starts the use case	• e.g., "Customer phones Sales Rep with complaint" • May be the first step in the use case • Not "essential" (like event) –"who and how" • Optional step
7	Preconditions (optional)	• What the system can ensure is true at beginning	• e.g., "Service Rep has transaction authority" • Checked once, at the start • Not the same as all the entity state, data value, etc. checking that occurs later • Optional step – really only useful for out-of-context use cases
8	Milestones or steps (optional)	• Main phases or steps in main success case	• Note if sequence is mandatory or optional • Alternate and failure conditions and handling will be documented later • Optional step – service specification covers it
9	Postconditions (optional)	• Important states or data values on completion	• e.g., "Complaint is recorded, and escalated if necessary" • Optional step – service specification covers it

Figure 15.4   Format for the initial use case description, including optional components.

workshop participant referred to this as a "cognitive walkthrough," which is an apt description. Rather than a highly generalized description, we find that something closer to a specific scenario yields better results. We have the group identify a typical case that incorporates some interesting but plausible wrinkles that will get people thinking about how the use case should unfold. For the use case Student Completes Enrollment via Kiosk, the brief might begin "Sam Student is a first year student, unfamiliar with school practices, who comes in out of a rainstorm with headphones blaring and an overweight backpack and approaches the kiosk." We ask the group to "close your eyes, visualize the actor and their environment, and everything involved in getting to the use case, and then working through it." We collect ideas, and then write them up as a short vignette that has (surprise!) 5 ± 2 sentences. This example might yield ideas such as:

- Because of the headphones, the kiosk should provide visual as well as auditory feedback, and possibly other modes.
- Sam probably doesn't know his student number, so another means of identifying the user should be provided.
- A shelf for gloves, hat, pack, and so on would be helpful.

Stakeholder Interests

The purpose of the stakeholder interests is to uncover rules that would otherwise be missed, but must be enforced by the use case and the service being accessed. First identify who else (other than the actor) cares about the progress or outcome of the use case being studied. These are the stakeholders. For instance, for Student Completes Enrollment, the stakeholders will include other students waitlisted for the same section, the instructor assigned to that section, and the department offering that course and section. Cockburn's trick, brilliant in its simplicity, is to ask, "what would make each of these stakeholders unhappy?" When the question is phrased that way, people seem to have no problem identifying rules and interests. For instance:

- Students want to ensure that other students can't jump the queue and complete enrollment in a section for which they are already waitlisted. This might uncover the rule that we would expect—waitlisted students are given newly available spots on a first-waitlisted, first-confirmed basis. However, that could open a discussion at which we find that some students are given higher priority, depending on how urgently they need the course for their pending graduation.
- The instructor will obviously not want more students than the maximum to be able to enroll, but there could be other, more esoteric, rules, such as a minimum allowable GPA for enrolling students.
- The department, of course, will want to ensure that students have the prerequisite courses and might also want preference given to students who have declared their major in that department.

Important rules can be reflected in the use case brief or in the milestones if you choose to complete that section. Others will be noted for inclusion as rules in the final service specification and possibly as conditions for the dialogue to reflect, possibly as extensions.

Milestones

Of the optional components of the initial description, this is the one we do most often. You will list the milestones or main steps within the use case, but not each individual interaction in the dialogue. For enrolling a Student in a Section, the milestones might be simply Student is identified, Course is selected, Course Prerequisites are verified, Section is selected, and Enrollment is confirmed. Consider and note any mandatory sequence. For example, could a Section be selected and checked for available space before the Student is identified? This can have a significant impact—for instance, some retail sites on the Internet support browsing through flexible dialogues that allow customers to fill up electronic shopping carts before identifying themselves.

For a use case that serves multiple actors, this is a good time to check if it should be the same for each actor. If so, leave the use case as is, but if there is real doubt, create multiple use cases. They can be consolidated later if the details prove to be the same, but unless you separate them, unique details are unlikely to emerge

Remember, all of this might be revised after you complete use case dialogues for the normal and extension cases, and complete one or more use case scenarios.

Step 3: Complete Final Service Specifications (Detail)

As the specifications get more detailed, it takes fewer words to explain them, because the components are more granular and self-explanatory. The final service specification adds input and output message formats, and expands on the expected actions using this framework:

- Validation—these are the business rules that are enforced before the service can begin its core functions, further divided into:
  - Entity existence: which entities must already exist? For instance, there must be a record for the Student that is enrolling in a Section, and the Section must exist.
  - Entity state: what is the allowable status (or states) of the involved entities? For instance, the Student must be "active" and the Section must be "open."
  - Attribute or relationship values: what data values must be checked? For instance, the Student's GPA must be equal or higher to the minimum GPA for the Section.
- Functions—these are the core operations, methods, calculations, and so on that comprise the heart of the service, which often take the form of more business rules (e.g., for a successful Enrollment, reflect the appropriate fee in the Student's Account).
- Updates—the entities are created, updated, or deleted (e.g., an Enrollment record is created, linked to the Student and the Section, with Status set to either "active" or to "waitlisted" if the Section is currently full and the user indicated they would like to be waitlisted).

The input message is the minimum list of attributes that the UI must provide in order to invoke the service. Remember, for the most part all that this will require is record identifiers and new data from the user. A common mistake is to specify all of the attributes the service will need, but remember, most of these will be retrieved from stored data. To complete an Enrollment, all that has to be passed to the service is Student Number, Course Code, Section number, and optionally a waitlist indicator. Similarly, the output message is the minimum list of attributes that the service must send back to the UI, typically some sort of Result Code and any other confirmation information.

Figure 15.5 illustrates the basic format we use, and provide additional tips.

You could say that the documentation follows the universal "input-process-output" framework for documenting system processes:

Component	Description	Example	Tips
① Name	• Action verb-noun	Transfer enrollment	• *Avoid "mushy" verbs*
② Expected Result	• A statement of how the "state of the world" has changed on successful completion	An Enrollment in one Section of a Course is ended, and a new Enrollment in a different Section of the *same* Course is established	• *Precisely describe the result both in business terms and with respect to the data model*
③ Input Message ⟹❘	• The minimal list of attributes necessary to initiate the service	Student Number, From Section Number, To Section Number	• *Different message formats imply different services*

④ Validation	• The rules that determine whether the service can proceed
	• Read stored data and check:
	  - entity existence
	  - entity states
	  - specific values
		The Enrollment record for the Student in the "from" Section must exist ("existence") and currently be in "active" state ("active") and the available spaces in the "to" Section >= 1 ("value")	• *Check the other entities "in the neighborhood"*
			• *Almost all important entities will have a "state" attribute*

⑤ Functions $X+Y = Z$	• Implements calculations, algorithms, rules e.g., limits, totals, taxes, charges, etc.	If the transfer request is AFTER the class start date, APPLY transfer penalty	• *Be careful with time and date ranges, checking for conditions such as contiguous ranges, or gaps or overlaps.*
⑥ Data Updates	• All of the creates, updates and deletes made to the entities	Set the old enrollment record to the status "ended" AND create new enrollment record with the status of "active"	• *More common to change the status of a record and date stamp it than to delete it*
⑦ Output Message ⟸❘	• The list of attributes sent back to the user interface	Result Code, Confirmation Number	• *The minimum output message is usually a result/ status code*

Figure 15.5 Formats for final service description.

- Input—message from the UI, plus validation and reference data retrieved from databases;
- Process—the expected actions and rules;
- Output—message back to the UI, plus updates to the databases.

Figure 15.6 provides an example of a final business service description—it's not rigorous, but it illustrates the intent.

After this, you can get into complete, excruciating detail such as attribute-level validation and setting, algorithm details, error and exception handling, and handling complex transactions. Documenting the detailed logic might require other techniques, such as state-transition diagrams, flowcharts, decision trees, truth tables, and pseudocode. How fully you document services before turning them over for development depends on the environment in your organization and how involved the designers and programmers are in the analysis.

Service Name
Transfer Enrollment
Result (Description)
A Student's Enrollment in one Section of a Course is ended, and a new Enrollment in a different Section of the same Course is established
Input Message
Student Number, From Section ID, To Section ID
Output Message
Result Code, Confirmation Number
Actions—Validation
• Student must be in "registered" state • "from" Section must be in "filled" or "available" state • "from" Section Enrollment must be in "active" state • "to" Section must be in "available" state • "to" Section Enrollment must not exist • Transaction date must be on or before Semester last drop date
Actions—Operations and calculations
• If start date has passed, calculate transfer fee and new student account balance • Calculate new enrollment count for "from" Section, and set state to "available" if it was "filled" before • Calculate new enrollment count for "to" Section, and set state to "filled" if enrollment count is at maximum • Set Result Code • Set Confirmation Number (as per rules in data model) • Etc.
Actions—Updates
• Set "from" Section Enrollment to "ended" state, and set state change date • Create "to" Section Enrollment in "active" status • Update "from" Section as determined • Update "to" Section as determined • Update Student Account balance due.
Notes
• Investigate need to provide transfer fee exemption number • Investigate need to provide late transfer approval number

Figure 15.6 A final business service description.

Step 4: Begin Final Use Case Descriptions (First Pass at Detail)

Create Use Case Dialogues

The first pass of the final use case descriptions focuses entirely on the dialogue between actor and system for the normal, successful case. Start with a review of the initial description. Keep it low tech, using flipcharts and/or handouts—using a projector can be distracting at this point, and the facilitator will use the flipcharts later to keep the group on track. Having the conceptual data model available at this point helps, because the relationships and dependency among the entities often constrain the path the dialogue can follow. If you listed the main steps while completing the initial description, have that posted as well.

Next, have the group identify the first step in the use case, which the facilitator writes up, such as the following:

- "When client telephones the service center";
- "When customer insets bank card into ATM";
- "When student accesses the university's URL."

Have the group complete the first clause, for instance:

- "Then IVR system routes call to next available service rep."
- "Then ATM prompts for password."
- "Then system displays the university home page including a student sign-on box."

From that point on, simply work through the rest of the dialogue, letting the actors in the session define how they would like the dialogue to progress. You will refer to the use case description and data model as guides, so the dialogue might later have to change, but it's best to let the participants first describe how they *want* it to progress, because you will uncover new requirements. If you find yourself regularly saying, "sorry, it can't work that way" you might be correct, but you might also be stifling the session. *Always* use the form "when action then response." For instance:

- When Advisor enters Student Number and selects Enroll Student, then system verifies Student and Account status and displays basic Student data.
- When Advisor selects Semester/Session they are enrolling for, then system verifies that Semester/Session is available.
- When Advisor selects Course Code (e.g., "math") for next Course to enroll in, then system returns list of all Courses for that Course Code available in selected Semester/Session that Student has prerequisites for, with a list of available Sections.
- When advisor selects Section... and so on.

Eventually, the clauses will be numbered to make it easier to describe extensions during the second pass of the final use case description, but we don't do that until it has stabilized.

Each "when-then" clause extends from an action by an actor through to control returning to that actor. After we first read about this form (on a Web site maintained by students at Eindhoven University in the Netherlands) and began using it, we were surprised at how much more useful the use cases became. "When-then" forces explicit dialogues that drive out ambiguity about use case behavior. This is because every action is essentially a decision point—did the actor provide the right information for the system to proceed, and did the system provide the right information and guidance for the actor to proceed? For instance, if the actor is choosing which account to withdraw cash from, then the system must have provided the ability to make this choice by displaying the options. It's surprising how many important points like this can be missed, so "when-then" helps the facilitator ensure the group considers the following:

- For each actor's part of the clause:
  - Do they have the right information to proceed?
  - What choices will they make, and what information will they provide?
- For each system part of the clause:

  - What data (in general) will it access/store, and what rules or validations will it perform? Check the conceptual data model—are the basic entities available, and can you get to them in the desired sequence?
  - What will it display (visible to user), and what choices will it offer?

For some clauses you'll want to capture notes such as operational needs and wants or explanatory points (e.g., "matching names are listed with exact matches first, then alphabetically" or "multiple notification modes because it is a noisy, distracting environment"). This column could also be used to indicate points where the service will be invoked or ideas about specific UI features. If you are an overachiever, you can add an additional column for data requirements. Each row is a single "when-then" clause, although you will generally have notes or data requirements that are specific to the "when" or "then" parts. The purpose of the data column is to itemize the individual data items (attributes) that are being captured from the UI or displayed on it so you can ensure the necessary data is in the data model and update it as necessary. This illustrates how use cases drive the refinement of the logical data model.

Be sure to start at the real beginning of the use case, or at least early enough to demonstrate how the actor will see things. A common mistake is to begin at the desired system function without showing how the actor gets there. For instance, in a Web-based application, it's a good idea to be sure that some use cases or scenarios begin with the actor accessing the appropriate home page or portal URL. Some "friendly" dialogues will allow the actor to immediately enter their account ID, password, and selected function, while others require a ridiculous number of back and forth interactions (e.g., select customer geography, select customer type [corporate, small business, home, government, educational], select product family, and select service, each requiring a separate interaction [when-then clause]). This might make marketing happy with the data it provides, but it doesn't usually please the customer.

While developing the dialogue, differences of opinion will naturally arise. Don't waste time wrangling about which option is best—develop the dialogue for each alternative, and then let the appropriate actor representatives decide. System considerations shouldn't dominate, because the first priority is to produce a satisfying dialogue for the actors. After that, you can ensure that it's feasible with respect to system considerations.

Once the end of the use case is reached, walk through the dialogue from the beginning, refining it until the team is satisfied with the flow. You'll also have to ensure that the use case will support the goals of the process, provide the information and incentive for the actor to use it, and provide the attributes to invoke the service. Most important of all—will it actually work for the actor, in a satisfying fashion, in their environment? Bear in mind this might include stringent performance measures, challenging environmental issues, and difficult clients.

Some guidelines to consider when assessing the usability of the use case dialogue:

- Have you made the actor go through multiple steps when fewer (even one) would do? Many systems (especially interactive voice response systems!) force people through cascading menus for technical reasons or out of sheer design laziness. You should never have to navigate hierarchical menus to access common cases—they should be instantly accessible.

- Good e-commerce sites are easy to do business with the first time, and "instant" thereafter (think of Amazon.com and "one-click" ordering).

- Consider different types of actors ("archetypes")—the "normal" user; plus nervous, first-time users; and impatient, experienced users.

If further confirmation of usability is required, prototypes can be developed from the information gathered so far.

You will also want to assess the feasibility of the dialogue from a more technical perspective, but with a great deal of caution. Again, do not let convenience for the programmer disproportionately drive the behavior of the application. This is a central point from Alan Cooper's *The Inmates Are Running the Asylum*, referenced earlier. We don't want to unnecessarily restrict the dialogue, just make sure it's feasible by considering:

- Will interface technology support the intended dialogue? That is, are functions like "display" and "select" supported by the voice response or Smartphone interface you are working with?

- Does the UI gather the right information to support invocation of the business service?

- Is the use case indicating that services might need to be redefined to include more or fewer actions?

- Are data model accesses valid with respect to dependency? For instance, do we ever try to create a dependent entity without confirming that the parent(s) exist? Through direct entry or searching, will the dialogue provide the keys to access the correct data?

As you progress through the use cases you'll find that conventions emerge and you'll need to refine earlier dialogues. This might seem a little discouraging, but it actually demonstrates a benefit of the approach—you're improving the design before going to the expense of detailed analysis or prototyping.

Step 5: Refine Final Use Case Descriptions (Final Pass at Detail)

This step has two, straightforward goals:

1. Identify recurring use case "fragments" that will each be standardized and documented once as an "out-of-context" use case that will then be "included" (referenced) by other use cases.
2. Add extensions to the use cases to handle alternate or exception situations.

Identify Out-of-Context Use Cases

Out-of-context use cases, also referred to as *sub-use cases*, are a mechanism for ensuring that a portion of use case dialogue comprising multiple clauses isn't needlessly and inconsistently documented in many separate use cases. The obvious, generic examples are the use case fragments to log on, search, print, get help, and so on. Others will typically arise that are specific to your application, such as Search Product Catalogue or Display Organization Structure. In either case, they generally provide access to some defined service that does not meet our criteria to be called a business service, because it doesn't provide significant value on its own.

There isn't any great mystery to uncovering these, because some are generic and for others it is usually obvious when the same functionality is being documented multiple times. Simply create a new use case, named appropriately, and list the clauses. Many of these are not specific to a particular actor, and might simply be named with a verb-noun pair, such as lookup employee or access help. They are included in the use cases that use them with a name reference, for instance, When Administrative Assistant Lookup Employee ...or When Customer Search Product Catalogue.

There is probably a more rigorous way to accomplish this, but we find this is adequate.

Describe Extensions

Your initial use case dialogue described a normal, successful flow of interactions, but, of course, things aren't always normal or successful. Errors will arise at certain parts of a dialogue, exceptions in others, and alternative paths to the same outcome in yet others. How we handle any one of these situations is called an *extension*, because it extends the capabilities of the use case beyond the normal case. In the earlier days of use case analysis, these situations were separated into alternatives, exceptions, failures, or some other categorization scheme, but it eventually became clear that more time was spent trying to categorize the situation than deciding how to handle it. Now, they're all extensions.

Again, there is no great mystery to uncovering these, just a clause-by-clause walkthrough of the use case dialogue, asking for each clause, "what else could happen?" More to the point, "what else *could* happen, and *will* happen often enough for us to need a way to handle it?" Then describe the extension to the use case in either a brief narrative or a separate "when-then" dialogue. In virtually all cases, unless the extension represents a large piece of a use case, we use a narrative description, finding that inserting a "subdialogue" is awkward. If you are using a tabular form, in the "notes" column you can list any significant rules. For instance, "if the desired Section is full, system will allow waitlisting in any number of Sections in addition to enrolling in one Section, if it is available." Consider the following few clauses from a use case:

1. When Customer calls Service Center, then IVR routes call to next Service Rep.
2. When Service Rep accepts call and greets Customer and asks for Customer ID, then Customer provides Customer ID.
3. When Service Rep enters Customer ID, then System locates Customer and displays Customer profile.
4. And so on.

At each clause, situations can arise requiring an extension. Each is identified by stating the condition, prefixed with the clause at which the condition arises:

1. Too many calls to add customer's call to the queue;
2. Call is not accepted within target maximum wait time;
3. Customer doesn't know their Customer ID;
4. Customer ID not found;
5. Customer's "special handling flag" is set;
6. And so on.

Note that there are many possible extensions for some clauses, such as clause 3, each of which will be described separately. We always collect the possible extensions and then see if the list can be reduced before describing any single extension. Sometimes, conditions are so infrequent or implausible that it isn't worth designing a way to handle them, and, in other cases, conditions should be combined because they are minor variations of each other. For instance, you might be able to reduce "3. Customer doesn't know their customer ID" and "3. Customer ID not found" to simply "3. Customer ID unknown/not found." To document the extension, we simply add a brief narrative describing how it would be handled:

3. Customer doesn't know their customer ID:
    The system will present a Find Customer facility that provides multiple search criteria (Name, Postal Code, and so on). The Service Rep will obtain identifying information from the Customer and enter it into the search facility, which in turn will present a list of potential matches. In conversation with the Customer, the Service Rep will determine which is the correct Customer and proceed with that Customer ID. A predetermined question might be employed to confirm the Customer's identity.

In this example, it would have been just as feasible to document the extension in when-then form. In fact, it would probably already have been documented in that form as an out-of-context use case. Figure 15.7 illustrates a template we have used for use case descriptions.

Are We Finished Yet?

At this point, depending on time and resources, you might decide that you have done enough use case work. On the other hand, the criticality of your project might

Use Case Name
Departmental Advisor completes enrollment (of Student in Section(s))
Description
When the Student has submitted their enrollment form (by mail, fax, e-mail, etc.) their Advisor will complete the enrollment process for that student, including enrolling them in alternative Sections or even other courses as necessary. (Also see postconditions.)
Actor(s)
Departmental Advisor or management staff in the Registrar's Department (Students have separate use cases for self-service enrollment)
Distinctions from the essential use case (optional)
Departmental Advisor has capability to override certain rules such as prerequisites.
Preconditions (optional)
• Advisor is logged on, and has a menu of functions available • Assumption: The student has completed the appropriate enrollment form, and the advisor has it.
Primary Course (Normal success steps)

1. When Advisor enters Student Number and selects "Enroll Student"
    Then system verifies Student and Account status and displays basic student data
2. When Advisor selects Semester/Session they are enrolling for
    Then system verifies that Semester/Session is available
3. When Advisor selects Course Code (e.g., "Math") for next Course to enroll in
    Then system returns list of all Courses for that Course Code available in selected Semester/Session that Student has prerequisites for, with list of avail. Sections
4. When Advisor selects Section...etc.

Postconditions (optional)
• The Student will have a verified or waitlisted Enrollment in each selected Section. • Available space in Sections will be updated. • The Student's Account will be updated either by withdrawing funds electronically, or indicating an account due for handling by the A/R system. • A confirmation report will be produced for the Student.
Extension Courses (Alternate and failure steps)

1. Student Number not provided:
    • The Advisor can enter any number of characters of the last name. The system will produce a list of matching Students to select from.
4. Desired Section full:
    • If the desired Section is full, "waitlist" can be selected for any number of Sections (of the same Course) in addition to enrolling in one.

Comments, issues, and design notes
• For Student search, may need a mechanism for restricting the number of entries in the list. • For Student search, need a way to indicate whether the whole name or a subset is being entered.

Figure 15.7 A completed use case description.

dictate that you should do even more. If this is the case, then you will want to confirm and extend your use case descriptions by testing them further. That is what we will do in the final two sections, by identifying, describing, and developing a representative set of use case scenarios.

Step 6: Identify and Describe Use Case Scenarios (Conditions and Outcomes)

The goal of this phase is a set of use case scenarios that represent useful variations on the basic use cases. On larger, process-oriented assignments, we begin by inventing "process scenarios" that help us use the process workflow model as a framework for discovering use case scenarios. Just as a use case scenario illustrates a particular variation of one or more basic use cases, a process scenario illustrates a particular variation of the overall process or a plausible series of events for more transaction-related projects. Each process scenario has a named cast of characters and demonstrates a unique combination of conditions by tracing a single path through the process.

Creating these scenarios is an iterative, trial-and-error process. You could begin by asking the participants to identify a reasonable set of scenarios based on their experience. We've never used fewer than three or more than ten. For the student enrollment process, there might be four scenarios:

1. A scholarship-winning Student who is given early registration and gets into all of their chosen Sections;
2. A returning Student in good standing, who encounters the usual problems of missing prerequisites and full Sections, but is generally satisfied;
3. A problem Student on academic probation who also has financial issues and requires various waivers and other special handling;
4. A mature Student requiring extensive appeals and "life experience" credit to meet the prerequisites for the Sections they want.

Then, trace the path each scenario takes through the entire process workflow by identifying the branch taken at each major decision point. Sometimes we use a different color pen to show each scenario's path. The intent is to ensure that each branch containing significant steps is exercised at least once, and more if it is a core piece of the process that most real-life cases would go through. You might find it easier to start with tracing the paths and then proposing a likely scenario for each unique path

Once you're satisfied that you have a representative set of process scenarios, describe each one, including the actors' names and characteristics, the preconditions, the main conditions to be demonstrated, and the outcome of the scenario. We often separate the group into subteams, with each working on a specific process scenario. Whatever you do, don't split into subteams until the overall set of use cases and process scenarios has been defined; otherwise, you'll never get all the different ideas reconciled.

Each process scenario will involve several use case scenarios, which will be identified next.

Establish Use Case Scenarios

Again, this is not a mechanical step—it requires imagination, trial and error, and iteration. However, the process scenarios and the path traced by each through the process workflow will provide useful structure. Each process scenario could include just a few use case scenarios or many, depending on how complex the path is through the entire process and how many actors are involved. Don't be surprised if you end up with 40, 50, or more use case scenarios—after the first few, they go fairly quickly.

We'll identify the use case scenarios for one process scenario at a time. Choose a simple process scenario and begin by following its path in the workflow. Each contiguous (done "all at a time") sequence of steps by an actor represents a probable use case scenario, as long as it involves use of the information system. Note that contiguous steps by an actor are represented as a single step in the to-be handoff-level workflow model, so that can be a useful aid. If you annotated the workflow model with the use case or cases for each step, that will be very useful as well. Using a workflow diagram (annotated or not) and the process scenario description (especially the list of conditions it demonstrates), decide which use cases should be demonstrated in this candidate use case scenario. Have the group refine the scenario by identifying the conditions, with basic data values and expected handling. Some of these conditions will demonstrate out-of-context (or "uses") use cases (logon, customer search, product search, help, print, ...) that will appear in many use cases. Without getting into the actual dialogue, refine the scenario description by describing the order of the main steps or milestones. You might even discover a few new use cases. The focus here is on identifying what use cases are involved and what conditions to demonstrate, not on actually working through the scenario. Figure 15.8 shows a format containing the essential elements.

After going through all of the process scenarios, check the "by actor" lists for use cases that haven't been covered yet. These will likely be error and exception cases that didn't appear in your basic workflow model. They can be worked into the appropriate process scenarios, either by creating additional use case scenarios or adding them to existing ones.

	Component	Description	Notes
1	Description	• Describe the essence of the scenario, the actors involved, and what is to be demonstrated	• This is essentially a "Use Case *Scenario* Brief"
2	Contents	• Which use cases are included • Also out of context use cases	• Impact on scenario
3	Preconditions & Impacts	• State of system • State of actors and key entities	• Impact on scenario
4	Conditions & Handling	• Specific conditions to demonstrate • Expected handling for each	• Impact on scenario
5	Dialogue (Later)	• "When/then" format • Optional notes	• Do this AFTER steps 1–4 have been agreed

Figure 15.8 Format for the use case scenario description.

Step 7: Complete Use Case Scenario Descriptions (Dialogues); Refine Use Cases As Necessary

In this final step, you develop a dialogue for each use case scenario and then assess whether it indicates that changes to the use case are necessary. Developing the dialogue is quite a mechanical step that usually goes smoothly because of the structured preparation you've done—you have a use case description that defines the dialogue for both the main flow and the extensions, and you have a use case scenario description specifying the actors, data values, and specific conditions or decision outcomes to be demonstrated.

Start by reviewing the process scenario description and then the description of the first use case scenario. You will then build up the dialogue for the use case scenario, one clause at a time, by taking clauses from the use case dialogue and "plugging in" actor names and data values as defined in the use case scenario description. You will stick to the main path when that is appropriate and use the extension paths where the scenario conditions dictate that. Remember, there will be no alternate flows, because the use case scenario traces exactly one path through one or more linked use cases. What will emerge is a dialogue like this:

- When Joan (the Customer) calls the Service Center,
  Then IVR routes call to Adam (the next available Service Rep).
- When Adam greets Joan and requests her Customer ID,
  Then Joan says she doesn't know and provides her last name "Jonnsen."
- When Adam selects Customer Search,
  Then system displays search window.
- When Adam enters "Johnson" and selects "phonetic,"
  Then system retrieves all Customer records with last names that sound like "Johnson" and displays them, including Last Name, First Name, Telephone Number, Address, and City.
- When Adam selects...

You and the group might even choose not to write out the dialogue. Instead, you will just "walk the flow," confirming that it works or noting any difficulties. Alternatively, to save session time, you can develop the dialogues before the session and then walk through them with the group. Either way, the intention is the same: to ensure that the series of interactions is functional and satisfying, given the specifics of the scenario. If it is not, then the use case dialogues will require refinement. The example in Figure 15.9 conveys the important aspects of use case scenarios.

Closing Thoughts

More Uses of Use Cases

Use cases are typically developed only for the to-be process, to guide the design of systems that will provide the best support for process performers. They are used in the design of prototypes and production applications, and, later in the systems

Use Case(s)	Scenario description/purpose
Dept. Advisor enrolls student in classes Dept. Advisor searches for student by name	Departmental Adviser "EdVisor" enrolls Student "StuDent" in his selected classes. Normal flow with a few minor problems.

Precondition	Impact
1. Stu Dent is a second year student 2. Stu is in good standing, with no outstanding debts to the university 3. Ed is already signed on to RegMan app.	1. Already registered at the university with all student data in place 2. None 3. No sign-on for this scenario

Condition	Expected Handling
1. Stu failed to provide Student Number 2. Prerequisite to Math 210 is missing 3. Section 3 of Chem 205 is full 4. Successful enrollment in Phys 220, Span 200, and Math 221	1. Use student name search 2. Prompt for waiver which Ed grants 3. Suggest alternate classes; one will be selected, but waitlist Class 3 4. Successful enrollment in Phys 220, Span 200, and Math 221

Dialog	Notes
When Ed selects "Enroll" from "menu" Then system presents a dialog box to select the student (either by number or by name)	
When Ed enters first five characters of last name Then system lists several matching students, showing student's full name, birth date, permanent residence city, and student number	Should have option to display full info about any student in the list. Should it take two steps to get to this point?
When Ed selects Stu from list and selects "enroll" Then system verifies Stu's academic and account status, displays Stu's basic personal/student data (to be determined,) declared major, course history list, and department selection list	
When Ed selects "Phys" from Dept. list and enters "220" Then system checks that Smith has the necessary prerequisites, and lists all classes plus their current status (open, full, pending, ...)	Should allow selection of department name either from pulldown list or direct entry.
When advisor selects "Phys 220, Class 3" Then system initiates transaction to enroll Smith in that class and displays confirmation	
When Ed selects "Math" from Dept. list and enters "210" Then system checks that Smith has the necessary prerequisites – he doesn't – so system displays waiver dialog.	If Ed had just entered "Math", the system would list all of the courses that Stu had the prerequisites for— Math 210 would not be on the list.
etc.	

Figure 15.9 A completed use case scenario description.

development process, they are invaluable for system testing and acceptance testing. Still later, they are a valuable adjunct to training materials in support of new systems and processes, and some clients even embed them in online help functions. It's usually overkill to get down to the details of individual use cases when describing the as-is process. However, if your existing systems provide poor support, use cases can expose particular deficiencies so improvement resources can be efficiently targeted. Some of our clients have used use cases and use case scenarios for existing applications in the ways we just suggested for new applications, as system documentation, as training tools, to assess their current systems, and for use in online help functions.

For many years, we have used data models and event-based scenarios as tools for evaluating purchased applications. Now, we sometimes go a little further and produce use cases for a candidate purchased application as an evaluation tool. These aren't idealized use cases designed by the client, but the actual human-computer interaction for the application depicted as use cases. Seeing a use case dialogue clearly laid out, whether it is clean and elegant or convoluted and primitive, is a powerful evaluation tool. It helps clients get past flashy GUIs and performance promises and see the support an application will actually provide to their people. One client inspected a dialogue like this and offered the opinion that "This application is like an old truck—it will probably get you there, but it won't be comfortable." Other clients have said they would have handled their ERP software implementation very differently if they'd had use cases to see how the system actually behaved. One found their data entry workload had increased by a factor of five after implementation of their chosen ERP, which required much higher staffing levels. In a phrase worthy of Yogi Berra, they later told us, "If we had developed a core set of use cases for this system before we selected it, we wouldn't have!"

But Why Do They Work So Well?

After diving into the details, let's resurface and remind ourselves why use cases and business services work so well as requirements definition frameworks. We hope to have demonstrated this already but will close with a reminder of the specific strengths so you get the most from these techniques.

The first reason is simply that subject matter experts from the business can see, via the use case, whether the behavior evident at the system's presentation layer will support their tasks and processes. System developers can gather requirements from the use cases, not just for user interface design, but for business services and data management as well.

The second is almost self-evident, but it bears pointing out. A use case, and especially a use case scenario, is better than the traditional bland list of requirements because it's a story, and everyone loves a story. By working within the context of a scenario that includes specific people and situations, participants are much more effective at visualizing the new system in operation and describing how it should behave. They involve clients in a real and meaningful way in specifying requirements, giving them confidence that their true requirements are understood and documented in a form that easily lets them decide whether the delivered system conforms to those requirements.

Business services contribute integrity, flexibility, and reuse once they are deployed, but they are also invaluable during the requirements discovery process because they make discovery of use cases, at the right granularity, so much easier.

Compared to these benefits, the techniques outlined here have proven to be disproportionately simple and cost-effective. Someday, we will write a book on the topic of requirements modeling with use cases and services, but in the meantime we hope to have provided a baseline that you can get started with right away.

Reference

[1]   Gray, J., and A. Reuter, *Transaction Processing: Concepts and Techniques*, San Francisco, CA: Morgan Kaufmann Publishers, 1992.

Appendix

The example:

This brief example is a composite created by Brianna Knox and Dennis Korevitski of Covestic (www.covestic.com) and Alec Sharp, the author. It is based on work performed at similar agencies in the United States, Canada, and the United Kingdom. Because it is an amalgam from various organizations, and because there's only room to provide a short sample of the work products, it is simplified and certainly isn't totally complete or accurate. However, we hope it will provide a useful example of some of the main products that are developed, and their sequence, during a typical process improvement initiative. Further material will appear and the example can be discussed at www.workflowmodeling.com.

Background:

"The Agency," as we'll call them, is mandated by the government to ensure workplace health and safety for the workers and employers within their jurisdiction. They accomplish this through education, consultation, monitoring, inspection, and enforcement. In your area, the equivalent organization might have phrases such as "workplace safety,""occupational safety and health,""workers' compensation,"or "labor regulation" in its name.

The agency finds itself under ever increasing pressure. Workers, employers, the public, the media, and the government all have higher than ever expectations for the safety of workers. They also have high expectations for the competitiveness of employers in an age where work (and employment) can move freely to lower-cost jurisdictions. On top of that, the prevailing laws and regulations are much more complex than they used to be, and cooperation with other agencies and organizations is expected.

The agency has determined that in order to improve stakeholder perceptions, ensure its survival, and, most of all, meet its mandate to improve workplace safety, health, and economic well-being, it must:
- Provide the very best quality of service to its customers, the workers, and employers of the region. In particular, they must be perceived as being less bureaucratic and more appropriate and sensitive—their actions must be predictable, justified, rational, and both cost- and time-effective.
- Improve workplace safety, not just anecdotally, but be able to quantitatively demonstrate their achievements.
- Improve the work environment for the health and safety professionals they employ by eliminating needless frustration.
- Prove that they are "best of breed" when compared to other public and private agencies in terms of cost-effectiveness and customer service.
- Earn the support of the government in enacting enabling legislation by demonstrating their effectiveness and needs.

Toward these ends, the agency has initiated a comprehensive program of fundamental process redesign.

Figure A.1   Background for Inspect Employer process.

Accident
Account Balance
Account Manager
Adjudication
Adjudicator
Administration
Agency Staff
Analytics
Appeal
Appeal Admin
Appeal Type
Assessment
Backlog
Certificate
Citation
Client
Collections
Communication
Complaint
Compliance
Consultant
Consultation
Consultation Request
Contractor
Document
E-mail

Employee
Employer
Employer Account
Employer ID
Employer List
Employer Event
Employer Services Ass't
Employer Status
Enrollment Request
Event
Event Location
Facilitator
Facility
Fine
Hearing
Incident
Incident Frequency
Indicia
Industry Class Code
Infraction
Injunction
Injured Worker
Inspection
Inspection Admin
Inspection Date
Inspection Finding

Inspection Outcome Rpt
Inspection Plan
Inspection Report
Inspection Request
Inspection Result
Inspection Supervisor
Inspection System
Inspector
Investigation
Investigator
Invoice
Issuance
Lead Time
Letters
Litigation
Location
Logging
Mainframe
Monitoring
Notification
Notification Letter
Officer
Order
Payment
Penalty
Plant

Premium
Premium Amount
Prev'n Analysis Team
Protest
Receipt
Referral
Refund
Regional Director
Registration Date
Regulation
Report
Response Time
Risk Class
Risk Class Code
Safety Infraction
Self-Employed
Severity
SIC
Site
Statement
Threat
Trend
Violation
Worker
Workload
Workload Report

Figure A.2   Collected terms.

Selected nouns	Synonyms
Appeal	Adjudication, Protest, Hearing
Application	Enrollment Request
Complaint	Inspection Request, Referral
Consultation	Proactive Inspection
Employer	Client, Employer Account, Account
Event	Employer Event
Incident	Accident
Inspection	Investigation
Indicia	Certificate, License
Inspection Outcome	Inspection Finding, Citation, Injunction
Inspection Result	Safety Infraction, Infraction, Violation
Inspection Report	Report, Notification, Issuance, Statement
Location	Site, Facility, Plant
Officer	Inspector, Investigator, Facilitator, Adjudicator, Account Manager
Penalty	Assessment, Fine
Worker	Contractor, Employee

Facts
Account Balance, Appeal Type, Self-employed, Employer Status, Employer ID, SIC, Industry Class Code, Registration Date, Risk Class Code, Inspection Date, ...
Metrics
Workload, Lead time, Backlog, Compliance, Incident Frequency, Response Time, ...
Organizations, departments, jobs, roles, ...
Account manager, Administration, Analytics, Appeal Admin, Employer Services Assistant, Collections, Regional Director, ...
Processes, functions, activities, tasks, ...
Assessment, Monitoring, Logging, Litigation, ...
Systems, tools, equipment, mechanisms, ...
Mainframe, e-mail, document, letters, eDRM imaging system, Word letter templates, PPT presentations, ...
Reports, forms, screens, queries, ...
Workload report, Employer list (Note: almost none!)
Others too vague, single instance, not tracked, out of scope
Agency, agency staff, trend, premium, threat ,...

Figure A.3   Sorted terms, including core nouns.

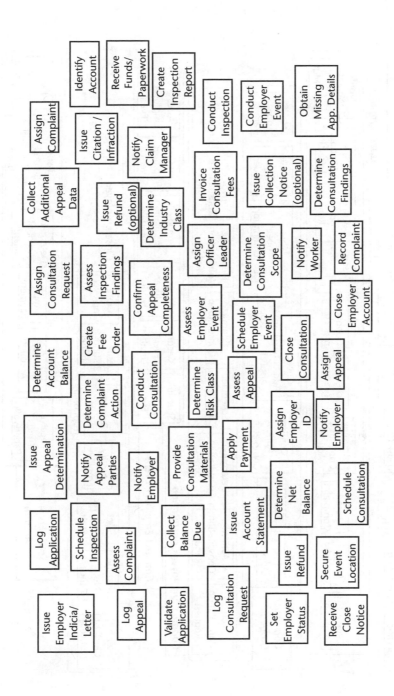

Figure A.4 Collected activities.

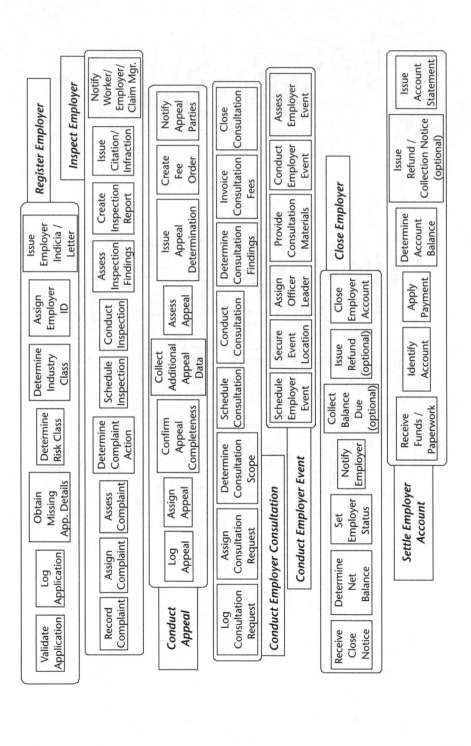

Figure A.5 Discover processes by organizing activities, analyzing linkages.

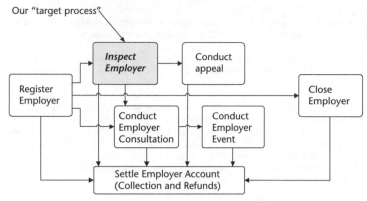

Figure A.6   Overall process map (process landscape).

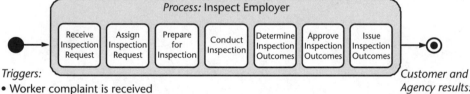

Figure A.7   Process framing (trigger, result, subprocesses, cases).

Figure A.8   Process versus Organization chart.

Stakeholder assessment

- Workers: Procedure to register a complaint and initiate an inspection request is opaque and daunting, which discourages workers; fear that they will be revealed as a whistleblower; no visibility to inspection status and outcomes.
- Employers: Expectations for inspections (and compliance) seem subjective and are not understood; lack of clarity leads to many follow-up discussions and back-and-forth sending of documents; communication paths are cumbersome and archaic.
- Agency staff: Massively inefficient mechanisms to obtain historical information (e.g., inspection outcomes) and record new information; inspection preparation takes longer than the inspection itself; constantly changing priorities; frustration due to lack of measures to assess effectiveness; frustration with rewards for "shuffling paper" rather than improving safety; moving data from tablets / laptops to the mainframe by transcribing it onto paper is very frustrating; no access to other agency's data, especially licensing, taxation, and environmental information.
- Agency: Inability to demonstrate performance compared to other agencies; fear of losing experienced staff due to frustration; poor customer satisfaction ratings; complex and convoluted processes are difficult to manage; lack of metrics to manage by; burdened by politically-driven metrics; no visibility into operational activities.

Context (changes in the environment)

- Workers and the public have become intolerant of poor workplace safety; expectation is that employers should provide safe workplace conditions, and the agency should enforce it.
- Extreme competition from other jurisdictions leads to employers needing to drive down costs such as insurance and settlements.
- Regulatory environment is much stricter, in some cases driven by international treaties.
- Much greater workload with the same staffing levels.
- Agency is now expected to justify its existence in the face of alternatives.

Consequences of inaction

- Unacceptably high levels of injured, disabled, and deceased workers.
- Increasing complaint volumes to handle due to workplace dissatisfaction.
- Increasing levels of agency staff dissatisfaction.
- Unacceptably high levels of employer closure, leading to loss of employment and tax base.
- Increased costs for employer insurance, making employers and the region less competitive.
- Outsourcing of agency functions is likely if benefits can't be demonstrated at an acceptable cost.

Figure A.9   Initial as-is process assessment—issues by stakeholder, context, consequences.

Stakeholder goals

Workers:

- Without fear, register a complaint and initiate an inspection;
- Have visibility to inspection status and outcomes for their own workplace and others;
- Perceive a distinct improvement in their workplace safety environment.

Employers:

- Realize a real reduction in lost-time incidents, which will also positively impact their insurance rates;
- Have real-time visibility to inspection processes, data, and status, and to relevant regulations;
- Have clear and standardized processes for interaction with the Agency;
- Alternate communication channels (e.g., Web-based forms) that will free up resources that currently fill in the Agency's paper forms.

Agency staff:

- Spend less time preparing for inspections, leaving more time for site work—should go from a 60/40 ratio of preparation to inspection to 20/80 within six months of implementation;
- Modern reporting and business intelligence capabilities for better targeting and justification;
- Metrics that will allow the actual effectiveness of Inspectors and Employers to be measured based on safety outcomes, rather than focusing on tasks such as completion of a form;
- Clear methods for prioritizing inspections, and elimination of constant reprioritization—fewer than 5% of inspections should be reprioritized once preparation is initiated.

Agency:

- Elimination of the entirely paper-based workflow with an electronic system that would provide full monitoring and visibility into operational activity, as well as high-quality metrics;
- Modern systems that would be easier to maintain and add new capabilities to as needs change, and be easier to recruit support staff for;
- Metrics that will demonstrate the actual safety outcomes achieved through Agency interventions;
- Increased job satisfaction for staff—target is a 50% reduction in the turnover rate within one year.

Figure A.10   Initial to-be process goals—subjective and objective.

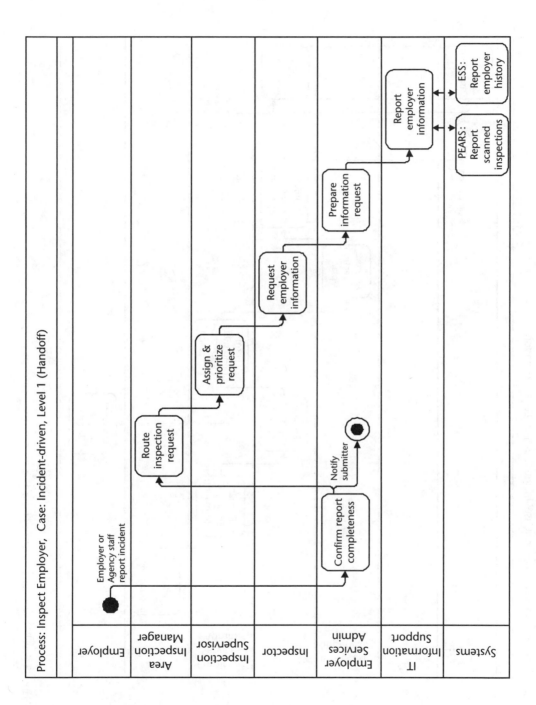

Figure A.11 Handoff (level 1) swimlane diagram of the as-is process, main case (page 1).

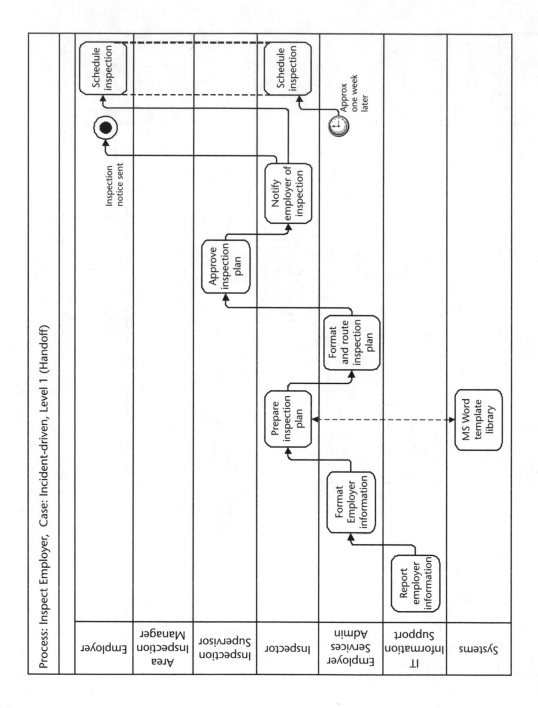

Figure A.12 Handoff (level 1) swimlane diagram of the as-is process, main case (page 2).

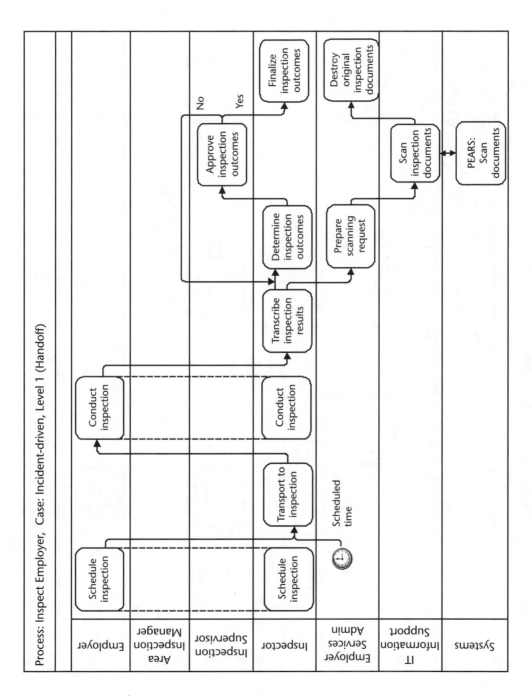

Figure A.13 Handoff (level 1) swimlane diagram of the as-is process, main case (page 3).

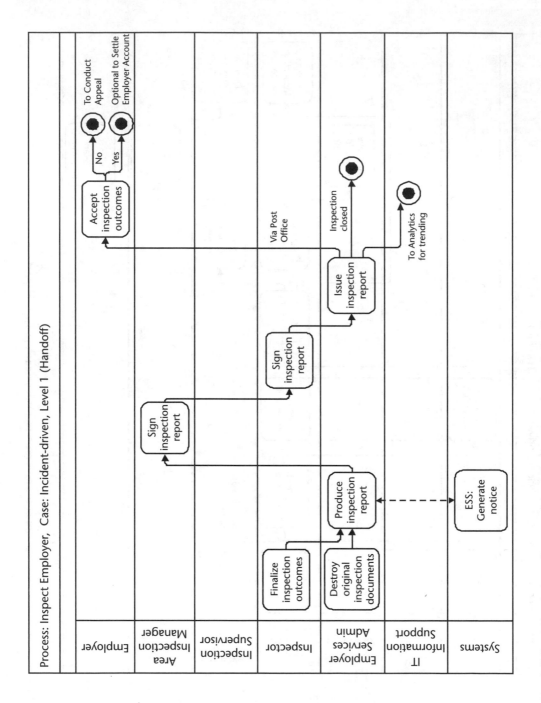

Figure A.14 Handoff (level 1) swimlane diagram of the as-is process, main case (page 4).

Issue Workflow	Potential Solution
Far too many handoffs because of support staff doing systems work, for approval, for signatures, etc.	• Provide Inspectors with tools to gather the information needed for preparation. • See note under "policies and rules."

Issue Information Systems	Potential Solution
Absolutely no "canned reports" or other facilities are available to aid inspection preparation.	• Develop a standardized suite of reports • Acquire business intelligence and analytics tools
Communication between the Employer and the Agency is paper-based and cumbersome.	• Notifications and reports should make use of Web presentment technology.
Inspectors capture data on laptops or tablets, then manually transcribe it, after which it is scanned into a non-queryable form. Pictures and video are also captured, but can't be maintained in shared form.	• Modern database technology should be used seamlessly from the point of inspection onwards, eliminating transcription and scanning. • Facilities for capturing video and images.

Issue Motivation and Measurement	Potential Solution
Inspectors are not measured and rewarded for improvements in workplace safety, only for the volume of paper they produce.	• The ability to capture workplace data, develop safety metrics, and incent inspectors must be developed.

Issue Human Resources	Potential Solution
Inspectors spend too much time on paperwork, as do their support people.	• Modern solutions and business process management technology will free up resources.
Admin support people have much higher potential than is currently being used.	• With tools and training, Admin Support could play a greater role in preparing for and interpreting inspections.

Issue Policies and Rules	Potential Solution
Policies such as requirement for approvals and signatures add no value and introduce delay.	• Eliminate our policies on requiring approvals and signatures—spot checks and audits will suffice.
Assignment of inspection to Inspector isn't done consistently, nor is prioritization.	• Heuristics should be developed to allow automated assignment and prioritization.

Issue Facilities	Potential Solution
The cost to maintain facilities for document storage and scanning is growing, and maintaining the scanning equipment is becoming a major expense.	• As noted before, eliminate paper-based methods and scanning with the right combination of process management and database technology.

Figure A.15   Final as-is assessment by enabler with potential improvements (potential characteristics).

Visit www.workflowmodeling.com for discussion of the book, and additions to the case study including:

• Expanded framing information (actors, responsibilities, metrics, etc.)
• Expanded handoff-level diagrams for the as-is and the to-be processes.
• Service-level diagrams for the as-is and the to-be processes.
• Assessment by enabler of critical improvement suggestions.

Figure A.16   Further resources.

About the Authors

Alec Sharp has managed his own consulting and education business, Clariteq Systems Consulting Ltd., for more than 25 years. Serving clients from Ireland to Illinois to India, his expertise includes facilitation, strategy development, application requirements specification, data management, and business process improvement. He is a popular conference presenter and conducts workshops on workflow process modeling and other topics for large organizations globally.

Patrick McDermott is the president of McDermott Computer Decisions, Inc., in Oakland, California. He received a B.A. in economics from California State University at Sacramento. He has served as the director of the Data Management Association (DAMA).

Index